# COLERIDGE'S
# SECRET MINISTRY

# COLERIDGE'S SECRET MINISTRY

## The Context of the Conversation
## Poems 1795-1798

### KELVIN EVEREST

*Lecturer in English*
*St. David's University College*

THE HARVESTER PRESS · SUSSEX
BARNES & NOBLE · NEW YORK

First published in Great Britain in 1979 by
THE HARVESTER PRESS LIMITED
*Publisher: John Spiers*
2 Stanford Terrace, Hassocks, Sussex.

and published in the USA by
HARPER & ROW PUBLISHERS, INC.,
BARNES & NOBLE IMPORT DIVISION
10 East 53rd Street, New York 10022

*British Library Cataloguing in Publication Data*

Everest, Kelvin
    Coleridge's secret ministry.
    1.   Coleridge, Samuel Taylor — Criticism and
    interpretation
    I.   Title
    821'.7        PR4484

ISBN 0-85527-655-x

Barnes & Noble
ISBN 0-06-492043-7


Printed in Great Britain by
Redwood Burn Ltd., Trowbridge and Esher

*In memory of*
**CELIA KENDALL**

# CONTENTS

# ACKNOWLEDGEMENTS

I should like to express my thanks to the friends and colleagues who have helped me to complete this study of Coleridge. I had the good fortune to be supervised in my postgraduate work on Coleridge by two fine scholars of Romanticism, Geoffrey Matthews and Christopher Salvesen, who have both managed to remain good-humoured and encouraging throughout all the many demands I have made on their time. I am grateful to Gavin Edwards and Valerie Pitt for their helpful comments on various parts of the manuscript, and to Peter Mann for his exacting reading of the whole book. Cedric Brown gave me the benefit of his expert knowledge of Neoplatonism. I must acknowledge a special debt to the late Donald Gordon, for the rare privilege of his teaching.

The book could never have been written without the kindness and generosity of Lionel Kelly, or the practical and critical help of Faith Everest.

*St. David's University College*
*1978*                                                            *K.E.*

# Introduction

The historical context of Coleridge's poetry has been neglected. It is a commonplace of English literary criticism that the first generation Romantic poets were enthusiastic about the early progress of the French Revolution, and that, like everybody else, they later became disillusioned. Their experience, and the poetry that developed from it, appears to confirm that 'liberty' is a frail ideal, an aspiration that sensible people grow out of, like adolescence. English poets of the twentieth century have substantiated the experience in their response to Stalinism and the Spanish Civil War; W.H. Auden's *New Year Letter* ('January 1, 1940') looks back on the excitement of Wordsworth, in France in the 1790s, with an urbane disenchantment that anticipates more recent literary judgements (for example those of M.H. Abrams):

> Thus WORDSWORTH fell into temptation
> In France during a long vacation,
> Saw in the fall of the Bastille
> The Parousia of liberty,
> And weaving a platonic dream
> Round a provisional regime
> That sloganized the Rights of Man,
> A liberal fellow-traveller ran
> With Sans-culotte and Jacobin,
> Nor guessed what circles he was in,
> But ended as the Devil knew
> An earnest Englishman would do,
> Left by Napoleon in the lurch,
> Supporting the Established Church,
> The Congress of Vienna and
> The Squire's paternalistic hand.[1]

Professor Abrams quotes part of this passage in his *Natural Supernaturalism: Tradition and Revolution in Romantic Literature,* and adds:

> Herschel Baker has rightly said that Wordsworth's *Prelude* recorded 'the spiritual biography of his generation'. Auden,

*1*

writing in 1940, reminds us that it also anticipated remarkably the spiritual biography of Auden's own generation, and mine:

> We hoped; we waited for the day
> The State would wither clean away,
> Expecting the Millennium
> That theory promised us would come,
> It didn't.[2]

But this disenchantment, that informs the whole of Professor Abrams's account of the social context of Romanticism, is not the only perspective that is available. Shelley, for example, saw things differently in his 'Preface' to *The Revolt of Islam*:

> If the Revolution had been in every respect prosperous, then misrule and superstition would lose half their claims to our abhorrence, as fetters which the captive can unlock with the slightest motion of his fingers, and which do not eat with poisonous rust into the soul. The revulsion occasioned by the atrocities of the demagogues, and the re-establishment of successive tyrannies in France, was terrible, and felt in the remotest corner of the civilised world. Could they listen to the plea of reason who had groaned under the calamities of a social state according to the provisions of which one man riots in luxury whilst another famishes for want of bread? Can he who the day before was a trampled slave suddenly become liberal-minded, forbearing, and independent? This is the consequence of the habits of a state of society to be produced by resolute perseverance and indefatigable hope, and long-suffering and long-believing courage, and the systematic efforts of generations of men of intellect and virtue. Such is the lesson which experience teaches now. But, on the first reverses of hope in the progress of French liberty, the sanguine eagerness for good overleaped the solution of these questions, and for a time extinguished itself in the unexpectedness of their result. Thus, many of the most ardent and tender-hearted of the worshippers of public good have been morally ruined by what a partial glimpse of the events they deplored appeared to show as the melancholy desolation of all their cherished hopes. Hence gloom and misanthropy have become the characteristics of the age in which we live, the solace of a disappointment that unconsciously finds relief only in the wilful exaggeration of its own despair. This influence has tainted the literature of the age with the hopelessness of the minds from which it flows.[3]

There is no doubt that the first English Romantics, and Wordsworth and Coleridge in particular, did react against their early commitment to the ideals and achievements of the French Revolution. But in thus establishing the pattern of their 'spiritual biographies', it is critically important that we determine whether their withdrawal from the party of revolutionary change was a real and effective withdrawal from their social context in England (an 'internalisation' of social experience and response), or whether it was rather a reaction essentially conditioned, still, by the tensions and conflicts of the society in which they lived. There was nothing inevitable, no timeless quality of the human spirit, in their progress from radicalism to reaction; Shelley's 'Preface' makes that clear. Coleridge's intellectual development is inseparable from his specific historical experience, a developing response to the conditions of his social experience in England, at a certain time.

Good criticism of Coleridge begins with William Hazlitt. 'Mr Coleridge' in *The Spirit of the Age* (1825) is a useful point of departure, and not as a simple sketch of character; Hazlitt's subjects emerge as representative figures in the pattern of a revolutionary age:

> It was not to be supposed that Mr Coleridge could keep on at the rate he set off; he could not realize all he knew or thought, and less could not fix his desultory ambition; other stimulants supplied the place, and kept up the intoxicating dream, the fever and the madness of his early impressions. Liberty (the philosopher's and the poet's bride) had fallen a victim, meanwhile, to the murderous practices of the hag, Legitimacy. Proscribed by court-hirelings, too romantic for the herd of vulgar politicians, our enthusiast stood at bay, and at last turned on the pivot of a subtle casuistry to the *unclean side*: but his discursive reason would not let him trammel himself into a poet-laureate or stamp-distributor, and he stopped, ere he had quite passed that well-known 'bourne from whence no traveller returns' – and so has sunk into torpid, uneasy repose, tantalized by useless resources, haunted by vain imaginings, his lips idly moving, but his heart for ever still, or, as the shattered chords vibrate of themselves, making melancholy music to the ear of memory! Such is the fate of genius in an age, when in the unequal contest with sovereign wrong, every man is ground to powder who is not either a born slave, or who does not willingly and at once offer up the yearnings of humanity and the dictates of reason as a welcome sacrifice to besotted prejudice and loathsome power.[4]

It is part of Hazlitt's great value that he allows insight into what was in some ways an inaccessibly private response; Coleridge never recovered from the self-isolating effect of his activities as a radical, dissenting intellectual of the 1790s in England. The sense of dislocation from English society is a darkening presence in his life, up to the departure for Germany in September 1798; and this quality of his experience lies at the heart, not only of his succeeding efforts to construct a philosophy of unity (that yet contrived to stay within the bounds of the Church of England, and English Conservative thought), but also of his endeavour, in the poetry he wrote during the 1790s, to establish the presence of a sympathetic audience. This endeavour is most striking in the blank-verse poetry of meditation and description, *The Eolian Harp, Reflections on having left a Place of Retirement, This Lime-Tree Bower my Prison, Frost at Midnight, Fears in Solitude,* and *The Nightingale,* that are now referred to as the conversation poems (after Coleridge's sub-title for *The Nightingale,* in the 1798 *Lyrical Ballads*). These poems provide a particularly interesting point of focus for a discussion of Coleridge's social experience in the 1790s, because they celebrate values – retirement in nature, friendship, domestic happiness, the directly benevolent influence of the physical world – that were central to the specific character of his radicalism.

The causes and effects of Coleridge's social experience in the nineties require very careful examination. Again, Hazlitt's essay offers a most useful perspective, that has never properly been followed through in its implications:

It was a misfortune to any man of talent to be born in the latter end of the last century. Genius stopped the way of Legitimacy, and therefore it was to be abated, crushed, or set aside as a nuisance. The spirit of the monarchy was at variance with the spirit of the age. The flame of liberty, the light of intellect, was to be extinguished with the sword - or with slander, whose edge is sharper than the sword. The war between power and reason was carried on by the first of these abroad – by the last at home. No quarter was given (then or now) by the Government-critics, the authorised censors of the press, to those who followed the dictates of independence, who listened to the voice of the tempter, Fancy. Instead of gathering fruits and flowers, they soon found themselves beset not only by a host of prejudices, but assailed with all the engines of power, by nicknames, by lies, by all the arts of malice, interest and hypocrisy, without the possibility of their defending themselves 'from the pelting of the pitiless storm', that poured down upon them from the strong-holds of corruption and authority. The philosophers, the dry abstract reasoners, submitted to this reverse pretty well, and armed themselves with patience 'as with triple steel', to bear discomfiture, persecution, and disgrace. But the poets, the creatures of sympathy, could not stand the frowns both of king and people. They did not like to be shut out when places and pensions, when the critic's praises, and the laurel-wreath were about to be distributed. They did not stomach being sent to Coventry, and Mr Coleridge sounded a retreat for them by the help of casuistry, and a musical voice. – 'His words were hollow, but they pleased the ear' of his friends of the Lake School, who turned back disgusted and panic-struck from the dry desert of unpopularity, like Hassan the camel-driver,

> 'And curs'd the hour, and curs'd the luckless day,
> When first from Shiraz' walls they bent their way.'

They are safely inclosed there, but Mr Coleridge did not enter with them; pitching his tent upon the barren waste without and having no abiding place nor city of refuge![5]

Hazlitt's account is extremely acute, and we shall see how many of its details accurately predicate the kind of pressures that were actually brought to bear on Coleridge. His emphasis on the political atmosphere in England is perhaps rather less familiar than the many well-known views of near contemporaries on the various effects of momentous political events on the continent. Too much attention has been devoted to the spectacular impact of the French Revolution on English life; too much attention, that is, at the expense of the peculiarly English conditions which met that impact. Hazlitt himself writes, in a vein closely paralleled by many commentators, of the Revolution's influence, and distinguishes the emergence of a new poetic style amongst the significant forms of that influence. Wordsworth is the great poet of this revolution; his verse

> is one of the innovations of the time. It partakes of, and is carried along with, the revolutionary movement of our age: the political changes of the day were the model on which he formed and conducted his poetical experiments. His Muse (it cannot be denied, and without this we cannot explain its character at all) is a levelling one.[6]

The last of Hazlitt's *Lectures on the English Poets* (1818-19), 'On
the Living Poets', describes in detail the relation of English
poetry to the Revolution. The Lake School of poetry

> had its origin in the French Revolution, or rather in those
> sentiments and opinions which produced that revolution; and
> which sentiments and opinions were indirectly imported into
> this country in translations from the German about that period.
> Our poetical literature had, towards the close of the last century,
> degenerated into the most trite, insipid, and mechanical of all
> things, in the hands of the followers of Pope and the old French
> school of poetry. It wanted something to stir it up, and it found
> that something in the principles and events of the French
> revolution. From the impulse it thus received, it rose at once
> from the most servile imitation and tamest common-place, to the
> utmost pitch of singularity and paradox. The change in the
> belles-lettres was as complete, and to many persons as startling,
> as the change in politics, with which it went hand in hand.[7]

The liberation of subject-matter was one crucial effect of this
stylistic revolution. A 'levelling' spirit was pervasive in the new
poetry of humble life, outside the context of 'Society', and
especially of rural life, outside the context of the pastoral
tradition. The characters of Wordsworth's poetry have no
urbane significance; rather, he finds in them a grandeur and
dignity deriving from their quotidian contact with nature and a
stable rural community, even if this community is under threat.
A carefully unaffected simplicity of style characterises the new
voice, a language of primordial integrity that is a polemical
rejection of corrupt sophistication. Hazlitt gestures drily
towards the contribution of Coleridge in this change; he lists
examples of the 'mixed rabble' of Lake School egalitarianism,
'Botany Bay convicts, female vagrants, gipsies, meek daughters
in the family of Christ',[8] and this last allusion, to *The Eolian
Harp*, suggests by its comically incongruous juxtaposition, that
there is something uncertain in Coleridge's commitment and
his achievement. It is important that we take this uncertainty
into account.

Hazlitt had a political axe to grind, but his estimate of
Coleridge does not seem less fair because of that. He seems
constantly to hint at something profoundly disturbed in
Coleridge's work and personality, a kind of neurotic devious-
ness. Professor Norman Fruman's recent study *Coleridge the*

*Damaged Archangel* has explored in great detail this quality in Coleridge, his extensive and artfully concealed plagiarisms, his various kinds of dishonesty and their elaborate mechanisms of defence, and has suggested that we should look for the causes of these features of personality in a fundamentally unbalancing childhood experience, deprived of love and family security. An important strand of Professor Fruman's argument is the connection he establishes between Coleridge's lifelong concern to project himself as a many-sided genius, an adult *wunderkind*, and the psychological effects of his unhappy childhood and youth. The autobiographical letters that Coleridge wrote at the request of Tom Poole are our main source for the early years of his life, and they betray Coleridge's sense of himself as unloved within his family, neglected and literally rejected by them. He did not get on well with his brothers, and his father, who obviously took greatest interest in him, died when Coleridge was eight. Most seriously, he appears to have had little love from his mother; no letters to her have survived, and letters to other members of his family end with a most pointed distinction between the 'duty' he sends his mother, and the love he bestows elsewhere. Professor Fruman grounds his arguments against large areas of Coleridge's supposed reputation on an analysis of his personality that is Freudian in assumptions and terminology. His book was intended to initiate controversy, and to a certain extent it has done so. He has been attacked and defended; oddly, his most violent opponent, Professor Thomas McFarland, has since published an essay on 'Coleridge's Anxiety' that appears to reach very similar conclusions, using an explicitly Freudian terminology in the discussion of Coleridge's early life.[9]

It seems that there is common ground in the matter of Coleridge's unbalancing childhood, but violent disagreement as to the difference that this makes to our estimate of his philosophical and literary achievements. It is no accident that Professor McFarland is a leading exponent of Coleridge's philosophy, who has argued that the undeniable plagiarisms are really one more dimension of the unifying impulse in Coleridge's thought, which 'reticulates' together large and apparently disparate chunks of other people's ideas.[10] Many of Professor Fruman's examples, though, of Coleridge's dishonesty, are simply unanswerable, and he is surely right to place them in the whole context of Coleridge's extreme anxiety about his relationship with his audience. He is always seeking to impress, to be accepted and respected for the brilliant and attractive mind that could cut across divisions of party and class with its power. But this concern developed quite as much out of his social experience as a young man in the nineties, as it did from the wretched deprivations of his childhood. The cast of his personality, its desperate efforts to realise a need to belong, was moulded in a dialectical process of psychological and social forces that cannot be separated out and ranged in any order of importance.

Another recently published book on Coleridge, E.S. Shaffer's *'Kubla Khan' and The Fall of Jerusalem*, has stressed the need, increasingly serious in English studies, to consider 'the entire milieu of a work of art, in its intimate relations with artistic creation, and not simply to offer superficial and perfunctory 'background' history'.[11] Continental critics, Lukacs, Goldmann, Barthes, and in England Raymond Williams, have prepared the ground for a methodology that may enable such an approach to the study of literature, but theory is still at an experimental stage, and now forms in itself a major area of research. Ms Shaffer suggests a solution of the problem that is also, from her own point of view, a way of avoiding a marxist basis for her argument; she proposes the isolation of what Goldmann has called 'a sufficiently autonomous subject matter',[12] and she cites Michel Foucault's *Histoire de la folie* as an example of such an approach. Raymond Williams is quoted in support of this solution, which in Ms Shaffer's words implies 'selection of a subject-matter which cuts across the boundaries of the traditional disciplines, yet which in practice, to be manageable, must be smaller than any traditional discipline'. Or as Raymond Williams put it:

> It is not then a question of relating the art to the society, but of studying all the activities and their interrelations, without any concession of priority to any one of them we may choose to abstract.[13]

The present work seeks to develop an argument that places one specific area of Coleridge's art, the conversation poems written between 1795 and 1798, in a context of their 'interrelations', with certain central preoccupations of Coleridge's thought in the 1790s, and with the general pattern of his life in English society in that decade. No particular one of these different subjects has been allowed a special 'priority'; the intention has been to proceed, by a series of different perspectives on Coleridge in the 1790s, towards a larger understanding of Coleridge's various 'activities', the things that he did, and thought, and wrote, over a period of time that was very importantly formative, for Coleridge himself, and for the development of English culture as a whole. Coleridge certainly made his own distinctive contribution to this cultural develop-ment, but it is one major implication of my argument that Coleridge's importance, the influence of his ideas about literature and society, and his own work as an artist, owes a great deal of its special character to the determining influence of his social context in the last decade of the eighteenth century.

Coleridge's conversation poems articulate a certain form of consciousness, an activity of mind that explores the emotional and intellectual resources of a personal context that is essen-tially narrow and limited, and most often explicitly domestic. Family and friends, in a particular place, at a particular time, provide the basis for the characteristic development of the conversation poems, towards the affirmation of community between man, nature, and God. This form of consciousness is in part a development of traditions in English meditative nature poetry, and most strikingly it is a development of the 'retirement' tradition that enters English poetry in the second half of the seventeenth century. In one of the following chapters I attempt to trace in some detail the relationship between Coleridge's conversation poems and the tradition of English retirement poetry; but exclusively literary analysis is not in itself adequate to account for the ways in which Coleridge's poetry modifies its inherited literary form. We need to think in larger terms about the sources of the power that Coleridge can generate in his ideal of a stable domestic community of family and friends in nature. We need in particular to think about the implications of Coleridge's intellectual position in the mid 1790s, as a Unitarian radical, a follower of Hartley and Joseph Priestley. His radical Unitarianism involved a commitment not only to the concept of a revolutionary élite, a small group of dedicated reformers on the model of Christ's disciples (and, a little self-consciously, like the ill-fated Girondistes in revolutionary France), but also to Hartleian associationism, with its direct emphasis on the morally educative force of nature, and of the family environment of the child. These ideas lay behind the scheme to found a 'Pantisocracy' in America, and Pantisocracy itself lay behind the community that Coleridge actually succeeded in bringing about, briefly, in Nether Stowey. And Nether Stowey is one defining context of the best conversation poems. I have tried to present this complex of ideas and personal history in a way that helps us to understand the force that Coleridge could give to various elements within the rhetoric of the conversation poems, friends, family, nature, and in a way, too, that brings out the social and political resonance of Coleridge's poetic language. For Coleridge *was* a radical; his beliefs in the 1790s constituted in one perspective the theoretical framework of a critique of the society in which he lived. And an awareness of this radical dimension of Coleridge's thought leads on to one further aspect of Coleridge's experience in the 1790s; the extent to which his conviction that enduring personal and social values sprang from, and were sustained in, the relationships of family and private friendship, was itself a conviction formulated as a self-defensive and compensatory response to the general hostility of English society as a whole (a hostility disturbingly particularised in Coleridge's relations with the very respectable members of his own family, vicars and soldiers that they were).

The problem of audience is central. Coleridge's efforts to realise his social ideals were quite at one with his efforts to establish a sympathetic audience, and the rhetoric of the conversation poems is, in effect, precisely an effort to create relationship, a sense of connectedness, between particular men and women (and, especially important for Coleridge, between adults and children), and between man and his particular world. The endeavour has much in common with the work of other Romantic poets, in its concern to utilise 'the very language of man', and it shares with Wordsworth in particular a rhetoric that seeks deliberately to give the intimacy, with its implicit polemical commentary, of close private relationship, rather than the formal, public language of eighteenth-century

English poetry, a language confident in the assent of its public. There is indeed much in Wordsworth's views on poetry, and in his poetic practice in the 1790s, that bears most interestingly on Coleridge's problematic sense of relationship with an audience. Wordsworth engages directly with this relationship, in full awareness of its social dimension, in the 'Advertisement' to *Lyrical Ballads:*

> The majority of the following poems are to be considered as experiments. They were written chiefly with a view to ascertain how far the language of conversation in the middle and lower classes of society is adapted to the purposes of poetic pleasure. Readers accustomed to the gaudiness and inane phraseology of many modern writers, if they persist in reading this book to its conclusion, will perhaps frequently have to struggle with feelings of strangeness and aukwardness: they will look round for poetry, and will be induced to enquire by what species of courtesy these attempts can be permitted to assume that title.[14]

But the frank confidence of Wordsworth's tone, its superb self-possession, draws attention at once to the considerable gulf that separates the whole character of Wordsworth's mind from Coleridge himself, with his insecurities and anxiety, the vulnerability that qualified his response to social hostility of every kind.

That vulnerability, the fineness and intensity of his social consciousness, is Coleridge's distinctive and pervasive quality, and the argument of the present work is an attempt to display its presence in all the diverse activities, in their connectedness, that formed Coleridge's mind in the 1790s. The poetry itself gives us our fullest sense of the quality of his experience in those years, but we do not properly understand the poetry without a knowledge of the full range of experience that it draws on. In my efforts to uncover the connectedness between Coleridge's poetry, his thought, and his social experience, I have tried to avoid any obscuring disproportion in my account of the diverse forces at work; a certain degree of autonomy has therefore been allowed to each section of the discussion, as this seemed the best way to preserve clarity of focus. The method that I have adopted assumes a dialectical process in the formation and interpretation of human activity, and I have tried simply to separate out and describe what I take to be the most important forces at work in one particular and limited context.

# 1
# Coleridge and the French Revolution

The Bastille fell on 14 July 1789, and Coleridge celebrated the event in a poem, *Destruction of the Bastile*. The poem was not published until 1834, but a MS transcribed around 1793 exists in Coleridge's hand, and there is no doubt that the poem represents Coleridge's contemporary response to the events in France. The last stanza confirms this contemporaneity:

> Shall France alone a Despot spurn?
> Shall she alone, O Freedom, boast thy care?
> Lo, round thy standard Belgia's heroes burn,
> Tho' Power's blood-stain'd streamers fire the air,
> And wider yet thy influence spread,
> Nor e'er incline thy weary head,
> Till every land from pole to pole
> Shall boast one independent soul!
> And still, as erst, let favour'd Britain be
> First ever of the first and freest of the free!
>
> (*PW*,i,11)

This clearly echoes the voice of popular reaction; Charles James Fox had led the applause of a nation who prided themselves on the constitution of 1688, and welcomed the belated reforms of their national neighbours almost as much as they welcomed the confusion of a great national rival. The solidly Whig approval of Coleridge's closing couplet demonstrates the power of the Revolution to fire even the slightest political consciousness, but demonstrates also that Coleridge's political consciousness was at this time only slight. The political statement of *Destruction of the Bastile* is an isolated example; Coleridge does not emerge as in any real sense politically conscious before 1794 and the meeting with Southey at Oxford. The point is important for two reasons; it provides a good example of the extraordinary problems presented by Coleridge's sense of his audience, and stresses that Coleridge missed the early freshness of the revolution, and did not share directly in the exitement of the period before Robespierre's rise to power.

France declared war on England and Holland on 2 February 1793, and England reciprocated on 10 February. Coleridge was in radical Cambridge at the time, and wrote on 7 February to Mary Evans:

> Have you read Mr Fox's letter to the Westminster Electors? It is quite the *political Go* at Cambridge, and has converted many souls to the Foxite Faith.
>
> (*CL*,i,51)

This is not the tone that we might have anticipated; Coleridge is informed but detached, toying with commitment, at the very moment which he recalled five years later in *France: an Ode*:

> And when to whelm the disenchanted nation,
> Like fiends embattled by a wizard's wand,
> The Monarchs marched in evil day,
> And Britain joined the dire array;
> Though many friendships, many youthful loves
> Had swoln the patriot emotion
> And flung a magic light o'er all her hills and groves,
> Yet still my voice, unaltered, sang defeat
> To all that braved the tyrant-quelling lance,
> And shame too long delayed and vain retreat!
> For ne'er, O Liberty! with partial aim
> I dimmed thy light or damped thy holy flame;
> But blessed the paeans of delivered France,
> And hung my head and wept at Britain's name.
>
> (*PW*,i,245)

Mary Evans was presumably intended as one of the 'many youthful loves' that had made Coleridge's 'unaltered' voice difficult to maintain, but the letter he wrote to her is obviously not stained with tears, is in fact in his most playful manner (the letter was one of a packet to the Evans family; another letter, to Mary's sister Anne, dated 10 February, begins 'A little before I had received your Mamma's letter, a bird of the air had informed me of your illness. . . ': (*CL*,i,54). Either Coleridge is lying in *France: an Ode*, or he is deliberately misleading the Evans family about his political views (in which case *France: an Ode* is still not based on Coleridge's actual experience). Coleridge, the poet, and especially the letter writer, fed on love and approval, and tended to become like the audience he addressed. *France: an Ode* appeared in the *Morning Post* on 30 July 1798. The paper had swung away from a pro-French, anti-ministerial bias through 1797-8, but impelled as much by government pressure as editorial control. On 2 March 1798, the editor, Daniel Stuart, had published a lengthy account of the arrest of the radical John Binns (Coleridge, at this time writing editorials for the *Morning Post*, had championed an earlier Binns cause in the *Watchman*)[1], and had been summoned before the Privy Council to explain the sources of his information. Stuart became very careful after this in reporting government suppression of radical activity, and editorial attitudes towards France, and notably towards French aggression in Switzerland, became increasingly antipathetic in April (France had invaded Switzerland in January, and the Helvetic Republic was created in April). When *France: an Ode* appeared on 16 April, it was prefaced by an editorial note:

> The following excellent Ode will be in unison with the feelings of every friend to Liberty and foe to Oppression; of all who, admiring the French Revolution, detest and deplore the conduct of France towards Switzerland. It is very satisfactory to find so zealous and steady an advocate for Freedom as Mr Coleridge concur with us in condemning the conduct of France towards the Swiss Cantons. Indeed his concurrence is not singular; we know of no friend to Liberty who is not of his opinion. What we most admire is the *avowal* of his sentiments, and public censure of the unprincipled and atrocious conduct of France.[2]

Coleridge changes with the background against which he writes. The case of *France: an Ode* involves some very large questions about the nature of the forces at work in changing the background, and we must return to these questions later. Coleridge was quite exceptionally anxious about his relationship with an audience (no poet ever changed his work so much on the advice of reviewers), and much of his best poetry was a tribute to what he considered his best audience. Coleridge's politics are always involved in the audience that provides a context for any given statement; the comment to Mary Evans about Cambridge enthusiasm for Fox is probably conditioned in sentiment and tone by Coleridge's sense of what she wanted to hear, and as such is not reliable evidence of Coleridge's real attitude in February 1793. But we still have to decide what statements *are* reliable evidence, and we meet this problem often in trying to trace the development of Coleridge's mind.

We cannot talk in terms of the shock of Coleridge's disillusionment with the French Revolution until we have established the existence and character of his illusions. Coleridge became a Unitarian at Cambridge; he was at Jesus College, where David Hartley had been an undergraduate and fellow. Hartley's great expositor was Joseph Priestley, the most eminent Unitarian in the second half of the eighteenth century, and one whose history would by 1793 have taught Coleridge the kind of pressure that could be brought to bear on the radical elements in English dissent. But Coleridge learned this lesson in a more immediate way in May 1793, when Cambridge witnessed the trial, for sedition and defamation of the Church, of the Unitarian William Frend, a mathematics don. Gillman's *Life of Coleridge* (1838) recounts an anecdote that has been cited as proof of Coleridge's fearless radicalism at the time of Frend's trial;

> The trial was observed by Coleridge, to be going against Frend, when some observation or speech was made in his favour; a dying hope thrown out as it appeared to Coleridge who, in the midst of the Senate, whilst sitting on one of the benches, extended his hands and clapped them. The Proctor in a loud voice demanded who had committed this indecorum. Silence ensued. The Proctor in an elevated tone, said to a young man sitting near Coleridge, 'Twas you, sir!' The reply was as prompt as the accusation; for, immediately holding out the stump of his right arm, it appeared that he had lost his hand – 'I would, sir', he said, 'that I had the power.' – That no innocent person should incur blame, Coleridge went directly afterwards to the Proctor, who told him that he saw him clap his hands, but fixed on this person who he knew had not the power. 'You have had', said he, 'a narrow escape.'[3]

Hazlitt describes, in 'My First Acquaintance with Poets', how Coleridge had once made allegations of plagiarism against Hume, and comments 'Credat Judaeus Apella!' (Professor Fruman thinks this best translated 'tell that to the Marines').[4] The passage quoted really insists on a similar response; Professor Fruman has taught us a rational scepticism in dealing with this kind of wildly unlikely story from Coleridge, especially when the story serves to promote the image of Coleridge as morally unimpeachable (Coleridge is seen as both undauntedly courageous in the declaration of his affiliations, and scrupulously honest in his conduct; 'That no innocent person should incur blame . . . .'). The status of the story as reliable evidence is dubious, even though Gillman, probably recalling Coleridge's own words, refers to Frend's trial as a 'disturbing cause, which altered the course of his path in life'.[5] No doubt Coleridge was caught up in the excitement of the trial, but we sense the tone of his involvement in University politics more accurately in an account, by a contemporary of Coleridge's at Cambridge, of a more likely episode:

> I recall a juvenile Scene to my mind, in which [Coleridge was] with myself engaged – I think, in my first or second Term at Trinity. Frend, the Algebraist, had published a pamphlet named Peace and Union, and was called upon to answer for the Opinions expressed in it before the Vice Chancellor's Court, in the Senate House. He appeared to Us an oppressed Man and a party was suddenly made up to chalk his Name in triumph upon the University Walls. Copley, although of a higher Year, joined Us, and also so did the late Legh Richmond, who afterwards adopted opinions like those of Cargill & Mason. Richmond had a stump leg, but was very active – the Pavement rang with his Steps and drew after us the Proctor and his Beadles – it became necessary for Richmond to screen himself under a post. The work however was prosecuted and hardly was a Wall of a College left unmarked by 'Frend for Ever'. We were at it three or four Hours.[6]

This is no dramatic confrontation with authority, but a spontaneous 'rag', as much for the thrill as the principle, Coleridge taking his cue from the mood of the moment. This image fits the voice of *Destruction of the Bastile*, and makes sense of the other glimpses that we catch of the undergraduate Coleridge, moving with many of his young contemporary intellectuals towards a radical position, but without commitment to the full-blooded republicanism that he was suddenly to adopt in his first letters to Southey. Against his interest in Frend we can balance an early and enduring respect for Burke; Coleridge's old schoolfellow C.V. Le Grice recalls a regular activity in Coleridge's room in Jesus:

> Aeschylus, and Plato, and Thucydides were pushed aside, with a pile of lexicons, to discuss the pamphlets of the day. Ever and anon, a pamphlet issued from the pen of Burke. There was no

need of having the book before us. Colerigde had read it in the morning, and in the evening he would repeat whole pages verbatim.

This doesn't imply Coleridge's approval of Burke; he was following the debate on the French Revolution closely, for example during Frend's trial, when

pamphlets swarmed from the press. Coleridge had read them all; and in the evening, with our negus, we had them *viva voce* gloriously.[7]

This suggests a catholicity of interest, an open-mindedness, that points to a radical whig in the making rather than a nascent jacobin. Coleridge wrote a prize-winning Greek Sapphic *Ode on the Slave-Trade* (*PW*,i,147) which is of course opposed to the trade, but is hardly directed to the inspiration of violent revolution. He introduces the poem with some helpful information:

The slaves in the West-India Islands consider Death as a passport to their native country. The sentiment is thus expressed in the Introduction to a Greek Prize Ode . . . .

(*PW*,i,147)

The poem begins (in Coleridge's own literal translation), 'Leaving the gates of Darkness, O Death ! hasten thou to a Race yoked to Misery!' (*PW*,i,147). And we should remember that at about the same time that Coleridge was winning a Cambridge prize with an ode to the earthly hopelessness of slaves (3 July 1792), Pitt was attacking the slave trade in Parliament. We have no reason to suppose that the Coleridge who set out in June 1794 for a tour of Wales was a jacobin, or anything like one; but Coleridge stopped at Oxford on the way to Wales and was introduced by his companion Joseph Hucks to Robert Southey. We hear Coleridge's democratic voice for the first time in his first letter to Southey, written on 6 July 1794. There is, out of nowhere, a flood of jargon, a firm sense of political orientation discriminating between 'aristocrat' and 'democrat' as the poles of human worth. Coleridge is a virulent republican for his exciting new audience:

The Cockatrice is a foul Dragon with a *crown* on its head. The Eastern Nations believe it to be hatched by a Viper on a *Cock's* Egg. Southey. – Dost thou not see Wisdom in her *Coan* Vest of Allegory? The Cockatrice is emblematic of Monarchy – a *monster* generated by *Ingratitude* on *Absurdity*. When Serpents *sting*, the only Remedy is – to *kill* the Serpent, and *besmear* the *Wound* with the *Fat*. Would you desire better Sympathy?

(CL,i,84)

Southey could scarcely have asked for better proof of Coleridge's sympathy. The 'disturbing cause' that changed Coleridge's path in life was no abstraction, no public event, but the warm actuality of a personal relationship. This involvement of the public, political life within the intimate confines of Coleridge's personal life, his affections, his private happiness, is pervasive and crucial. Coleridge's radicalism starts with Southey, not the intellect but the strong, sympathetic man. And much of his best poetry will grow out of an essentially private mode of vision, the deep self-absorption of complete domestic security; but it is poetry about belief, about value, and in this aspect its vision transcends the narrow limits of a basis in domesticity. We cannot understand the conversation poems in particular unless we realise the special resonance for Coleridge of the public in the private.

Coleridge's sudden immersion in radical commitment was well-timed. Robespierre had risen in power through the preceding eighteen months, but he fell in July, providing a good moment for Coleridge to join in; he wasted no time, and by September had published *The Fall of Robespierre*, a drama in three acts, the first by Coleridge, the other two by Southey (Coleridge in fact pretended the whole play was his own, which disturbed Southey's democratic sympathies). Southey's third act closes with 'Barrere' reaffirming the integrity of the Revolution's principles:

never, never
Shall this regenerated country wear
The despot yoke. Though myriads round assail,
And with worse fury urge this new crusade
Than savages have known; though the leagued despots
Depopulate all Europe, so to pour
The accumulated mass upon our coasts,
Sublime amid the storm shall France arise,

> And like the rock amid surrounding waves
> Repel the rushing ocean. – She shall wield
> The thunder-bolt of vengeance – she shall blast
> The despot's pride, and liberate the world!
>
> (*PW*,ii,516-7)

There had been a rapid radicalisation within the French Revolutionary government after 1792. In the summer of that year Austro-Prussian armies attacked France, which precipitated the arrest of the king and queen and the start of the terror against supporters of the ancien régime. In September the National Convention met and proclaimed the first year of the Republic, Louis was executed in January 1793, war with England came in February. We have seen that in *France: an Ode* Coleridge remembered his reaction to have been that of many of his friends, particularly Wordsworth. Wordsworth's analysis of the course of events is close to Coleridge's in his lecture 'On the Present War', published in *Conciones ad Populum* (1795); he blames the aggression of the French on panic stimulated by the counter-revolutionary campaigns of the worried European monarchies, prompted by England:

> In France, the Men who for their desperate ends
> Had pluck'd up mercy by the roots were glad
> Of this new enemy. Tyrants, strong before
> In devilish pleas were ten times stronger now,
> And thus beset with Foes on every side
> The goaded Land wax'd mad.
>
> (*Prelude*,X,307-12)

Wordsworth is recollecting in disenchantment, and like everything else the French Revolution was for him a very personal experience, but France as goaded into retaliation was a stock argument for French supporters. His familiar account of the shock of war is, however, perhaps rather more exclusively personal:

> No shock
> Given to my moral nature had I known
> Down to that very moment; neither lapse
> Nor turn of sentiment that might be named
> A revolution, save at this one time,
> All else was progress on the self-same path

> On which with a diversity of pace
> I had been travelling; this a stride at once
> Into another region.
>
> *(Prelude*,X,233-41)

The importance of the Revolution for English radicals lay fundamentally in the possibilities it opened out for change in England; things were not to be so simple, and suddenly democratic principles, support for the French, became treason. The outbreak of war dislocated the relation of political theory to political action, deracinating a generation of intellectuals and forcing an internalisation of the apocalyptic revolutionary impulse. Pitt's ministry was behind this forcing, and we should interpret the process of disenchantment much more as a function of the political situation *in England* than as something that happened to a generation channel-gazing in political innocence. We must be careful about arguing from Wordworth to Coleridge and his contemporaries; war intensified the struggle between a selfish monarchy and an oppressed people (this is how Coleridge saw it), and not all democrats were as badly winded as Wordsworth. Wordsworth's was from the start an emotional response. He had actually been in France in 1791-2, had shared in, been carried away by the boundless popular elation of success, had even, confusingly, got a young royalist pregnant (that would have been beyond Coleridge at any time). Wordsworth is historically valuable for his evocation of the mood of the early revolutionary years, the millennial state of mind.

The mood is remembered and the memory coloured by Wordsworth's development through the intervening years, imparting an aura of vanished promise, dreamlike:

> custom, law, and statute took at once
> The attraction of a Country in Romance
>
> *(Prelude*,X,695-6)

and the attraction had as much to do with the young Wordsworth as with the changes he witnessed:

> Bliss was it in that dawn to be alive,
> But to be young was very heaven.
>
> *(Prelude*,X,692-3)

The impact of the Revolution, as seeming to offer confirmation
of the millennium as a political and social reality, is fixed at a
moment in past time, when

> Not favoured spots alone, but the whole earth
> The beauty wore of promise,
>
> *(Prelude*,X,701-2)

a moment when 'The inert/Were rouz'd, and lively natures rapt
away', for all

> Were call'd upon to exercise their skill,
> Not ĥ Utopia, subterraneous Fields,
> Or some secreted Island, Heaven knows where,
> But in the very world which is the world
> Of all of us, the place in which, in the end,
> We find our happiness, or not at all.
>
> *(Prelude*,X,722-7)

The subtle modulation from past to present tense registers
Wordsworth's sense of the difference between then and now;
an earth of promise recedes back into the utopian, the world
('the very world which is the world'), intransigent, remains as it
always is. Book ten of the *Prelude* is carefully structured. Its
central strategy is a mode of prolepsis; we learn of how
Wordsworth learned of the death of Robespierre, and his
reaction to the news, *before* the passage in which he describes
the atmosphere of the revolution in 1791-2. The temporal
sequence is re-ordered, heightening the distanced unreality of
the millennial passage because we come to it in knowledge of
subsequent events and the disillusion they entailed.
Wordsworth describes his response to the news of Robespier-
re's death in a verse paragraph that must be quoted in full as a
helpful example of the way in which temporal perspectives are
overlaid, establishing a sense of the self's continuity in time as a
concern overriding the temporal flux in which the poet lived
and remembers:

> Great was my glee of spirit, great my joy
> In vengeance, and eternal justice, thus
> Made manifest. 'Come now ye golden times,'
> Said I, forth-breathing on those open Sands
> A Hymn of triumph, 'as the morning comes

Out of the bosom of the night, come Ye:
Thus far our trust is verified; behold!
They who with clumsy desperation brought
Rivers of Blood, and preached that nothing else
Could cleanse the Augean Stable, by the might
Of their own helper have been swept away;
Their madness is declared and visible,
Elsewhere will safety now be sought, and Earth
March firmly towards righteousness and peace.'
Then schemes I framed more calmly, when and how
The madding Factions might be tranquillised,
And, though through hardships manifold and long,
The mighty renovation would proceed;
Thus, interrupted by uneasy bursts
Of exultation, I pursued my way
Along that very Shore which I had skimm'd
In former times, when, spurring from the Vale
Of Nightshade, and St. Mary's mouldering Fane,
And the Stone Abbot, after circuit made
In wantonness of heart, a joyous Crew
Of School-boys, hastening to their distant home,
Along the margin of the moonlight Sea,
We beat with thundering hoofs the level Sand.

(*Prelude*,X,539-66)

Wordsworth's memories of the period and its moods are not simply private, and in fact the superiority of style, the careful decorum discriminating between levels of tone, has a more generalised solidity now than Coleridge's frantically topical enthusiasm. But the *Prelude* is a personal, contemplative history, the ordered presentation of a firm-contoured, imaginatively composed past. Coleridge could never have written such a poem, could never have emancipated himself from the ideas and excitements of the present; this perpetual contemporaneity appears in its negative aspect as a chameleon-like relationship with every kind of audience, and this is a manifestation of the need to belong, to share the life of 'head and heart' with a home, a community, a nation. This is why the process, government-instigated and controlled, in which English intellectual radicals became through the 1790s increasingly alienated from all classes of English society, constituted such a serious and damaging problem for Coleridge. Wordsworthian distance is not the right approach to understanding these problems; they require, as E.P. Thompson has stressed, 'close attention to the actual lived historical experience'.[8] One positive aspect of Coleridge's contemporaneity is an acute sensitivity and responsiveness to his intellectual milieu. Coleridge in the early 1790s is essentially an enlightenment figure. Wordsworth, in *An Evening Walk* and *Descriptive Sketches*, obviously shares qualities with the immediate literary tradition in which he wrote, but more obvious, even this early, is his enormous, self-sufficient originality. Coleridge is peculiarly indebted to surrounding voices. He could assume with remarkable facility the manner of his poetic models, and indeed at first he did nothing else. He was completely alive to developments in political and social theory, in science and philosophy; his reading was probably more in secondary sources, as Professor Fruman and others have shown, than in the primary sources that J.L. Lowes influentially assumed himself to have traced, but Coleridge was undoubtedly in touch with a very wide range of contemporary thought at a relatively early age. His awareness was intelligently discriminative, but fundamentally that of a thoroughly representative mind in search of new directions. We can raise our eyebrows (with Professor Fruman) at the extreme rapidity with which Coleridge recognised, assimilated and utilised Wordsworth's profound originality, but we can also respect the insight that this involved; the impact of Wordsworth required in Coleridge an effort of sympathy and re-orientation that he did not hesitate to make.

Coleridge's impressionable contemporaneity responded in 1794 to the impact of Southey. When the two ardent young democrats ended their play with an affirmation of the continuing regeneration of France they picked up the clarion-call of the day; Wordsworth recalled the 'mighty renovation' that could proceed again after the removal of Robespierre, and the idea of the Revolution as a return to glorious beginnings derived from the millennial character of English response. The particular spark that stung Burke into his *Reflections on the Revolution in France* was Dr Richard Price's famous sermon preached on 4 November 1789, to the Society for Commemorating the Revolution in Great Britain.[9] Price was, after Priestley, the most famous Unitarian of the day; like most dissenting writers he was used to turning at moments of political stress to the advice of the Almighty, and had for example done so during the American war:

> In this hour of tremendous danger, it would become us to turn
> our thoughts to Heaven. This is what our brethren in the Colonies
> are doing.[10]

In addressing a society that, having been established to
commemorate the Glorious Revolution of 1688 had discovered
a new cause for celebration, and so for continued existence, in
1789, Price took the opportunity to offer his thoughts on the
French Revolution; thoughts which now asserted with trium-
phant optimism the presence of the Divine in the political:

> What an eventful period is this! I am thankful that I have lived
> to see it: and I could almost say, *Lord, now lettest thou thy servant
> depart in peace, for mine eyes have seen thy salvation*. I have lived to
> see a diffusion of knowledge, which has undermined supersti-
> tion and error – I have lived to see the rights of man better
> understood than ever; and nations panting for liberty, which
> have seemed lost to the idea of it – I have lived to see over
> THIRTY MILLIONS of people, indignant and resolute, spurn-
> ing at slavery, and demanding liberty with an irresistible voice:
> their king led in triumph and an arbitrary monarch surrender-
> ing himself to his subjects . . . .
> . . . . Tremble all ye oppressors of the world!
> Take warning all ye supporters of slavish governments and
> slavish hierarchies! Call no more (absurdly and wickedly)
> REFORMATION, innovation. You cannot now hold the world
> in darkness. Struggle no longer against increasing light and
> liberality. Restore to mankind their rights; and consent to the
> correction of abuses, before they and you are 'destroyed
> together.[11]

Price set the tone of non-conformist enthusiasm for the
Revolution. The millennialism of that enthusiasm is already
discernible, the anticipation of an apocalyptic return to golden
times. 'Reformation' was a loaded word, its reference both
political and religious; Major John Cartwright, a Unitarian who
provides one of the links between Wilkes and the parliamen-
tary reform movement of the 1770s and 1780s, and the
radicalism of the 1790s and the early nineteenth century, had
based his arguments for parliamentary reform in *Take Your
Choice* (1776) on the common assumption that the Anglo-Saxon
Constitution had expressed a pure and original democracy,

distinguishing like Price between reform and 'innovation'. Dissent, particularly in its close connections with opposition to the American War, and the slave trade, provided a focus for political discontent in England. The conditions in which the Anglican Church had been created necessitated a self-defensiveness which its close relationship with the state facilitated in terms of parliamentary legislation. Catholics were of course the primary object of this legislation, but the Test and Corporation Acts discriminated against Protestant dissenters. The protestant stress on individual responsibility, the origin of its spiritual disposition in a return to dogma and organisation uncorrupted by the Catholic tradition, to a Christianity of vague, primitive integrity, fostered fragmentation into minority sects. These sects were in their nature enthusiastic and proselytising, and bitterly resentful of the political and social disabilities under which they operated. Locke influenced Priestley's theory of natural rights, which was itself a logical implication of the Protestant appeal to personal judgement. But dissent was fragmented, polarised into the rational faith of the intelligent, educated Unitarians, who continued through the 1790s to channel their energies into agitation for parliamentary reform, and the basically working class vitality of the Methodists and their off-shoots, which found its political analogue in the activities of the Corresponding Societies,a much more profoundly radical movement working outside the context of parliament altogether. The sweeping changes in France effected a momentary unity of mood and direction in the diverse elements of English non-conformity, and this is Price's mood in the *Discourse*. The language of *Revelation* and the other appropriate texts blurred, in the apocalyptic fervour that welcomed the Revolution, a distinction between the dissent of middle-class intellectuals and the chiliasm of a working-class gradually awakening to political consciousness under the pressure of an increasingly exploitive restructuring of industry. The millennial enthusiasm of the Unitarians, and of Coleridge, never broke the bounds of their very rational faith; it supplied an imagery and diction equally available to the atheist; 'Hey for the New Jerusalem! The Millenium! And peace and eternal beatitude be unto the soul of Thomas Paine!', wrote Thomas Holcroft to Godwin.[12] Working-class sects were more literal,

though Methodist leaders discouraged confusion of develop-
ments in this world with the destined rewards of the next.

Richard Brothers, a retired naval captain on half-pay, sent
letters in May and July 1792 to the King, the Queen, the Prime
Minister and the Speaker of the House of Commons warning
them that war with France would constitute fulfillment of the
prophecy in *Revelation* 19:14-21. Brothers believed himself the
leader of the lost tribes back to Jerusalem (he estimated their
time of arrival as 19 November 1798), and issued prophecies
numerous and varied enough to meet with some success.
London was due for destruction by earth-quake in August
1793; a terrific thunderstorm one week before the appointed
day shook the nerve of his followers, who cowered for shelter
in ale-houses or on boats (a safer bet) from the imminent
consummation of all things. Nothing happened, which
Brothers explained by telling of his personal last-minute
intercession with the Almighty, thus consolidating his credibili-
ty. In 1794 he published *A Revealed Knowledge of the Prophecies
and Times*, which proved popular enough in its anticipation of
rivers of blood flowing through London, overturned govern-
ments and headless monarchs, to earn a charge of treason and
conviction for criminal lunacy in March 1795. Coleridge found
this funny; 'Poor Brothers! They'll make him know the *Law* as
well as the *Prophets!*' (*CL*,i,156)[13] Coleridge would naturally
respond in this way; his Unitarianism (and here again he moves
with the drift of his contemporaries) represented the obvious
compromise between a solid Christianity (his father was a
country vicar, and the autobiographical letters to Poole give no
indication of any reaction away from his beliefs and influence),
and the implications of eighteenth-century developments in the
sciences. Natural philosophy had itself become, by the end of
the century, a contributive factor to the rational millenarianism
which came to Coleridge through Priestley, and through his
reading in such writers as Thomas Burnet and Erasmus
Darwin. It was quite typical that Brothers should have
envisioned an earthquake as the agent of his apocalypse; the
Christian scheme of history could be conceived of as working
itself out in terms of the evolution of the physical world.
Priestley's materialism lent to his millenarianism the authority
of science; Anthony Lincoln's lucid account of Priestley's

thought in his *English Dissent 1763-1800* makes the point succinctly:

> For Priestley the necessarian, the ultimate millenium on earth had all the certainty of the last term in a scientific series.[14]

Priestley's millenarianism was positive and unequivocal and the French Revolution simply intensified a pervasive assumption of his work. He had, for example, made his position clear in a published *Fast Sermon* of 1783:

> As a believer in revelation and consequently in prophecy, I am led by the present aspect of things to look forward to events of the greatest magnitude and importance, leading to the final happy state of the world.

In his *Essay on the First Principles of Government* (1771) Priestley had emphasised the presence of a Divine controlling will in the evolution of social organisation:

> The Divine Being sends conquests and Revolution as opportunities for mankind for reforming their systems of government.[15]

Priestley's *Letters to Burke* (1791), with their detailed explanation of the practicalities of an imminent post-revolutionary society, are thoroughly consistent with the rational optimism of the Unitarians.[16] Coleridge found it easy in 1796 to accommodate his scientific reading to his Christianity:

> Millenium, an History of, as brought about by progression in natural philosophy – particularly, meteorology or science of airs and winds – Quaere – might not a Commentary on the Revelations be written from late philosophical discoveries?

It is important to notice Coleridge's assumption of the centrality of the personal will in bringing about the millennium. He hypothesises the *use* of science in order to bring about a new heaven on earth (Professor Coburn cites parallels in Priestley, Burnet, Darwin, and in the work of Coleridge's friends Thomas Beddoes and Humphrey Davy);[17] the millennium as a culmination towards which the race works implied the necessity of a general change in attitude towards individual responsibility, and this necessity informs Coleridge's most serious and sustained contribution to the millenarianism of the earlier 1790s. Coleridge began *Religious Musings* in December 1794, and was still working on it a few weeks before it appeared in *Poems on Various Subjects* in April 1796.[18] He took the poem very seriously, writing to Cottle in October 1795 'it has cost me much labour in polishing, more than any poem I ever wrote – and I believe, deserves it more' (*CL*,i,162). He still regarded the poem as his most important in April 1796; a letter to Benjamin Flower (Unitarian radical publisher of *The Fall of Robespierre*, and the *Cambridge Intelligencer*, to which Coleridge contributed poetry from 1794 to 1798) concludes 'I rest for all my poetical credit on the *Religious Musings*' (*CL*,i,197), and he makes almost the same remark to Poole ten days later (*CL*,i,203). The poem 'echoes' an anti-war pamphlet by a Unitarian, Gilbert Wakefield's *The Spirit of Christianity Compared with the Spirit of the Times* (1794). Herbert Piper's *The Active Universe* has demonstrated Coleridge's heavy debt to Wakefield, and Professor Fruman clears away any ambiguities about Coleridge's failure to acknowledge it.[19] The plagiarisms of *Religious Musings* do not diminish the value of the poem as representative of Coleridge's mind in the mid-nineties, but they do emphasise the curious dependence of his thought and creativity on an immediate context. This is not an excuse. Coleridge's emotional insecurity was very serious and deepened under various pressures in the 1790s. The pressures were both public and private, forcing desperate measures, in both spheres, designed to preserve an image of himself as worthy of love and respect, of belonging. The plagiarisms are a part of his anxiety about his audience, a fear of trusting his own voice. It is most interesting that *Religious Musings* should embrace so fervently the ideal of an egalitarian community of selflessness in God's 'vast family', the kind of community that would resolve his personal problems as well as those of the society in which he lived. Coleridge regarded the disposition of the interior self as an indispensable precondition of the self-transcending love that would bring about a millennial society. The collapse of confidence in that society as an actual political possibility was, in Coleridge's case, a consequence of the collapse of the personal, the domestic life. Coleridge's personal millennium

and his conception of the public millennium were ultimately
the same thing, and the possibility of a re-located 'apocalypse of
imagination' was not open to him. It is nevertheless true that
*Religious Musings* declares a confidence in the imminence of an
apocalyptic climax of social evolution that Coleridge never
regained. He addresses the

> numberless,
> Whom foul Oppression's ruffian gluttony
> Drives from Life's plenteous feast!
>
> (ll.276-8)

and comforts them with the knowledge that they approach the
hour of relief and retribution:

> Rest awhile
> Children of Wretchedness! More groans must rise,
> More blood must stream, or ere your wrongs be full.
> Yet is the day of Retribution nigh:
> The Lamb of God hath opened the fifth seal:
> And upward rush on swiftest wing of fire
> The innumerable multitude of wrongs
> By man on man inflicted! Rest awhile,
> Children of Wretchedness! The hour is nigh
> And lo! the Great, the Rich, the Mighty Men,
> The Kings and the Chief Captains of the World,
> With all that fixed on high like stars of Heaven
> Shot baleful influence, shall be cast to earth,
> Vile and down-trodden, as the untimely fruit
> Shook from the fig-trees by a sudden storm.
> Even now the storm begins.
>
> (ll.300-315)

'The French Revolution', reads a note to this last line in the
1796 *Poems*; Coleridge also gives plainly gratuitous references
to *Revelation*. The passage would probably have given scant
comfort to any child of wretchedness who happened across it,
its effect deriving entirely from a generalised optimism that
manipulates the biblical associations, only a gesture. But
Coleridge believed that such a gesture should be made, the
facts appeared to justify it; and the passage brings out an
important contrast between the attitudes to the Revolution of
Coleridge and Wordsworth. Wordsworth remembered the
millennial excitement as a crucial moment in his personal

history, and Professor Abrams is surely right in maintaining
that Wordsworth structures the *Prelude* to

> pivot on his experience of the French Revolution in order to
> show how he as the exemplary poet 'in these times of fear,/This
> melancholy waste of hopes o'erthrown', has been restored in
> imagination and had succeeded in reconstituting the grounds for
> hope.[20]

Wordsworth's experience of France (and it *was* an intensely
personal, immediate experience) helped to convince him that
external events mattered in the end far less than the moods
they engendered, and that his imaginative endeavour should
be the re-creation, 'reconstitution', of those moods. Moments of
shadowy exultation were more valuable than the conditions of
their birth, and Wordsworth achieved a style that could, in
re-enacting, preserve them:

> the soul,
> Remembering how she felt, but what she felt
> Remembering not, retains an obscure sense
> Of possible sublimity, to which,
> With growing faculties she doth aspire,
> With faculties still growing, feeling still
> That whatsoever point they gain, they still
> Have something to pursue.
>
> (*Prelude*, II, ll,334-41)

Colerige recognised with his contemporaries the shift in French
attitudes away from the early desire for an international
fraternité of the people, and towards a frankly aggressive
imperialism. But it was not this recognition that undermined
his belief in the importance and possibility of changing society;
that was the effect of a more insidious process, that struck at
the foundations of his personal security. The millennarianism
of *Religious Musings* is an intellectual quality. The poem's climax
envisions an apocalypse heralded by very erudite trumpeters:

> . . . such delights, such strange beatitudes
> Seize on my young anticipating heart
> When that blest future rushes on my view!
> For in his own and in his Father's might
> The Saviour comes! While as the Thousand Years
> Lead up their mystic dance, the Desert shouts!

> Old Ocean claps his hands! The mighty Dead
> Rise to new life, whoe'er from the earliest time
> With conscious zeal had urged Love's wondrous plan,
> Coadjutors of God. To Milton's trump
> The high groves of the renovated Earth
> Unbosom their glad echoes: inly hushed,
> Adoring Newton his serener eye
> Raises to heaven: and he of mortal kind
> Wisest, he first who marked the ideal tribes
> Up the fine fibres through the sentient brain.
> Lo! Priestley there, patriot, and saint, and sage,
> Him, full of years, from his loved native land
> Statesmen blood-stained and priests idolatrous
> By dark lies maddening the blind multitude
> Drove with vain hate. Calm, pitying he retired,
> And mused expectant on these promised years.
>
> (ll.355-76)

Milton is present in his capacity as the greatest republican poet, and as the poem's most obvious literary model; Coleridge claimed in his title that the poem was 'written on the Christmas Eve of 1794', which is certainly was not; but the reminiscence of the 'Nativity Ode' is thematically legitimate, and Coleridge referred to the poem as his 'nativity' more than once (e.g. *CL*,i,147,162). Newton, Priestley and Hartley ('he first who marked the ideal tribes . . .'; Coleridge identified him in a note) earn their places through the 'conscious zeal' with which they have 'urged Love's wondrous plan'. Coleridge had two kinds of hero in the mid-nineties; the 'patriot heroes', soldiers and statesmen, men of action like Washington or Kosciusko, and the 'patriot sages', those thinkers and scientists whose preparatory work was equally indispensable to the work of revolution.[21] Coleridge placed himself in this second group (as the writer, for example, of poems like *Religious Musings*), with Milton and Newton (who had written a commentary on *Revelation*), Priestley and Hartley. Coleridge shared the Unitarian wariness of mysticism, and *Religious Musings* itself offers a good example of the rational, scientific 'proof' that a Hartley or Priestley provided of the millennium's ultimate inevitability. Coleridge describes early in the poem the process by which the soul develops into a selfless identity with God. The passage is slightly confused by Coleridge's attempt to describe the development of the collective soul, and to prescribe the ultimate goal of that development (the tenses get tangled). The account itself seems to derive in part from a neo-platonic source, but Coleridge was anxious to correct this impression in 1797; the passage reads, in the text of 1797:

> Lovely was the death
> Of Him whose life was Love! Holy with power
> He on the thought-benighted Sceptic beamed
> Manifest Godhead, melting into day
> What floating mists of dark idolatry
> Broke and misshaped the omnipresent Sire:
> And first by Fear uncharmed the drowsed Soul.
> Till of its nobler nature it 'gan feel
> Dim recollections; and thence soared to Hope,
> Strong to believe whate'er of mystic good
> The Eternal dooms for His immortal sons.
> From Hope and firmer Faith to perfect Love
> Attracted and absorbed: and centered there
> God only to behold, and know, and feel,
> Till by exclusive consciousness of God
> All self-annihilated it shall make
> God its Identity: God all in all!
> We and our Father one!
>
> (ll.28-45)

A note to line 43 ('All self-annihilated . . .') tries to ensure that the reader does not assume that Coleridge is simply speculating here:

> See this *demonstrated* by Hartley, vol.1, p.114, and vol.2, p.329. See it likewise proved, and freed from the charge of Mysticism, by Pistorius in his Notes and Additions to part second of Hartley on Man, Addition the 18th, the 653rd page of the third volume of Hartley, Octavo Edition.
>
> (*PW*,i,110)

The very precision of the reference seeks to provide a kind of 'scientific' basis for the ideas. Up to the middle of 1796, Coleridge preserved his confidence in France as an example of the sort of society towards which all modes of social organisation were evolving, but the loss of confidence in France did not simultaneously involve a loss of all confidence. He lost the milennial optimism, but continued for at least two years to use 'liberty' as a central ideal. Two years may not seem a long time, but Coleridge's life and work from 1795-98 was the most formative period of his life, and we shall need to follow him through this period in detail.

The first number of the *Watchman* appeared on 1 March 1796, and was plainly pro-French in reporting the unwillingness of Parliament to engage in peace negotiations. Having quoted Pitt's cagey response to the motion for peace of the whig Charles Grey, Coleridge affirmed his faith in the Directory:

> . . . in the fourth year of this bloody contest, we are exactly where we should have been at the beginning of any other war. Yet must not these motions be considered as having been altogether ineffectual: they have beyond all doubt removed the prejudices of many, and have inspired notions and feelings which will not die with the subject that caused them.
>
> Still survives
> Th'imperishable seed, soon to become
> That tree, beneath whose vast and mighty shade
> The Sons of Men shall pitch their tents in peace,
> And in the unity of Truth preserve
> The bond of Peace. For by the eye of God
> Hath VIRTUE sworn, that never one good deed
> Was worked in vain!
>
> What the language and professions of the French Legislature are, how little they consider themselves as distressed and exhausted, and how high the views which they entertain, our readers will be able to judge by the following extract . . .[22]

By the end of April, Coleridge had begun seriously to rethink his position. Bonaparte opened his Italian campaign in April, and perhaps the new force this gave to the image of France as a real threat to English national security, a threat now not to the King and his ministers but to the whole people, contributed to Coleridge's change of attitude. The decisive moment was a French rejection of the English offer of peace negotiations; the offer had been transmitted on 8 March through William Wickham, English minister to Switzerland, to the French ambassador in Switzerland, François Barthelemy, who communicated the French rejection on 26 March. Coleridge included the correspondence in the *Watchman* (No.7), 19 April.[23] The *Watchman* (No.8) that appeared on 27 April opened with a 'Remonstrance to the French Legislators' that strikes a new note of disenchantment, anxiously probing the motivation of the French in its increasingly military aspect.[24] Coleridge's enthusiasm for the Revolution never rekindled after this; his references to France are isolated though, given the right audience, hardly disgusted. He wrote to Flower in December 1796:

> Indeed, I am out of heart with the French. In one of the numbers of my Watchman I wrote 'a remonstrance to the French Legislators': it contain'd *my* politics, and the splendid Victories of the French since that time have produced no alterations in them. I am tired of reading butcheries and altho' I should be unworthy of the name of Man, if I did not feel my Head & Heart awefully interested in the final Event, yet, I confess, my Curiosity is worn out with regard to the particulars of the Process. *(CL,i,268-9)*

Even writing in March 1798 to his brother George, a correspondent who always elicited a most embarrassing strain of the contrite schoolboy in Coleridge, he did not disparage the faith he had lost:

> Of the French Revolution I can give my thoughts the most adequately in the words of Scripture—'A great & strong wind rent the mountains & brake in pieces the rocks *before* the Lord; but the Lord was not in the wind; and after the wind an earthquake; but the Lord was not in the earthquake: and after the earthquake a Fire—& the Lord was not in the fire'. *(CL,i,395)*

We are not concerned here with Coleridge's later attitudes to the Revolution (those, for example, of the *Friend*), which are not only very different from anything that we find before Coleridge left for Germany in 1798, but often downright dishonest in their recollection of Coleridge's attitude in the 1790s. He was disappointed in the direction taken by the Revolution; and it was not the only revolution that seemed to have failed in the nineties: 'Poor Poland! They go on sadly there', comments Coleridge in a letter to Southey of July 1794 *(CL,i,86)*. A poem that Coleridge published in the *Watchman* (No.6), *On Observing a Blossom on the First of February 1796*, describes a flower tempted into fatally premature bloom by a false spring:

> with indignant grief
> Shall I compare thee to poor Poland's hope,
> Bright flower of hope killed in the opening bud?
>
> (*PW*,i,149)

Poland's attempt to replace an absolute monarchy with a more popular form of government had made it a whig cause, and Coleridge published a sonnet in the *Morning Chronicle* (16 December 1794) to the Polish revolutionary Thaddeus Kosciusko; the failure of the Polish insurrection (the country was partitioned between Austria, Russia and Prussia in 1795) did not affect his belief in its principles and objectives, any more than French imperialism affected his belief in the principles of the Revolution as he conceived them. He attributed the failure of the Revolution to ignorance and misunderstanding on the part of the French and their enemies, and this was still his position in July 1798 when he published *Original Poetry. A Tale* in the *Morning Post* (the poem is entitled *Recantation* in *Sibylline Leaves* (1817) and subsequent editions). The poem was introduced, somewhat heavy-handedly, as a comic story:

> The following amusing Tale gives a very humourous description of the French Revolution, which is represented as an Ox.
>
> (*PW*,i,299)

The Ox, we learn, liberated after long captivity, naturally frolics to 'shew his huge delight', and is regarded as mad by the 'neighbours', who in treating him as such actually do drive him mad. 'A sage of sober hue' had tried to prevent them:

> 'STOP, NEIGHBOURS, STOP!' aloud did call
> A sage of sober hue.
> But all at once, on him they fall,
> And woman squeak and children squall,
> 'What? would you have him toss us all?
> And dam'me, who are you?'
>
> Oh! hapless sage! his ears they stun
> And curse him o'er and o'er!
> 'You bloody-minded dog! (cries one,)
> To slit your windpipe were good fun,
> 'Od blast you for an *impious* son
> Of a Presbyterian wh—re!'
>
> (*PW*,i,300,ll.25-36)

This 'amusing', 'very humourous' account is historically accurate (Coleridge knew what had happened to Priestley); when the poem appeared in Southey's *Annual Anthology* (1800) the italicised 'impious' was justified in a footnote:

> One of the many fine words which the most uneducated had about this time a constant opportunity of acquiring, from the sermons in the pulpit and the proclamations on the—corners.
>
> (*PW*,i,300)

Later in the poem, with the Ox now rampaging, the 'man that kept his senses' reappears, urging suitable defensive measures as the dictate of common sense:

> *'A bare-faced dog! just now he said*
> *The Ox was only glad—*
> *Let's break his Presbyterian head!'*
> 'Hush!' quoth the sage, 'you've been misled;
> No quarrels now! let's all make head,
> YOU DROVE THE POOR OX MAD.'
>
> (ll. 109-14)

This clear, reasonable voice is Coleridge's within the poem, in spite of the attempt in the last stanza to make the poem into a defence of the renegade Foxite George Tierney. The uncomfortable 'comic' manner cannot obscure the seriousness of the experience; Coleridge is trying to joke his way into the approval of a public whose hostility had been profoundly damaging. It is the strategy of an isolated man.

*France: an Ode* had appeared in the same paper some three months earlier. As we have seen, the poem falsified Coleridge's response to the declaration of war in 1793. Coleridge made himself more representative of the audience whose disillusion the poem catered for, a disillusion that Stuart's interview with the Privy Council had clarified and accelerated. *Recantation* deals exclusively with the development of English response to the Revolution, and *France: an Ode* should be read in the context of the English political situation. The poem rejects the possibility of a 'liberty' achieved in terms of the 'forms of human power', and urges the friends of freedom to look for her in nature:

> O Liberty! with profitless endeavour
> Have I pursued thee, many a weary hour,
> But thou nor swell'st the victor's strain, nor ever

> Didst breathe thy soul in forms of human power.
> Alike from all, howe'er they praise thee,
> (Nor prayer, nor boastful name delays thee)
> Alike from Priestcraft's harpy minions,
> And factious Blasphemy's obscener slaves,
> Thou speedest on thy subtle pinions,
> The guide of homeless winds, and playmate of the waves!
> And there I felt thee!—on that sea-cliff's verge,
> Whose pines, scarce travelled by the breeze above,
> Had made one murmur with the distant surge!
> Yes, while I stood and gazed, my temples bare,
> And shot my being through earth, sea, and air,
> Possessing all things with intensest love,
> O Liberty! my spirit felt thee there.
>
> (ll.89-105)

The optimism of *Religious Musings* has disappeared, but 'Liberty' has still a political resonance. She has become the 'guide of homeless winds', winds which find no abiding place in France or England, and the universal brotherhood of man that had been anticipated is scaled down to a personal, elemental unity with nature. The pines and the distant surge join in one murmur, as Coleridge's individuality is dissolved through 'all things' in a state of 'intensest love'; this experience of nature is not an alternative to the bigger dream of unity, but a part and condition of it, all that is now possible. Coleridge considered the familial community life in nature as a social model, and a socially affective example, a means of effecting a slow revolution through cultivation of the healing values of nature and home. He tried in the 1790s to live this ideal, and for a time he succeeded. It was a life that provided the conditions, and to a very important extent the subject, of his creativity.

Mario Praz offers a most interesting argument on the quality of domesticity in Coleridge and other Romantics in his *The Hero in Eclipse in Victorian Fiction*

> Coleridge, who at first had preached fervently in favour of liberty and against violence and the sceptred and bloody tyrants, fell back upon a defensive, Christian ideal, with *Fears in Solitude* (1798). The beginning and ending of this poem, inspired by a love of his own land in the gentler and humbler aspects of its landscape, have a pastoral tone, a tone of elegiac quietism that might well be termed Biedermeier.[25]

Professor Praz considers Coleridge's retreat into the quiet refuge of a localised nature (which is also a secure home) as a mode of bourgeois defensiveness characteristic of the art that evolved concomitantly with the development of capitalist society and the rise of the middle class. He finds the forerunners of this bourgeois art in the Dutch genre painters, Vermeer, Terborch, De Hooch, whose work 'descends in a direct line from the portrait of the merchant Arnolfini and his wife, painted by Jan Van Eyck in 1434'. In the work of these painters:

> Realism is spiritualised through intensity of vision, attaining, in the highest examples, the quality of inwardness and becoming 'intimism'; and, since it reproduces the joys of prosperity and peace, it suffuses these paintings with an air of great earthly security: moments of everyday life thus become intimations of eternity.[26]

This strongly suggests the atmospheric quality of the conversation poems; but Professor Praz's argument implies a straightforward apostasy in Coleridge's retreat into privacy, 'all enthusiasm for the French Revolution having been extinguished . . . thanks to the influence of the anti-Jacobin Burke',[27] which is too simple, begs too many questions. It is not true that Coleridge 'fell back upon a defensive, Christian ideal'; Coleridge's radicalism was always Christian, his millennnarianism not a mood but an intellectual commitment. Neither is *Fears in Solitude* (as a representative conversation poem in this respect) 'inspired by a love of his own land'; it is rooted in a domesticated nature, a known and familiar landscape expressive of ideals that are not national. Professor Praz's argument works much better with Wordsworth; we meet in his poetry a very strong sense of the 'earthly security', the 'prosperity and peace' of 'bourgeois expansiveness and good nature'.[28] *Home at Grasmere*, and more especially the Lucy poems, embody an ideal presentation of the achieved paradise in retreat from the pressure of political reality. *I travelled among unknown men* (written in alien Germany) explicitly links a domestic paradise with the release of tension accompanying apostasy, where 'patriot' has ceased to mean 'democrat', and has merged with an insular nationalism:

I travelled among unknown men,
In lands beyond the sea;
Nor, England! did I know till then
What love I bore to thee.

'Tis past, that melancholy dream!
Nor will I quit they shore
A second time, for still I seem
To love thee more and more.

Among thy mountains did I feel
The joy of my desire;
And she I cherished turned her wheel
Beside an English fire.

Thy mornings showed, thy nights concealed,
The bowers where Lucy played;
And thine too is the last green field
That Lucy's eyes surveyed.

The issues here are personal but not particularised; they hover vaguely in the mysterious serenity of Wordsworth's mood. The voice is resolute, independent, fallen back from any sense of community with external things, on to the imaginative resources of the self's integrity. The conversation poems, in contrast, *are* remarkably particularised, specifically personal and local, rooted in the sense of community not as the ideal projection of a state of mind, but as the literal condition of a good society.

# II
# Domesticity and Retirement in Coleridge's Poetry

The conversation poems represent Coleridge's most clearly articulated statement of a theme that is present in all his poetry. It is. in fact more accurate to speak of a number of related themes and images; friendship, family, marriage, the retired, self-sufficient 'dell' or 'vale' or 'nook' providing an intimately known home in nature. The genesis and evolution of this group of recurring images is closely related to his private life, and Coleridge's conception of the values of this life is inseparable from his sense of the home in nature as an agent of social progress. The ideal of a retired familial community grows out of an emotional insecurity that became an intellectual commitment; Coleridge shaped his life in the image of an ideal conception, and the life and ideal both collapsed under private and social pressure. Coleridge discovered that the inter-relation of public and private could be quite as destructive as it was, for him, creative.

Images of domesticity and retirement in Coleridge's poetry have been discussed by various commentators in the context of specific areas of Coleridge's life and work. Sister Eugenia Logan's study of 'Coleridge's Scheme of Pantisocracy and Americal Travel Accounts', for example, compares Coleridge's images of the ideal retired dell with descriptions in contemporary travel literature of community life in rural America.[1] George Whalley's absorbing study of *Coleridge and Sara Hutchinson and the Asra Poems*, an excellent discussion of the poems that Coleridge wrote about his love for Sara Hutchinson, includes a brief account of the image of the 'jasmine-bower' as prefiguring in the earlier poetry (*The Eolian Harp, To Joseph Cottle, Reflections on having left a Place of Retirement*) an image that becomes dominant in the Asra poems:

> The word 'bower' does not appear significantly in the early poems; but from the time of his meeting with Asra, Coleridge endows the image with an especial marital warmth until it becomes his most persistent emblem of the ecstasy of secluded peaceful love.[2]

The 'bower' image is one version of a preoccupation that we can trace in development from Coleridge's earliest poetry. Coleridge's poetry of love for Asra appropriated a language that had been used in most of the poetry before 1802; the greatest Asra poem, the *Letter to Sara Hutchinson,* is in this sense the point towards which Coleridge's poetic language evolves through the decade of the 1790s. But as early as 1795, in the opening section of *The Eolian Harp,* the idea of 'marital warmth' as one aspect of the secure familial community is Coleridge's most consistent theme. Coleridge's earliest surviving poem, *Easter Holidays* (1787), celebrates the boarding-school boy's joy at the prospect of a return home in vacation, and offers an idealised picture of the happiness of children at home:

> With mirthful dance they beat the ground,
> Their shouts of joy the hills resound
> And catch the jocund noise:
> Without a tear, without a sigh
> Their moments all in transports fly
> Till evening ends their joys.
>
> (*PW*,i,ll.13-18)

The poem turns on a warning, in the manner of Gray, of how 'little think their joyous hearts Of dire Misfortune's varied smarts', which reminds us how slight and derivative are most of the poems that Coleridge wrote before the second half of 1794. Coleridge's earliest poetic models were Johnson, Gray, Collins, the Milton of *L'Allegro* and *Il Penseroso,* and the contemporaries, Bowles, Anna Seward, Darwin, that we would expect a mind so acutely responsive to its contemporary atmosphere to admire. The earliest poetry is unrelievedly conventional in style and subject, but displays a striking consistency in its concern with home and family; even *Easter Holidays* three times associates 'joy' with domestic happiness, an association that grows in strength towards the affirmation of the conversation poems, and the despair of the *Letter to Sara Hutchinson. Dura Navis* (1787) emphasises the bliss of domestic security by contrasting it with life at sea (which seems unfair and pretty pointless; perhaps Coleridge simply wanted an opportunity to use the dreadful pun of the title); the sailor's life is particularly unpleasant because

No tender parent there thy cares shall soothe,
No much-lov'd Friend shall share they every woe.

(*PW*,i,2,ll.3-4)

This does not tell us much about the mutinies at Spithead and
Nore, but it shows us how Coleridge predicates a domestic ideal
that is in strong contrast with the childhood he actually lived.
The ideal is more powerful, more irresistibly attractive, because
it reflects an emotional need rather than a firmly-grasped
reality. Coleridge advises the aspiring mariner that he should

. . .with the joys of home contented rest—
Here, meek-eyed Peace with humble Plenty lend
Their aid united still, to make thee blest.
To ease each pain, and to increase each joy—
Here mutual Love shall fix thy tender wife,
Whose offspring shall thy youthful care employ
And gild with brightest rays the evening of thy Life.

(ll.58-64)

The early poetry offers many such passages on 'the joys of
home', often highly idealised, sometimes associated with a
particular place, a refuge from the conventional 'misery' that
dogs Coleridge's youthful poetic persona. *An Effusion at
Evening* (1792) is specific in locating the retired domestic
paradise in Coleridge's own childhood home (the blanks in the
following lines are presumably 'Otter'—'dear native streamlet' in
the later version published as *Effusion XXXI* in the volume of
1796 (*PW*i,54,1.81) – and 'Ottery', which makes the relevant
line scan and must be the place through which 'Pleasure's
streamlet glides'):

. . .lost by storms along life's wild'ring Way
Mine eye reverted views that cloudless Day,
When,——!on thy banks I joy'd to rove
While Hope with kisses nurs'd the infant love!

Sweet————!where Pleasure's streamlet glides
Fann'd by soft winds to curl in mimic tides;
Where Mirth and Peace beguile the blameless Day;
And where Friendship's fixt star beams a mellow'd Ray;
Where Love a crown of thornless Roses wears;
Where softened Sorrow smiles within her tears;

> And Memory, with a Vestal's meek employ,
> Unceasing feeds the lambent flame of Joy!
>
> *(PW*,i,50,11.43-54)

Memory feeds here the flame it has lit; the 'joy' that Coleridge persistently remembers of home life was never actually his, and we feel this most when he most insists ('that cloudless', 'blameless Day', when neither 'Friendship', nor 'Love', nor even 'Sorrow', ever hurt) on the domestic ideal. *Nil Pejus est Caelibe Vita* (1789) presents the friendship, the love, the children, the pervasive joy of marital life, with a naive confidence that is quite tragically ironic in the context of the married life he was to lead:

> What pleasures shall he ever find?
> What joys shall ever glad his heart?
> Or who shall heal his wounded mind,
> If tortur'd by Misfortune's smart?
> Who Hymeneal bliss will never prove,
> That more than friendship, friendship mix'd with love.
>
> Then without child or tender wife,
> To drive away each care, each sigh,
> Lonely he treads the paths of life
> A stranger to Affection's tye:
> And when from Death he meets his final doom
> No mourning wife with tears of love shall wet his tomb.
>
> Tho' Fortune, Riches, Honours, Pow'r,
> Had giv'n with every other toy,
> Those gilded trifles of the hour,
> Those painted nothings sure to cloy:
> He dies forgot, his name no son shall bear
> To shew the man so blest once breath'd the vital air.
>
> *(PW*,i,4-5)

The condition of this inflated idealisation of domestic security is a dark anxiety betraying Coleridge's extreme personal insecurity. This negative quality is less apparent in the poetry but sometimes floats uneasily to the surface, as in *On Receiving an Account that his only Sister's Death was Inevitable* (1791):

> Say, is this hollow eye, this heartless pain,
> Fated to rove thro' Life's wide cheerless plain—

> Nor father, brother, sister meet its ken—
> My woes, my joys unshared! Ah! long ere then
> On me they icy dart, stern Death, be prov'd;—
> Better to die, than live and not be lov'd
>
> (*PW*,i,20,ll.9-14)

Anxiety of this sort is discernible, though half-suppressed, in Coleridge's references to his mother; in a *Sonnet: on quitting School for College* (1791) he compares leaving the 'parental scenes' of Christ's Hospital (of necessity a surrogate home) to the time

> ...when erewhile, my weeping childhood, torn
> By early sorrow from my native seat,
> Mingled its tears with hers—my widow'd Parent lorn.
>
> (*PW*,i,29)

The final periphrasis is conventional, but it is nevertheless a way of not saying 'mother'. Professor Fruman discusses the biographical details and speculates convincingly on the psychological impact of Coleridge's 'weeping childhood'; he was neglected by his mother and conscious of it, while his father, whom Coleridge loved and thought of as loving, died in 1781, the 'early sorrow' that 'tore' him from his 'native seat'.[3] Father images are relatively uncommon in the poetry; God is often hailed as 'father', or 'mighty parent', as in *Morienti Superstes (PW*,i,62; but this poem may well not be Coleridge's),[4] though this, of course, is scarcely unique. There is, however, an unmistakable emphasis on the familial quality of God's King-dom; *Religious Musings* uses 'father' for God four times (ll.45,52,61,358), and describes how knowledge of oneself, as a member of 'His vast family' (1.119), 'fraternises man' (1.129). These details are more interesting in the light of other passages in the poem that are considered below. Coleridge became more conscious, as he moved into adulthood, of his need for a surrogate father. His brother George was an obvious candidate, and the *Poems* of 1797 are dedicated 'To the Reverend George Coleridge of Ottery St. Mary, Devon. Notus in fratres animi paterni.' Coleridge wrote a note to the dedication in a copy of the 1797 *Poems*:

N.B. If this volume should ever be delivered according to its direction, *i.e.* to Posterity, let it be known that the Reverend

George Coleridge was displeased and thought his character
endangered by the Dedication.

(*PW*,i,173)

*To the Reverend George Coleridge* brings home to us how hurt
Coleridge must have been by his brother's response:

> Thee, who didst watch my boyhood and my youth;
> Didst trace my wanderings with a father's eye;
> And boding evil yet still hoping good,
> Rebuk'd each fault, and over all my woes
> Sorrow'd in silence!

(*PW*,i,175,ll.44-8)

Coleridge had printed the poem as part of the dedication.
Where Coleridge uses the abstraction of fatherhood in his
poetry, it is as a comfortably idealised aspect of the idealised
domestic haven; the prisoners who suffer from their confine-
ment in *Destruction of the Bastile* (1789) are tortured by delusive
dreams of their inaccessible 'children dear' (*PW*,i,10,l.14), an
idea that recurs in the sonnet to *La Fayette* (1794), where the
imprisoned bird is deprived of a 'Father's joy' (*PW*,i,82,l.6).
Again we notice how consistently 'joy' is associated with family
life; the phrase 'father's joy' is to appear in the *Letter to Sara
Hutchinson*, though there the father is Coleridge himself, and
the children have become part of the prison. The concern with
family and friendship in Coleridge's poetry follows an ascend-
ing and then receding movement that parallels the unfolding
of his private life. Idealisation against the background of
deprivation develops into the secure, creative confidence of
happy marriage and friendly community (though the anxiety
persists, a strong undercurrent); this recedes into a nostalgic
yearning for a lost or unattainable domestic paradise with Asra,
idealised but much stronger than the first phase because
drawing on the resources of experience and its language.
Coleridge becomes a husband and father, watches his children
grow, finds them first a projection of all he might have been,
might have had, and then as living incarnations of all that he is,
all he has lost. The images of mother, lover, wife, and friend,
meet in Sara, who sustains them uneasily but adequately; these
images become again unreal, centering on Asra, the impossible

love that Coleridge wrote poems about into old age. The conversation poems are the highest point of the ascending movement, with the *Letter to Sara Hutchinson* and *Dejection Ode* embodying a moment of great tension, resisting recession.

Mother images are frequent in the poetry. They have a double-edged force that demonstrates how Coleridge's most extreme deprivations produce his most extreme idealisations. The image oscillates between savage perversion and marvellous perfection. *An Effusion at Evening* remembers how 'Hope with kisses nurs'd the infant love'; in the sonnet to *Burke* (1794), 'the sainted form of FREEDOM' wishes

> That Error's mist had left thy purged eye:
> So might I clasp thee with a Mother's joy.
>
> *(PW,*i,81,ll.13-14)

We read in *On a Discovery made too late* (1794) of the 'agony of care' with which a mother nurses 'her sweet infant heir / That wan and sickly droops upon her breast' (*PW*,i,72,ll.13-14), and a *Sonnet* (1796) tells of 'the cries / With which a Mother wails her darling's death' (*PW*,i,155,ll.3-4). There are many such characterisations; 'a seeking Mother's anxious call' (*PW*,i,125, 1.14), 'who that beauteous Boy beguil'd . . .has he no friend, no loving mother near?' (*PW*,i,287; it is interesting that in many cases Coleridge thinks of a mother's intense love as lavished on a child, sick or lost, who particularly needs it). *Translation of a Passage in Ottfried's Metrical Paraphrase of the Gospel* (1799) is a celebration of the Virgin Mary, but also of abstract mother-hood and its relation with the child (*PW*,i,306). The *Ode to Georgiana, Duchess of Devonshire* (1799) wonders how an aristoc-rat can make a good radical Whig, and finds the solution in the Duchess's experience of motherhood:

> You were a Mother! That most holy name,
> Which Heaven and Nature bless,
> I may not vilely prostitute to those
> Whose infants owe them less
> Than the poor caterpillar owes
> Its gaudy parent fly.
>
> *(PW*,i,337,ll.52-7)

Coleridge is referring to the brave, and then quite scandalous,

decision of the Duchess to breast-feed her children,[5] but there
is the suggestion too of something more bitterly personal.
Coleridge's sister Anne died in 1791 (her death prompted two
poems, *PW*,i,20,21): *To a Friend* (1794), written to Charles
Lamb partly as a comment on *Religious Musings*, partly to
comfort him in the illness of his sister, recalls the motherly
attentions of his own sister:

> I too a Sister *had*, an only Sister—
> She lov'd me dearly, and I doted on her!
> To her I pour'd forth all my puny sorrows
> (As a sick Patient in a Nurse's arms)
> And of the heart those hidden maladies
> That e'en from Friendship's eye will shrink asham'd.
> O! I have wak'd at midnight, and have wept,
> Because she was not!
>
> (*PW*,i,78,ll.12-19)

No reminiscence exists of such care from his mother, in the
poetry or elsewhere. Coleridge's consciousness of his mother's
deficiencies emerges partly through his silences; the opening of
*To the Reverend George Coleridge,* for example, invokes the
'blessed lot' of one who 'retreats' to 'the same dwelling where
his father dwelt', and 'haply views his tottering little ones', but
nowhere in this poem (easily his frankest discussion of isolation
from his own family) is his mother mentioned. Grotesque
mothers and fiendish women are powerfully present, however,
in the poetry of 1798. The sexually and morally perverse
mother of *The Three Graves* destroys the happiness of her
children:

> Beneath the foulest mother's curse
> No child could ever thrive:
> A mother is a mother still,
> The holiest thing alive.
>
> (*PW*,i,227,ll.256-9)

Marital stability is irrationally shattered by the mother's
influence, and the image of home, like that of the mother,
becomes more ideal in contrast with a stark reality:

> Lingering he raised his latch at eve,
> Though tired in heart and limb:

> He loved no other place, and yet
> Home was no home to him.
>
> (ll.452-5)

The nightmare woman 'Life-in-Death' of the *Ancient Mariner* is a suggestive figure in this context (*PW*,i,194,ll.190-4), and we think also of the 'woman wailing for her demon-lover' in *Kubla Khan* (*PW*,i,297,1.16). *Christabel* is pervaded by a horror of disturbed familial relations; the sinister and powerfully sensual Geraldine usurps the influence of Christabel's dead mother, poisoning the love of her father. The 'Conclusion to Part II' of the poem places in perspective Sir Leoline's unnatural rejection of his own child, a rejection prompted by the apparently beautiful but really hideous usurping mother ('Behold! her bosom and half her side / Are lean and old and foul of hue'):

> Why is thy cheek so wan and wild,
> Sir Leoline? Thy only child
> Lies at they feet, thy joy, thy pride,
> So fair, so innocent, so mild;
> The same, for whom thy lady died!
> O by the pangs of her dear mother
> Think thou no evil of thy child!
> For her, and thee, and for no other,
> She prayed the moment ere she died:
> Prayed that the babe for whom she died,
> Might prove her dear lord's joy and pride!
> That prayer her deadly pangs beguiled,
> Sir Leoline!
> And wouldst thou wrong thy only child,
> Her child and thine?
>
> (*PW*,i,234,ll.621-35)

Coleridge sets this against an ideal father's 'joy', which was in fact his own; the 'Conclusion to Part II' was written of Hartley Coleridge in April or May 1801, and sent in a letter to Southey on 6 May (the text as quoted here is that of the first published edition of *Christabel* (1816); cp. *CL*,ii,728):

> A little child, a limber elf,
> Singing, dancing to itself,
> A fairy thing with red round cheeks,
> That always finds, and never seeks,
> Makes such a vision to the sight

As fills a father's eyes with light;
And pleasures flow in so thick and fast
Upon his heart, that he at last
Must needs express his love's excess
With words of unmeant bitterness.
Perhaps 'tis pretty to force together
Thoughts so all unlike each other;
To mutter and mock a broken charm,
To dally with wrong that does no harm.
Perhaps 'tis tender too and pretty
At each wild word to feel within
A sweet recoil of love and pity.
And what, if in a world of sin
(O sorrow and shame should this be true!)
Such giddiness of heart and brain
Comes seldom save from rage and pain,
So talks as it's most used to do.

(*PW*,i,235-6,ll.656-77)

In the few years that Coleridge realised his ideal of familial community, he achieved an articulation of great sensitivity, introspective but accessible, the language of hard-won emotional security; it is a distinctive and completely original voice.

*Christabel* contains a very famous passage on the tragedy of broken friendship (Hazlitt singled it out for praise in *The Spirit of the Age*). It is probably based on the quarrel with Southey:

They stood aloof, the scars remaining,
Like cliffs which had been rent asunder;
A dreary sea now flows between;—
But neither heat, nor frost, nor thunder,
Shall wholly do away, I ween,
The marks of that which once hath been.

(*PW*,i,229,ll.421-6)

Friendship was as important to Coleridge as family, and he often describes one in terms of the other; *To a Young Ass* (1794), one of his best political poems, asserts the sympathy and kinship that Coleridge feels for a 'Poor little Foal' wandering near its tethered mother:

It seems to say, 'And have I then *one* friend?'
Innocent foal! thou poor despis'd forlorn!
I hail thee *Brother*—spite of the fool's scorn!

(*PW*,i,75,ll.24-6)

In spite of the warning to fools, less sensitive than Coleridge, Byron ('obvious as ever', comments Professor Empson) still couldn't resist it:

> Yet none in lofty numbers can surpass
> The bard who soars to elegise an ass.
> So well the subject suits his noble mind,
> He brays, the laureat of the long-ear'd kind.[6]

The poem anticipates precisely this kind of response, and the Coleridge of 1794 would doubtless have interpreted it as exactly the attitude that perpetuated the oppression of the animal, and its master:

> Poor Ass! thy master should have learnt to show
> Pity—best taught by fellowship of Woe!
> For much I fear me that *He* lives like thee,
> Half famish'd in a land of Luxury!
>
> (*PW*,i,75,ll.19-22)

Coleridge would renovate the miserable animal (and, by implication, its master) by inviting it to join his familial community 'in the Dell/Of Peace and Mild Equality'. Many of the poems that Coleridge wrote between leaving Cambridge and leaving his wife are addressed in title or substance to personal friends; Lamb, Lloyd, Cottle, the Wordsworths, both Saras, his children. These friends are more explicit regarded by Coleridge as members of his family in the letters, perhaps because Coleridge was worried about the political connotations of brotherhood. This connotation is certainly intended in *To a Young Ass*, and is clear, for example, in *The Dungeon* (extracted from *Osorio*, 1797):

> And this place our forefathers made for man!
> This is the process of our love and wisdom,
> To each poor brother who offends against us
>
> (*PW*,i,185,ll.1-3)

George Coleridge, on the other hand, is a better brother because he is also a friend, 'my earliest friend!' (*PW*,i,174,l.9.). Friends, like family, are especially important for Coleridge because he found them hard to keep. He was well aware of this; *To an Infant* (1795) is an excellent example of the penetrative quality of Coleridge's introspection, that is always likely to surprise by the harsh accuracy of its self-analysis:

> A babe art thou—and such a Thing am I!
> To anger rapid and as soon appeased,
> For trifles mourning and by trifles pleas'd,
> Break Friendship's mirror with a tetchy blow,
> Yet snatch what coals of fire on Pleasure's altar glow!
>
> (*PW*,i,91)

There are countless examples in the poetry of the warmth of Coleridge's affection for his close friends. Sometimes the expression is unpalatably idealised:

> Together thus, the world's vain turmoil left,
> Stretch'd on the crag, and shadow'd by the pine,
> And bending o'er the clear delicious fount,
> Ah! dearest youth! it were a lot divine
> To cheat our noons in moralising mood,
> While west-winds fann'd our temples toil bedew'd:
> Then downwards slope, oft pausing, from the mount,
> To some lone mansion, in some woody dale,
> Where smiling with blue eye, Domestic Bliss
> Gives *this* the Husband's, that the Brother's kiss!
>
> (*PW*,i,156)

The lines are from *To a Young Friend* (1796), addressed to Charles Lloyd 'on his proposing to domesticate with the author' (*PW*,i,155). The last line exposes a confidence in Sara's willingness to embrace the wealthy young banker's son that was to prove totally unfounded. There are fortunately many more successful meditations on friendship in the poetry. The *Hexameters* (1798-9) he wrote in Germany to the Wordsworths are a fine instance of this quality, and of the loneliness that is its dark converse:

> William, my head and my heart! dear William and dear
> Dorothea!
> You have all in each other; but I am lonely, and want you!
>
> (*PW*,i,305)

This loneliness conditions the ideal of community. Herbert Piper has explained the reference of *Religious Musings* as

Unitarian and Hartleian, and Professor Abrams finds it 'a strange amalgam of Neoplatonic Christianity and Hartleian philosophy' in which 'man's highest state is to experience his familial participation in the One.'[7] But there is a simple personal resonance in those passages that are certainly Hartleian, and perhaps borrow the imagery of Neoplatonism, that we recognise as related to the central themes of friendly, familial community and its antitheses. Deprived of identity with God's 'vast family',

> No common centre Man, no common sire
> Knoweth! A sordid solitary thing,
> Mid countless brethren with a lonely heart
> Through courts and cities the smooth savage roams
> Feeling himself, his own low self the whole;
> When he by sacred sympathy might make
> The whole one Self! Self, that no alien knows!
> Self, far diffused as Fancy's wing can travel!
> Self, spreading still! Oblivious of its own,
> Yet all of all possessing! This is Faith!
> This the Messiah's destined victory!
>
> (*PW*,i,114-5,ll.148-58)

Coleridge is prescribing here from an intellectual position based in his reading of Hartley and Priestley (and possibly Cudworth)[8], and the millennial fervour requires a very undomestic rhetoric. But the lines nevertheless place in a political and spiritual context the harmful effects of a 'lonely heart', the misery of 'a sordid solitary thing'. Coleridge's consciousness, and this includes the way he responded to and used his reading, is conditioned by the life he was living when he wrote *Religious Musings*. A desolating loneliness is at the heart of Coleridge's poetry. Christabel's incommunicable consciousness, her helpless isolation, becomes increasingly disturbing throughout the poem. *The Ancient Mariner* locates the extreme of human despair in an enforced solitude that is antithetical to community, to 'joy' (as the condition that Coleridge associated with community), to a Christianity whose God is the 'mighty parent' of a 'vast family of love':

> Alone, alone, all, all alone,
> Alone on a wide wide sea!

> And never a saint took pity on
> My soul in agony.
>
> The many men, so beautiful!
> And they all dead did lie:
> And a thousand thousand slimy things
> Lived on; and so did I.
>
> (*PW*,i,196-7,ll.232-9)

Here is a 'sordid solitary thing' among 'a thousand thousand'
('a million million' in 1798; *PW*,ii,1036); but we know from
*Religious Musings* that the self, however tortured by the
projections of guilt, by an act of 'sacred sympathy might make
/ The whole one Self'. The Mariner achieves such an act,
achieves a consciousness of the possibilities of community (even
if his 'horrible penance' (marginal gloss, *PW*,i,196) is to be
conscious of but still excluded from community) when 'by the
light of the moon' he sees the 'creatures of the great calm' in
'their beauty and their happiness' (marginal gloss, *PW*,i,198),
and blesses them:

> O happy living things! no tongue
> Their beauty might declare:
> A spring of love gushed from my heart,
> And I blessed them unaware:
> Sure my kind saint took pity on me,
> And I blessed them unaware.
>
> (*PW*,i,198,ll.282-7)

The Mariner learns the value of the community he has lost; the
desperate intensity of the words spoken directly to the
wedding-guest is generated by an awareness of the simple
values of community, so accessible and yet so easily lost, that
the wedding itself asserts:

> O Wedding-Guest! this soul hath been
> Alone on a wide wide sea:
> So lonely 'twas, that God himself
> Scarce seemed there to be.
>
> (*PW*,i,208,ll.597-600)

Home, friendship, family, values that spring from a sense of
belonging; ideally, a Christian family of all mankind, united in

prayer with a parent of infinite love. The word 'together' insists
on these values:

> O sweeter than the marriage-feast,
> 'Tis sweeter far to me,
> To walk together to the kirk,
> With a goodly company!—
>
> To walk together to the kirk,
> And all together pray,
> While each to his great Father bends,
> Old men, and babes, and loving friends
> And Youths and maidens gay!
>
> *(PW*,i,208,ll.601-9)

The 'kirk' is left behind by the Mariner as he sets out on his
journey, and left behind too, in a sense, is the wedding that
proceeds as the tale is told. The Mariner's return to his 'own
countree', to the home whose value he has learnt in loss, is a
return to 'joy':

> Oh! dream of joy! is this indeed
> The light-house top I see?
> Is this the hill? is this the kirk?
> Is this mine own countree?
>
> *(PW*,i,204,ll.464-7)

And the mariner's discovery of value sustains him in the
dreadful reality of his situation:

> The Pilot and the Pilot's boy,
> I heard them coming fast:
> Dear Lord in Heaven! it was a joy
> The dead men could not blast.
>
> *(PW*,i,206,ll.504-7)

The word 'joy' occurs in three other contexts in *The Ancient
Mariner;* the becalmed crew, dying of thirst, grin 'for joy' on
seeing a distant sail with its promise of help, sympathy ('a flash
of joy', reads the gloss, *PW*,i,193). The other appearance of the
word is in the marginal gloss that explains the significance of
the 'moving Moon' that the mariner sees immediately before
blessing, 'by the light of the moon', the sea creatures:

> In his loneliness and fixedness he yearneth towards the journeying moon, and the stars that still sojourn, yet still move onward; and every where the sky belongs to them, and is their appointed rest, and their native country and their own natural homes, which they enter unannounced, as Lords that are certainly expected and yet there is a silent joy at their arrival.
>
> *(PW*,i,197)

This beautiful passage embodies a central aspect of the Mariner's experience, and is a statement that suggests, more than any other in the poem, the identification of the Mariner with Coleridge himself. The moon is one of Coleridge's most consistent poetic symbols, appearing here as in *Frost at Midnight, The Nightingale,* the *Letter to Sara* and *Dejection Ode* in crucial conjunction with the values of stable familial community, with 'joy'.

We find these values pervasive in Coleridge's poetry, and consistently associated with the retired natural setting. *To a Young Friend* places its idyll, as we have seen, in 'some lone mansion, in some woody dale'. The earliest appearance of this image, a version of the retirement of eighteenth-century nature poetry, is in *To Disappointment,* a poem that Coleridge included in a letter to Mrs Evans (one of a packet to the whole family) of 13 February 1792 (*CL*,i,21-4). The Evans family was the first of a series of families that Coleridge spent his life trying to join, an endeavour which was in fact ultimately successful, with the Gilmans. Coleridge calls Mrs Evans both friend and parent; he is consoling her in her disappointment at his own inability to join the family in a Welsh holiday:

> Then haste thee, Nymph of balmy gales!
> Thy poet's prayer, sweet May! attend!
> Oh! place my parent and my friend
> 'Mid her lovely native vales.
>
> Peace, that lists the woodlark's strains,
> Health, that breathes divinest treasures,
> Laughing Hours, and Social Pleasures
> Wait my friend in Cambria's plains.
>
> Affection there with mingled ray
> Shall pour at once the raptures high
> Of filial and maternal Joy;
> Haste thee then, delightful May!
>
> *(PW*,i,34,ll.13-24)

Wales is a secluded nook on a rather large scale, but the language is characteristic of the way in which Coleridge conceived the life in 'lovely native vales'. 'Native' is a loaded word in this context; the moon has its 'native country' in *The Ancient Mariner,* but negatively Coleridge invariably thinks of his native place as somewhere in a lost past. The Otter is remembered as his 'Dear native brook' (*PW*,i,48), and Ottery and the surrounding countryside as his 'Dear native haunts' (*PW*,i,54), and these native places are invoked with nostalgia as forming a contrast to present woes. Wales will be the scene, for the returning native, of the 'affection', 'laughing hours' and 'social pleasures' of 'filial and maternal joy'. If we except the conversation poems themselves, Coleridge's domestic retreats are always distanced by a world-weary nostalgia, or projected into a paradisal future. In 1796, in *Poems on Various Subjects,* he published a *Song* which was in fact extracted from his part of *The Fall of Robespierre;* in the 1797 *Poems* and thereafter he called the poem *Domestic Peace,* and because of its appearance in one of Coleridge's earliest overt political statements it has attracted a good deal more critical attention, from writers on his early political views, than any of his other minor poems on this theme:

> Tell me, on what holy ground
> May Domestic Peace be found?
> Halcyon daughter of the skies,
> Far on fearful wings she flies,
> From the pomp of Sceptered State,
> From the Rebel's noisy hate.
>
> In a cottaged vale She dwells,
> Listening to the Sabbath bells!
> Still around her steps are seen
> Spotless Honour's meeker mien,
> Love, the sire of pleasing fears,
> Sorrow smiling through her tears,
> And conscious of the past employ
> Memory, bosom-spring of joy.

(PW,i,71-2)

'Domestic Peace' is personified in the eighteenth-century manner, and the lines are if anything less interesting in their presentation of the theme than others that we have noted. But the poem is interesting in its specific placing of the 'cottaged vale' in the context of a society polarised between radicalism and reaction. The comments of Lewis Patton and Peter Mann in the introduction to their edition of the *Lectures 1795: on Politics and Religion* draw attention to this aspect of the poem:

> It has several times been noted that Adelaide's Song in *The Fall of Robespierre* expressed some of [Coleridge's] deeper feelings . . . . In it memory, love, honour, domestic peace, holiness, joy are all associated with retirement and private life and placed in opposition to both 'sceptr'd state' and the 'rebel's noisy hate'. Although conventional in language, the Song successfully evokes a mood of nostalgic longing for the 'cottag'd vale' remote from the political violence that the play dramatises, and looks forward to those later poems, such as *Frost at Midnight* and *This Lime-Tree Bower*, in which the longed-for contentments are achieved.[9]

This is accurate except in its implication that Coleridge's ideal retirement is essentially apolitical, a rejection of responsibility towards actual or potential modes of social organisation. This reading of the poem in its reference to Coleridge's own position (the poem is spoken by a character in a play that is unquestionably about the significance of political events in France) is shared by Geoffrey Carnall, who thinks that *Domestic Peace* 'indicates where the deepest sympathies of both poets lay' [i.e. both Coleridge and Southey], [10] and by Carl Woodring, for whom

> The 'cottag'd vale' in which Domestic Peace resides, far not only from 'the pomp of Sceptered State' but also from 'the Rebel's noisy hate', and within listening distance of 'Sabbath bells', admittedly gives a strong anti-political hue to Pantisocracy; Adelaide anticipates by two years her author's protest that 'local and temporary Politics are my aversion'.[11]

But it is difficult to see how Pantisocracy, a theory of social organisation, could be regarded as 'anti-political'. It certainly assimilates Coleridge's stress on the values of friendship and familial community, but this argues for the politicality that developed in these values, rather than for Coleridge's resort to these values as an alternative, transcending social and political issues, to involvement in the life of his times. Coleridge felt that personal problems, and the problems created by his relation to

English society in the 1790s, could both be resolved in a single way.

Coleridge's scheme of Pantisocracy is discussed in a following chapter, but we need to look here at the poetry Coleridge wrote about it, for Pantisocracy clarifies and strengthens the image of the familial community in retirement. Coleridge sent a sonnet on *Pantisocracy* in a letter to Southey of 18 September 1794. It opens with a familiar contrast between present woes and past 'joys', and we can interpret the terms of the contrast as either political or personal:

> No more my visionary soul shall dwell
> On joys that were; no more endure to weigh
> The shame and anguish of the evil day,
> Wisely forgetful!
>
> (*PW*,i,68,ll.1-4)

Coleridge's envisioned new life in America is conceived as a re-creation of his 'native haunts', a new start away from the errors of his troubled personality, and away from troubled England:

> O'er the ocean swell
> Sublime of Hope, I seek the cottag'd dell
> Where Virtue calm with careless steps may stray,
> And dancing to the moonlight roundelay,
> The wizard Passions weave an holy spell.
>
> (ll.5-8)

Coleridge enthusiastically invited all those who suffered under personal and political injustice to join him in this new life; the ass, for instance, that made Byron laugh:

> Innocent foal! thou poor despis'd forlorn!
> I hail thee Brother—spite of the fool's scorn!
> And fain would take thee with me, in the Dell
> Of Peace.and mild Equality to dwell.
>
> (*PW*,i,75,ll.25-8)

The lines quoted are from the politically emasculated text of *Poems on Various Subjects*,[12] but we know from a manuscript of 1794 that the Dell Coleridge meant was that 'Where high-soul'd Pantiscocracy shall dwell!' (*PW*,i,75). The first version of the

*Monody on the Death of Chatterton* (1790) faintly suggests some sort of social pressure as the reason for the young poet's suicide:

> Is this the land of liberal Hearts!
> Is this the land, where Genius ne'er in vain
> Pour'd forth her soul-enchanting strain?
>
> (*PW*,i,13,ll.13-15)

Chatterton, like Butler and Otway, 'sank beneath a load of Woe':

> This ever can the generous Briton hear,
> And starts not in his eye th'indignant Tear?
>
> (ll.22-3)

These generous Britons of liberal Heart, indignantly tearful, are whiggish figures who would have helped Chatterton if they could; as it was, he had nearly been saved by a distinctly Coleridgean vision:

> . . .filial Pity stood thee by,
> Thy fixed eyes she bade thee roll
> On scenes that well might melt thy soul—
> Thy native cot she held to view,
> Thy native cot, where Peace ere long
> Had listen'd to thy evening song;
> Thy sister's shrieks she bade thee hear,
> And mark thy mother's thrilling tear,
> She made thee feel her deep-drawn sigh,
> And all her silent agony of Woe.
>
> (ll.59-68)

'Filial Pity' failed in the version of 1790, but Coleridge kept on working at the poem (he was still changing it quite substantially in 1829; *PW*,i,125), and though he could not revive Chatterton he did conceive a way of keeping him immortal. Coleridge had published a revised *Monody* in a subscription edition of the Rowley poems in aid of Chatterton's family, and another, longer version appeared in *Poems On Various Subjects*. This *Monody* ends with the hope of commemorating Chatterton in a monument on the banks of the Susquehannah, the planned home of Pantisocracy. The lines not only show how sustained was the attraction of the plan for Coleridge, but are a swipe at Southey, who by this time had forsaken Pantisocracy and gone to live with his rich uncle in Portugal:[13]

> Yet will I love to follow the sweet dream,
> Where Susquehannah pours his untamed stream;
> And on some hill, whose forest-frowning side
> Waves o'er the murmurs of his calmer tide,
> Will raise a solemn Cenotaph to thee,
> Sweet Harper of time-shrouded Minstrelsy!
> And there, sooth'd sadly by the dirgeful wind,
> Muse on the sore ills I had left behind.
>
> (*PW*,i,131,ll.158-65)

The 'sore ills' are partly personal, partly like Chatterton's, whose destructive isolation was the fault of society. In *Religious Musings*, Pantisocracy is placed in a wider context, as the salvation of all those whose suffering is the corollary of a political situation. Coleridge sees a 'blest future' approaching, a familial society of love that equates with the society that Pantisocracy would gradually develop into:

> each heart
> Self-governed, the vast family of Love
> Raised from the common earth by common toil
> Enjoy the equal produce.
>
> (*PW*,i,122,ll.340-3)

Coleridge's familial retirement is not a renunciation, a recoil from social man, but a positive new start, releasing new potential.

Coleridge's destined partner in Pantisocracy was Sara Fricker, the sister of Southey's fiancée. Coleridge met her in August 1794, so that by the summer of 1795, when Pantisocracy was abandoned as a viable proposition, the friendship had lengthened into an engagement, at least in the determined view of Southey. Coleridge was less emphatic, but hounded by Southey he accepted the obligation and married Sara on 4 October 1795. Coleridge thus found himself in the summer months of 1795 approaching the actuality that constituted his highest ideal of happiness; but this actuality was approaching under conditions less than ideal, Coleridge's life and mind diverging in the way that lends a peculiar poignancy to his

emphasis on familial community. The poems that he wrote
during his 'courtship' of Sara are interesting because they
embody a tension between the ideal role that Coleridge
required her to play, and his sense that she was somehow less
than adequate to that role. They provide also a context for *The
Eolian Harp,* and its famous failure of tone in the introduction
of Sara. *The Silver Thimble* (1795) is slight and light-hearted,
and when it appeared in *Poems on Various Subjects* was
attributed, by implication, to Sara herself. Mrs Coleridge many
years later told her daughter that only a very few lines of the
poem were hers. The poem presents Coleridge's matchless
attentiveness to Sara as such a thing,

> I thought, one might not hope to meet
> Save in the dear delicious land of Faery!
> (*(PW*,i,104,ll.11-12)

which sets the tone of Coleridge's approach to his courtship,
and the early months of marriage. *To the Nightingale* (1795)
finds Sara superior in voice, 'What time the languishment of
lonely love / Melts in her eye', to Philomel, 'Sister of love-lorn
Poets', whose songs

> Are not so sweet as is the voice of her,
> My Sara—best beloved of human kind!
> When breathing the pure soul of tenderness,
> She thrills me with the Husband's promis'd name!
> ( (*PW*,i,94,ll.23-6)

This is not merely stiltedly conventional in sentiment, but so
impossibly idealised as to suggest that Coleridge could only
anticipate his marriage with closed eyes, overcompensating by
dreams of an emotional fairyland. Coleridge is more successful
writing strictly within the stylistic conventions of his immediate
literary tradition. *Lines,* 'composed while climbing the left
ascent of Brockley Coomb, Somersetshire, May 1795', describes
a picturesque landscape observed by a solitary figure who longs
for the company of a soul-sharing friend or lover. The scene is
composed and affective in the manner of Dyer or Thomas
Wharton:

> Up scour the startling stragglers of the flock
> That on green plots o'er precipices browze:
> From the deep fissures of the naked rock
> The Yew-tree bursts! Beneath its dark green boughs
> (Mid which the May-thorn blends its blossoms white)
> Where broad smooth stones jut out in mossy seats,
> I rest:—and now have gain'd the topmost site.
> Ah! what a luxury of landscape meets
> My gaze! Proud towers, and Cots more dear to me,
> Elm-shadowed Fields, and prospect-bounding Sea!
> Deep sighs my lonely heart: I drop the tear:
> Enchanting spot! O were my Sara here!
>
> *(PW*,i,94,ll.5-16)

Sara is little more than a formality, and Coleridge can fit her easily into the conventionally moulded experience; but *Lines in the Manner of Spenser* (1795) is an elaborately artificial presentation of Coleridge's apprehension of the contrast between his idealised conception of Sara, and the disgruntled reality. Coleridge wishes he could pluck a quill from the Dove of Peace,

> For O! I wish my Sara's frowns to flee,
> And fain to hear some soothing song would write,
> Lest she resent my rude discourtesy,
> Who vow'd to meet her ere the morning light,
> But broke my plighted word—ah! false and recreant wight!
>
> *(PW*,i,95,ll.5-9)

Very amusing, from one fairy lover to another; Coleridge goes on to explain that he failed to turn up only because he was having a pleasant dream of Sara and

> Such joys with sleep did 'bide,
> That I the living image of my Dream
> Fondly forgot.
>
> (ll.42-4)

Coleridge found this forgetfulness less easy to come by in later years, and there is an uneasiness in his sense of the difference between the Sara of his dream:

> My Sara came, with gentlest look divine;
> Bright shone her eye, yet tender was its beam;

> I felt the pressure of her lip to mine!
> Whispering we went, and Love was all our theme—
> Love pure and spotless, as at first, I deem,
> He sprung from Heaven!
>
> (ll.37-42)

and the real Sara:

> Too late I woke, and sigh'd—
> 'O! how shall I behold my Love at eventide!'
>
> (ll.44-45)

This half-realised insecurity and anxiety is felt most strongly in *Lines written at Shurton Bars...September 1795...*Coleridge describes the 'dread' of loneliness that his marriage, his love for Sara, overcomes; but the horror of loneliness haunts the poem, more powerful than its positive emphasis on 'the heart's big ecstasy'. Coleridge is addressing his absent Sara, 'in answer to a letter from Bristol' (*PW*,i,96):

> O ever present to my view!
> My wafted spirit is with you,
> And soothes your boding fears:
> I see you all oppressed with gloom
> Sit lonely in that cheerless room—
> Ah me! You are in tears!
>
> Beloved Woman! did you fly
> Chill'd Friendship's dark disliking eye,
> Or Mirth's untimely din?
> With cruel weight these trifles press
> A temper sore with tenderness,
> When aches the void within.
>
> But why with sable wand unblessed
> Should Fancy rouse within my breast
> Dim-visag'd shaped of Dread?
>
> (*PW*,i,97,ll.7-21)

Love has changed Coleridge's attitude towards the indulgence of a solitary melancholy in a setting of sympathetically wild, storm-torn nature:

> Time was, I should have thought it sweet
> To count the echoings of my feet,
> And watch the storm-vex'd flame.
> And there in black soul-jaundic'd fit
> A sad gloom-pamper'd Man to sit
> And listen to the roar.
>
> (ll.46-51)

The experience of familial community that Sara brings is to purge Coleridge of this kind of self-indulgent sensibility, and heighten his consciousness of stormy nature's grim reality for those who have no social defences against it:

> When stormy Midnight howling round
> Beats on our roof with clattering sound,
> To me your arms you'll stretch:
> Great God! you'll say—To us so kind,
> O shelter from this loud bleak wind
> The houseless, friendless wretch!
>
> (ll.73-8)

This positive function of the domestic retreat, providing a healing environment, gains in strength in the poetry as it gains in strength as a condition of Coleridge's life after August 1795. But *Lines written at Shurton Bars* remains an indefinably disturbing poem, with the tonal stress falling strongly on those negative, isolating and isolated states of mind that make the achievement of community more valuable in contrast. Coleridge's nervousness about Sara, a fear of anti-climax, is paralleled in the three sonnets he wrote on the birth of his first son (Hartley was born in September 1976). He is overwhelmed by the reality of fatherhood, and the three poems record a curious vacuity of response that is nearer to dread than elation:

> When they did greet me father, sudden awe
> Weigh'd down my spirit: I retired and knelt
> Seeking the throne of grace, but inly felt
> No heavenly visitation upwards draw
> My feeble mind, nor cheering ray impart.
> Ah me! before the Eternal Sire I brought
> Th'unquiet silence of confused thought
> And shapeless feelings: my o'erwhelmed heart
> Trembled, and vacant tears stream'd down my face.
> And now once more, O Lord! to thee I bend,
> Lover of souls! and groan for future grace,
> That ere my babe youth's perilous maze have trod,
> Thy overshadowing Spirit may descend,
> And he be born again, a child of God.
>
> (*PW*,i,152-3)

The effort to correlate the existence of the child with his conception of its importance is too much for Coleridge (this is a common experience of fatherhood, but Coleridge's resistance to the fact is extreme):

> O my sweet baby! when I reach my door,
> If heavy looks should tell me thou art dead,
> (As sometimes, through excess of hope, I fear)
> I think that I should struggle to believe
> Thou wert a spirit, to this nether sphere
> Sentenc'd for some more venial crime to grieve;
> Did'st scream, then spring to meet Heaven's quick reprieve,
> While we wept idly o'er thy little bier!
>
> (*PW*,i,154,ll.7-14)

This slightly macabre reaction is superseded by an accommodation of the child to Coleridge's idealisation of the domestic retreat; Sara becomes more convincing as a mother, and the baby becomes the projection of Coleridge's ideal self-image (Coleridge's children always retain this significance in the poetry):

> Charles! my slow heart was only sad, when first
> I scann'd that face of feeble infancy:
> For dimly on my thoughtful spirit burst
> All I had been, and all my child might be!
> But when I saw it on its mother's arm,
> And hanging at her bosom (she the while
> Bent o'er its features with a tearful smile)
> Then I was thrill'd and melted, and most warm
> Impress'd a father's kiss: and all beguil'd
> Of dark remembrance and presageful fear,
> I seem'd to see an angel-form appear—
> 'Twas even thine, beloved woman mild!
> So for the mother's sake the child was dear,
> And dearer was the mother for the child.
>
> (*PW*,i,154)

Coleridge's 'dim-visag'd shapes of Dread' became more palpable in time, and the anxiety always present in his attitude to domestic retirement was disastrously confirmed in the course of his family life. The *Letter to Sara* is obviously a most crucial poem in this respect, just as the other conversation poems are products of the positive in ascendence over the negative pole of Coleridge's emotional and intellectual oscillation. *The Old Man of the Alps*, published in the *Morning Post* of 8 March 1798, is a reverential treatment of family life, a community of lovers, children, friends, with its attendant joy. The poem is Wordsworthian in its simple narrative movement, its attempt at the unforced grandeur of character and idea in preference to metaphor, that Coleridge had seen in *The Ruined Cottage;* but the diction and movement are Coleridge's ('But sweet is pity to an aged breast'), and the values of the poem are those of his best poetry:

> . . .oft she prattled with an eager tongue
> Of promised joys that would not loiter long,
> Till with her tearless eyes so bright and fair,
> She seem'd to see them realis'd in air!
> In fancy oft, within some sunny dell,
> Where never wolf should howl or tempest yell,
> She built a little home of joy and rest,
> And fill'd it with the friends whom she lov'd best:
> She named the inmates of her fancied cot,
> And gave to each his own peculiar lot;
> Which with our little herd abroad should roam,
> And which should tend the dairy's toil at home.
>
> (*PW*,i,249,ll.29-40)

Coleridge realised the promise of this joy, not 'in air' but in fact, in the cottage in Nether Stowey, and more briefly still in the cottage at Clevedon in the early weeks of his marriage. The self-sufficiency of the community is pantisocratic, emphasising the importance of that scheme in the genesis of his real and poetic 'little home of joy'. Coleridge left England for Germany in September 1798, and from that moment the reality of this community faded. He wrote (or rather 'imitated' from the German) a handful of poems about home-sickness, loneliness, a yearning for the domestic community he had left; *Hexameters, Something Childish, but very natural* (23 April 1799; *PW*,i,313), *Home-Sick* (6 May 1799):

> And sweet it is, in summer bower,
> Sincere, affectionate and gay,
> One's own dear children feasting round,
> To celebrate one's marriage-day.
>
> (*PW*,i,314,ll.5-8)

Coleridge met Sara Hutchinson in October 1799, three months after returning from Germany; he could never have left home for so long, and have travelled so far, had he felt secure in his domestic happiness, and Sara Hutchinson simply helped to focus the problem. The initial shock of the disintegrating domestic situation produced some poems of stature, of which *Love* is the finest, a transparently veiled account of his covert 'courtship' of Sara Hutchinson. The association of 'joy' with love and friendship persists, 'my hope, my joy, my Genevieve'; but the ideal of domestic retirement in the poetry is reduced, after 1799, to the sad evocation of a hopelessly distant paradisal happiness. *Ode to Tranquillity* (1801) is stylistically regressive, the tranquillity very domestic but ringing hollow, and *To Asra* (1801) confirms that a real, achieved security of domestic life was receding into the unattainable ideal of Asra's love reciprocated. A great majority of the poems that Coleridge wrote between 1799 and his death in 1834 are more or less 'Asra' poems, with the early domestic values appropriated to an image of the perfect friend and lover that Coleridge never had. We find constantly an eerie re-emergence of the Stowey happiness as a disturbing dream of thwarted happiness. *Constancy to an Ideal Object* (which may be as early as 1805, or as late as 1828) contrasts two conditions between which Coleridge oscillated throughout his life, reconciling their opposition (and the reconciliation was more than anything a triumph of the creative imagination) only briefly, for a few weeks in 1795, a few months in 1797 and 1798. One condition is the familial community, a way of life that Coleridge considered, and proved to be, fruitful and happy; the other condition is, unmistakably, that of the Ancient Mariner:

> Yet still thou haunt'st me; and though well I see,
> She is not thou, and only thou art she,
> Still, still as though some dear embodied Good,
> Some living Love before my eyes there stood
> With answering look a ready ear to lend,
> I mourn to thee and say—'Ah! loveliest friend!
> That this the meed of all my toils might be,
> To have a home, an English home, and thee!'
> Vain repetition! Home and Thou are one.
> The peacefull'st cot, the moon shall shine upon,
> Lulled by the thrush and wakened by the lark,
> Without thee were but a becalmed bark,
> Whose Helmsman on an ocean waste and wide
> Sits mute and pale his mouldering helm beside.
>
> (*PW*,i,456,ll.11-24)

# III
# Pantisocracy and the Theory of Retirement

Coleridge wrote to Southey, in August 1795, urging him not to succumb to family pressure by allowing himself to be forced out of Pantisocracy and into the Church:

> Domestic Happiness is the greatest of things sublunary—and of things celestial it is perhaps impossible for unassisted Man to believe any thing greater—:but it is not strange that those things, which in a pure form of Society will constitute our first blessings, should in its present morbid state, be our most perilous Temptations—!
>
> (*CL*,i,158)

Pantisocracy was not simply an elaborate rationalisation of the ideal of familial community (though this aspect of the scheme has been neglected),[1] but involved a differentiation between kinds of domesticity. The pattern of Coleridge's poetry, where antipathetic social realities intensify his sense of value in a community, a family, outside an existing social structure and its circles of affection, shapes the Pantisocracy scheme as Coleridge conceived it. The family provided an ideal social model, but it also provided an effective agent of social pressure in the 'present morbid state' of the social context from which Coleridge projected his 'pure form of Society'. Early on in a painful letter that Coleridge wrote to the wavering Southey on Friday, 13 November 1795, he reminded his Godwinian friend that Pantisocracy had originally (Southey had introduced Coleridge to the scheme in Oxford in 1794) represented not merely a rejection of conventional domesticity, but a rejection of any social morality structured around the family unit:

> Before I quitted Oxford, we had struck out the leading features of a Pantisocracy: while on my Journey thro' Wales, you invited me to Bristol with the full hopes of realizing it—:during my

abode at Bristol, the Plan was matured: and I returned to
Cambridge hot in the anticipation of that happy Season, when
we should remove the *selfish* Principle from ouselves, and
prevent it in our children, by an *Abolition* of Property: or in
whatever respects this might be impracticable, by such similarity
of Property, as would amount to a *moral Sameness,* and answer all
the purposes of *Abolition.* Nor were you less zealous: and
thought, and expressed your opinion, that if any man embraced
our System, he must comparatively disregard 'his father and
mother and wife and children and brethren and sisters, yea, and
his own Life also': or he could 'not be our disciple'.

                                        (*CL*,i,163-4)

There were obviously Godwinian elements in the theory of
Pantisocracy, and they certainly came from Southey; Col-
eridge's Christianity kept him dubious about Godwin until he
had succeeded in converting him.[2] Southey's conviction, as
recalled in Coleridge's letter, that the disciple of Pantisocracy
would never allow the claims of personal and familial affection
to override those of a generalised rational benevolence, was
thoroughly Godwinian. Godwin's attitude to family affection is
epitomised in a famous passage of *Political Justice* (1793), where
it is proposed that a perfectly rational, and therefore perfectly
benevolent being, confronted with the alternatives of sacrific-
ing either Fenelon or Fenelon's valet, would save Fenelon; even
if the valet were oneself, or one's 'wife or mother'.[3] A central
aspect of the Godwinian 'perfectibility', the continual evolution
of rational man, was its stress on the necessity of the increasing
ascendance of rational benevolence over private affection. The
Godwinian radical had necessarily to scorn the comforts and
affections of home, but 'home' was and is a concept that may
readily be expanded to include the whole range of social
custom and mannerism that place a class or homogeneous
region within a wider social context of all classes and regions,
the nation: Coleridge and Southey in the first flush of hot
democratic rage were far from able to resist the frequent
opportunities for baiting the provincial bourgeois that every-
where surrounded them in Somerset. We can guess that the
scheme of Pantisocracy to which Southey first introduced
Coleridge was extreme in its Godwinism, just as Southey was at
the time extreme in his 'democratic' manner. Coleridge,
impressionable, picked up Southey's tone, and the two young

Pantisocrats appear to have spent good crusading time in a pointless ostentatious show of radical virulence. The impression that Coleridge made at this time accentuated later the strong local distrust of 'jacobins' that came to drive the Wordsworths out of Alfoxden. A tradition of the Poole family preserves the reactions of Coleridge and Southey to the news of Robespierre's death. John Poole, visiting his cousin Tom, found him in the company of two young men, introduced to him

> by the names of Coleridge and Southey, who not only did not show the feelings any right-thinking people might have been expected to manifest at such a piece of intelligence, but one of them—Southey—actually laid his head down upon his arms and exclaimed, 'I had rather have heard of the death of my own father'.[4]

A reaction by Godwin out of Gothic romance, which anyway cost nothing as Southey's father had been dead for two years.[5] Southey out-paced Coleridge in extravagance of commitment, and indeed Coleridge must have had uneasy qualms about the bristling indignation on the faces of his audience; his social manner was never pure performance, but struggled always towards the communication of some idea or experience that could be shared (of course, his monologues became famous for their exclusiveness, and we think of the image in Beerbohm's cartoon, Coleridge blandly preaching to a sleeping audience).[6] Tom Poole's description of the two young radicals is interesting:

> [Coleridge's] aberrations from prudence, to use his own expression, have been great; but he now promises to be as sober and rational as his most sober friends could wish. In religion he is a Unitarian, if not a Deist; in politicks a Democrat, to the utmost extent of the word.
>
> Southey, who was with him, is of the University of Oxford, a younger man, without the splendid abilities of Coleridge, though possessing much information, particularly metaphysical, and is more violent in his principles than even Coleridge himself. In Religion, shocking to say in a mere Boy as he is, I fear he wavers between Deism and Atheism.[7]

Poole's sensitive eye detected a restraining self-consciousness in

Coleridge, but the less sympathetic John Poole found no reason for distinguishing between shades of black:

> One is an undergraduate of Oxford, the other of Cambridge. Each of them was shamefully hot with Democratic rage as regards politics, and both Infidel as to religion. I was extremely indignant.[8]

Sixty years later the Reverend John Poole still had no time for Coleridge, and recalled the 'sad democratic nonsense' that he used to talk.[9]

Southey's fervour abated a good deal more rapidly than Coleridge's, and the differences between the two men, Southey's greater self-confidence and his shorter period of radical commitment, are illuminated by a comparison of family backgrounds. Southey's place in his own family was obviously secure, though the family itself laboured under financial difficulties and had been saved from bankruptcy only by the intervention of Southey's ferociously respectable aunt, Miss Tyler of Bath.[10] Coleridge's financial embarrassments were strictly his own, and he had to beg to be bailed out by his brothers. Southey had been expelled from Westminster School for an audaciously rebellious attack on corporal punishment in the school magazine, appositely entitled *The Flagellant,* but the expulsion did not alienate Southey from his family: 'Not one reproach have I heard concerning Westminster. It does not hurt me, for I have not acted improperly.' Doubtless this self-confidence was easier to sustain in a domestic atmosphere free from recrimination. Geoffrey Carnall has drawn attention to Southey's characteristic 'assurance of rectitude', and has seen this unattractive quality as a defence against 'unmanageable emotional insecurity';[11] this is very plausible, and fits in persuasively with the well-argued thesis of Mr. Carnall's book, but there is a sense in which all social manners are defensive in this way, and the serenity of Southey's 'assurance', while perhaps admirable, does betray a certain superficiality of self-consciousness in comparison with Coleridge's anxious introspection, however destructively intense that may have been. It is not surprising that Southey should have seemed to the Poole family the more aggressively assertive of the two radicals (another family legend of the Pooles records that

Southey 'had positively said that Robespierre was a ministering angel of mercy, sent to slay thousands that he might save millions';)[12] Coleridge's uneasy awareness of the social discomfort inherent in his self-isolating radical stance was based in his experience of alienation that had operated perpetually at the quotidian level of domestic relations, while Southey had no such experience to worry over. Coleridge too had got himself into trouble in the course of his education, running up alarming debts at Cambridge.[13] But unlike Southey, who had reacted to his expulsion with anger,[14] Coleridge spun in wild recoil away from the confrontation with his family entailed in the mismanagement of his own affairs. He joined the army as a common solider. The episode of 'Silas Tomkyn Comberbache' has been recorded with a smug paternal indulgence from commentators, has been obscured, in fact, by the same hearty trivialisation accorded to Coleridge's early years in most accounts of Pantisocracy, and of Coleridge's subjection to the attentions of a government spy in 1798 (and there is no real excuse in the fact that Coleridge himself came to encourage this attitude). It is worth pointing out that to enlist in the King's Light Dragoons in December 1793, aften ten months of war with France, was for a supporter of the French a quite extraordinarily desperate resource. The differences between the two enthusiasts who met at Oxford in July 1794 were in reality far greater than they seemed, and Southey's Godwinian scheme of an ideal society could hardly have been congenial to Coleridge as such; under Coleridge's influence Pantisocracy (a name provided by Coleridge, together with the important technical term 'aspheterize'—'we really *wanted* such a word': *CL*,i,84) became Hartleian and Unitarian, and very firmly based in the idea of a familial community informed by private affection as the precondition of benevolence. Carnall describes Southey's horror of the 'common, cold, lip-intercourse of life',[5] a disposition that suited very well the isolation of the middle-class radical, but a disposition absolutely foreign to Coleridge, whose best medium was the 'lip-intercourse' of conversation. Coleridge often tried to laugh off his isolation from the local life of the community in Somerset:

> I am here [Stowey] after a most tiresome journey; in the course of which, a woman asked me if I knew one Coleridge, of Bristol.

> I answered, I had heard of him. 'Do you know, (quoth she) that
> that vile jacobin villain drew away a young man of our parish,
> one Burnet,' &c. and in this strain did the woman continue for
> near an hour; heaping on me every name of abuse that the
> parish of Billingsgate could supply. I listened very particularly;
> appeared to approve all she said, exclaiming 'dear me!' two or
> three times, and, in fine, so completely won the woman's heart
> by my civilities, that I had not courage enough to undeceive
> her....
>
> (*CL*,i,321)

Whether or not this actually happened, what is sadly apparent
is Coleridge's fundamental need to share the common experi-
ence of his humanity, to have himself accepted. Pantisocracy
was a means of escape from the hostility of anti-jacobin
England, an attempt to resolve the conflicts that were by the
end of 1794 beginning to loom large in Coleridge's life; and
Pantisocracy was created in the image of that happy family in
nature which Coleridge idealised.

In contrast to Hartley, Godwin considered mind as deter-
mined not by the physical but by the psychological environ-
ment. This environment is embodied in the political institutions
of a people, and it is in the interests of these institutions to
retard the development of mind, a development which inevita-
bly finds any institution obstructively inflexible, unresponsive
to change. The progress of man towards perfectly rational
benevolence thus depended on the dissolution of governments,
and of the contracts that they involved. But Pantisocracy as
described in a letter of Thomas Poole to a prospective
pantisocrat (the letter, sketchy as it is, is the most detailed
account of the scheme that survives) was not to be a rational
anarchy in the Godwinian sense:

> Every one is to enjoy his own religious and political opinions,
> provided they do not encroach on the rules previously made,
> which rules, it is necessary to add, must in some measure be
> regulated by the laws of the state which includes the district in
> which they settle.[16]

Pantisocracy was obviously envisaged as involving some sort of
social contract, and was therefore fundamentally opposed to
Godwin's stress on the necessity for an absolute freedom from
constraint in the operation of the objective reason. Coleridge's

own description of Pantisocracy emphasised the contractual obligations under which members of the new society would live:

> A small but liberalized party have formed a scheme of emigration on the principles of an abolition of individual property. Of their political creed, and the arguments by which they support and elucidate it they are preparing a few copies—not as meaning to publish them, but for private distribution. In this work they will have endeavoured to prove the exclusive justice of the system and its practicability; nor will they have omitted to sketch out the code of contracts necessary for the internal regulation of the society; all of which will of course be submitted to the improvements and approbation of each component member.
>
> (*CL*,i,96-7)

It is a great pity that Coleridge's account of the 'code of contracts necessary for the regulation of the society' was never written, but the circumstances in which the scheme evolved suggest that Coleridge anticipated a small community composed of friendly couples with numerous children, situated in a landscape of uncorrupted (and therefore uncorrupting) purity. The nucleus of this community was to be formed by Coleridge, Southey, George Burnet (Southey's contemporary at Balliol, and like Coleridge and Southey a native of the west country), and the Fricker family, a widow with five daughters and a son. The Fricker girls were Sarah, Edith, Martha, Mary and Eliza; Coleridge became engaged to Sarah, Southey to Edith, Burnet tried hard with Martha but, to the exasperation, presumably, of the others, was repeatedly rebuffed. Mary was already married to the quaker Robert Lovell, who threw himself heartily into the scheme (dragging with him, in imagination at least, his brother and two sisters). Coleridge also recruited old school friends. He had first met Southey at Oxford through Robert Allen, a Christ's Hospital boy then at University College, and Allen joined the party; and while in London in September 1794 Coleridge managed to fire the enthusiasm not only of George Dyer (who confidently predicted that Joseph Priestley himself, already in America, would join the pantisocrats), but also of his contemporaries at Christ's Hospital, notably Le Grice and Favell. Coleridge was building his new society on family and friends, and on the principle of 'aspheterism' ('the generalisation of individual property');[17] the problem of where to draw the aspheteric line was rather tricky, as Tom Poole solemnly acknowledged:

> The regulations relating to the females strike them as the most difficult; whether the marriage contract shall be dissolved if agreeable to one or both parties, and many other circumstances, are not yet determined.[18]

Coleridge and Southey misunderstood each other over the delicate issue of 'the regulations relating to the females'; this hardly needs stressing, but we should notice that the problem of marriage was closely related to that of ownership, and that Godwin's attitude to property was opposed in principle to Coleridges's position. Godwin devoted Chapter III of the third book of *Political Justice* to a discussion 'Of Promises', and his rejection of contracts as binding irrespective of changing circumstances naturally involved a consideration of the rights of property:

> Property is sacred: there is but one way in which duty requires the possessor to dispose of it, but I may not forcibly interfere, and dispose of it in the best way in his stead. This is the ordinary law of property, as derived from the principles of universal morality.

Godwin proceeds to qualify this statement by drawing attention to those situations in which the right of the possessor would be superseded by the claim of another individual to a more basic right, for example the right to live.[19] Godwin regarded inequality in the distribution of property as a social evil; but he advocated equality of property only as one means to the end of personal freedom in the exercise of benevolent reason, a condition of freedom from government in which 'the principles of universal morality' would find free play:

> Two of the greatest abuses relative to the interior policy of nations, which at this time prevail in the world, consist in the irregular transfer of property, either first by violence, or secondly by fraud. If among the inhabitants of any country there existed no desire in one individual to possess himself of the substance of another, or no desire so vehement and restless

as to prompt him to acquire it by means inconsistent with order and justice, undoubtedly in that country guilt could scarcely be known but by report. If every man could with perfect facility obtain the necessaries of life, and, obtaining them, feel no uneasy craving after its superfluities, temptation would lose its power. Private interest would visibly accord with public good; and civil society become what poetry has feigned of the golden age.[20]

Marriage was evil because it constituted an 'irregular transfer of property' as a contract usually undertaken in direct opposition to the principle of objective reason, and because it fostered a damagingly irrational sense of possession:

The method is, for a thoughtless and romantic youth of each sex, to come together, to see each other, for a few times, and under circumstances full of delusion, and then to vow eternal attachment. What is the consequence of this? In almost every instance they find themselves deceived. They are reduced to make the best of an irretrievable mistake. They are led to conceive it their wisest policy, to shut their eyes upon realities, happy, if, by any perversion of intellect, they can persuade themselves that they were right in their first crude opinion of each other. Thus the institution of marriage is made a system of fraud; and men who carefully mislead their judgements in the daily affair of their life, must be expected to have a crippled judgement in every other concern.

Add to this, that marriage, as now understood, is a monopoly, and the worst of monopolies. So long as two humans beings are forbidden, by positive institution, to follow the dictates of their own mind, prejudice will be alive and vigorous. So long as I seek, by despotic and artificial means, to maintain my possession of a woman, I am guilty of the most odious selfishness. Over this imaginary prize, men watch with perpetual jealousy; and one man finds his desire, and his capacity to circumvent, as much excited, as the other is excited, to traverse his projects, and frustrate his hopes. As long as this state of society continues, philanthropy will be crossed and checked in a thousand ways, and the still augmenting stream of abuse will continue to flow.[21]

One imagines that this passage would have struck Coleridge with some force in his later years, as indeed, though for different reasons, it must have struck Godwin himself after his brief but transforming experience of married life with Mary Wollstonecraft.[22] Young Southey was far more likely to adopt the attitudes of such a radical attack on marriage; unlike

Coleridge, he could enjoy the luxury of setting small store by the comfortable reality of his domestic life (but one must anyway suspect the consistency of Southey's Godwinism; he proposed taking with him to America his mother and various brothers and sisters.)[23]

Coleridge's Hartleian Unitarianism placed him in direct opposition to Godwin's views on the value of domestic affection as expressed in *Political Justice*. Coleridge insists, in a letter to Southey, that 'Some home-born Feeling is the *centre* of the Ball, that, rolling on thro' life collects and assimilates every congenial Affection' (*CL*,i,86). His discussions of Pantisocracy always reveal the Hartleian basis of its theory:

> Wherever Men *can* be vicious, some *will* be. The leading Idea of Pantisocracy is to make men *necessarily* virtuous by removing all Motives to Evil—all possible Temptations.
>
> (*CL*,i,114)

Pantisocracy would remove 'all Motives to Evil' partly by its location in a nature of pristine purity. Coleridge's belief in the educative force of nature is present in the early poetry; *To an Infant* (1795) provides an obvious example:

> Ah! cease thy tears and sobs, my little Life!
> I did but snatch away the unclasp'd knife:
> Some safer toy will soon arrest thine eye,
> And to quick laughter change this peevish cry!
> Poor stumbler on the rocky coast of Woe,
> Tutor'd by pain each source of pain to know!
> Alike the foodful fruit and scorching fire
> Awake thy eager grasp and young desire.
>
> (*PW*,i,91,ll. 1-8)

Joseph Priestley's abridgement of Hartley's *Observations on Man, Hartley's Theory of the Human Mind* (1775) (a book that Coleridge must surely have known), is prefaced by three introductory essays, by Priestley, the first of which, 'A general view of the doctrine of Vibrations', selects the example of heat as a phenomenon about and through which nature instructs.[24] Hartley's own words parallel Coleridge's poem:

> when our Love and Hatred are excited to a certain Degree, they put us upon a Variety of Actions, and may be termed Desire and

Aversion; by which last Word I understand an active Hatred. Now the Actions which flow from Desire and Aversion, are entirely the Result of associated Powers and Circumstances.... The young Child learns to grasp, and go up to the Plaything that pleases him, and to withdraw his Hand from the Fire that burns him, at first from the Mechanism of his Nature, and without any deliberate Purpose of obtaining Pleasure, and avoiding Pain, or any explicit Reasoning about them. By degrees he learns, partly from the Recurrency of these mechanical Tendencies, inspired by God, as one may say, by means of the Nature which he has given us; and partly from the Instruction and Imitation of others; to pursue everything which he loves and desires; fly from every thing which he hates; and reason about the Method of doing this, just as he does upon other Matters.[25]

Hartley elsewhere approves in more general terms the benevolent effects of beautiful natural scenery, and offers an associational analysis of the means by which these effects are achieved; he also stresses the value of retirement:

To [the pleasures of country sports and pastimes] we may add, the Opposition between the Offensiveness, Dangers, and Corruption of populous Cities, and the Health, Tranquillity, and Innocence, which the actual View, or the mental Contemplation, of rural Scenes introduces; also the Pleasures of Sociality and Mirth, which are often found in the greatest Perfection in Country Retirements, the amourous Pleasures, which have many Connexions with rural Scenes, and those which the Opinions and Encomiums of others beget in us, in this, as in other Cases, by means of the Contagiousness observable in mental Dispositions, as well as bodily ones.[26]

Escape from the 'offensiveness, dangers and corruption of populous cities' meant for the pantisocrats escape from the influence of corrupt political institutions, and from the social structure that those institutions sought to preserve. But the escape that Coleridge envisaged did not constitute an abdication of social responsibility; Pantisocracy was to enshrine the spirit of a good society, was to be a purification of the springs of benevolence. Exposure to the divine influence of nature would be one means to this purificiation, but another, equally important means would be constituted in the healing paradise of familial community. *To an Infant* celebrates the relationship between mother and child:

> Untaught, yet wise! mid all thy brief alarms
> Thou closely clingest to thy Mother's arms,
> Nestling thy little face in that fond breast
> Whose anxious heavings lull thee to thy rest!
>
> (ll.11-14)

These most elemental 'home-born Feelings' are an ultimate source of what Hartley called 'Sociality', 'the Pleasure which we take in the mere Company and Conversation of others, particularly of our Friends and Acquaintance, and which is attended with mutual Affability, Complaisance and Candour'. The child develops 'sociality' through contact with 'Parents, Attendants, or Play-fellows'. 'Good-will, or benevolence', 'that pleasing affection which engages us to promote the welfare of others to the best of our power', 'is nearly connected with Sociality, and has the same Sources.'[27] We can understand why Coleridge was so worried that the children who were to travel with the pantisocrats might already have suffered too much exposure to the polluting environment of a corrupt society and its institutions:

> These children—the little Fricker for instance and *your* Brothers—Are they not already *deeply* tinged with the prejudices and errors of Society? Have they not learnt from their Schoolfellows *Fear* and *Selfishness*—of which the necessary offspring are Deceit, and desultory Hatred? *How* are we to prevent them from infecting the minds of *our* Children? By reforming their Judgements?—At so early age *can* they have *felt* the ill consequences of their Errors in a manner sufficiently vivid to make this reformation practicable? Reasoning is but *Words* unless where it derives force from the repeated experience of the person, to whom it is addressed.—*How* can we ensure their silence concerning *God* &c—?
>
> (*CL*,i,119-20)

It might have been objected that Coleridge's objections to the children were equally applicable to himself, and indeed *To an Infant* articulates Coleridge's consciousness of his own childish disregard for the natural morality of nature's teaching (he is still prone to 'snatch what coals of fire on Pleasure's altar glow!'). But it was Coleridge's consciousness of his situation that would have enabled him to control the conditions in which the children of Pantisocracy would grow up, and it is the inevitable inadequacy of just such consciousness, in the 'corrupted' children, that worries him in his letter. Godwin's emphasis on prevailing political institutions as a most important factor in the determination of consciousness lies behind Coleridge's anxiety; and even if his knowledge of Godwin was taken second-hand from Southey,[28] he acknowledged Godwin's influence in the sonnet *To William Godwin* that appeared in the *Morning Chronicle* on 10 January 1795:

> O form'd t'illume a sunless world forlorn,
> As o'er the chill and dusky brow of Night,
> In Finland's wintry skies the Mimic Morn
> Electric pours a stream of rosy light,
>
> Pleas'd I have mark'd OPPRESSION, terror-pale,
> Since, thro' the windings of her dark marchine,
> Thy steady eye has shot its glances keen—
> And bade the All-lovely 'scenes at distance hail'.
>
> Nor will I not thy holy guidance bless,
> And hymn thee, GODWIN! with an ardent lay;
> For that thy voice, in Passion's stormy day,
> When wild I roam'd the bleak Heath of Distress,
>
> Bade the bright form of Justice meet my way—
> And told me that her name was HAPPINESS.
>
> (*PW*,i,86)

But while Godwin was a major figure in the highly-charged political atmosphere of the mid-nineties, there were questions on which Coleridge, as a Unitarian, could not countenance Godwin's views. '*How* can we ensure their silence concerning *God?*' he wrote to Southey of the children already '*deeply* tinged with . . . prejudices and errors'; Coleridge certainly thought the established Church as corrupt an institution as any,[29] but he was never anything less than a devout Christian, and as such could not regard the atheist Godwin as an acceptable hero. Coleridge was anyway repelled by Godwin's views on the value of private affection, views which he came to attack very directly in the *Watchman*;[30] and he disagreed also with Godwin over the nature of the right to property. Where Godwin respected the right to such possessions as were necessary to the continuation of life, but recommended equalisation of property, Coleridge insisted, most particularly in his Unitarian lectures of 1795, on the complete abolition of personal property, and advocated a thoroughgoing communism of work and wealth.

An institutionalised means of access to God was at the very best supererogatory within the Hartleian scheme; human consciousness, and the objects of which it was conscious, evolved in reciprocity up through Hartley's seven increasingly complex levels, beginning in simple sensation and issuing finally (after incorporating 'Imagination', 'Ambition', 'Self-interest', and 'Sympathy') in 'Theopathy', and 'The Moral Sense'.[31] Hartley summarised (in words that Coleridge echoed in *Religious Musings)* the ultimately revelatory quality towards which perception developed:

> Since God is the Source of all Good, and consequently must at last appear to be so, i.e. be associated with all our Pleasures, it seems to follow, even from this Proposition, that the Idea of God, and of the Ways by which his Goodness and Happiness are made manifest, must, at last, take place of, and absorb all other Ideas, and He himself become, according to the Language of the Scriptures, *All in All.*[32]

Coleridge's ideals of private affection and domesticity in retirement thus found a Christian rationalisation in Hartley's associationism; they constituted the necessary bases for a love of abstract qualities in man,[33] and for the love and consciousness of God. Coleridge's 'Lectures on Revealed Religion', delivered in Bristol in 1795, demonstrate the way in which Coleridge's Christianity incorporated political ideas that broadened the rational basis of his ideal community in nature.[34] The second of Coleridge's six lectures included a defence of the Mosaic dispensation, and an admiring account of the Jewish Constitution (although the account leans heavily on Moses Lowman's *A Dissertation on the Civil Government of the Hebrews* (1740), a standard work approved by liberal dissenters):

> The Constitution was presented to the whole nation by Moses, and each individual solemnly assented to it. By this Constitution the Jews became a federal Republic consisting of twelve Tribes. The Country contained 15 millions of acres, which were equally divided among the People, 25 acres to each man, the People being about 700,000.

'To preserve this equal division', Coleridge went on, 'it became necessary to prevent Alienation'; this was done by the prohibition of interest on money, and by an act for the abolition of all debts every sixth year, thus rendering the lending of money 'unadvantageous and insecure'. To prevent any 'Abuses' that 'might gradually creep in',

> On every 50th year a solemn Jubilee was appointed, in which all Lands were restored, and the Estate of every Family discharged from all incumbrances returned to the Family again.

Coleridge found 'the terms of this Law' so 'beautiful',

> and so replete with practical Wisdom and Benevolence that it would be almost criminal to leave any part of it unobserved.

The contemporary resonance of this historical argument emerged in an unusually forceful statement of Coleridge's position on the rights of property:

> Liberty was proclaimed through the whole nation—the whole nation were informed by divine authority that it was unlawful to acknowledge any human superior. Every Hebrew was thus the Subject of God alone. Nor was an end proposed without means established. The Lands were restored. Property is Power and equal Property equal Power. A Poor Man is necessarily more or less a Slave. Poverty is the Death of public Freedom—it virtually enslaved Individuals, and generates those Vices, which make necessary a dangerous concentration of power in the executive branch. If we except the Spartan, the Jewish has been the only Republic that can consistently boast of Liberty and Equality.[35]

Pantisocracy as Coleridge explained it was based in the conviction that 'Property is Power', and in the last of the 'Lectures on Revealed Religion' he pointed to Christ's teaching as the source of this conviction:

> I have asserted that Jesus Christ forbids to his disciples all property—and teaches us that accumulation was incompatible with their Salvation! An assertion so novel may require proof . . . . In Matthew VI.25-33 the most plausible defences of accumulation are declared to be of no avail. "Therefore take no thought what shall we eat and what shall we drink? or Wherewithal shall we be clothed? But seek ye first the Kingdom

of God and his Righteousness—and all these things shall be added unto you. Take therefore no thought for the morrow"!

This 'positive Precept of our Saviour', Coleridge argued, must imply either 'that we are to be idle and expect miraculous subsistence', or 'that we are to gain our daily bread by our daily labour, and not accumulate from any prudential Fears of Tomorrow'. Coleridge then attempted to prove by further reference to Christ's teaching that the second interpretation was correct, and proceeded to attack in very strong terms the evils inherent in accumulated property:

as long as anyone possesses more than another, Luxury, Envy, Rapine, Government & Priesthood will be the necessary conse-quence, and prevent the Kingdom of God—that is the progres-siveness of the moral world.[36]

Coleridge's communism was a Hartleian, Unitarian commit-ment, and was in terms of practical politics more radical than anything implied by Godwin. His only criticism of the Jewish Constitution was a suggestion that its equalisation of property did not go far enough:

An abolition of all individual Property is perhaps the only infallible Preventative against accumulation, but the Jews were too ignorant a people, too deeply leavened with the Vices of Egypt to be capable of so exalted a state of Society—[37]

Coleridge's commitments in politics and philosophy were the rationalisations of attitudes adopted in resistance to social and personal pressure. Pantisocracy evolved as a response to Coleridge's own financial embarrassments, his isolation from family, his estrangement from English society. A Christian, intellectual radical, not working class, without real vocation, without home, Coleridge's beliefs issued in the conception of a small, independent community whose values and activities would embody resolution of the problems inherent in his social context. It is dangerously easy to simplify the nature of the relationship between Coleridge's life in society, and the life of his mind; to ignore it is hardly more absurd than, for example, to assume that he adopted a communistic theory of property simply to facilitate a scheme of emigration that he would not otherwise have been able to afford, though even that kind of crudity is sometimes difficult to resist:

> With regard to pecuniary matters it is found necessary, if twelve men with their families emigrate on this system, that 2000£ should be the aggregate of their contributions; but infer not from hence that each man's quota is to be settled with the littleness of arithmetical accuracy. No; *all* will strain *every* nerve, and then I trust the surplus money of some will supply the deficiencies of others.
>
> (*CL*,i,97)

Coleridge developed the ideas of Pantisocracy within a social context that ensured the continuing 'idealism', rather than the actual realisation, of the scheme; the conditions that necessitated Coleridge's conception of a new society were also the conditions that operated in various ways to keep that conception ideal, unrealiseable. The force of family as the unit of social organisation in England proved too strong for the idea of family as a radical political model. Southey left Pantisocracy as a result of his family obligations, his proper sense of the necessity not to let his family down or waste their money. One suspects that Mrs Fricker only ever tolerated the wild talk of her children's friends because of her determination to see her daughters married. Of course, Coleridge could never have raised a sufficient amount of money to carry through a journey to America, and once the projected personnel of Pantisocracy started to backslide he must have felt that the unbalancing disaffection of his own family life was in fact the condition of all family life; he certainly thought of Pantisocracy as a family:

> SHAD GOES WITH US. HE IS MY BROTHER! I am longing to be with you—Make Edith my Sister—Surely, Southey! we shall be frendotatoi meta frendous. Most friendly where all are friends. She must therefore be more emphatically my Sister.
>
> (*CL*,i,103)

The Pantisocratic ideal of a small, self-sufficient familial community, a physical and psychological environment both healing and morally progressive, appears in the lectures of 1795 as an intellectual, a theoretical imperative, and this imperative re-emerges in significantly modified forms

throughout Coleridge's life. The years which see Coleridge's
radicalism nullified, his belief in the necessity and imminence
of social change destroyed, are years that witness also Col-
eridge's movement from materialism to philosophical idealism,
from Hartley to Kant. The ideal of a healing, educating
community also undergoes metamorphosis, beginning as a
radical ideal and ending as the central element in a work of
conservative political theory. This metamorphosis is the change
from the Coleridge of *A Moral and Political Lecture* (1795) to the
Coleridge of *On the Constitution of the Church and State* (1830);
and it is a transformation that tells, in the end, as much about
Coleridge's England, as about the man himself.

A *Moral and Political Lecture* discriminates between three types
of 'the friends of Freedom',[38] of which only the third type is
approved by Coleridge:

> that small but glorious band, whom we may truly distinguish by
> the name of thinking and disinterested Patriots. These are the
> men who have encouraged the sympathetic passions till they
> have become irresistable habits, and made their duty a necessary
> part of their self-interest, by the long continued cultivation of
> that moral taste which derives our most exquisite pleasures from
> the contemplation of possible perfection, and proportionate
> pain from the perception of existing *depravation*. Accustomed to
> regard all the affairs of man as a process, they never hurry and
> they never pause; theirs is not that twilight of political know-
> ledge which gives us just light enough to place one foot before
> the other; as they advance, the scene still opens upon them, and
> they press right onward with a vast and various landscape of
> existence around them. Calmness and energy mark all their
> actions, benevolence is the silken thread that runs through the
> pearl chain of all their virtues. Believing that vice originates not
> in the man, but in the surrounding circumstances; not in the
> heart, but in the understanding; he is hopeless concerning no
> one . . . he looks forward with gladdened heart to that glorious
> period when Justice shall have established the universal frater-
> nity of Love. These soul ennobling views bestow the virtues
> which they anticipate. He whose mind is habitually imprest with
> them soars above the present state of humanity, and may be
> justly said to dwell in the presence of the most high.[39]

This 'small but glorious band' who look forward to the
'universal fraternity of Love', who inhabit ' a vast and various
landscape', who ennoble their souls with 'the virtues which they

anticipate', are Coleridge's first extended acount of an 'elect,'[40] a group of intellectuals necessarily small, necessarily confined in the initial sphere of its operations (confined, as it happened, almost exclusively to the sphere of personal relationship), but holding within their circle of affection and influence the potential of a new world. The conversation poems represent the language of this community, containing a voice that is subsequently echoed in the work of other Romantic radicals who found themselves forced onto private resources by an increasingly hostile political atmosphere. Hazlitt's deep pleasure in the local life and colour still vigorous in rural, pre-industrial England is suggestive in this context; but a quality of domestic intensity, the sense of value in personal relationship and the small, closed group, is powerfully present in Leigh Hunt and De Quincey, and provides what is almost a defining characteristic of Charles Lamb's 'Elia' essays. Shelley in particular comes nearest to Coleridge in the use of a poetic voice that is peculiarly that of friendship, an intimate voice shared in opposition to a common threat, the language of a small, close audience. The 'Letter to Maria Gisborne', the late lyrics to Jane:

> There seemed from the remotest seat
> Of the white mountain waste,
> To the soft flower beneath our feet,
> A magic circle traced,—
> A spirit interfused around,
> A thrilling, silent life,—
> To momentary peace it bound
> Our mortal nature's strife;
> And still I felt the centre of
> The magic circle there
> Was one fair form that filled with love
> The lifeless atmosphere,[41]

this delicate fragility of mood, the extreme transience of its 'momentary peace', is pervaded by the darkening, elegiac vision of Shelley's maturity; but the poetry is Coleridgean in its address to an audience that holds in itself the highest value that the poet celebrates. Shelley, like Coleridge, creates a social context for his utterance, a magic circle. Shelley is closest to Coleridge, though, in such a passage as this, from *Prometheus Unbound* (III,iii, Prometheus to Asia):

> all around are mossy seats,
> And the rough walls are clothed with long soft grass;
> A simple dwelling, which shall be our own;
> Where we will sit and talk of time and change,
> As the world ebbs and flows, ourselves unchanged.
>
> (ll.20-24)

The retreat that is also a preserve of human potential is explicitly invoked by Shelley in the final section of 'Lines written among the Euganean Hills'; the passage provides an excellent gloss on the quality in Coleridge that we are bringing into focus. Shelley meditates, prayerfully, on the possibility of a 'flowering isle' in the 'sea of Life and Agony':

> some calm and blooming cove,
> Where for me, and those I love,
> May a windless bower be built,
> Far from passion, pain, and guilt,
> In a dell mid lawny hills,
> Which the wild sea-murmur fills,
> And soft sunshine, and the sound
> Of old forests echoing round,
> And the light and smell divine
> Of all flowers that breathe and shine:
> We may live so happy there,
> That the Spirits of the Air,
> Envying us, may even entice
> To our healing Paradise
> The polluting multitude;
> But their rage would be subdued
> By the clime divine and calm,
> And the winds whose wings rain balm
> On the uplifted soul, and leaves
> Under which the bright sea heaves;
> While each breathless interval
> In their whisperings musical
> The inspired soul supplies
> With its own deep melodies,
> And the love which heals all strife
> Circling, like the breath of life,
> All things in that sweet abode
> With its own mild brotherhood:
> They, not it, would change; and soon
> Every sprite beneath the moon
> Would repent its envy vain,
> And the earth grow young again.
>
> (ll.342-73)

Coleridge considered Pantisocracy as a means to the millennium, as a society that would renovate the earth (like Shelley in *Prometheus Unbound,* Coleridge would have regarded a new earth as the product of a change in human consciousness; but where for Coleridge this change is the means to an end, it represents for Shelley the unimagined change itself, only imaged in the language of revelation); he wrote to Southey, in August 1795, of Pantisocracy as 'perhaps a miraculous Millennium' of which the 'realization is distant' (*CL*,i,158). The Bible offered to the Unitarian Coleridge authoritative sanction for the kind of intellectual elite that he advocated in *A Moral and Political Lecture* and in the theory of Pantisocracy:

> Where the Causes of evil exist, Good cannot be—in the moral world there is a constant Alternation of Cause and Effect—and Vice and Inequality mutually produce each other. Hence the necessity of Governments and the frequency of Wars—Jesus Christ therefore commanded his disciples to preserve a strict equality—and enforced his command by the only thing capable of giving it effect. He proved to them the certainty of an Hereafter—and by the vastness of the Future diminished the Tyranny of the Present. If not with hereditary faith but from the effect of our examination and reflection we are really convinced of a state after Death, then and then only will Self-interest be wedded to Virtue—Universal Equality is the object of the Messiah's mission not to be procured by the tumultuous uprising of an indignant multitude but this final result of an unresisting yet deeply principled Minority which gradually absorbing kindred minds shall at last become the whole.[42]

Christ's disciples formed the original model for Coleridge's ideal community of familial equality, a point which emphasises the Christian basis of Pantisocracy and its successive forms, and the millennial quality of its value. Coleridge's disappointment in the French Revolution did not immediately destroy his faith in its principles; in a similar way, the failure to make Pantisocracy into a social reality intensified his yearning for the sort of life it represented, and this yearning was still strong enough in the ageing, conservative Coleridge of the late 1820s to throw a great deal of weight onto the notion of the 'clerisy' in *On the Constitution of the Church and State.* In the concept of the 'clerisy', by which Coleridge denominated that group of men who comprised in themselves 'all the so called liberal arts and sciences, the possession and application of which constitute the civilization of a country',[43] we find the re-emergence of a small intellectual elite as providing a 'healing paradise' for the 'polluting multitude'; but the ideal has been re-constituted in response to the dissolution of the private audience and its radical potential, and Coleridge now addresses a general public as the apologist of its own status quo. Coleridge grew into acceptance of the only kind of society to which intellectuals could be allowed to belong. The re-emergence of Coleridge into relationship with an audience was a gradual process, a process which arrived at its crucial point in the presentation of himself as a shy, retired academic, unused to the harsh light of public notice, in the opening paragraph of *Biographia Literaria:*

> It has been my lot to have had my name introduced, both in conversation, and in print, more frequently than I find it easy to explain, whether I consider the fewness, unimportance, and limited circulation of my writings, or the retirement and distance in which I have lived, both from the literary and political world.

The tone that Coleridge adopts here confirms the impression of the epigraph from Goethe that followed the title page, the impression of a careful, defensive return, full of self-justification, to the bosom of the society that had rejected him:

> Little call as he may have to instruct others, he wishes nevertheless to open out his heart to such as he either knows or hopes to be of like mind with himself, but who are widely scattered in the world: he wishes to knit anew his connexions with his oldest friends, to continue those recently formed, and to win other friends among the rising generation for the remaining course of his life. He wishes to spare the young those circuitous paths, on which he himself had lost his way.[44]

The failure of Pantisocracy had not, however, been the end of Coleridge's efforts to establish a domestic, communal way of life; that was in fact an endeavour which did, to some limited but rewarding extent, find success, in the cottage at Nether Stowey. There he lived with wife and child, in rural retirement, in daily contact with Poole, and later the Wordsworths, often visited by friends, Lamb, Thelwall, Lloyd. It is important to realise that for Coleridge the cottage at Nether Stowey was, quite consciously, a version of the pantisocratic ideal. Coleridge did not finally give up the effort to live in a manner that asserted his highest values until his escape to Germany and the first immersion in philosophical idealism. Towards the end of 1796, Coleridge became obsessed with the idea of moving into a cottage that Tom Poole had discovered to be available in his own village of Nether Stowey. There were two major factors that contributed to Coleridge's extreme anxiety about the success of this plan; his growing awareness of the harsh economic reality of his situation ('there are two Giants leagued together whose most imperious commands I must obey however reluctant—there names are BREAD & CHEESE: *CL*,i,222), and his persistent desire for the small community of kindred souls in nature. The ideal of home was to be a refuge from the obligations and responsibilities that loomed larger as Coleridge's life took form within society; it was also, however narrowly by now, to provide the germ of a new society in which such obligations and responsibilities did not inhere. When in December Tom Poole began to have second thoughts about bringing Coleridge to live on his doorstep (it seems likely that Poole's neighbours had tried to urge him against allowing the well-known Jacobin into their midst,)[45] Coleridge wrote a succession of over-wrought, almost desperate letters in an effort to carry the plan through. These letters tell of the life that Coleridge anticipated in Nether Stowey:

> If I live at Stowey, you indeed *can* serve me effectually, by assisting me in the acquirement of agricultural practice. —If you can instruct me to manage an acre and a half of Land, and to raise on it with my own hands all kinds of vegetables, and grain, enough for myself & my Wife, and sufficient to feed a pig or two with the refuse, I hope, that you will have served me *most* effectually, by placing me out of the necessity of being served.
>
> (*CL*,i,270)

The affinities with Pantisocracy are strong, if for example we compare Poole's account of the Scheme:

> Their opinion was that they should fix themselves at—I do not recollect the place, but somewhere in a delightful part of the new back settlements; that each man should labour two or three hours in a day, the produce of which labour would, they

imagine, be more than sufficient to support the colony. As Adam Smith observes that there is not above one productive man in twenty, they argue that if each laboured the twentieth part of time, it would produce enough to satisfy their wants.[46]

Coleridge had himself stressed the self-sufficient agricultural economy of Pantisocracy:

> In the course of the winter those of us whose bodies, from habits of sedentary study or academic indolence, have not acquired their full tone and strength, intend to learn the theory and practice of agriculture and carpentry, according as situation and circumstances make one or the other convenient.
>
> (*CL*,i,97)

Coleridge's descriptions of the Stowey life become more detailed with the increasing anxiety of his letters to Poole:

> I shall have six companions—My Sara, my Babe, my own shaping and disquisitive mind, my Books, my beloved Friend, Thomas Poole, & lastly, Nature, looking at me with a thousand looks of Beauty, and speaking to me in a thousand melodies of Love.
>
> (*CL*,i,271)

This is later supplemented by a fuller account that again echoes earlier descriptions of Pantisocracy:

> To Mrs Coleridge the Nursing and Sewing only would have belonged—the rest I took upon myself—& since our resolution have been learning the practice.—With only two rooms, & two people—their wants severely simple—& no great labour can there be in their waiting upon themselves. Our Washing we should put out.—I should have devoted my whole Head, Heart, & Body to my Acre and a Half of Garden Land—& my evenings to Literature.
>
> (*CL*,i,274)

'Their wants severely simple'; Coleridge would have necessarily to devote his evenings to literature, for the necessity of earning a living was rapidly becoming a dominant force in his life, and literature was the only source of income that he anticipated:

> I receive about forty guineas yearly from the Critical Review &

New Monthly magazine. It is hard if by my greater works I do not get twenty more. I know how little the human mind requires when it is tranquil—and in proportion, as I should find it difficult to simplify my wants, it becomes my duty to simplify them. For there must be a vice in my nature, which woe be to me if I do not cure . . . . Sixteen shillings would cover all the weekly expences of my Wife, infant, and myself—this I say from my Wife's own calculation.

(*CL*,i,270)

He is just about in control of himself, and the tone, here, trying as he is to convince Poole of the reasoned plausibility of his proposals. We notice the close connection in Coleridge's mind between the happiness of self-sufficient, domestic community, and the ability to cope with economic pressure. At other moments, really frightened about the prospects of the Stowey plan, he betrayed the intensity of his insecurity, now both social and economic; 'What am I do do then?—I shall be again afloat on the wide sea unpiloted and unprovisioned', he wrote, unable to focus on anything but his dreams:

my time was to have been divided into four parts—1. Three hours after breakfast to studies with CL1.—2. the remaining hours till Dinner to our Garden—3. From after dinner till Tea to letter-writing, and domestic Quietness. 4. From Tea till Prayer time to the Reviews, Magazines, & other literary Labours.

(*CL*,i,273)

Coleridge could see no other viable life offered by the contingencies of his social situation:

I can accept no place in State, Church, or Dissenting Meeting. Nothing remains possible, but a School, or Writer to a Newspaper, or my present Plan.—I could not love the man, who advised me to keep a School or write for a Newspaper.

(*CL*,i,274)

Tom Poole decided that the irritation of neighbours (and probably his own awareness of the responsibilities he took on) did not outweigh the pleasure of allowing Coleridge to realise his dream of 'domestic Quietness', 'the realization', as Coleridge put it, 'of my innocent Independence' (*CL*,i,274). He secured the cottage, and Coleridge moved in on the eve of the new year of 1797.

Coleridge's financial difficulties were not over, indeed they had scarcely begun; and Coleridge's radicalism was still to earn him much social discomfort, even as it lost rapidly in commitment. But in Nether Stowey Coleridge's sense of security, however imaginary, allowed him the congenial social context that his distinctive poetic language needed. He had written to Thelwall, on 17 December 1796, of his scheme for a 'farm', pre-empting the criticisms that he anticipated from the very active political lecturer:

> I doubt not, that the time will come when all our Utilities will be directed in one simple path. That Time however is not come; and imperious circumstances point out to each one his particular Road. Much good may be done in all. I am not *fit* for *public* Life; yet the Light shall stream to a far distance from the taper in my cottage window. Meantime, do *you* uplift the torch dreadlessly, and shew to mankind the face of that Idol, which they have worshipped in Darkness!
>
> (*CL*,i,277)

The taper image has long been celebrated by Coleridgeans as providing the perfect apotheosis of Coleridge in his *annus mirabilis,* and of course the image has been accommodated all too easily to our well-worn conception of the Platonist in his lonely tower. The light that Coleridge hoped would stream from his window has served that dominant aspect of his reputation which constitutes a 'chapter' in the history of ideas, a chapter in which Coleridge's mind is seen as a charming if elusive butterfly that managed to struggle free from the unpromising ugliness of his quotidian life. The context of Coleridge's image is, however, very plainly political, and the 'face of that Idol' that will be illuminated by Thelwall's torch and Coleridge's candle can hardly refer to the higher life of unchanging forms. It might be suggested that Coleridge is simply taking his colour from the background provided by his correspondent, here certainly more red than blue; but Thelwall inspired a certain relaxed discursiveness in Coleridge, argumentative without strain, that produced the best of his early letters. Coleridge's personality was formed, to an extreme degree, by its rootless subjection to the social and economic forces by which his society defended itself, but the fundamental sympathies of the man are still discernible through his constant efforts to hedge bets. Even his brother George, who represented for Coleridge the private and the public institutions that he always dreaded would shun him, could not quite eradicate the egalitarian temper:

> I have been asked what is the best conceivable mode of meliorating Society—My Answer has been uniformly this—'Slavery is an Abomination to every feeling of the Head and Heart—Did Jesus teach the *Abolition* of it? No! He taught those principles, of which the necessary *effect* was—to abolish all Slavery. He prepared the mind for the reception before he poured the Blessing—.' You ask me, what the friend of universal Equality *should* do—I answer—'Talk not of Politics—*Preach the Gospel!*'
>
> (*CL*,i,126)

This is not sleight of hand; we have seen that Coleridge's Unitarianism found solid radical principles in the Bible, and this was so whether Coleridge's correspondent was George, or Thelwall, or the radical Benjamin Flower:

> My answer to Godwin will be a six shilling Octavo; and is designed to shew not only the absurdities and wickedness of *his* System, but to detect what appear to me the defects of all the systems of morality before & since Christ, & shew that wherein they have been right, they have exactly coincided with the Gospel, and that each has erred exactly where & in proportion as, he has deviated from that perfect canon.
>
> (*CL*,i,267)

The move to Nether Stowey was, then, an attempt to realise a Christian, radical ideal. As such, the scheme failed; it is obviously not possible, in any terms, to present Coleridge as a great, or an influential, or even a minor radical thinker. But the real life of his mind began in radicalism, and the nature of this beginning cannot be ignored when we come to the chaotic voices of his more familiar work. The ideal of the small, politically affective community turned from a radical to a conservative aspiration, and this was a change, clearly enough, from resistance to capitulation. The ideal was, anyway, never confined to radical thought. Just as the family could be regarded as the unit of a new society, while it actually operated as the highly effective unit of an existing social structure, so the ideal of community had also two opposed political functions. Coleridge's radical version had counterparts in the textbooks of radicalism, for example in the Godwinian system of 'parishes'.[47] Early practical experiments in the social effects of an improved environment, for instance the Owenite communities, fell naturally into the form of small, self-sufficient groups, but the inevitable artificiality of such experiments, instituted not as the product of change but as a defence against it, only confirmed the eternal impracticability of utopias. But we find in Burke a social model of startling similarity:

> To be attached to the subdivision, to love the little platoon we belong to in society, is the first principle (the germ as it were) of public affections. It is the first link in the series by which we proceed towards a love to our country and to mankind.[48]

As a radical, it was from precisely this sort of national community that Coleridge was excluded. The process of his development into a philosophical idealist, and a great conservative theorist, was the process of his assimilation into the national community as Burke conceived it. Coleridge found that English society could not and would not join him in Nether Stowey; but he needed, above all, to belong, and he returned to that society as a prodigal son, becoming the centre of a slightly grotesque 'family' in Highgate, and the champion of a theory of Church and State that made careful, reasoned allowance for the accommodation of the forces of progress.[49]

The central conversation poems, *This Lime-Tree Bower my Prison, Frost at Midnight,* and *The Nightingale,* enact Coleridge's development from materialism to idealism. Their vision is located beyond the phenomenal nature, the present world, which yet remains the inescapable condition of vision. In Nether Stowey, Coleridge was wrested away from the conviction that his ideal community would ever become a millennium known through the senses, and present on the faces of his neighbours; he came there to a point at which the culmination of his search for a life that enacted value merged into the beginning of a life-long effort to find the intellectual unity that would hold together the fragments of his life.

# IV
# Politics and the Problem of Audience

Coleridge's stress on 'principles', as the essential prerequisite for useful thinking about politics, philosophy, and criticism, has been used as evidence for a continuity in his thought, a consistent development from beginning to end, that begins in *A Moral and Political Lecture:*

> It will be . . .our endeavour, not so much to excite the torpid, as to regulate the feelings of the ardent: and above all, to evince the necessity of *bottoming* on fixed Principles, that so we may not be the unstable Patriots of Passion or Accident, or hurried away by names of which we have not sifted the meaning, and by tenets of which we have not examined the consequences.[1]

Coleridge did consistently maintain the necessity of an adherence to unchanging conceptions, that could be brought to bear on all kinds of problem, and which could place these problems within a framework capable of reconciling apparently opposed systems of belief. This insistence was characteristic of the Sage of Highgate:

> My system, if I may venture to give it so fine a name, is the only attempt I know ever made to reduce all knowledges into harmony. It opposes no other system, but shows what was true in each; and how that which was true in the particular, in each of them became error, *because* it was only half the truth. I have endeavoured to unite the insulated fragments of truth, and therewith to frame a perfect mirror. I show to each system that I fully understand and rightfully appreciate what that system means; but then I lift up that system to a higher point of view, from which I enable it to see its former position, where it was, indeed, but under another light and with different relations;—so that the fragment of truth is not only acknowledged, but explained.[2]

The impressive claims of this passage are in a way substantiated in the works that Coleridge actually published in his lifetime. The Constitution of Church and State is examined 'according to the idea of each':

*i.e.,* as a *principle,* existing in the only way in which a principle can exist—in the minds and consciences of the persons, whose duties it prescribes, and whose rights it determines. In the same sense that the sciences of arithmetic and of geometry, that mind, that life itself, have reality; the constitution has real existence, and does not the less exist in reality. because it both *is,* and *exists as,* an IDEA.[3]

The *Friend* announced itself as a series of essays designed 'to aid in the formation of fixed principles in politics, morals and religion', and its main sections discuss 'the Principles of Political Knowledge' and 'the Grounds of Morals and Religion'.[4] We are not directly concerned here with the very complex question of Coleridge's 'system', as it is or is not consistently present as an implied structure in the later lectures and prose works. We can say, however, that there are indisputable inconsistencies between Coleridge's stated commitments in the 1790s, and those he claimed after the turn of the century. He came to reject an earlier self, but, more puzzlingly, he tried to pretend that an earlier self, with its different commitments, had never existed. Some of Coleridge's attempts to disclaim his early radicalism are frankly outrageous: an example of the extraordinary lengths to which he was prepared to go is his claim in 1807 that the sonnet *To Earl Stanhope* (1795) 'was written in ridicule of Jacobinical Bombast [,] put into the first Edition by a blunder of Cottle's, rejected indignantly from the second & ... maliciously reprinted in my Absence'.[5] The attempt to transform an enthusiastic celebration of the radical peer ('Thyself redeeming from that leprous stain / Nobility', *PW,*i,89) into a parody of itself by the super-imposition of an ironic distance, in the manner of the *Anti-Jacobin,* which is not contained by the language of the poem, betrays an anxiety in relation to the sympathy between poet and audience that was obviously profoundly disturbing. And this sort of anxiety in Coleridge centres in the main on the insecurity that attended the expression of political belief. Coleridge's political views were characteristically modified to meet what he felt to be the demands of the social context in which he spoke; a change of context could require embarrassing elaboration in the explaining away of what must have seemed to him a terrifying personal past, lying in wait to undercut the sympathy of the moment's listeners. A continuous self-defensive consciousness of audience is the pervasive rhetorical strategy of Coleridge's prose style. How far a philosophy of unity might require a prose style calculated to offend no-one is an interesting question; how far a philosophy of unity may develop as the rationalisation of such a style is perhaps an even more intriguing problem.

Coleridge's system 'opposes no other system', but appreciatively comprehends all other structures of meaning; his modest, tolerant omniscience is the means to a harmony of all 'insulated fragments' within one comprehensive structure. Not only the problems of philosophy disappear within this system, but also the insecurity of his relationship with an audience. No-one is alienated, because everyone is right once the proper 'lights' and 'relations', the accommodating perspectives, are discovered. Coleridge's 'perfect mirror' reveals disagreement, antagonism, as nothing more than a failure of perspective. The man holding the mirror is everybody's friend. This is the mode of relationship that Coleridge tried to create with his audience in *A Moral and Political Lecture*, where he adopted the role of mediator between opposed parties precisely because an overt commitment to either side would have involved the hostility, from one side or the other, that Coleridge dreaded. 'Companies resembling the present', he noted in his lecture, 'will from a variety of circumstances consist chiefly of the zealous Advocates for Freedom'.[6] There can be no doubt that he was at the same time keenly aware that those present in the lecture hall did not comprise the whole of his audience, for by February 1795 the ears of the government were extremely sensitive to the zealous advocacy of freedom. Soon after the publication of the lecture, Coleridge wrote to George Dyer explaining that he had been '*obliged* to publish, it having been confidently asserted that there was Treason in it' (*CL*,i,152). The 'Advertisement' that prefaced the published form of the lecture confirms that Coleridge had decided to publish from fear of persecution (which could, for example, have taken the simple form of a threat to revoke the licence of any publican allowing Coleridge the use of a lecture room; public houses commonly rented space for public meetings):

> They, who in these days of jealousy and Party rage dare publicly explain the Principles of Freedom, must expect to have their Intentions misrepresented, and to be entitled like the Apostles of Jesus, "Stirrers up of the People, and men accused of Sedition". The following Lecture is therefore printed as it was delivered, the Author choosing that it should be published with all the inaccuracies and inelegant colloquialisms of an hasty composition, rather than that he should be the Object of possible Calumny as one who had rashly uttered sentiments which he afterwards timidly qualified.[7]

Coleridge's first publication thus begins with the first of many prefatory apologies, by which he attempted to preempt hostile criticism. The political hostility that threatened Coleridge is registered in the lecture in the terms by which he sought to establish a harmless neutrality; 'the necessity of *bottoming* on fixed Principles' was an emphasis that Coleridge used in making common ground between the advocates of freedom, and the guardians of English society. In placing this emphasis on 'principles' he neatly appropriated an argument often used in the context of the debate that had followed in the wake of the French Revolution. Mrs Barbauld, the poetess and educational reformer whom Coleridge knew and admired in the 1790s, had published in 1790 *An Address to the Opposers of the Repeal of the Corporation and Test Acts* (Mrs Barbauld was married to a dissenting minister), in which she had described with excitement the dawning era: 'Systems are analysed into their first principles, and principles are fairly pursued to their legitimate consequences'.[8] Burke himself had placed the political debate over the Revolution in a wider context of fundamental issues:

> Whatever may be the success of evasion in explaining away the gross error of *fact*, which supposes that his Majesty (though he holds it in concurrence with the wishes) owes his crown to the choice of his people, yet nothing can evade their full explicit declaration, concerning the principle of a right in the people to choose; which right is directly maintained, and tenaciously adhered to. All the oblique insinuations concerning election bottom in this proposition.[9]

But the context of basic principles was equally available to Burke's radical opponents; to Mary Wollstonecraft, for example, in *A Vindication of the Rights of Women* (1792):

> In the present state of society it appears necessary to go back to first principles in search of the most simple truths, and to dispute with some prevailing prejudice every inch of ground.[10]

Coleridge could conveniently appropriate 'principles' as a defensive measure, by which the opposed elements in his audience could each be satisfied; and especially so, as the exact nature of his principles remained obscure. The *Critical Review* reviewed *A Moral and Political Lecture* in April 1795, and drew attention to the studied vagueness of Coleridge's actual commitment:

> Though, with one or two exceptions, we admire the style of this little work, we think it rather defective in point of precision; and, instead of saying we have shown the necessity of forming some fixed and determinate principles of action, he should have said, we have represented certain characters. We also think our young political lecturer leaves his auditors abruptly, and that he has not stated, in a form sufficiently scientific and determinate, those principles to which, as he expresses it, he now proceeds as the most *important point*.[11]

The pro-French *Critical Review* was understandably disappointed that the author of *The Fall of Robespierre,* which had been well reviewed by the magazine a few months earlier, could produce nothing more positive. But Coleridge was beginning to realise the genuine dangers of his position as a radical by reputation, and the sheltering neutrality of principles, of a commitment to nothing more awkward than the, idea of commitment, allowed the evasion of confrontation with an audience. Coleridge certainly had principles; in 1796 he still maintained that property was 'beyond doubt the Origin of all Evil' (*CL*,i,214), and the bias of his political lecturing throughout 1795 was undeniably anti-ministerial, opposed to the war, to the slave trade, to the Two Bills. In spite of the continued threat of prosecution he did in fact regain his nerve, to a certain extent, later in the year. One critic has argued that Coleridge's *The Plot Discovered* was published in December because the lecture on the Two Bills (delivered in November) on which it was based had, like *A Moral and Political Lecture,* aroused the suspicions of the government.[12] If that was the case, it must have renewed the anxiety with which he had been

coming to terms in, for example, the 'Preface' (dated 16
November 1795) to *Conciones ad Populum*, where Coleridge's
self-possessed confidence allows him a franker acknowledge-
ment of the political atmosphere:

> The two following addresses were delivered in the month
> February, 1795, and were followed by six others in defence of
> natural and revealed Religion. There is "a time to keep silence"
> saith King Solomon;—but when I proceeded to the first Verse of
> the Fourth Chapter of the Ecclesiastes, "and behold the Tears of
> such as were oppressed, and they had no comforter; and on the
> side of the oppressors there was power"—I concluded, that this
> was *not* the "time to keep silence".—For Truth should be spoken
> at all times, but more especially at those times, when to speak the
> Truth is dangerous.[13]

We must return to the dangers that Coleridge refers to here,
but a scrutiny of their specific forms may prove more useful if
we first bear in mind the development beyond the 1790s of
Coleridge's characteristic stress on the importance of fixed
principles.

We may take a single example, one strand in a very elaborate
pattern, from the second number of the *Friend* (8 June 1809) as
it first appeared in serial form between 1 June 1809 and 15
March 1810. The number begins with a quotation from a
speech of Burke's delivered in 1780 (before the French
Revolution had changed his political colour without changing
his principles), 'on presenting to the House of Commons a plan
for the better security of the independence of Parliament'.
Coleridge then proceeds to introduce his opinions on '[the]
most hazardous subject' of politics:

> Conscious that I am about to deliver my sentiments on a subject
> of the utmost delicacy, to walk
> > "per ignes"
> > "Suppositos cineri doloso"
> I have been tempted by my fears to preface them with a motto
> of unusual length, from an Authority equally respected by both
> of the opposite parties.

Burke's great recommendation is that 'he has almost uniformly
made the most original and profound general principles of
political wisdom, and even the recondite laws of human

passions, bear upon particular measures and events'. It is clear that there can only be a specious consistency between the principles that Coleridge urges here, and those that he meant to propose in *A Moral and Political Lecture*. The stance of 'purity and disinterestedness in Politics' (the phrase is Burke's, from the speech that Coleridge quoted), the stance of the man above party rage, facilitated the preservation of intellectual integrity, so important in Coleridge's projected self-image, while enabling him to adjust his commitments to meet the demands of his audience. It is fascinating to observe the way in which Coleridge's discomfort, in the consciousness of his own tortuous efforts to appear consistent, manifests itself, and in fact often draws attention to itself; for the second number of the *Friend* is almost entirely devoted to self-justification before the event, an anxious refusal to take responsibility for any wrong impression he may make, a constant effort not to offend. Effectively nothing is said about the principles or practice of politics. Coleridge includes a very long footnote (later omitted), directed to those

> who from various printed and unprinted calumnies have judged most unfavourably of my political tenets; and to those, whose favour I have chanced to win in consequence of a similar, though not equal mistake. To both I affirm, that the opinions and arguments, I am about to detail, have been the settled convictions of my mind for the last ten or twelve years, with some brief intervals of fluctuation, and those only in lesser points, and known only to the Companions of my Fire-side.[14]

Coleridge's hesitation between 'ten or twelve years' means in effect the difference between 1797 and 1799, before and after Germany; and there is no doubt that in Germany Coleridge's home-sickness, his yearning to belong, began to merge with a yearning to belong to England, and a new willingness to accept the limitations imposed by English society (the anti-French and strongly pro-English feeling amongst German society seems to have placed England, for Coleridge, in a much more agreeable light).[15] But 1797 was a critical year in Coleridge's political development, as we sense in the note that Coleridge attached to the passage just quoted:

> I may safely defy my worst enemy to shew, in any of my few

writings, the least bias to Irreligion, Immorality, or Jacobinism:
unless in the latter word, be implied sentiments which have been
avowed by men who without recantation, direct or indirect, have
been honoured with the highest responsible offices of Govern-
ment.

   This is the first time, that I have attempted to counteract the
wanton calumnies of unknown and unprovoked persecutors.
Living in deep retirement, I have become acquainted with the
greater part only years after they had been published and
individually forgotten.[16]

Southey's comment, in a letter written a few days after this
appeared, is no less than fair: 'if he was not a Jacobine, in the
common acceptation of the name, I wonder who the Devil
was.'[17] A note of Thelwall's, in the same frankly unequivocal
manner, confirms this judgement:

   That Mr Coleridge was indeed far from democracy, because he
   was far beyond it, I well remember—for he was a downright
   zealous leveller, and indeed in one of the worst senses of the
   word he was a Jacobin, a man of blood. Does he forget the
   letters he wrote to me (and which I believe I yet have)
   acknowledging the justice of my castigation of him for the
   violence and sanguinary tendency of some of his doctrines?[18]

Coleridge's published work in the 1790's had not, it is true,
shown any bias towards 'Irreligion' in the sense of atheism, or
even Deism, though he had been open in opposition to the
established Church and its institutions. But his work had been
Jacobin, 'in the common acceptation of the name' as a
contemptuous blanket term for all radicals, in its attitudes to
the government, the war, and individual property.

   We notice the 'deep retirement' in which Coleridge has lived,
in ignorance of the slanders against him (curiously now
'individually forgotten'—presumably by all but Coleridge). The
function of ideal retirement has changed in its relation to
English society, and has become the quiet retreat of the thinker
working within society, providing, from something like a
conventional pastoral perspective, the rationale of a society that
is assumed as his own. The suggestion of past heresy could be
profoundly damaging in this context, threatening to disturb
the relationship with an audience, threatening to turn retire-
ment into the isolation that is its reflex. Coleridge's retirement

ideal develops essentially as a re-direction of his work away
from a particular kind of private audience, and out to a general
audience known largely through the prevalence of its institu-
tions and tastes (the 'reading public').[19] The re-direction is
registered as a modification of style, more particularly of tone;
and we can locate an intermediate stage of this development in
the appalling letter that Coleridge wrote, on 1 October 1803, to
Sir George and Lady Beaumont (*CL*,i,998-1005). This long,
agonised letter opens out for us the chaos of Coleridge's mind,
the extraordinary manner in which his political life, and his life
in society, is inextricably woven into the anxieties and neuroses
of his personality. We do not find it difficult to blame the
Coleridge who devises elaborate falsifying rationalisations of
his own past, in the *Friend,* or in the passage in Chapter 10 of
*Biographia Literaria* that so incensed an acquaintance from
Coleridge's Bristol days.[20] But the personality that informs the
Beaumont letter requires a more strenuous act of sympathy, a
reading that takes properly into account both Coleridge's
extreme instability, and the extreme hostility of his social
environment in the formative years of the mid-nineties. The
letter begins with familiar explanations of delay, and detailed
description of illness; then, after insisting that the 'only
medicine' of 'a hot climate' is unacceptable because 'it seems
better to die than to live out of England', he suddenly turns to
the impact made on him by the recent execution of the Irish
patriot Robert Emmet, for his part in a violent uprising:

> I have been extremely affected by the death of young
> Emmett—just 24!—at that age, dear Sir George! I was retiring
> from Politics, disgusted beyond measure by the manners &
> morals of the Democrats, & fully awake to the inconsistency of
> my practice with my speculative Principles.
>
> (*CL*,ii,999)

Coleridge's identification with Emmet, it later becomes clear, is
a good deal more complicated than a simple similarity in early
radical commitments which Coleridge lost and Emmet did not;
but we are immediately aware of Coleridge's falsifying memory
as it tugs a recently past self into acceptable form. Coleridge
had written in July 1796 (about eight weeks before his
twenty-fourth birthday) of his 'aversion' to 'local and temporary

Politics'; 'they narrow the understanding, they narrow the heart, they fret the temper' (*CL*,i,222). But these remarks have to be read in context. Coleridge was unhappy about the prospect of leaving Bristol to take up a post with Perry's *Morning Chronicle*, and unhappy about the economic circumstances that were pushing him into ephemeral commentary on literature and politics. The aversion to local and temporary politics was also a response to the hostility that Coleridge met with as a radical. This hostility, the atmosphere of an unsympathetic audience, made a large part of the public reaction to Coleridge's earliest political lectures:

> Since I have been in Bristol I have endeavoured to disseminate Truth by three political Lectures—I believe, I shall give a fourth— / But the opposition of the Aristocrats is so furious and determined, that I begin to fear, that the Good I do is not proportionate to the Evil I occasion—Mobs and Mayors, Blockheads and Brickbats, Placards and Press gangs have leagued in horrible Conspiracy against me—The Democrats are as sturdy in the support of me—but their number is comparatively small— / Two or three uncouth and unbrained Automata have threatened my Life—and in the last Lecture the Genus infimum were scarcely restrained from attacking the house in which the 'damn'd Jacobine was jawing away'.
>
> (*CL*,i,152)

Two months after this he wrote a postscript to his political lectures: 'I was soon obliged by the persecutions of Darkness to discontinue them' (*CL*,i,155). By October 1796, when the twenty-four year old Coleridge was still hoping for some means to illuminate this 'Darkness', he was writing to Cottle about ways in which to increase the sales of a new edition of his poems: 'by omitting everything political, I widen the sphere of my readers' (*CL*,i,241). Coleridge's claim in the Beaumont letter that he had by 1796 become 'fully awake to the inconsistency of my practice with my speculative Principles', was a misleading half-truth; it seems clear, on the other hand, that Coleridge had begun, in the months before moving to Nether Stowey, to notice a disturbing incongruity between his public image as it actually was, and the kind of image through which he could feel a security of relationship with his audience. The reference to Emmet's death leads into a remarkable account of the effects, as Coleridge felt them, of his 'misunderstood' political position. The account is full of inconsistencies and confusions, that arise from a self-mitigating attempt to display the effects of 'aristocratic hostility' while denying the democratic sympathies that made him an object of persecution. He reviews briefly, and accurately, the basic ideas of Pantisocracy:

> They were Christian, for they demanded the direct reformation & voluntary act of each Individual prior to any change in his outward circumstances, & my whole Plan of Revolution was confined to an experiment with a dozen families in the wilds of America: they were philosophical, because I contemplated a possible consequent amelioration of the Human Race in its present state & in this world; yet christian still, because I regarded this earthly amelioration as important chiefly for its effects on the future State of the Race of man so ameliorated.
>
> (*CL*,ii,1000)

These 'philosophical', 'Christian' principles, Coleridge explains, had helped him to 'know what is right in the abstract, by a living feeling, by an intuition of the uncorrupted heart', to 'body forth this abstract right in beautiful Forms', and to 'project this phantom-world into the world of Reality', or 'rather, to make ideas and realities stand side by side, the one as vivid as the other'. He had seen, as a substantial possibility, the prospect of a consequent amelioration of the Human Race, but this vision of brotherhood (the metaphor of family was especially resonant for Coleridge) was, bitterly, destructive of actual social relations:

> . . .my relations, & the Churchmen & 'Aristocrats', to use the phrase of the Day—these two conceited my phantoms to be substances / only what I beheld as Angels they saw as Devils, & tho' they never ceased to talk of my Youth as a proof of the falsehood of my opinions they never introduced it as an extenuation of the error. My *opinions* were the Drivel of a Babe, but the Guilt attached to them, this was the Grey Hair & rigid Muscle of inveterate Depravity. To such Bigotry what was an enthusiastic young man likely to oppose? They abhorred my person, I abhorred their actions: they set up the long howl of Hydrophoby at my principles, & I repayed their Hatred & Terror by the bitterness of Contempt. Who then remained to listen to me? to be kind to me? to be my friends—to look at me

with kindness, to shake my hand with kindness, to open the door, & spread the hospitable board, & to let me feel that I was a man well-loved—me, who from my childhood have had no avarice, no ambition—whose very vanity in my vainest moments was 9/10ths of it the desire, & delight, & necessity of loving & of being beloved?—These offices of Love the Democrats only performed to me; my own family, bigots from Ignorance, remained wilfully ignorant from Bigotry. What wonder then, if in the heat of grateful affection & the unguarded Desire of sympathizing with these who so kindly sympathized with me, I too often deviated from my own Principles?

(*CL*,ii,1000)

Through the self-justification, the embarrassed meanderings of indulgent self-pity, we feel in this passage something peculiarly Coleridgean, something distinctive; a sad, stark simplicity in the admission of loneliness, vulnerability, the overriding need for love. We meet this mood in the conversation poems, where it is present, paradoxically, as the condition of a self-redeeming growth in consciousness; we meet it in *The Pains of Sleep:*

To be beloved is all I need,
And whom I love, I love indeed

(*PW*,i,391)

Most obviously, we know it as the pervasive mood of the *Letter to Sara*. The Beaumont letter helps us to see this condition as a failure in Coleridge's relation to community. Coleridge's expressions of loneliness contain a response to pressures inescapably personal, but also, inescapably, political, economic, and social, because Coleridge suffered through the effects of a cultural dislocation that took place in England in the 1790s, a dislocation that issued not only in the clearer manifestation of class conflicts developing with the Industrial Revolution, but in the separation of the creative intellect from its accustomed audience.

The hostility that helped to define the value of retirement for Coleridge, and which was powerful in restricting his ideals to a shadowy potentiality, to the imagination as their only operative medium, was one consequence of the French Revolution. The conditions that shaped this consequence, and some leading features of subsequent developments in the 1790s, need now to be sketched in a little more distinctly. The more or less radical political activity engendered in England by the impact of the Revolution was extensive, and was met by the government's campaign of repression. We have already noted the close connection between the movement in agitation for Parliamentary reform before 1789, and the interests of the dissenting community; dissent was still a 'most important element in the radicalism of the 1790s, but its relative importance was to change very seriously in the course of the decade. Articulate and organised radicalism of the working class, on the other hand, became in this decade, for the first time, a force that demanded serious consideration. The recognition of this force, the realisation of its potential, was perhaps a greater and more far-reaching shock to English society than the Revolution itself. The English working class, in the form in which it began to become self-conscious, was a function of the Industrial Revolution. It emerged (though the fact of its emergence is clearer in retrospect) as the largest of various groups, newly urbanised, newly confined in the quality of working life, produced by a long process of change in English society. The technological advances of the eighteenth century, the large and unusually mobile work force created by changes in the structure of the agricultural economy, the consolidation of trade and commerce within the context of England's political stability through the hundred years or so that preceded the French Revolution, constantly shifting inter-relations in the development towards a capitalist economy produced, under the cohesive agency of the French example, a political consciousness that Coleridge met in his 'democrat' friends. The political identity of the common people, their power, their capacity as a new force in society, were indeed questions that scarcely worried the young Coleridge; but these were issues that were to affect his life and work no less powerfully than other aspects of industrial change whose connection with English Romanticism is rather easier to specify. The rich ambivalence of a Wordsworthian vision of nature, the keen eye for fact, the transmuting eye of self-projection, is a development of the various values found in nature by a society responding to the effects of its own economic expansion. Enclosure had lent to the dwindling wild nature of common

land an intensified appeal; an elegiac strain entered very
powerfully into the poetic language of nature; the picturesque
aesthetic of dilapidation trained the eye to a pleasure in the
abandoned rural community; these were ways to accommodate
the shock of rural depopulation and poverty, the shift in the
economic emphases towards the towns. The changing relation
of country to town necessitated by change in the economic basis
of society is crucial in the history of English Romanticism, but
the more immediate political upheaval, still a part of the larger
process of change, exerted in its way a pressure no less telling.

Coleridge's letter to the Beaumonts turns at one point to his
involvement in political organisations:

> ...fortunately for me, the Government, I suppose, knew that
> both Southey & I were utterly unconnected with any party or
> club or society—(& this praise I must take to myself, that I
> disclaimed all these Societies, these Imperia in Imperio, these
> Ascarides in the Bowels of the State, subsisting on the weakness
> & diseasedness, & having for their final Object the Death of that
> State, whose Life had been their Birth & growth, & continued to
> be their sole nourishment—. All such Societies, under whatever
> name, I abhorred as wicked Conspiracies—and to this principle
> I adhered immoveably, simply because it was a principle, & this
> at a time when the Danger attached to the opposite mode of
> conduct would have been the most seducing Temptation to
> it—at a time when in rejecting these secret associations, often as
> I was urged to become a member now of this & now of that, I
> felt just as a religious young officer may be supposed to feel,
> who full of courage dares refuse a challenge—& considered as a
> Coward by those around him often shuts his eyes, & anticipates
> the moment when he might leap on the wall & stand in the
> Breach, the first & the only one.—) This insulation of myself
> and Southey, I suppose, the Ministers knew.
>
> (*CL*,ii,1001)

Coleridge's vision of fearless energy in the fusion of principle
and commitment, idea and action, was not forced to a crisis. He
was always conscious that the Government were in fact very
ready to identify him with party; and the threat of imprison-
ment was not idle, a fact that he seems to have brooded on: 'if
in that time I had been imprisoned, my health and constitution
were such as that it would have been almost as certain Death to
me, as the Executioner has been to poor young Emmett'
(*CL*,ii,1002). As far as we know, Coleridge never was a paid-up

member of any party or club, but his political position was of a
sort that could be, and which by his own admission definitely
was, a target for the aristocrats. The growth of the political
societies after 1791, and their repression by the government
with increasing severity and, as it appeared at the time,
increasing effectiveness, has been treated thoroughly by his-
torians since the beginning of the present century. There is no
need to rehearse in detail the course of events from Dr Price's
sermon in 1789, to the passing in July 1799 of 'An 'Act for the
more effectual Suppression of Societies . . . .'[21] The atmosphere
of the period has been realised with brilliant lucidity in E.P.
Thompson's *The Making of the English Working Class*,[22] but
Thompson's emphasis falls strongly on the excitement of
nascent political consciousness in the common people, and this
is an emphasis that throws slightly out of focus the experience
represented by these years for a man of Coleridge's class and
personality. There is no doubt that Coleridge shared in the
millennial optimism engendered by the French Revolution, but
it is important to remember that his political consciousness did
not emerge to any significant degree before the middle of
1794. By this time an active radical commitment had already
become dangerous in a real sense, as Coleridge knew perfectly
well. The lines on Priestley in *Religious Musings* for example,
demonstrate an awareness of the sort of pressure that could be
brought to bear on radical dissenters, even the most eminent:

> Lo! Priestley there, patriot, and saint, and sage,
> Him, full of years, from his loved native land
> Statesmen blood-stained and priests idolatrous
> By dark lies maddening the blind multitude
> Drove with vain hate. Calm, pitying he retired,
> And mused expectant on these promised years.
> 
> (*PW*,i,123,ll.371-6)

The sonnet on Priestley that Coleridge contributed to the
*Morning Chronicle* (11 December 1794) had made the same
point:

> Though rous'd by that dark Vizir Riot rude
> Have driven our PRIESTLEY o'er the Ocean swell;
> Though Superstition and her wolfish brood
> Bay his mild radiance, impotent and fell;
> Calm in his halls of brightness he shall dwell!
> 
> (*PW*,i,81)

The 'dark Vizir' manipulating 'Riot rude' is undoubtedly Pitt, called 'dark Scowler' by Coleridge in another of the *Morning Chronicle* sonnets (23 December 1794; *PW*,i,83). Priestley's calm, pitying, expectant retirement had, as Coleridge claims, been forced upon him. On 14 July 1791, the anniversary of the fall of the Bastille, a celebration in Birmingham attended by leading local dissenters (Priestley did not himself attend; he had antagonised the town with a patronising pamphlet attacking the disabilities of the dissenters, *A Familiar Letter to the Inhabitants of Birmingham* (1789) ) was the occasion of a riot by a 'Church and King' mob, incited by government *agents provocateurs*. Two Unitarian meeting-houses were burnt, together with Priestley's house and laboratory. After two days of rioting the local magistrates issued a proclamation reminding the people of Birmingham that the destruction of property was unlawful. Priestley fled to London.[23] The episode is famous as prefiguring much that was to come, but it has a special interest in relation to the position in society of a man of Coleridge's sympathies and background. It is not simply that the Unitarians were estranged, as intellectuals, from the large majority of the English people, though this was certainly the case and introduces what looks now like an element of paradox into their radicalism. In Halévy's succinct terms, 'when Price and Priestley by their imprudent declarations had compromised the sect of which they were the luminaries, the aristocracy and the populace combined against it';[24] and the inherently self-isolating tendency of the Unitarians extended also, it is worth recalling, into a theological argument by which their resistance to the doctrine of the divinity of Jesus alienated most adherents of other dissenting sects. But the isolation of the sect with which Coleridge, by frequent public affirmation, identified himself, was not solely a matter of political and religious principles; this simply ensured the hostility of the aristocrats, and of the loyal, God-fearing Englishman. More fundamentally, the Birmingham riots were 'an explosion of latent class hatred and personal lawlessness triggered-off by the fortuitous coming together of old religious animosities and new social and political grievances'.[25] 'Class hatred' is a phrase that introduces an entirely new element into our assessment of Coleridge's situation; and the presence of this element, the first intermittent signs of a new and alarming energy, effectively cut off for the Unitarians the possibility of identification with any significant group in English society. Priestley had nowhere to turn, by 1794, but America, and it is no accident that Pantisocracy too was planned for that promised land. A good deal has been written on the influence on the Pantisocracy scheme of Coleridge's reading in American travel literature, where he would have found the obvious appeal of the new republic enhanced by accounts of magnificent natural scenery, and an idyllic life of agricultural self-sufficiency. It is ironic that Coleridge, for whom the attraction of America was, as we have seen, partly the attraction of a haven from economic pressure, shoud have allowed the appeal of the new world to be heightened by a rhetoric inspired to a considerable extent by the desire to bring money into America, and to make money out of it. Brissot de Warville's *Travels in the United States, Performed in 1788* (Dublin 1792), which appeared in a second edition in 1794, and from which Coleridge quoted in *Conciones ad Populum*,[26] was the record of a journey financed by a Genevan banker who had formed a company to speculate in the American national debt;[27] while Thomas Cooper's *Some Information Respecting America* (1794), which specifically recommended the Susquehannah, was a part of the joint endeavour by Cooper and his father-in-law, Priestley, to make money from the auction of land.[28] But Brissot and Cooper, together with other writers whose work on America Coleridge probably knew, notably Gilbert Imlay (whose *Topographical Description of the Western Territory of North America* appeared in 1792), shared more in common than travel books (though their interest in America was hardly fortuitous); they had all been in France in the early 1790s, and had been associated with the Girondists. In emigrating to America, Coleridge and Southey would have been following what was by 1794 almost the classic pattern of radical intellectuals isolated by class from the common people, and by principle from their social and intellectual fellows. One suspects that Coleridge was in fact identifying with Brissot when in the 'Introductory Address' to *Conciones ad Populum* (which is a revised version of *A Moral and Political Lecture*) he characterised the plight of the Girondists:

The Annals of the French Revolution have recorded in Letters of Blood, that the Knowledge of the Few cannot counteract the Ignorance of the Many; that the Light of Philosophy, when it is confined to a small Minority, points out the Possessors as the Victims, rather than the Illuminators, of the Multitude . . ..

The Girondists, who were the first republicans in power, were men of enlarged views and great literary attainments; but they seem to have been deficient in that vigour and daring activity, which circumstances made necessary. Men of genius are rarely either prompt in action or consistent in general conduct; their early habits have been those of contemplative indolence; and the day-dreams, with which they have been accustomed to amuse their solitude, adapt them for splendid speculation, not temperate and practicable counsels. Brissot, the leader of the Gironde party, is entitled to the character of a virtuous man, and an eloquent speaker; but he was rather a sublime visionary, than a quick-eyed politician; and his excellences equally with his faults rendered him unfit for the helm, in the stormy hour of Revolution. Robespierre, who displaced him, possessed a glowing ardour that still remembered the *end*, and a cool ferocity that never either overlooked, or scrupled, the means.[29]

Thomas Poole, and indeed most English radicals of the middle class, shared Coleridge's sympathetic admiration of Brissot.[30] The Girondists had been overtaken in 1793 by the radicalisation of the French revolutionary impulse under the leadership of Robespierre; Brissot, together with Madame Roland and other leaders of the party, had been guillotined in October, but Imlay and Cooper had escaped. Cooper, a well-known radical who had attended the Jacobin Club in Paris, in the Spring of 1792, as a representative of the Manchester Constitutional Society (and had been carefully watched by an agent of the British Foreign Office) would have found England almost as inhospitable, in 1794, as Robespierre's France; it is scarcely surprising that he decided to join Priestley in making a new life in America.[31] It was in 1793 that radicalism became positively dangerous in England, and that it became so is a measure of ministerial response to the great increase in organised political groups outside the traditional Parliamentary context. These groups included the 'Societies' from which Coleridge dissociated himself in the Beaumont letter. The dishonesty of his dissocation is easily exposed; the 'Prospectus' to the *Watchman*, for example, listed amongst the 'chief objects' of the paper the desire to 'co-operate' with the Whig Club (a party group formed in opposition to the passage of the Two Bills) and 'with the PATRIOTIC SOCIETIES, for obtaining a Right of Suffrage general and frequent.'[32] Many of the names we find acclaimed in the lectures, Muir, Palmer, Margarot, Gerrald, had provided the martyrs of the radical cause.

The societies provide us with a simplified but helpful perspective on the range of political and class interests that identified with French revolutionary principles, and that concealed beneath the appearance of unity in a common cause an opposition as fundamental as that between revolutionary France and the continental counter-revolutionary alliance. 'Revolution Societies', formed in anticipation of 1788 and the centenary of the 'Glorious Revolution', had existed in London and elsewhere in the 1780s and were easily accommodated to the millennial intensification of commitment after 1789. The London Revolution Society, for example, included in its membership Dr. Price, and the radical peer Lord Stanhope (whom Coleridge celebrated in verse in 1795), and enjoyed the support of radical Whigs, which reinforced the bias towards Parliamentary reform that came naturally from a substantial dissenting presence. The Parliamentary context of this sort of group was in powerful contrast to the working class 'Corresponding Societies', which sought to establish and maintain contacts with each other and with the French. In addition to the London Corresponding Society, for which the remarkable shoemaker Thomas Hardy acted as secretary, there were large and active societies in most industrial towns by 1793. The efforts of these societies to hold a National Convention, effectively to establish an alternative national representative body, elicited a reaction from the government that led to the notorious political trials in Scotland and England in 1793 and 1794, and to repressive legislation. In May 1792, a ministerial proclamation had been issued against 'seditious meetings and proclamations', an act 'ever memorable as the commencement of the struggle between the House of Commons and the People';[33] The situation deteriorated after the successful prosecution of active radicals, and later of delegates to the British Convention in Edinburgh in 1793. Habeas Corpus was suspended in England on 17 May 1794, on the arrest of fourteen members of the Constitutional Society on charges of treason (Thelwall, Holcroft, Hardy, and Horne Tooke were amongst those held in the Tower); the prisoners, defended by Erskine (praised by Coleridge in another of the *Morning Chronicle* sonnets for having 'dreadless' stood when 'British Freedom for an happier land / Spread her broad wings'; *PW*,i,79), were acquitted in October and November (Mr Windham, Secretary-at-War, described them as 'acquitted felons'), but Habeas Corpus was suspended again in December, regardless of the celebrations that had greeted the release of the prisoners. The most important legislative measures taken against the radicals came in 1795, when an attack on the King on his way to open Parliament on 29 October (an attempt was made to pull him from his carriage), following three days after a mass meeting in Islington in support of universal suffrage, prompted Lord Grenville to introduce into the Lords, in November, an 'Act for the Safety and Preservation of his Majesty's Person and Government against Treasonable and Seditious Practices and Attempts.' In the Commons, Pitt introduced an 'Act for the more effectually preventing Seditious Meetings and Assemblies'; the legal machinery thus established (the new offences were punishable by imprisonment or, on a second offence, by up to seven years transportation; the Scottish victims had received sentences from Lord Justice Braxfield of between seven and fourteen years transportation), and the steadily increasing threat of a French invasion, ensured that any radical still publicly active after the end of 1795 lived in the disturbing consciousness of a viciously hostile social environment. The members of the Constitution Society prosecuted for their activity obviously felt more immediately than most the effects of mounting ministerial concern; the Society had been formed in 1780 (by Sheridan, amongst others, who was yet another subject for Coleridge's *Morning Chronicle* sonnets; *PW*,i,87-8) as the Society for Promoting Constitutional Information, and having almost entirely lapsed by the end of the decade had been rejuvenated in March 1792, gaining new momentum, like other societies, from the proclamation against sedition in May. Its membership comprised a range of interests that was never again possible after the first years of post-revolutionary excitement; veteran

campaigners from the days of Wilkes, Horne Tooke and Major
Cartwright, combined with Hardy of the Corresponding
Society, the intellectual atheist Holcroft, the radical lecturer
Thelwall. But 1792 saw a change in the character of the
membership as distinguished founder members, leading Whigs
and nobility amongst them, gave way to men who placed their
emphases very differently, men like the Mackintosh of *Vindiciae
Gallicae* (1791), the young radical Lord Daer, Joseph Gerald
and Maurice Margarot (both transported after the Scottish
trials); Tom Paine himself attended meetings. The Constitution
Society found itself in 1792 beginning to part ideological
company with such a representative group as the Friends of the
People, a reform club formed in 1791 that attracted 'the flower
of the Foxite Whigs', and quickly dissociated itself from such
early members as Cartwright and Daer, to assert its identity as
'a stronghold of moderation and gentlemanly politics'.[34]
The Friends of the People, unlike the Constitution Society, had
at least a future; its members were absorbed into the ranks of
Parliamentary party as pressures mounted in the mid-nineties,
but Thelwall, Holcroft, and the rest, identifying with no class
interest, were scattered and isolated by the sweep of events.
Their Society never met again after the trials of 1794.

Thelwall, Holcroft, Godwin, Priestley: the best-known of
those who formed themselves into isolated enclaves of middle-
class radicalism, dissenting or atheist, were also to provide the
company that constituted Coleridge's social world in the 1790s.
We need to employ a dual historical perspective in the
interpretation of Coleridge's relation to this social context. The
1790s is a period that must provide the real starting-point in
any history of British radicalism, and the work of Hardy, even
Thelwall, the sacrifice of transported radicals, assumes now a
significant aspect that, if not quite triumphant, suggests at least
the achievement of painful birth. The structure we impose
retrospectively on events can take into account subsequent
developments that can scarcely have been recognised contem-
poraneously; and our structural principle can utilise ideas
about the nature of class that were not available to those whose
lives were involved. Coleridge would have experienced an
imperious, ungovernable hostility, impinging constantly
through the minutiae of his social experience on any sense of

security, personal or ideological, that had survived his damaging estrangement from the comforts of family affection. Indeed, Coleridge's family was itself an agency of social and political pressure, certainly by example and attitude, that he must have found peculiarly difficult to cope with. Lord Coleridge's *The Story of a Devonshire House*, the history of the Coleridge family, conveys more precisely than is perhaps part of any conscious intention the baffled disapproval with which the family, in process of creating by careful application a very respectable posterity, met the challenge of a renegade youngest child. Coleridge's brothers, John, Francis Syndercombe (there is an odd resemblance between Frank's peculiar middle name, and the 'Comberbache' under which Coleridge enlisted in the army; Frank was the object of Coleridge's open resentment and bitterness as the favourite of the family nurse),[35] William, James, Luke, Edward, and George, were not the sort of Englishmen to find patience for Coleridge's principles or his personality. John, Frank and James all joined the army, John and Frank both dying in the Indian service; William, Edward and George all took degrees at Pembroke, all took orders, all became schoolmasters; Luke, who like Frank and William died in his twenties, took a double first at Christ Church, Oxford, and became a brilliantly promising physician (Coleridge was the only brother who, having attended University, failed to take a degree; throughout the nineties, he solemnly signed himself 'S.T. Coleridge, of Jesus College, Cambridge'). The Coleridges were to produce scholars, bishops, and judges in the nineteenth century, including the Lord Coleridge, great-grandson of James, who provides a mouthpiece for the family attitude to Coleridge himself:

> He was never a fighter, his spirit shrank from conflict. It is mayhap a vain regret, but who can say what the poet might not have accomplished, had destiny enabled him through life to walk in peace the cloistered precincts of his early home, where Nature ever lavishes her gifts of beauty, curtained from the rougher winds and storms of life, and protected from the buffets of ill-health, fortune, and the world?

The irony of this splendidly patronising passage does not consist solely in the fact that the ideal of a sheltering home in nature was a yearning intensified in Coleridge by his deprivation of its familial equivalent; for his family also made its contribution to the political atmosphere that made retirement a necessary resource. James in particular, 'the Colonel', is a suggestive figure in this context. Lord Coleridge's characterisation of him is in the sharpest contrast to the family version of their poet, who 'certainly did not possess the practical side' of his brothers. James, 'in manner abrupt, yet genial, ... commanded respect from all':

> His family looked up to him with unbounded affection, not unmingled with a certain awe. He had a high temper, sternly kept under control. His emotions lay deep, and, when aroused, for the time completely mastered him. Yet no man was more worldly wise, or a better steward of his own or other's property. His duty was to him a living thing, no cold abstraction, and he walked through life as in the constant recognised presence of Almighty God.

As we would expect, James was active in preparing the defence of his country against the French threat:

> He took a leading part in the Volunteer movement, becoming in 1795 Captain, in 1797 Major-Commandant, and in 1799 Lieutenant-Colonel of the Exmouth and Sidmouth Volunteers.[36]

This feature of James's career is singled out for commemoration in a wall plaque that can still be seen in the 'Dorset' aisle of the church in Ottery St Mary (Coleridge is represented by a photocopy, in a glass case, of the document by which Mrs Coleridge secured the removal of her son to Christ's Hospital).

Volunteer movements and loyalty oaths were details in the pattern of Coleridge's social experience in Somerset from 1794 to 1798, and this pattern, of barely muted hostility in the quotidian life of intercourse with neighbours and a local rural population, of distressing persecutions endured by friends, emerges with, if anything, increased clarity even as Coleridge's attitudes change and his radicalism dissolves after 1796. The most serious problem was an inevitable consequence of the necessarily *rural* situation of retirement; the birth of working class political consciousness, and the comfort such consciousness derived from the evidence of flourishing political discus-

sion societies (with a rapidly expanding membership), were far
less potent factors in the life of a rural community, where the
radical's isolation was accentuated. Bristol harboured a Corres-
ponding Society, but like most large industrial centres there
was little, after 1794, in the way of organised intellectual
radicalism that could offer Coleridge a sympathetic audience.
It was exactly this radical, intellectual (and dissenting) audience
that Coleridge sought to establish for the *Watchman*, and the
contacts he made on a tour undertaken early in 1796, to collect
subscriptions for the paper, give us a useful idea of the sort of
public to which he felt his views would appeal. The tour took
him to Birmingham, Nottingham, Sheffield, Manchester,
Liverpool, Lichfield; he soon encountered typical difficulties,
in Worcester for example:

> With regard to BUSINESS, there is no chance of doing any
> thing in Worcester—the Aristocrats are so numerous and the
> influence of the Clergy so extensive, that Mr Barr thinks that no
> Bookseller will venture to publish THE work.
>
> (*CL*,i,175)

Booksellers were wisely cautious; in Sheffield Coleridge found
James Montgomery, radical poet and editor of the *Sheffield Iris,*
in prison, ostensibly for libelling a local magistrate. Coleridge
agreed not to have the *Watchman* sold in Sheffield, in order not
to damage the sales of the *Iris*.[37] But it is the company that
Coleridge kept in Birmingham, Nottingham and Derby that is
most interesting. He met Joseph Wright in Derby (who was
certainly alive to the new visual presence of a revolution in
manufacturing techniques), and was introduced to Erasmus
Darwin (amongst the many activities of this extraordinary man
was the leading role that he played in the Birmingham Lunar
Society), and Jedediah Strutt, inventor and cotton spinner. It is
certain that Coleridge would have met with members of the
Lunar Society in Birmingham, many of whom were, like Strutt,
making a great deal of money out of their contributions to the
new industrial technology. Tom and Josiah Wedgewood, whose
grant of an annuity to Coleridge in 1798 was to ensure that he
remained unemployed (and was to make possible the trip to
Germany), were in close touch with the Society, whose
membership included, besides Priestley, James Watt, Matthew

Boulton, Samuel Galton, James Keir, and the land-owning philanthropists and amateur engineers Richard Edgeworth (father of the novelist), and Thomas Day.[38] In Birmingham too Coleridge first met Charles Lloyd, the son of a wealthy Quaker banker; and in Nottingham he attended a dinner in celebration of Fox's birthday presided over by 'Mr Wright... a man of immense fortune' (*CL*,i,178). This was the generation of benevolent philanthropists, self-made men or their sons, whose position in English society was to change drastically as the political alignments that emerged in the wake of the French Revolution gradually solidified into the more fundamental oppositions of class created by the Industrial Revolution, oppositions inherent in new relations of production. And this generation represented the audience that Coleridge envisaged for the *Watchman;* though even this small public made demands on his sense of relation to an audience that he simply could not meet.

The area of Bristol did not offer in itself a suitable public large enough to maintain the *Watchman,* but there were other ways in which the city was less than ideal for Coleridge. His lecture against the slave trade, delivered 16 June 1795, and published in a revised version in the fourth *Watchman*,[39] can have won him few friends in the centre of the British slaving industry. The sympathetic 'democrat' supporters at Coleridge's lectures were easily outnumbered by 'aristocrats', which was not surprising; Burke had served as Member of Parliament for Bristol from 1774 to 1780 (not quite the Burke of *Reflections on the Revolution in France,* but the outspoken Irish Whig), and had lost his seat after falling out with the commercial interest in the city, largely a slaving interest, over trade with Ireland, and religious prejudice. 'The inhabitants of Bristol' had, it is true, submitted a petition to Parliament, in November 1795, objecting to the passage of the Two Bills,[40] but anxiety over the exact scope of the measures proposed by Grenville and Pitt was almost universal at first, without breaking the bounds of a traditional constitutionalism that was not prepared to argue with the fact of an established article of law. Coleridge was well aware that the commercial interest was predominant in Bristol (the city still testifies to-day to the presence, in endowed schools and public buildings, of the great slave-trading families; a

visitor to Bristol meets everywhere the name of Colston), and
we recall the lines in *Reflections on having left a Place of Retirement*
on 'A wealthy son of Commerce . . . Bristowa's citizen', with his
'thirst of idle gold'. Coleridge's political audience in Bristol was
always a narrowing circle, but his audience in the rural
community outside Bristol, the community in which he actually
lived after 1796, was confined quite literally to a handful of
friends. The real vitality of radicalism was urban, a response to
new urban conditions; rural England, changing no less funda-
mentally but more gradually, could be appropriated by the
machinery of reaction to the idea of 'old England', could be
seen as representing a deep-rooted, traditional way of life that
embodied 'timeless' social values sturdy in resistance to Jacobin-
ical discontent. This function of rural life was powerfully
realised as propaganda in the *Cheap Repository Tracts* of Hannah
More, who had lived since 1784 in Wrington Vale, near Bristol;
by July 1795, some 700,000 copies of the *Tracts* had been sold,
and less than a year later the figure had passed two million.[41]
Coleridge, Southey and Lovell had met Hannah More through
Cottle in 1794 and had been sufficiently impressed to consider
dedicating to her *The Fall of Robespierre*;[42] she would presuma-
bly have had for Coleridge the same sort of appeal as Bowles,
an abolitionist, a philanthropist, patron of the low. Her
propagandist *Tracts* (114 appeared between 1795 and 1798;
Mrs Piozzi called them 'antidotes to Tom Paine')[43] need to be
considered in the larger context of the extensive and pro-
longed battle of books that began with Price's sermon and
Burke's reply. *Reflections on the Revolution in France* inspired an
articulate radical minority to eloquent defence of the swinish
multitude; at least thirty-eight formal replies were published,
William Cowper complaining that the appearance of his
Homer was delayed by the rush on presses: 'Burke's pamphlet
stood in my way when I wrote last; for every press, and
consequently mine, groaned with answers to it.'[44] The replies
are familiar now as various attempts at the rationalisation of
the post-revolutionary optimism. Mackintosh's *Vindiciae Gal-
licae*, Mary Wollstonecraft's *Vindication of the Rights of Man*
(1791), and, less directly, *Political Justice*, are the best-known
volumes, and we might unwarily receive from them an
impression of Burke as an isolated and outmoded voice of

crumbling conservatism. Such an impression is misleading in important ways; no single work by any of the radical intellectuals came near to the early sales of the *Reflections* (about 30,000 copies), but more significant from Coleridge's perspective was the fact that Burke's book was successful with the middle class. One reply to the *Reflections*, the first part of Tom Paine's *Rights of Man* (1791), did indeed achieve sales on a completely new scale; distributed by the London Constitutional Society, 50,000 copies were sold within a few weeks at the same price, three shillings, as Burke's book (it had been supposed that the price of Paine's book would keep it out of the wrong hands). Part two of the *Rights of Man* was published in 1792, in a sixpenny edition as well as in the more expensive form, and with a cheap reprint of the first part. Within two years, sales had reached an estimated 200,000; Paine's book, tapping new resources of literacy, became the bible of working class radicalism, enjoying a success that again tends to obscure the strength of Burke's appeal. For Coleridge, not sharing in the life or the cultural tradition of the working class, but rooted in another life, another tradition, would have felt the success of Burke, as the spokesman of his own class, a consolidating influence in the assertion of a massive dominance by the governing interests.[45] Coleridge respected Paine's political thought, at least in 1795, but from the start he rejected Paine's Deism:

> Had his political writings resembled his theological the British Constitution might have scorned the puny Assailant—the fort would have seemed strong contrasted with the Impotence of the Besieger, and Thomas Paine had been pensioned for having written a Panegyric when he intended a Satire.[46]

Coleridge's Christianity necessarily qualified his alignment with the extreme radicals, Paine as well as Godwin, and Paine's frank aggression was a mode of commitment far too divisive for Coleridge's self-conscious unsteadiness of orientation in society. But Paine was the popular hero, the voice of the people, in a way that Godwin was certainly not. Godwin's appeal was to that intellectual radical minority with which Coleridge tried to identify, and while even this comforting sympathy of audience was soon closed to Coleridge, he could at least meet and talk with Godwin on common intellectual

ground. Paine represented an energy inaccessible to Coleridge;
to commit himself to the radicalism with direction, with a
future, constituted a social dislocation that his personality
would not have survived. We must remember his insecurity, his
anxiety, his yearning for home, the disabilities that made for
such a strong contrast with Tom Poole's brave integrity:

> Tom Poole was not the kind of person to reserve an unpopular
> opinion, or to be silent when any of his cherished ideals were
> attacked or misrepresented. His sense of the misery of the
> French people through centuries of grinding oppression, his
> sympathy with their efforts, however wild and convulsive, to
> achieve their just freedom, was exceedingly deep, and, in season
> or out of season, he never scrupled to proclaim what he thought.
> He became for a while, and this especially after the publication
> of Paine's *Rights of Man* as a reply to Burke's celebrated
> *Reflections on the French Revolution,* a kind of political Ishmaelite
> in his own neighbourhood, his hand against every man, and
> every man's hand against him. It was probably at this time that
> he made his appearance amongst the wigs and powdered locks
> of his kinsfolk, male and female, without any of the customary
> powder in his hair; which innocent novelty was a scandal to all
> beholders, seeing that it was the outward and visible sign of a
> love of innovation, a well-known badge of sympathy with
> democratic ideas. If he did not find himself literally in a
> minority of one, being happy in the comprehension and
> adherence of his brother Richard, yet his cousin's journals show
> that the household at Marshmill—the little circle whose support,
> if he could have obtained it, would have been grateful to him
> beyond all others—bristled with disapproval; whilst the small
> world of Stowey and Bridgewater made no secret that it was very
> much shocked, and at times almost inclined to believe that Tom
> Poole ought to be denounced as a public enemy.[47]

Coleridge, living in the same community, was not capable of
sustaining this kind of singleness, this kind of integrity; and
while we acknowledge the dependency of his character as a
psychological disability, we have also to acknowledge this
dependency as a quality intensified by, in many ways insepara-
ble from, the pervasive hostility of his social environment. It
was in 1792, just as Tom Poole was gesturing against the
stirring uneasiness with which rural England demonstrated its
distrust of French behaviour, that Hannah More's *Village
Politics* appeared; 'in form it is typical: a dialogue in which the

solid blacksmith inevitably wins the argument over the silly radical mason. How often in such publications the victor is identified with the rural complex—he is frequently a farm labourer—while the vanquished is an artisan or small shop-keeper'.[48] The appeal to the 'rural complex' was, unhappily for Coleridge, well-judged; the loyal, God-fearing Englishman was scarcely a myth of the propagandists, and Coleridge encountered him every day as the serving-man at Alfoxden, or the local squire, or the inn-keeper, or his own brother. The morale of loyal subjects was strengthened by a steady flow of government-sponsored publications directed at all classes of society, but finding their best audience in the middle class; such a representative work as Paley's *The British Public's Reasons for Contentment, addressed to the Labouring Part of the British Public* (1792) was addressed in fact quite specifically to people of Coleridge's class, but even the simpler truths of *Village Politics* found their warmest enthusiasts not so much in 'the Labouring Part' as in their masters.[49] Both these works, and many others like them, were produced and distributed by the Association for Preserving Liberty and Property against Republicans and Levellers, an organisation formed in 1792, probably with government support, under the leadership of John Reeves, a barrister in contact with the circle of the *Anti-Jacobin*. The Association was based in London, but in the mid-nineties branches were formed throughout the country, and joined the many local organisations that had been formed in opposition to the popular societies. The activities of the conservative societies were not confined to publication; organised harassment of 'Jacobins' was fairly common, and the residual violence of a mob with an effigy of Tom Paine to burn was turned often into physical assault on targets obviously chosen, by someone, with care.[50] The violence was familiar to Coleridge, in a way that brings home to us the unnerving immediacy of reaction; he delivered sermons in Taunton, in 1797 and 1798, for the Unitarian minster there, Dr. Joshua Toulmin, and we read in a letter of 1798 Coleridge's account of the death of his daughter, who 'in a melancholy derangement suffered herself to be swallowed up by the tide on the coast between Sidmouth and Bere' (*CL*,i,409). It has been suggested that 'it may have been the period of persecution that unhinged the mind of the

Toulmin daughter', and it does seem at least plausible that a sensitive nature should break under the strain imposed on the Toulmin family in the nineties. An effigy of Paine was burnt before the house, windows were smashed by stones, the house itself was threatened with attack. Toulmin's friends actually formed vigilante bands for the protection of his home and family.[51] But far more personally distressing for Coleridge were the persecutions endured by a man who emerges from the letters as a correspondent who won Coleridges's profound respect. The memoir of Thelwall that prefaces his *Poems, chiefly written in Retirement* (2nd edition, 1801), written by himself, but in the third person, outlines with sad restraint the political career of an intellectual who was, as political lecturer and radical poet, in striking ways a larger-scale, metropolitan version of Coleridge in Bristol. Thelwall recalls briefly in his memoir the confiscation of his private papers, books, and engravings ('there should be no war against the mind'), and his solitary confinement in the Tower for five months, in Newgate for seven weeks. He draws attention to the suppression of his paper the *Tribune* (with heavy financial loss) as a consequence of the Two Bills; then he turns to the more crudely physical forms of his persecution:

> The suppression of the Political Lectures; his further efforts to revive discussion, under the title of Lectures on Classical History; and the successive interruptions at Yarmouth, Lymn, Wisbeach, Derby, Stockport, and Norwich, are recent in the remembrance of every one. At four of these places he narrowly escaped assassination (at the first perhaps, the still more terrible fate of being carried to Kamtschatka) by the sailors, the armed associators, and the Inniskilling dragoons, by whom he was successively attacked. And so active was the acrimony that pursued him, that, even on his way to the retreat, to which he shortly afterwards withdrew, having occasion to pass through Ashby de la Zouch, to claim a small debt, a mob of soldiers and loose people was hired, by certain zealots in that town, to assail him. Against these he was obliged to maintain his ground, singly, for a considerable time; till the Chief-Constable of the place arrived, and took him under his protection.

Thelwall brings sharply into focus the social isolation that led him, as it had helped to lead Coleridge, into retreat; the embittered and unillusioned awareness of social pressure goes with a sober consciousness that the Coleridgean defence, the escape into 'principles' which relaxes the tension of party alignment, was for the radical a useless strategy:

> ... with respect to his opinions *merely political* ... he desires no apology, and he is anxious for no vindication. It is enough for himself, that he remembers them without self-reproach. That he retains them in silence, *ought* to be enough, even for the most prejudiced and hostile. Since 'the age of Chivalry' humanized the European world, the time is past when mean submissions were expected, even from a vanquished foe—when courage could not be satisfied without 'slaying the mind'. He claims the benefit of this civilization. He expects that it should be extended to the victims of opinion, as well as of the sword: and that he should be permitted to walk in the uprightness of his own convictions, withou being hunted any longer, from society, by a proscription more ferocious than if assassination, or the other crime of Italy, had been proved against him. Some claims to this species of toleration he thinks he possesses from the example of his deportment: for he has never been one of those who make sect or party the test of moral rectitude. He has ever believed, and maintained, that Theories the most opposite were equally consistent with sincerity and moral feeling in the professors. In the pâmphlet above quoted, may be seen how he could feel, even for the most bitter and the most formidable of his antagonists ... Yet is there, scarcely, a consideration of private justice, or of human sympathy, that, in consequence of HIS opinions, has not been violated against him. The ordinary transactions of life have been interrupted—the intercourses of the closest relationship violated and impeded, and the recesses of the utmost security have been disturbed—even magistracy, that should have protected, has been the insidious prompter of hostility and insult; and the post itself, has been forbidden to him as a vehicle of confidential intercourse. The channels of vital sustenance have been dried up; and Friendship (the last stay of the human heart)—even Friendship, itself (a few instances of generous perseverance alone excepted) wearied and intimidated with the hostilities to which it was exposed, has shrunk from its own convictions, and left him in comparative insulation.

Thelwall's experience was ratified in the life of every radical, but the account has a peculiar relevance for Coleridge, whose 'generous perseverance' in friendship was surely in Thelwall's mind as an exception to the wearying and intimidatory effect of hostility. Thelwall sought, unsuccessfully as it turned out, to

escape the influences of the political atmosphere by moving to
a small farm in Wales. The pantisocrats, prompted by South-
ey's dawning realisation of the connection between family
affection and income, had at one time displaced the original
plan of emigration by the scheme of an experiment in
community to be located in Wales; they would certainly have
found, with Thelwall, that the taint of radicalism became
increasingly obnoxious in relation to the degree of rural
simplicity, with its corresponding wild and uncontaminated
nature, that characterised an isolated agricultural community.
Thelwall explains the relief he had anticipated in retirement:

> Such a retreat could not but appear, to an enthusiastic
> imagination, as a sort of enchanted dormitory, where the
> agitations of political feeling might be cradled to forgetfulness,
> and the delicious day dreams of poesy might be renewed . . .
> Thelwall flattered himself that agriculture . . . and the visitation
> of the Muse . . . might secure that humble sort of subsistence to
> which he had determined to accommodate his desires. In the
> choice of this situation he was, also, further influenced by its
> remoteness from all political connection. For, determined
> himself to observe the most inviolable silence respecting his
> opinions, he took it for granted, that there, where they had
> never yet been heard of, he should be equally out of the way of
> all solicitations to revive the discussion, and all the animosities
> they had excited against him.

We need not emphasise the similarities between Thelwall's
retirement, and Coleridge's decision to move into the cottage at
Nether Stowey. Thelwall was to be disappointed in his
expectations:

> . . . altho to his resolution he steadfastly adhered, in his hopes of
> consequent tranquility he was most woefully disappointed.
> Politics, hiterto unknown in that neighbourhood, were now
> injected, in their most acrimonious form, into the ears of the
> ignorant inhabitants, in order to stimulate a vulgar hostility,
> more harrassing and more irritating than all the open oppres-
> sions of power: and the officiating clergyman of the parish
> seems to have thought it the duty of his function, to aggravate
> these hostilities, by the most pointed and inflammatory allusion
> from the pulpit.[52]

Thelwall found himself feared as a conjuror by his neighbours;

he was assaulted with a pick-axe, his home was threatened; and this kind of social experience was really very close to Coleridge's own in Nether Stowey.

We should notice one feature that appears as an obvious disparity between Thelwall's conception of retirement, and that of Coleridge. Thelwall identifies retreat with defeat, with the conscious admission of a personal inability to withstand further pressure. Nature offered release from social tension; we remember Coleridge's famous anecdote:

> John Thelwall had something very good about him. We were once sitting in a beautiful recess in the Quantocks, when I said to him, "Citizen John, this is a fine place to talk treason in!"—"Nay! Citizen Samuel", replied he, "it is rather a place to make a man forget that there is any necessity for treason!"[53]

We need, as so often, a degree of judicious circumspection in the validation of Coleridge's memory. It is not likely that he would have called his conversation with Thelwall 'treason'; Wordsworth's phrasing, in his memory of the exchange recorded in the Fenwick note to 'Anecdote for Fathers', is more convincing:

> Coleridge exclaimed, "This is a place to reconcile one to all the jarrings and conflicts of the wide world". —"Nay", said Thelwall, "to make one forget them altogether".[54]

Thelwall's retirement, lacking the Christian basis, the positive aspect of Coleridge's ideal, implied a tranquil ending rather than quiet beginnings. And poetry was for Thelwall a pleasant source of 'delicious day dreams', the appropriate indulgence of an intelligence forced to concede the superior power of reaction. Thelwall at first thought of retiring to Stowey in 1797, to make permanent, as he wrote to his wife,

> the delightful society of Coleridge and of Wordsworth, the present occupier of Allfox Den. We have been having a delightful ramble to-day among the plantation, and along a wild, romantic dell in these grounds, through which a foaming, rushing, murmuring torrent of water winds its long artless course. There have we ... a literary and political triumvirate, passed sentence on the productions and characters of the age, burst forth in poetical flights of enthusiasm, and philosophised

our minds into a state of tranquillity, which the leaders of
nations might envy, and the residents of cities can never know.[55]

Implicit here, present perhaps in just the suggestion of a sharp
critical edge in that last sentence, is a conception of the relation
between a civilised life, with poetry as its highest mode of
expression, and society. The poet operates in a sphere beyond
the political, almost, it might seem, beyond the social, at a cool
pastoral distance; he speaks a language that is affective in terms
of a relatively limited audience, and this audience identifies in
the end with a class interest. Thelwall makes the point explicitly
in the memoir:

> On the renewal of his intercourse with the profession of
> Literature, he finds, indeed the profits (always scanty and
> precarious) almost annihilated by growing imposts: he finds,
> also, the press teeming, and, perhaps, the public already satiated
> with NATIONAL HEROICS, which, when his principal work
> was first projected, was a *desideratum* in English Poesy: and, what
> is more than all, he has to encounter prejudice and hostility in
> those classes of society, who alone can be expected to have a
> taste for such compositions, or to give them extensive encour-
> agement.[56]

'The language of poetry', as Hazlitt put it, 'falls in naturally
with the language of power'.[57] Thelwall's sense of failure in
retreat provides an important corrective to our interpretation
of Coleridge's retirement, for while it was, as we have seen, a
positive resource, a way of life potentially regenerative socially
as well as privately, it was, also, an enforced resource, a defeat
that contained, in imagination, the seeds of victory. The self
was driven into privacy, introspection, a destructive loneliness
that could yet be made to provide the context of an outward,
embracing movement of spirit, a willed growth into com-
prehending, unifying consciousness.

The community in Nether Stowey was, however, itself under
the same pressures that Thelwall recalled so bitterly. The diary
of Charlotte Poole, Tom's sister, preserves the tone of local
attitudes to radicalism. Her contempt would have been espe-
cially damaging for Coleridge, who liked to think of himself as
inside the families of his friends. Mrs Evans had been cast as
surrogate mother, and the whole family had been regarded by
Coleridge as comprising an intimate, sympathetic audience:

My very dear—
　What word shall I add sufficiently expressive of the warmth which I feel? You covet to be near my heart. Believe me, that You and my Sisters have the very first row in the front box of my Heart's little theatre—and—God knows! *You are not crowded.* There, my dear Spectators! you shall see what you shall see—Farce, Comedy, & Tragedy—my Laughter, my Cheerfulness, and my Melancholy. A thousand figures pass before you, shifting in perpetual succession—there are my Joys and my Sorrows, my Hopes and my Fears, my Good tempers, and my Peevishnesses: you will however observe two, that remain unalterably fixed—and these are Love and Gratitude. In short, my dear Mrs Evans! my whole heart shall be laid open like any sheep's heart: my Virtues, if I have any, shall not be more exposed to your view than my weaknesses. Indeed I am of opinion, that Foibles are the cement of Affection, and that, however we may *admire* a perfect character, we are seldom inclined to love or praise those, whom we cannot sometimes blame.—Come Ladies! will you take your seats in this play house? Fool that I am! Are you not already there? Believe me, you are—

(*CL*,i,21-2)

This characteristic stress on the familial audience became distressing in relation to the Pooles. Tom himself was an indispensable source of support, and encouragement, and admiration; Tom's mother, '*Our* Mother', Coleridge called her, appreciated the young man's affectionate nature. Tom wrote to Coleridge describing how his mother had wept 'with a mother's affection at hearing your letters read'.[58] These successes intensified the discomfort of a more general background of alienation, not simply from the local community of agricultural labourers who regarded the French Revolution as 'a fearful and unnatural catastrophe, to be shuddered at, and certainly not sympathised with',[59] but from the whole Stowey community, including almost all of the Poole family, who regarded Coleridge with 'chilling disapproval'. Charlotte's diary is a commentary on the development of this attitude. The early phase of the Revolution had struck no sympathetic chord:

December 14th [1792] —Amused ourselves with reading Dr More's journal while he was in Paris on the dreadful 10th of August; which sent us to bed in bad spirits, and not in charity with all mankind, but hating the French.[60]

In 1797 the estrangement of the democrats from English society was clarified by the news of Napoleon's victories in Italy; Poole and Coleridge, 'and two or three benevolent souls besides', 'read and re-read' the news, 'till the heart overwhelmed was sad with joy'.[61] Charlotte Poole, in contrast, was brought very low by the news in June of mutiny in the fleet:

> June 4th, 1797.—The newspapers are filled with melancholy news from the Fleet, which is still in a state of mutiny, occasioned by the black contrivances of the Democrats, who have got into the Fleet and poisoned the minds of the sailors.[62]

When Thelwall arrived in Nether Stowey, in July 1797, in search of peace, and friendship, and a home, he inspired in Charlotte an indignation that exceeded even the 'incurable suspicion, and mistrust' with which she had greeted Coleridge and Wordsworth:

> July 23rd, 1797—We are shocked to hear that Mr. Thelwall has spent some time at Stowey this week with Mr Coleridge, and consequently with Tom Poole. Alfoxton house is taken by one of the fraternity, and Woodlands by another. To what are we coming?[63]

But Charlotte had little real cause for alarm, locally or, indeed, nationally. In December she was able to observe, 'with satisfaction', the largeness of the congregation that gathered at Over Stowey church to observe a General Thanksgiving 'for the three signal victories obtained over the Fleets of the French, the Spaniards, and the Dutch'.[64] The mutinies had not damaged British sea-power; and while it seems certain that there were real connections between the mutinies at Spithead and the Nore, and such organisations as the United Irishmen and the Corresponding Societies,[65] we feel the mood of the sailors in the letter, written on the back of a song-sheet, sent by a leader of the mutineers to the Board of Admiralty: 'Dam my eyes if I understand your lingo or long proclamations, but, in short, give us our due at once, and no more of it, till we go in search of the rascals, the eneyms (sic) of our country.'[68]

The local hostility reached a crisis with the arrival of

Thelwall, and his proposal to live in the area, but before examining more closely the circumstances surrounding Thelwall's visit, it will be useful to bear in mind the aspect that political events on a national scale would have presented to Coleridge by the time of the arrival of his radical friend. Burke's *Reflections* had scorned as unrepresentative the ostentatious supporters of French liberty,[67] and had stirred up by that scorn what seemed like the evidence of substantial radical support. How far the radicals were truly representative of the majority of the nation in the nineties is a question that must, for our purposes, have two opposed answers; looking back, we can see a massive potential, but looking on, as Coleridge was, a handful of vociferous agitators could be seen as providing the opportunity for Pitt's Tory party to manoeuvre itself into an impregnable Parliamentary position. Burke saw the implications of the Revolution very early, but there was, too, something profoundly personal, and self-defensive, in his fear of the Revolution. Fanny Burney's diary has recorded a telling moment:

> [Burke] spoke... with an eagerness and a vehemence that instantly banished the graces, though it redoubled the energies, of his discourse. "The French Revolution", he said, "which began by authorising and legalising injustice, and which by rapid steps had proceeded to every species of despotism except owning a despot, was now menacing all the universe and all mankind with the most violent concussion of principle and order".... When he had expatiated upon the present dangers, even to English liberty and property, from the contagion of havoc and novelty, he earnestly exclaimed, "This it is that has made ME an abettor and supporter of Kings! Kings are necessary, and, if we would preserve peace, and prosperity, we must preserve THEM. We must all put our shoulders to the work! Ay, and stoutly, too!"... How I wish my dear Susanna and Fredy could meet this wonderful man when he is easy, happy, and with people he cordially likes! But politics, even on his own side, must always be excluded; his irritability is so terrible on that theme that it gives immediately to his face the expression of a man who is going to defend himself from murderers.[68]

Burke's massive alarm was, ultimately, from his perspective, justifiable; but it contained nevertheless a measure of personal insecurity, of panic. Pitt used this quality of response in contemporary political life to strengthen his Parliamentary hand, and the manufacture of panic represented a most useful tactic. The power of the Monarch and his ministers was effectively consolidated in 1794 and 1795 as many Whigs, notably the Duke of Portland (who was as Home Secretary in 1797 to be involved in the episode of Coleridge and the spy) and his followers, joined the ranks of the Tories. The repressive measures found little opposition in Parliament, but it is difficult to discriminate between their success as an index of serious public anxiety, and their success as a resounding political defeat for Fox.[68] The vast network of government spies was a precaution particularly against the establishing of a French connection, but it also served to supply propaganda with the victims and the materials for heightening tension. There can be no question that the government was alive to a new depth of intensity and commitment in British radicalism, and that Pitt cannot be seen as feigning public or personal worry; but radicalism was manipulated as a tool of Parliamentary politics, and was not recognised as dangerous in the way that later became obvious.

When Coleridge received the attention of a spy in 1797 he experienced at first hand a feature of contemporary life that had already provided a theme for his political lectures. Thelwall had published a pamphlet on *The Moral Tendency to a System of Spies and Informers,* and Coleridge had read at Cambridge a pamphlet by Fox that accused the 1792 Ministry of encouraging the habit of spying.[70] Coleridge's account of the episode of the spy in Nether Stowey, in Chapter 10 of *Biographia Literaria,* is often quoted; its tone is knockabout and has convinced most commentators, with Lawrence Hanson, that the incident must have 'afforded Coleridge some excellent fun'.[71] We remember the spy with 'his Bardolph nose', who misheard 'Spinoza' as 'Spy Nozy', who 'entered into conversation' with Coleridge, 'and talked of purpose in a *democrat* way in order to draw [him] out', only to find himself embarrassed by the manifest respectability of his subject.[72] A passage never quoted in relation to the affair, however, is Coleridge's attack on the spy system in *Conciones ad Populum:*

All our happiness and the greater part of our virtues depend on social confidence. This beautiful fabric of Love the system of Spies and Informers has shaken to the very foundation. There have been multiplied among us "Men who carry tales to shed blood!" Men who resemble the familiar Spirits described by Isaiah, as "dark ones, that peep and that mutter!" Men, who may seem to have been typically shadowed out in the Frogs that formed the second plague of Egypt: little low animals with chilly blood and staring eyes, that "come up into our houses and our bed-chambers!" These men are plenteously scattered among us: our very looks are deciphered into disaffection, and we cannot move without treading on some political spring-gun. Nor here has the evil stopped. We have breathed so long the atmosphere of Imposture and Panic, that many honest minds have caught an aguish disorder; in their cold fits they shiver at Freedom, in their hot fits they turn savage against its advocates; and sacrifice to party Rage what they would have scornfully refused to Corruption. Traitors to friendship, that they may be faithful to the Constitution—Enemies of human nature, that they may prove themselves the Adorer of the God of Peace—they hide from themselves the sense of their crime by the merit of their motive. Thus every man begins to suspect his neighbour, the warm ebullience of our hearts is stagnating: and I dread, lest by long stifling the expressions of Patriotism, we may at last lose the feeling.[73]

The use of spies was no less extensive when, less than two years after the publication of this passage, one George Walsh arrived in Nether Stowey with a £20 note in his pocket received from Mr J. King, Permanent Under-Secretary of State in the Home Office.[74] He had come from an interview, at Hungerford in Berkshire, with Charles Mogg, ex-servant at Alfoxton who had alarmed another ex-servant from the house, now cook to a Dr Lysons of Bath, with stories of the nest of French Jacobins established in Alfoxton. Dr Lysons had informed the Home Secretary (Portland), who had despatched an agent to investigate. It was apparently the strange accents of the Wordsworths, their continental habit of laundering on Sundays (and doubtless their social inaccessibility), and the long walks in the surrounding countryside taken, notebooks in hand, by Wordsworth and Coleridge (Coleridge explains in *Biographia Literaria* that he had been making studies for a projected Cowperian poem on 'The Brook'),[75] that had worried the local working people. Thomas Jones (a farmer), 'Christopher Trickie

and his Wife who live at the Dog pound at Alfoxton', and
Moggs himself had decided that 'these French people' were
'very suspicious persons and that They were doing no good
there. And that was the general opinion of that part of the
country'. The rural complex could hardly have provided a less
sympathetic context for the poets as they moved towards *Lyrical
Ballads;* and Mr Walsh, clearly no fool, speaks for Coleridge's
own class in his reports to the Home Office:

> I think this will turn out no French affair, but a mischiefous
> gang of disaffected Englishmen. I have just procured the Name
> of the person who took the House. His name is Wordsworth a
> name I think known to Mr Ford.

Coleridge's verbal scrupulosity in the preservation of his
self-image, the image of an intellect grounding its judgements
in principles that transcended party, this crucial nicety of
discrimination is trampled over by the crude stigmatisation of a
society under stress:

> The inhabitants of Alfoxton House are a Sett of violent
> Democrats. The House was taken for a Person of the name of
> Wordsworth, who came to It from a Village near Honiton in
> Devonshire, about five Weeks since. The Rent of the House is
> secured to the Landlord by a Mr Thomas Poole of this Town.
> Mr Poole is a Tanner and a Man of some property. He is a most
> Violent Member of the Corresponding Society and a strenuous
> supporter of Its Friends. He has taken with him at this time a
> Mr Coleridge and his wife both of whom he has supported since
> Christmas last. This Coleridge came last from Bristol and is
> reckoned a Man of superior Ability. He is frequently publishing,
> and I am told is soon to produce a new work. He has a Press in
> the House and I am informed He prints as well as publishes his
> *own productions.[76]

Poole in particular is considered dangerous because of his
leading part in the organisation of a Poor Man's Club in Nether
Stowey. He was blamed for Thelwall's visit, and for acting as
the 'protector' of Coleridge and the other 'Jacobins'; yet his
friendship never wavered, his support remained essential to
Coleridge, who was in his turn also capable of an impressive
dignity, a reasoned, sane humanity in the face of persecution.
This quality in Coleridge (it is strongest when the pressure is

most extreme, and we can recognise it for example, in
Coleridge's reaction to the very unpleasant quarrel with Lloyd
and Lamb)[77] emerges in his real exertions to find a home for
Thelwall; he writes to persuade a neighbour to procure a
cottage for Thelwall:

> ... by his particular exertions in the propagation of those
> principles, which *we* hold sacred & of the highest importance, he
> has become, as you well know, particularly unpopular, thro'
> every part of the kingdom—in every part of the kingdom,
> therefore, some odium, & inconvenience must be incurred by
> those, who should be instrumental in procuring him a cottage
> there—but are Truth & Liberty of so little importance that we
> owe no sacrifices to them? And because with talents very great,
> & disinterestedness undoubted, he has evinced himself, in
> activity & courage, superior to any other patriot, must his
> country *for this* be made a wilderness of waters to him? . . .. If the
> day of darkness & tempest should come, it is most probable, that
> the influence of T. would be very great on the lower classes—it
> may therefore prove of no mean utility to the cause of Truth &
> Humanity, that he had spent some years in a society, where his
> natural impetuosity had been disciplined into patience, and
> salutary scepticism, and the slow energies of a *calculating* spirit.
> (*CL*,i,342)

Coleridge in 1797 was quickly learning the discipline of
patience. On 19 August he wrote to Thelwall: 'The Aristocrats
seem determined to persecute, *even Wordsworth*'(*CL*,i,341; it
seems clear from this that Coleridge knew about the spy soon
after his arrival on 15 August, and clear too that he did not
find the situation funny). On 21 August he wrote again to
Thelwall, giving amongst his explanations of the decision
against finding a house in Stowey the probable effect on Poole:

> ... the hope, which I had entertained, that you could have
> settled here without any, the remotest interference of Poole, *has
> vanished*. To such interference on his part there are insuperable
> difficulties—the whole Malignity of the Aristocrats will converge
> to him, as to the *one* point—his tranquillity will be perpetually
> interrupted—his business, & his credit, hampered & distressed
> by vexatious calumnies—the ties of relationship
> weakened—perhaps broken—& lastly, his poor Mother made
> miserable—the pain of the Stone aggravated by domestic
> calamity & quarrels betweixt her son & those neighbours with
> whom & herself there have been peace & love for these fifty

years.—Very great odium T. Poole incurred by bringing *me* here—my peaceable manners & known attachment to Christianity had almost worn it away—when Wordsworth came & he likewise by T. Poole's agency settled here—/ You cannot conceive the tumult, calumnies, & apparatus of threatened persecutions which this event has occasioned round about us. If *you* too should come, I am afraid, that even riots & dangerous riots might be the consequence.

(*CL*,i,343)

We cannot accuse Coleridge of exaggeration. As it turned out, he decided within a year to leave Nether Stowey himself, and there is perhaps a clue to the decidedly hurried departure of Wordsworth and Coleridge for Germany (without waiting for the appearance and critical reception of *Lyrical Ballads*) in Coleridge's account, in a letter of January 1798 to Josiah Wedgewood, of the reasons behind his plan to take a Unitarian Ministry in Shrewsbury:

. . . by Law I shall be exempted from military service—to which, Heaven only knows how soon we may be dragged. For I think it not improbable, that in case of an invasion our government would serve all, whom they chose to suspect of disaffection, in the same way that good King David served Uriah— 'Set ye Uriah in the forefront of the hottest Battle, & retire ye from him, that he may be smitten & die'. I do not wish to conceal from you that I have suffered more from fluctuation of mind on this than any former occasion: and even now I have scarcely courage to decide absolutely. It is chilling to go among strangers—& I leave a lovely country, and one friend so eminently near to my affections that his society has almost been consolidated with my ideas of happiness.

(*CL*,i,367)

The atmosphere that helped Coleridge to decide in favour of a journey, 'chilling' as this was, into a strange country, far from the place and people that had been 'consolidated' with his ideas of happiness, was not confined in its direct influence on Coleridge to the immediate locality of Nether Stowey. Coleridge's fear of conscription was justifiable in the context of local volunteer movements, and the enthusiastic collection of loyalty oaths (we hear of a solicitor at Bridgewater in 1792 who 'collects oaths of loyalty like taxes').[78] In 1796 the head of the leading family in Coleridge's locality, Francis Egerton, 3rd

Duke of Bridgewater, had distinguished himself by subscribing 'a draft at sight for £100,000' to Pitt's loyalty loan.[79] But the ostentatious loyalty of Coleridge's neighbourhood was dwarfed as a disturbing influence by the emergence in 1798 of a national image of Coleridge as a dangerous Jacobin. Canning's *New Morality* [80] appeared in the *Anti-Jacobin* on 9 July 1798; the whole range of Coleridge's social milieu was represented in the poem as prostrate in praise of the botanist Louis-Marie de Laverellière-Lépaux, who had been the first of the new French Directory to be elected. Paine, Godwin, Holcroft, Thelwall, Priestley, Wakefield were invoked by name; and also

> . . . ye five other wandering Bards that move
> In sweet accord of harmony and love,
> C——dge and S—th–y, L——d, and L——be and Co.
> Tune all your mystic harps to praise LEPAUX![81]

Canning's poem was quickly realised by Gillray as an elaborate political cartoon, 'New Morality;—or The Promis'd Installment of the High-Priest of the Theophilanthropes, with the Homage of Leviathan and his Suite', which appeared in the new *Anti-Jacobin Review and Magazine*, and was also issued separately.[82] The cartoon closely follows the poem, and represents Lépaux on a three-legged stool, approached by 'a fantastic procession of English Jacobins' who 'wave their red caps'. The procession is headed by the poets, amongst them Coleridge (represented like Southey with an ass's head; Coleridge's *To a Young Ass* had appeared in the *Morning Chronicle* in December 1794) waving a book entitled *Coleridge Dactylics*. There is no record of Coleridge's reaction to either the poem or the cartoon, and he may well not have heard of them until returning from Germany. But soon after returning, on 24 December 1799 we find him writing to Southey with helpless indignation:

> I have bought the Beauties of the Anti-Jacobin—& Attorneys and Counsellors advise me to prosecute—offer to undertake it, so that I shall have neither trouble or expence. They say, it is a clear Case.
>
> (*CL*,i,522)

*The Beauties of the Anti-Jacobin* (1799), an anonymously edited compilation from the work of Canning, Gifford, Ellis, and Frere in the *Anti-Jacobin*, designed 'to occupy a place on the tables, or in the pockets, of the middle class of society',[83] had reprinted the *New Morality* with a footnote attacking Coleridge for his 'Deism': 'To the disgrace of discipline, and a Christian University, this avowed Deist was not expelled.' More accurately, and more savagely, the note drew attention to the fact that Coleridge had 'left his native country, commenced citizen of the world, left his poor children fatherless and his wife destitute. 'Ex uno disce' his associates Southey and Lambe'.[84] This attack made a profound impression on Coleridge, even if it is not difficult now to see how such a chasm could have developed between the image he had laboured to create, and the received image, the caricature, by which the reading public knew him.

Notwithstanding his 'principles', Coleridge's political colours would have been perfectly apparent to any intelligent contemporary. By July 1798 Coleridge had published poetry in the *Cambridge Intelligencer,* the *Morning Chronicle,* the *Morning Post,* and the *Monthly Magazine.* All these papers were anti-ministerial and francophile in editorial policy. Coleridge's 'Sonnets on Eminent Characters', a roll-call of liberal heroes, had appeared in the *Morning Chronicle* in December 1794 and January 1795; a glance at the index of the *Anti-Jacobin* tells us all we need to know about its attitude to the *Chronicle:*

> *Morning Chronicle*—its impiety—its blasphemy—its falsehood—its historical, geographical and political ignorance—its insolence—baseness—and stupidity. *Passim, passim.*[85]

The *Anti-Jacobin* devoted a weekly section to the correction of 'misrepresentations', 'mistakes', 'lies', and so on, taking the vast majority of its examples from the *Chronicle* and the *Post.* The *Cambridge Intelligencer* was 'detected and exposed' in the issue of 7 May 1798.[86] The image of Coleridge built up by the reviews of his early publications would also have attracted the animosity of the aristocrats. The pro-French *Critical Review* in particular had encouraged Coleridge from the start; it welcomed the author of *The Fall of Robespierre* as 'a genuine votary of the Muse',[87] and had given space to approving reviews of *A Moral and Political Lecture, Conciones ad Populum* and *The Plot Disco-vered*.[88] The paper later carried reviews of *Poems on Various Subjects, Ode on the Departing Year,* the second edition of *Poems, Fears in Solitude,* and *Lyrical Ballads,* which we need to consider in the context of other reviews of Coleridge's poetry. Coleridge certainly did not burst on the literary world with the force of a Byron, but he was respectably received by the liberal *Analytical Review* (edited by the radical publisher Joseph Johnson), by the *Monthly Review,* and by the *New Annual Register,* all politically sympathetic. The high-church and Tory *British Critic,* in contrast, supported by Pitt and leading churchmen, found Coleridge an irritating poet. It is likely that Coleridge was only reviewed at all through the influence of his Cambridge friend Francis Wrangham, whom Coleridge described to Cottle in April 1796 as 'a reviewer in the British Critic & a college acquaintance of mine, an admirer of me & a *pitier* of my principles' (*CL*,i,201). The critical reception of Coleridge takes us back to the problem, for the radical poet, of working in a medium that was considered the amusement of a particular class. Coleridge's public, polarised by political differences, still shared a received canon of poetic taste. The *British Critic* reviewed *Poems on Various Subjects* in May 1796, approving the volume's 'tenderness of sentiment' and 'elegance of expression' but criticising a manner not 'sufficiently chastened by experi-ence of mankind, or habitude of writing'. We detect Wran-gham's hand in the patronising concession that 'Mr Coleridge does not, in this volume, betray much of his politics, except in his violent rant to Lord Stanhope'.[89] The reaction of the *Critical Review* to the same volume found no incompatibility between the aspiring poet and an 'enthusiastic love of liberty', but shared the reservations about Coleridge's style: 'The versifica-tion is not sufficiently polished, and, by not having the pause and accent in the proper place, grates upon a correct ear.'[90] In the course of the nineties Coleridge lost contact with every sort of public audience; his politics cost him readers, and as he tried anxiously to cover his political tracks with an attitude that was both anti-ministerial and anti-French, he found (it must have seemed a bitter irony) that his politics cost him readers in both camps. The *British Critic* decided that, in spite of 'sensibility' and 'poetic taste', the poet of *Fears in Solitude* harboured 'absurd and preposterous prejudices against his country'. The *Critical Review,* on the other hand, observed drily that 'without being a ministerialist, Mr Coleridge has become an alarmist'.[91] It is not Coleridge's politics, but his poetry, that we consider most important now, which makes the muted approval that he met with, at first, as a poet, seem rather strange. He was oddly unselfconscious about the quality of his poetry; much of it (much, for example, of *Poems on Various Subjects*) was not particularly impressive, but by 1798 he had published *The Eolian Harp, Reflections on having left a Place of Retirement, Frost at Midnight, The Nightingale,* and a number of pieces that are less successful but still, undoubtedly, the work of a poet at least very interesting. *The Ancient Mariner* attracted some attention, however unconsidered and dismissive that was; but Coleridge's peculiarly original blank verse poems appear to have made no real impression at all, if we except scattered notes of approval or disapproval. This cannot have been reassuring, but the sense that he wrote for an audience both politically prejudiced against him, and oblivious to the quality of his language, deepened into public silence before the clever way in which the *Anti-Jacobin* group grasped the situation of the radical poets, and capitalised on it. On 20 November 1797, the first issue of the *Anti-Jacobin* announced, in an 'Introduction to the Poetry of the Anti-Jacobin', its intention of including weekly specimens of the *'Jacobin* Muse': 'such pieces as may serve to illustrate some of the principles on which the poetical as well as the political doctrine of the NEW SCHOOL is established'. The *'Jacobin* Art of Poetry' was recognised to involve a new conception of the proper objects of poetry, that also comprehended a conscious effort of stylistic innovation. Style was identified with party; Coleridge's art was to be constrained to a privacy of address not only by the radical taint, but by the assertion of style. The *Anti-Jacobin* was quick to point out the absurdity of a poet who thought of himself as distinguished from other men not qualitatively, but merely by the degree of his vision's intensity:

> It might not be unamusing to trace the springs and principles of this species of Poetry, which are to be found, some in the exaggeration, and others in the direct inversion of the sentiments and passions which have in all ages animated the breast of

the favourite of the Muses, and distinguished him from the 'vulgar throng'.[92]

Southey provided the target for the 'imitation', in the second issue of the *Anti-Jacobin*, of 'Sapphics';[93] the desire to ridicule experimentation in metre as ignorantly pretentious presumably accounts for the *Dactylics* that Coleridge carries in the Gillray cartoon.

Coleridge's isolation from a reading public was becoming serious as he left for Germany, but his isolation from fellow-radicals, an isolation made familiar to us in the work of Coleridge's critics,[94] had come earlier, and more deliberately. The *Watchman* had upset the dissenters by a youthful, ebullient facetiousness in reference to the Bible, and more particularly to the practice of fast-days.[95] The radicals had been alienated by the famous attack on Godwin in the essay on 'Modern Patriotism', in the third *Watchman*. Coleridge objected in the essay to Godwin's disregard of the domestic values:

> You have studied Mr Godwin's essay on Political Justice; but to think filial affection folly, gratitude a crime, marriage injustice, and the promiscuous intercourse of the sexes right and wise, may class you among the despisers of vulgar prejudices, but cannot increase the probability that you are a PATRIOT. But you act up to your principles.—So much the worse! Your principles are villainous ones! I would not entrust my wife or sister to you—Think you, I would entrust my country?[96]

The Christian emphasis that we have seen Coleridge placing upon domestic retirement clearly lies behind this slightly petulant attack (as so often, a failure of tone goes with the loss of audience); we feel the psychological pressure, the ideas in relation to a personal need, in Coleridge's unpleasantly gossipy personal attacks on the private lives of leading radicals in a letter to Thelwall of 13 May 1796. After asserting 'the moral uses of Marriage', which 'confines the appetites to one object', and 'gradually causes them to be swallowed up in *affection*', Coleridge restates to Thelwall his central position:

> The real source of inconstancy, depravity, & prostitution, is *Property*, which mixes with & poisons every thing good—& is beyond doubt the Origin of all Evil.—'But you cannot be a

Patriot unless you are a Christian'.—Yes! Thelwall! the disciples of Lord Shaftesbury & Rousseau, as well as of Jesus—but the man who suffers not his hopes to wander beyond the objects of sense will, in general, be *sensual*—& I again assert, that a Sensualist is not likely to be a Patriot.

(*CL*,i,213-4)

The association of the materialists with the 'Sensualist', and thus with sexual promiscuity, is firm in Coleridge's mind; he goes on to assert the truth of some ugly stories about Godwin, and passes on with relish a slanderous account of Joseph Gerrald, of whom he had been

informed by a West-Indian (a Republican) that to his knowledge Gerrald left a Wife there to starve—and I well know that he was prone to intoxication, & an Whoremonger. I saw myself a letter from Gerald to one of his FRIENDS, couched in terms of the most abhorred Obscenity, & advising a marriage with an old woman on account of her money.

(*CL*,i,215)

That sort of malice, directed against a man who had already been transported for his principles, is difficult to take;[97] it merges with much in Coleridge, the dishonesty, the endless self-justification, the unsubstantiated claims, that seems often to invite an irritation that can hover on the edge of contempt. Professor Fruman has suggested the great importance, throughout the products of Coleridge's life, throughout all the massively detailed records of his mental life, that we have now to assign to the influence of various sorts of mental disorder. But *Coleridge the Damaged Archangel* is a triumph of the sympathetic intelligence, its judgements urge compassion. There has to be an adjustment of perspective, and if we can see more clearly how firm is the psychological basis of Coleridge's achievement as well as his tragedy, we can begin also to modify Professor Fruman's emphases. Coleridge's personal vulnerability made particularly acute the discomfort of a social alienation that was importantly a representative condition. The effort to realise a form of his social ideal in Nether Stowey, the move to Germany, the return to find his reputation as a Jacobin confirmed, these experiences form a critically formative sequence. The tensions of public and private, of loneliness and community, of the actual and the possible, are present in his best poetry, and most characteristically in the conversation peoms, where they are absorbed into the texture of the poetic experience. But the influence of Coleridge's social experience in the nineties extends far beyond the poetry. The conversation poems themselves testify to this; they enact a development of consciousness which Coleridge comes in *Biographia Literaria* to invoke as the highest form of creative and critical activity. The experience of the conversation poems is structured around a self-redeeming growth of consciousness, a growth which encompasses the perceptual modes that Coleridge later called 'fancy' and 'imagination'.

# V
# The Literary Context of Retirement

Most discussions of Coleridge's poetry have had something to say about the various elements of literary tradition that it can be seen to draw on. There is general agreement on the specific areas of English poetry that the conversation poems may be referred to; we are •accustomed to think of the Augustan meditative manner in blank verse, a poetry most interested in nature, and in a pedestrian but self-assured habit of 'philosophical' speculation that borrows substance from stable and prevalent assumptions about the physical world, and man's place in it. Coleridge's own blank verse poetry shows up very well in this context, because it leaves him without real competitors. Cowper probably comes closest, but he has been placed in relation to Coleridge with firm precision by Humphrey House:

> In the Conversation poems Coleridge is carrying on where Cowper left off. The autobiographical element is given deeper psychological analysis, and the thought about it carries over into what is properly metaphysical poetry. The informal method is kept; but everything has greater import; the imagery leaves Cowper's direct statement; the descriptive passages are more intricately and closely knit to their psychological effects; the description is more minute, delicate and various in correspondence with the more minute and various states of mind on which it bears. Above all, the language of some of the poems, particularly "Frost at Midnight", has always the verbal concentration on which great poetry always depends, and Cowper so obviously nearly always lacks.[1]

And what is obvious in Cowper is much more so in Thomson and Akenside, Young and Mallett. The point that House made so well has been rehearsed and re-inforced many times; George Watson's discussion of the conversation poems says the same thing in more detail,[2] and Coleridge's achievement has been confirmed, at varying length, by Walter Jackson Bate, Max Schulz, Richard Fogle, indeed by almost all commentators on the conversation poems.[3] Some accounts investigate in considerable detail the specific shifts, in style, in theme, and in philosophical orientation, between Coleridge and his various literary antecedents. This kind of approach has yielded some fine and helpful essays; M.H. Abrams's 'Structure and Style in the Greater Romantic Lyric' is perhaps the best known, but there are also valuable studies by W.K. Wimsatt, Richard Haven, and Robert Langbaum.[4] Their work has shown that more needs to be stressed than the blank-verse meditative tradition; Dyer's graceful descriptive poetry uses octosyllabics, and Coleridge's early enthusiam, not just for Bowles but for many of the poets who contributed to the eighteenth century's rivival of the sonnet, does not strike us now as the oddity it once seemed.

It is clear that much useful work has already been done, and certainly there appears to be little point now in going yet again over the same tired ground. But there *are* things still to be said about the particular forms and conventions that Coleridge chose to appropriate to his own poetic language; the conversation poems, highly charged with Coleridge's powerful sense of the values he found in nature and in retirement, use existing poetic resources which emerge changed—in Coleridge, and in literary history, they serve a situation that is quite new—but still recognisable. The continuity of Coleridge's poetic language with its past is not separable from the continuous development of the society that poetic language addresses.

In the early years of their correspondence, Charles Lamb gave Coleridge a good deal of advice about poetry, with his engaging spontaneous sensitivity:

> Cultivate simplicity, Coleridge, or rather, I should say, banish elaborateness; for simplicity springs spontaneous from the heart, and carries into daylight its own modest buds and genuine, sweet, and clear flowers of expression. I allow no hot-beds in the gardens of Parnassus.[5]

This was written early in November 1796; Coleridge had published *Reflections on having left a Place of Retirement* in the October *Monthly Magazine*, but Lamb's first mention of that poem does not come until a letter dated 2 December:

> I have seen your last very beautiful poem in the Monthly
> Magazine—write thus, and you most generally have written
> thus, and I shall never quarrel with you about simplicity.[6]

There is on the face of it something a little puzzling here; we
know that Lamb admired Cowper and Burns at this time, and
his 'simplicity' is a term that we can understand in relation to
those writers. But how often, by December 1796, had Col-
eridge 'written thus'? *The Eolian Harp* had appeared in April, in
*Poems on Various Subjects,* and Lamb had praised it warmly.[7] But
it is surely surprising that the 'genuine, sweet, and clear'
simplicity of what we now look back on as the developing
conversational idiom should be recognised in this way by Lamb.
His tone is approving, but not unduly excited; definitely not
excited by anything as dramatically new as the conversation
poems are sometimes made to seem, even in the response of a
contemporary as sympathetic as Lamb, who recognised with
quite exceptional insight and generosity, far more alertly than
Wordsworth or Southey, that Coleridge had written a great
poem in *The Ancient Mariner.* Some of Coleridge's own earliest
statements about poetry are in fact puzzling like Lamb's,
appearing to assume, calmly, as a *fait accompli,* a poetic
achievement that seems now to have been of the very first
importance. The preface from Coleridge's little privately-
circulated anthology of *Sonnets from Various Authors,* which is the
earliest example that we have of Coleridge's characteristic
critical manner, appears to predicate with astonishing assur-
ance the whole direction of the immediate English poetic
tradition; Coleridge designates the qualities from which 'the
Sonnets of BOWLES derive their marked superiority over all
other Sonnets':

> ... moral Sentiments, Affections, or Feelings, are deduced
> from, and associated with, the scenery of Nature. Such composi-
> tions generate a habit of thought highly favourable to delicacy of
> character. They create a sweet and indissoluble union between
> the intellectual and the material world.
>
> (*PW*,ii,1139)

The passage offers a curious blend of idioms ('delicacy of
character' smacks of Fanny Burney), but W.K. Wimsatt's

brilliant short study of Coleridge and Bowles, 'The Structure of Romantic Nature Imagery', has formulated exactly the comment that one is tempted to make:

> . . . already, in 1796, Coleridge as poet was concerned with the more complex ontological grounds of association (the various levels of sameness, of correspondence and analogy), where mental activity transcends mere 'associative response'—where it is in fact the unifying activity known both to later eighteenth century associationists and to romantic poets as 'imagination'. The 'sweet and indissoluble union between the intellectual and the material world' of which Coleridge speaks in the introduction to his pamphlet anthology of sonnets in 1796 must be applied by us in one sense to the sonnets of Bowles, but in another to the best romantic poetry and even to Coleridge's imitation of Bowles [Wimsatt is investigating the similarities and differences between Bowles's 'To the River Itchin' and Coleridge's 'To the River Otter'].[8]

But this begs a crucial question; *is* Coleridge in any way conscious of the second sense that may be given to his famous comment on Bowles? Of course Wimsatt is in his own terms right, but there may also be something to be gained from an attempt to interpret the judgement of Bowles in Coleridge's own terms. Like Lamb, Coleridge did not think of his meditative blank-verse poems as an innovation, in style, or in the kind of mental action that they contained. 'Simplicity', the language of the feeling self in nature, was an available poetic mode, with its appropriate occasions, its shared associations. Its value had been learnt repeatedly; for example by Wordsworth's great favourite, 'Edwin', the hero of James Beattie's *Minstrel* (1771, 1774):

> Of late, with cumbersome, though pompous show,
> Edwin would oft his flowery rhyme deface,
> Through ardour to adorn; but Nature now
> To his experienced eye a modest grace
> Presents, where ornament the second place
> Holds; to intrinsic worth and just design
> Subservient still. Simplicity apace
> Tempers his rage: he owns her charms divine,
> And clears the ambiguous phrase, and lops the unwieldy line.
>
> (*Minstrel*, Canto II, Stanza 59)

The simple style that Beattie celebrates is a natural agent; it asserts the aesthetic norm of a properly clear-headed reference to the order of God, rather than the disorder of corruptly urbane metropolitan civilisation, as the basis of value. In the broadest terms, the simple style was a version of retirement.

The tradition of retirement in English poetry has been exhaustively surveyed in Maren-Sophie Rostvig's *The Happy Man: Studies in the Metamorphoses of a Classical Idea.* She demonstrates how the tradition enters English poetry around the middle of the seventeenth century, and makes the very interesting suggestion (unfortunately without pursuing any implications) that the idiom developed in the work of defeated and dispossessed refugees of the King's party. Her long and elaborate volumes really constitute a descriptive history of English nature poetry, as her search for traces of classical motif turns up specimens from an enormous range of writers and poets, from Vaughan and Waller and Denham, through Thomson and his followers, through Gray and Cowper, until her very last chapter actually deals with Coleridge's *Reflections of having left a Place of Retirement,* which she takes as marking a new departure (appropriately enough), and the end of the retirement tradition in her own definition. The strand of her argument that takes in Coleridge may be summarised very briefly; English poetry tended to represent the retired self in nature as disposed to a habit of philosophical meditation (taking its cue from the *rerum cognoscere causas* of Virgil's second *Georgic*), which realised with increasing intensity the presence of a Divine scheme in nature that was characteristically benevolent; this benevolence was instilled into the perceiving self (this was indeed the purpose of the scheme), which thus came ultimately to reject the abnegation of social responsibility implicit in retirement, and to arrive at commitment to social action which was necessarily metropolitan. Certainly, the argument illuminates part of the proper context in which we should read Coleridge's *Reflections,* though it is odd that Ms Rostvig should assume, as she seems to do, that the responsibility Coleridge learns from nature in the poem should diminish his commitment to domestic retirement. *Reflections* specifically does not do this; the poem's last line does not echo its opening simply to 'round things off'.

We should notice that Coleridge's conversation poems in fact borrow a good deal of their rhetoric from the tradition of retirement. They do not appear *conscious* of the conventions that they use; there is no formal statement of their relation to classical models, Horace or Virgil, Martial or Seneca,[9] and this is a very important departure. But some familiar elements of the conversational manner nevertheless point back to the earlier tradition. A basic contrast between town and country, for example, is always present, sometimes faintly, sometimes more positively. The elegant Horatian stoicism that finds in retirement a way to the virtuous life impossible in vain, fickle Rome, is even perhaps present, although not more than an association, in *The Eolian Harp:*

> For never guiltless may I speak of Him,
> Th' INCOMPREHENSIBLE! save when with awe
> I praise him, and with Faith that inly *feels;*
> Who with his saving mercies healed me,
> A sinful and most miserable man
> Wilder'd and dark, and gave me to possess
> PEACE, and this COT, and THEE, heart-honor' Maid!
> (1796 text, ll. 50-56)

This is generally agreed not to be a happy ending; there is an uncomfortable merging of this God's attributes with those of Sara, and Coleridge is trying to convince himself that he not only sees but feels how beautiful both God and Sara are. But there is too the sense of a successful emancipation from bewildering sophistication; Coleridge is saved by an impulse to simplicity which is identical with the situation of domestic retirement, even if the capitals are too strident. *To the Rev. George Coleridge* is in many respects a conversation poem, but it fails because Coleridge is too nervous about his audience to get talking. The poem's opening suggests in a similar but more positive way than *The Eolian Harp* that rural domesticity is the best antidote for a young man who has mixed in the world:

> A blessed lot hath he, who having passed
> His youth and early manhood in the stir
> And turmoil of the world, retreats at length,
> With cares that move, not agitate the heart,
> To the same dwelling where his father dwelt;

> And haply views his tottering little ones
> Embrace those aged knees and climb that lap,
> On which first kneeling his own infancy
> Lisp'd its brief prayer. Such, O my earliest Friend!
> Thy lot, and such thy brothers too enjoy.
> At distance did ye climb Life's upland road,
> Yet cheer'd and cheering: now fraternal love
> Hath drawn you to one centre. Be your days
> Holy, and blest and blessing may you live!
>
> (ll.1-14)

Most striking here is the psychological disturbance, inseparable in Coleridge from family relations, that is kept bravely under control by a stilted sentimentality. But again, the 'few paternal acres' of Horace's second *Epode* are not too far behind these lines; and the poem actually has an epigraph, '*Notus in fratres animi paterni*', from the *Odes*,II,ii. There is little life in the allusion, because it takes us into a suave cultural ethos of Horatian urbanity that is entirely foreign to Coleridge's too naive confessional manner. And yet we cannot be sure about this, for Horace's *Ode*,II,ii, is a recommendation of the stoic *nil admirari*, a habit of mind that is consistently active in the conversation poems. The opening paragraph of *Fears in Solitude* provides a good example of this quality in Coleridge's retirement:

> Oh! 'tis a quiet, spirit-healing nook!
> Which all, methinks, would love; but chiefly he,
> The humble man, who, in his youthful years,
> Knew just so much of folly, as had made
> His early manhood more serenely wise!
>
> (ll.12-16)

The opposition in these lines between the simple, healing purity of retirement and the 'folly' of the world, of society, is one that we meet often, most characteristically as an opposition of town to country. And Coleridge overlays the sense of value in place with a temporal perspective that contrasts the unhappy past, a lonely child's London schooldays, with a serene present, the grown man at home with his friends in the country, gently supervising his own children away from the wrong environment:

> My babe so beautiful! it thrills my heart
> With tender gladness, thus to look at thee,
> And think that thou shalt learn far other lore,
> And in far other scenes! For I was reared
> In the great city, pent 'mid cloisters dim,
> And saw nought lovely but the sky and stars.
> But thou, my babe! shalt wander like a breeze
> By lakes and sandy shores . . . .
>
> *(Frost at Midnight, ll.48-55)*

The emphasis on a Divine benevolence in nature is direct; the town is bad precisely because it obstructs the educative influxes of nature. Charles Lamb's experience is invoked to make the same point in *This Lime-Tree Bower my Prison:*

> Yes! they wander on
> In gladness all; but thou, methinks, most glad,
> My gentle-hearted Charles! For thou hast pined
> And hunger'd after Nature, many a year,
> In the great City pent, winning thy way
> With sad yet patient soul, through evil and pain
> And strange calamity!
>
> *(ll.26-32)*

And *The Nightingale*, confidently frank in its rejection of unnatural poetic conventions, still itself employs amongst a number of literary conventions the opposition of town and country (in the context of an attitude to 'fame' that is close to Horace); Coleridge celebrates the true poet's surrender of 'his whole spirit' to the influxes of nature,

> of his song
> And of his fame forgetful! so his fame
> Should share in Nature's immortality,
> A venerable thing! and so his song
> Should make all Nature lovelier, and itself
> Be loved like Nature! But 'twill not be so;
> And youths and maidens most poetical,
> Who lose the deepening twilights of the spring
> In ball-rooms and hot theatres, they still
> Full of meek sympathy must heave their sighs
> O'er Philomela's pity-pleading strains.
>
> *(ll.29-39)*

Even the most spontaneously uncontrolled of Coleridge's best poems, the *Letter to Sara*, can hint, partly through evident allusion to *Frost at Midnight,* at this same opposition; and we notice in passing that Coleridge's associationism persists, suggested with a beautiful lightness of touch:

> At eve, sky-gazing in 'ecstatic fit'
> (Alas! for cloister'd in a city school
> The Sky was all, I knew, of Beautiful)
> At the barr'd window often did I sit,
> And oft upon the leaded School-roof lay,
> And to myself would say—
> There does not live the Man so stripp'd of good affections
> As not to love to see a Maiden's quiet Eyes
> Uprais'd and linking on sweet Dreams by dim Connections
> To Moon, or Evening Star, or glorious western Skies—
> While yet a Boy, this Thought would so pursue me
> That often it became a kind of Vision to me!
>
> (*CL*,ii,791-2)

These lines are very strikingly original in manner, and it may seem unnecessarily forced to isolate them in the context of an effort to bring forward the conventional elements in Coleridge's reflective verse; it may indeed be perverse to go even further, and to consider a much better-known passage from the *Letter,* insisting on the same context:

> O Sara! we receive but what we give,
> And in *our* Life alone does Nature live.
> Our's is her Wedding Garment, our's her Shroud—
> And would we aught behold of higher Worth
> Than that inanimate cold World allow'd
> To the poor loveless ever-anxious Crowd . . . .
>
> (*CL*,ii,797)

An intimation of the higher values available through nature is closed to that crowd, the teeming social mass; Coleridge returns to them a few lines later, placing them this time a little more recognisably in the Christian perspective of fallen metropolitan man:

> JOY, innocent Sara! Joy, that ne'er was given
> Save to the Pure, & in their purest Hour,
> JOY, Sara! is the Spirit & the Power,
> That wedding Nature to us gives in Dower

> A new Earth & new Heaven
> Undreamt of by the Sensual & the Proud!
>
> (*CL*,ii,798)

Certainly Coleridge's sense of the contrast between the retired self and mankind at large involves entirely new emphases. A critical change has taken place; but we need to establish what is continuous between Coleridge and his literary predecessors, before we can be confident about what has changed. It may be useful to establish in some detail the particular character of English nature poetry that helped to shape the conversation poems.

Satan's serpentine approach to Eve in *Paradise Lost* shows the way in which the classical value in natural simplicity fitted into the Christian scheme:

> Much he the place admired, the person more.
> As one who long in populous city pent,
> Where houses thick and sewers annoy the air,
> Forth issuing on a summer's morn to breathe
> Among the pleasant villages and farms
> Adjoined, from each thing met conceives delight,
> The smell of grain, or tedded grass, or kine,
> Or dairy, each rural sight, each rural sound;
> If chance with nymph-like step fair virgin pass,
> What pleasing seemed, for her now pleases more,
> She most, and in her look sums all delight.
>
> (*Paradise Lost,* IX,ll.444-54)

There is no distinction between this urban view of nature, with its delighted eye alert to the possibilities of exploitation, and the fallen view of pre-lapsarian bliss in the Garden of Eden. Satan controls both views; the gap between our common experience, and the great struggle between God and Satan, is constantly bridged like this by Milton. Satan's cheeful, cavalier anticipation of the virgin jolts us out of the tourist's reductive complacency that we otherwise share with him absolutely. The urban idea of country life is always patronising because it is always potentially exploitative; the reality of country work (the georgic quality of 'tedded grass') shades into an abstraction, 'each rural sight, each rural sound', like the sense that one has of a holiday resort. Milton is urging on us the unreal holiday

atmosphere of values that we are supposed to live by; Satan is
not going to stay—he is far too conscious of being himself—and
he will leave wreckage behind. Retirement poetry in the
seventeenth and eighteenth centuries is written by metropoli-
tan outsiders in nature. We think of those Cavalier poets who
first began to use the convention, aching to be back at Court,
making the best of the peace and quiet, a handful of friends
and all the unbearable sheep. The ideas of nature that we find
in retirement poetry grow out of common assumptions that are
those of an urban culture. Retirement poetry differed from the
entirely abstracted ideal nature of pastoral (in the tradition of
Virgil's *Eclogues*, and the Greek pastoral poets), in its keen
awareness of the physical reality of nature. But even the most
relaxed and contented retirement poetry, Charles Cotton's for
example, is fundamentally pleased with itself for being so, for
not missing the parties and the balls, the social life that was
properly cultured. The celebration of nature was always formal
and public, the more or less graceful statement of what
everyone knew to be the appeal of an estate in the country.
This shared morality, constantly retaining a classical mode of
expression, is present everywhere; James Thomson arrived at
the best formulations:

> Oh! knew he but his happiness, of men
> The happiest he! who far from public rage
> Deep in the vale, with a choice few retired,
> Drinks the pure pleasures of the rural life.
> (*Autumn*, ll. 1235-8)

There are important similarities here with certain ideas about a
life in nature that Coleridge valued highly; there is the
function of social and political refuge that nature can perform;
the 'choice few' of a small congenial community; the physically
and spiritually healing influence of nature. It is only the public,
declamatory manner of Thomson's Virgilian paraphrase that
distinguishes his experience so sharply from Coleridge's; and
the shift in this respect between Thomson and Coleridge
represents one crucial change in the social and intellectual
orientation of English poetry, because Coleridge could not
substantiate and authenticate the values he found in nature by
reference to a stable, external, publicly received set of assump-

tions. The grounds of belief, of experience, need in Coleridge's poetry to be generated internally and subjectively, and tested against local, personal states of mind. The conversation poems cannot, as the *Seasons* or the *Essay on Man* could, take for granted a public audience to grasp and agree with what is said. Coleridge's finest achievement in the conversation poems is their manipulation of poetic tone as a structural principle. His experience is controlled and authenticated by tone, the index of personal mood that serves to replace a common language of public attitudes and commitments that was closed to Coleridge. His situation was part of a more encompassing development in English culture, reflected most accessibly in its literary forms, which began to remove the interpretation of experience from an objective to a subjective base. The sentimental novel clearly takes some of the strain of this transference, and Sterne's truly remarkable *Tristram Shandy*, with its headlong plunge into the endlessly distorting inconsistency of individual consciousness, and its emphasis on the central ambiguity of time, is perhaps the first work to imply the shift to subjectivity in the full extent of its significance.[10]

One dimension of this shift was political. The King's right, for example, was established in an external framework of value, and the whole security of the existing distribution of wealth and power was 'objectified' in the venerable Constitution. The objective status of these institutions was called seriously into question by regarding them as certain only when the particular individual consciousness could confirm them. Life was not now necessarily to be a process of the individual's gradual attunement to his place in the status quo; if things as they were did not suit, then they could perhaps be changed. And the determining power of consciousness was not a matter of arcane theoretical dispute, especially after 1789. In literature, the most influential work that placed a new emphasis on the structuring power of consciousness over reality was undoubtedly *Lyrical Ballads*. The focus on states of mind, with their sway over dependant reality, is central in that volume; Wordsworth's Preface points unequivocally to this aspect of the work's originality:

> ... it is proper that I should mention one other circumstance which distinguishes these Poems from the popular Poetry of the

day; it is this, that the feeling therein developed gives impor-
tance to the action and situation and not the action and situation
to the feeling.[11]

The passage goes on to draw our attention in particular to *Poor
Susan* and *The Childless Father;* but quite apart from those
poems in the volume that are very evidently concerned with the
power that consciousness may exert over its environment,
poems such as Coleridge's contributions *The Nightingale* and
*The Dungeon,* many of the most enduringly problematic poems
in *Lyrical Ballads* can be read as addressing themselves to the
dramatisation of peculiarly personal states of mind, with the
worlds that they inhabit. *The Thorn, The Idiot Boy,* and *The
Ancient Mariner* are examples;[12] and Wordsworth often seems
particularly interested in forcing on his bourgeois readers the
task of reviewing their *own* attitudes to the poetry's subjects, of
realising that consciousness, if it determines the judgements of
*The Thorn's* narrator (or of Peter Bell for that matter), also
determines the various limitations of their own perspectives on
the kind of people that the poetry deals with. The strategy is
employed most directly in *Simon Lee:*

> Few months of life has he in store,
>      As he to you will tell,
> For still, the more he works, the more
>      His poor old ancles swell.
> My gentle reader, I perceive
>      How patiently you've waited,
> And I'm afraid that you expect
>      Some tale will be related.
>
> O reader! had you in your mind
> Such stores as silent though can bring,
> O gentle reader! you would find
>      A tale in every thing.
> What more I have to say is short,
>      I hope you'll kindly take it;
> It is no tale; but should you think,
>      Perhaps a tale you'll make it.

(ll.65-80)

The polite step forward that Wordsworth's narrative voice
takes here is charged with a telling ambivalence in the epithet

'gentle'; it beckons to the reader's capacity for human sympathy, his readiness for natural kindess to his kind, but it also places the reader, with a mediator's delicate tact, in a social class that is not Simon's. And the consciousness of that gap between Simon and the reader can issue in a terrible witholding of sympathy.

The conversation poems that approach this problem in specifically social and political terms, *Reflections on having left a Place of Retirement* and *Fears in Solitude,* are seriously flawed, because when Coleridge feels that he is addressing directly the cultivated audience of poetry he takes refuge in a dilutedly miltonic and excessively declamatory public manner that ruins any sustained effort of tonal control. He is at his best when he can test and measure the developing and always relative judgements of consciousness against its relationship with nature, and when the control of tone can be sustained in the security of a sensitive and cultivated audience that is not public. We can turn back again to the preceding tradition of English nature poetry to place Coleridge's poetry as continuous with its past; for his achievement in the conversation poems gathers part of its impetus from the emerging direction of English nature poetry.

The real countryside does not become a significant theme of English poetry before the second half of the seventeenth century; it becomes a very prominent theme in the eighteenth century. It is important to consider the reasons for this sharpening of focus on the natural environment. We can grant that Renaissance modes of thought found a certain kind of value in nature that came to seem increasingly inadequate after the turn of the eighteenth century; Shakespeare's Duke could find books in the running brooks, sermons in stones and good in everything, but a poet like James Thomson, while continuing to accept that the moralist's response to nature should properly consist in reading off the Christian hieroglyphics buried in the Creation, was a little distracted from the task by the physical presence of the brooks and stones in their own right. It seems that nature began to mean less as the experience it represented grew more intense. Impressive attempts to account for this paradox have been made; by Earl Wasserman for example:

> ... the divine analogy remained for the eighteenth century the
> relational norm of image and value, and when it finally
> collapsed ... it was obvious to the Romantic that his first task was
> to put the two worlds together again.[13]

The very crispness of these terms is disconcerting; it is as if we
are invited to imagine Coleridge's deliberate decision that
worlds needed putting together, and then sitting down to write
the remedy. Certainly Professor Wasserman's way of putting
the problem is cogent and exact, but it is difficult to accept that
nature can have changed and reformed in meaning solely in
the opinions of men. We are only thinking, then, of one side in
a process that was dialectical. Consciouness is inseparable from
its material conditions, and a change in the way that nature is
perceived implies a change in the physical presence of nature,
and a concomitant change in the relations between nature and
man. Historians can be useful here:

> The enclosure of open fields into the smaller fields that form
> our familiar world today, and the reclamation of the wild lands,
> had been going on intermittently and at a varying pace in every
> century. But after the Restoration the government ceased to
> interfere with the enclosure of open field by private landlords,
> and the pace of change quickened sharply. Up to about 1730
> most of this enclosure was carried through by private agree-
> ments between the owners of the land in question. Very few
> enclosures were dealt with by act of parliament. But under
> George II, and above all from the 1750s onwards, enclosure by
> private act of parliament, working through special commisioners
> in each of the affected parishes, was the great instrument of
> change. From then onwards the transformation of the English
> landscape, or of a considerable part of it, went on at a
> revolutionary pace.[14]

We can read English nature poetry, the poetry written in the
hundred years or so preceding Coleridge's birth, as constitut-
ing in fundamental ways a sustained and various response to
rural change. The countryside was looking different, under the
impact of an increasingly rapid modification of the rural
economy which gradually came to notice as a driving of the
natural world into retreat. The terms provided by Professor
Wasserman usefully describe one effect of this change; much
eighteenth-century nature poetry is characterised by a formally

unbalancing divergence of the image and value of nature. But more encompassing terms may be proposed for a description of the poetic response of a new, a more radically intense consciousness of the diminishing wild lands, the growth of enclosure, rural depopulation and urban expansion. There are two broad and constantly overlapping categories of eighteenth-century nature poetry; there is one mode of response, which includes the picturesque, that emphasises a positive nature, valuable as a source of pleasure and benevolence. And there is another mode of response, not always opposed to the first, that emphasises in darkening, sober tones the fading of nature, or uses its fading (usually its literal fading at twilight) to point a stoic Christian moral. And here are really two ways of coping with a general cultural guilt, which does not have to be conscious (it may be unconscious—at least not explicitly formulated—like the guilt that a friend's death makes us feel), that registers the shock of finding nature not permanent after all, but in fact peculiarly vulnerable to human manipulation. The two kinds of response that have been distinguished represent quite predictable expressions of the consciousness of loss; a newly urgent stress on what is valuable and pleasurable in something suddenly inaccessible, or a melancholy disposition to generalise from the specific loss. Coleridge's experience of nature in the conversation poems is remarkably original in its merging of the two responses, its insistence, at twilight or in the night when the material presence of nature urges stoic resignation, on a happy pleasure of the senses and intellect that revives nature by deeming it a function of the self.

Changes in the countryside could occupy the eighteenth-century poets in obvious and immediate ways; there is the beautifully measured nostalgic solemnity of Goldsmith's *Deserted Village* (1770):

> Sweet smiling village, loveliest of the lawn,
> Thy sports are fled and all thy charms withdrawn;
> Amidst they bowers the tyrant's hand is seen,
> And desolation saddens all thy green:
> One only master grasps the whole domain,
> And half a tillage stints thy smiling plain:
> No more thy glassy brook reflects the day,

> But, choked with sedges, works its weedy way.
> Along thy glades, a solitary guest,
> The hollow-sounding bittern guards its nest;
> Amidst thy desert walks the lapwing flies,
> And tires their echoes with unvaried cries.
> Sunk are thy bowers in shapeless ruin all,
> And the long grass o'ertops the mouldering wall;
> And trembling, shrinking from the spoiler's hand,
> Far, far away, thy children leave the land.
>
> (ll.35-50)

The earlier, positive value that Goldsmith sets against this new state of the village turns out, in fact, to be a conventional Virgilian retirement in the classical idiom (*Deserted Village*, ll.97-112) having little to do with the actual village life that has gone. So perhaps there is something specious in Goldsmith's sadness. But what is most suggestive in the quoted passage is the ambivalence that a contemporary reader might have been disturbed by in the description; for this desolate scene would have been very pleasing to William Gilpin or Richard Payne Knight. The picturesque eye accommodated to contempoary taste exactly those features of the countryside that Goldsmith notes, ruin, wildness, uncultivated land, deliberately in preference to the smooth efficiency of 'tillage', the new techniques of production. Gilpin sometimes attempted, with inimitably parsonical discomfort, to explain the contradictions implicit in his ideal picture-frame:

> Moral, and picturesque ideas do not always coincide. In a moral light, cultivation, in all its parts, is pleasing; the hedge, and the furrow; the waving corn field, and rows of ripened sheaves. But all these the picturesque eye, in quest of scenes of grandeur, and beauty, looks at with disgust. It ranges after nature, untamed by art, and bursting wildly into all its irregular forms...It is thus also in the introduction of figures. In a moral view, the industrious mechanic is a more pleasing object, than the loitering peasant. But in a picturesque light, it is otherwise. The arts of industry are rejected; and even idleness, if I may so speak, adds dignity to a character.[15]

Ruskin, who took stones as seriously as he took men, was sternly to sort out these embarrassments.[16] The picturesque carried to sometimes foolish extremes a separation of nature's image from its value. Gilpin was shy of philosophy, but the

taste that he formed, like Burke's beautiful and sublime, found
a theoretical basis in the mechanistic philosophers. The purely
aesthetic picturesque pleasure in nature was assigned by the
more thoughtful Payne Knight to a mechanical function of
perception; the external stimulus was picturesque (or sublime,
or beautiful) in itself, and the judgements of the observer were
thus absolutely conditioned:

> Yet often still the eye disgusted sees
> In nature, objects which in painting please;
> Such as the rotting shed, or fungous tree,
> Or tatter'd rags of age and misery:
> But here restrain'd, the powers of mimic art
> The pleasing qualities alone impart;
> For nought but light and colour can the eye,
> But through the medium of the mind, descry;
> And oft, in filth and tatter'd rags, it views
> Soft varied tints and nicely blended hues,
> Which thus abstracted from each other sense,
> Give pure delight, and please without offence.
>
> (Payne Knight, *The Landscape*, (2nd
> edition 1795) Bk.I,ll.257-70)

Burke's account of the sublime had made the physiological
conditioning of the aesthetic response to nature more explicit
(though Payne Knight's notes to *The Landscape* show that he was
aware of the theoretical issues);[17] the eye's automatically
painful or pleasurable reaction to configurations of light took
out of the observer's hands any responsibility for moral
ugliness.[18] Behind Burke is Locke, but Locke's nature was not
determining of consciousness in a way that cut out the
possibility of moral judgement, for the mechanistic universe
was benevolent, and while the mind was formed by sensory
experience, it was formed in a Christian mould. The pictures-
que did not simply ignore the moral questions raised by the
eighteenth-century experience of change in the countryside; it
was one popular and fashionable means (and landscape
gardening was another)[19] to the actual concealment of the
effects of rural change. Gilpin's insipid 'ideal sketches', his
solemn recommendations of what to omit in a scene, and, most
obviously, the 'Claude glass', worked by turning one's back on
nature altogether, all point to the deliberate distortion involved

in picturesque seeing. The use of external aesthetic criteria in the judgement of visual nature, borrowed from the Dutch landscape painters and also, most typically, from the Italian and particularly the Claudian realisation of Virgilian pastoral, imposed a deceiving distance between the observer and the real countryside.

But whatever the cost, the dilettante proponents of picturesque technique did contribute to a heightening awareness of nature's physical presence, and their mild, well-mannered self-deceit was put firmly in its place by contemporaries of stronger mind, Cowper, and Wordsworth, and Jane Austen.[20] It is perhaps worth noting that the fashion for the picturesque, while usefully exemplifying the specific form that a basically guilty response to nature could take, demonstrates also that a certain new kind of word, a word such as 'picturesque', or 'romantic', was coined to signify new meanings in nature for the eighteenth century. 'Picturesque' and 'romantic' were both used to describe nature, in what were felt to be its appealing aspects, as if it were analogous to a work of fiction or of the visual imagination. And these usages indicate the new quality of wild, uncultivated nature as something quite suddenly more remote, even unreal; a proper context for the passionate and unbridled self of romance, the dangerously powerful capacities for feeling that had only a dubious status within the social framework of expanding capitalism.

The special pleasure that the picturesque eye sought in nature was a prosaic elaboration on earlier developments in English nature poetry. The literary picturesque, the strongest expression of a pleasurable response to benevolent nature, made its first significant appearance in 1726, with the publication of Thomson's *Winter,* and Dyer's *Grongar Hill.* Thomson is particularly interesting, because so much of his work is representative of various kinds of response and convention that are typical of nature poetry; and we recall that to speak of English nature poetry is virtually to speak of the retirement tradition, for there is scarcely any poetry that does not draw on the forms and resources of retirement, and Coleridge's own nature poetry is not exceptional in this sense. The closing passage of Thomson's *Autumn* (1730), for example, provides us with an interesting context for one feature that all the conversation poems share, their constant readiness to marry a high pitch of feeling in response to nature, with an impulse to explain or account for the experience, or to articulate it in terms that appear philosophical:

> This is the life which those who fret in guilt
> And guilty cities never knew—the life
> Led by primeval ages uncorrupt
> When angels dwelt, and God himself, with man!
> O Nature! all-sufficient! over all
> Enrich me with the knowledge of thy works;
> Snatch me to heaven; thy rolling wonders there,
> World beyond world, in infinite extent
> Profusely scattered o'er the blue immense,
> Show me; their motions, periods, and their laws
> Give me to scan; through the disclosing deep
> Light my blind way: the mineral strata there;
> Thrust blooming thence the vegetable world;
> O'er that the rising system, more complex,
> Of animals; and, higher still, the mind,
> The varied scene of quick-compounded thought,
> And where the mixing passions endless shift;
> These ever open to my ravished eye—
> A search, the flight of time can ne'er exhaust!
> But, if to that unequal—if the blood
> In sluggish streams about my heart forbid
> That best ambition—under closing shades
> Inglorious lay me by the lowly brook,
> And whisper to my dreams. From thee begin,
> Dwell all on thee, with thee conclude my song;
> And let me never, never stray from thee!

The *rerum cognoscere causas* motif testified, in its immense popularity in the eighteenth century, to the rational, investigative spirit which found in nature abundant evidence of a Divinely benevolent design. The Virgilian aspiration was echoed and translated repeatedly, and provided an intellectual perspective on the response to nature so distinctively anxious to enjoy and appreciate it, and to disavow allegiance to the encroaching town. Joseph Warton's version of the relevant passage from the second *Georgic* (ll.447-86) offers precisely this blend of worship that is also a morally improving form of knowledge, a rejection of urban civilisation, and a luxurious sensory and emotional enjoyment:

Teach me the ways of heav'n, the stars to know,
The radiant sun and moon's eclipses shew,
Whence trembles earth, what force old ocean swells
To burst his bounds, and backward what repels;
Why wintry suns roll down with rapid flight,
And whence delay retards the lingering night.
But if my blood's cold streams, that feebly flow,
Forbid my soul great nature's works to know,
Me may the lowly vales, and woodlands please,
And winding rivers, and inglorious ease![21]

The content and developing sequence of ideas, in Thomson and Warton (both following the same classical model), is strikingly similar in Coleridge's *Eolian Harp*, and indeed to a greater or lesser extent in all the conversation poems. Coleridge's contemplation of nature issues in an effort of comprehension:

And what if all of animated nature
Be but organic Harps diversly fram'd,
That tremble into thought, as o'er them sweeps,
Plastic and vast, one intellectual Breeze,
At once the Soul of each, and God of all?
                              (1796 text, ll.36-40)

The speculative impulse subsides to a chastened, 'inglorious' humility, prompted by the stabilising influence of Sara's simple faith; Coleridge relinquishes philosophy for the contentment of his domestic retreat. The crucial difference between Coleridge's verse and the earlier passages quoted is a difference of diction. The truly sustaining meaning that Coleridge finds in nature, its susceptibility to an embracingly connective mental activity, is validated by the language itself that embodies this activity. Nature's meaning is absorbed into the descriptive language, so that Coleridge is not at Thomson's disadvantage of having to confer the meaning by the use of a classical formula.

The neo-classical poetic langauge of natural description, 'stock diction', is typified in Thomson's *Seasons*. This was of course the kind of poetic language that Wordsworth and Coleridge claimed their work to react against, and many critics have found this claim reasonable. 'Stock diction' was charac-

terised in a number of ways; there is a pervasive use of
compound epithets, latinisms, personified abstractions, archa-
isms, technical terms, and these are found in conjunction with
certain common mannerisms of style, the frequent recurrence
of favourite words, the use of classical conventions, the
persistent habit of periphrasis, the use of the present participle
as epithet, and so on.[22] Virgil was the main source of this
diction, especially through the medium of Dryden's transla-
tions, though other works also exerted great influence (Sylves-
ter's Du Bartas, for example).[23] It is easy not to notice that even
Coleridge's best poetry owes something to the extraordinarily
stable diction of nature poetry. The earliest version of *The
Eolian Harp*, a draft of the first sixteen-and-a-half lines
(*PW*,ii,1021), exemplifies the presence of 'stock' elements in
Coleridge's evolving conversational idiom:

> My pensive Sara! thy soft cheek reclin'd
> Thus on my arm, how soothing sweet it is
> Beside our Cot to sit, our Cot o'ergrown
> With white-flowr'd Jasmine and the blossom'd myrtle,
> (Meet emblems they of Innocence and Love!)
> And watch the Clouds, that late were rich with light,
> Slow-sad'ning round, and mark the star of eve
> Serenely brilliant, like thy polish'd Sense,
> Shine opposite! What snatches of perfume
> The noiseless gale from yonder bean-field wafts!
> The stilly murmur of the far-off Sea
> Tells us of Silence! and behold, my love!
> In the half-closed window we will place the Harp,
> Which by the desultory Breeze caress'd,
> Like some coy maid half willing to be woo'd,
> Utters such sweet upbraidings as, perforce,
> Tempt to repeat the wrong!

We notice the familiar latinate vocabulary that goes with a
half-restrained impulse towards decorative periphrasis, 'pen-
sive Sara', 'reclin'd', 'polish'd Sense', 'perfume', 'noiseless gale'.
A feeling of the archaic here and there, 'meet emblems',
'perforce', a sprinkling of hyphenated compounds, even an
example of the adjectival suffix '—y', in 'stilly', combine with
the other elements to colour Coleridge's diction. Even the smell
of the beans was a common feature of descriptive language;
compare Thomson:

> Long let us walk
> Where the breeze blows from yon extended field
> Of blossomed beans.
>
> (*Spring*, ll.498-500)

And yet, Coleridge's lines do manage a certain purity, mannered as they are, that strikes us as something new. The pervasive stability of 'stock diction' has disappeared with the assumptions that it supported and articulated. This stability of 'stock diction' was a strength that it borrowed from the rational, investigative spirit in which eighteenth-century poets looked at nature. A stereotyped vocabulary aspired to the classificatory, Baconian habit of mind, and gave to Thomson's absorbed scrutiny the Christian authority of natural philosophy in the manner of the Royal Society, patiently working towards comprehensive knowledge of nature that held apocalyptic promise. Thomson places *The Seasons* in the context of Christian history, particularly in *Spring*, where Thomson's account of the fall, with man's subsequent alienation from nature, is supplemented by an insistence that much of the goodness in nature remains lost through a failure of human consciousness:

> Nature disturbed
> Is deemed, vindictive, to have changed her course.
>
> (ll.307-8)

> And yet the wholesome herb neglected dies;
> Though with the pure exhilirating soul
> Of nutriment and health, and vital powers,
> Beyond the search of art, 'tis copious blest.
>
> (ll.336-9)

> But man [opposed to the wolf], whom Nature formed of
> milder clay,
> With every kind emotion in his heart,
> And taught alone to weep,—while from her lap
> She pours ten thousand delicacies, herbs
> And fruits, as numerous as the drops of rain
> Or beams that gave them birth,—shall he, fair form!
> Who wears sweet smiles, and looks erect on Heaven,
> E'er stop to mingle with the prowling herd,
> And dip his tongue in gore? The beast of prey,
> Blood-stained, deserves to bleed: but you, ye flocks,
> What have ye done? ye peaceful people, what,

> To merit death? you, who have given us milk
> In luscious streams, and lent us your own coat
> Against the Winter's cold? And the plain ox,
> That harmless, honest, guileless animal,
> In what has he offended? he, whose toil,
> Patient and ever ready, clothes the land
> With all the pomp of harvest; shall he bleed,
> And struggling groan beneath the cruel hands
> Even of the clown he feeds? And that, perhaps,
> To swell the riot of the autumnal feast,
> Won by his labour?
>
> (ll.349-70)

This is just the kind of sentiment that would prompt a character in one of Henry Mackenzie's novels to burst into tears; it seems excessive now, even absurd (the miltonic resonance of Thomson's impassioned plea for vegetarianism—'luscious streams'—is irresistibly comic), but then the now characteristically British love of animals was one product of eighteenth-century 'sensibility' (it will presumably always be difficult to make a plausible case for sheep to the carnivorous audience of poetry).[24] Thomson's assumption would have been that nature itself impresses the necessary moral consciousness, as the agency of a benign God teaching benevolence. The 'physico-theological' perspective on nature, a scientific appreciation of the physical terms in which the Divine scheme was working out, lead also into a gentle social concern (with so many people living like animals, the actual animals must have been easy to include) that was part of the conventional response of the philosopher-poet in retirement. The scientific temper had its appeal for Coleridge, without driving him to the encyclopaedic lengths of a contemporary like Erasmus Darwin. The classificatory habit of mind is more diffuse in Coleridge, and peripheral to the poetry. But it is still there, rather as it is present in Wordsworth when he notes that 'The river is not affected by the tides a few miles above Tintern'.[25] Many of Coleridge's poems relegate his interest in natural philosophy to footnotes, and the interest broadens to embrace more than Gilbert White's fascinated curiosity, or the topographical observations of Gilpin, or Arthur Young. Coleridge's straightforwardly scientific notes are usually in the manner of Darwin; *Lines at Shurton Bars* (1795), for example, includes the following lines:

> 'Tis said, in Summer's evening hour
> Flashes the golden-colour'd flower
> A fair electric flame:

> (*PW*,i,99)

The image is explained by Coleridge in a very long note that begins:

> LIGHT *from plants*. In Sweden a very curious phenomenon has been observed on certain flowers, by M. Haggern, lecturer in natural history.

> (*PW*,i,99)

But there are other kinds of footnote that testify to broader, less definable interests; folk-lore, local custom and superstition (areas that now provide material for the anthropologist), for instance in the prefatory note to Coleridge's early poem *Songs of the Pixies* (1793), which draws attention to 'the superstition of Devonshire' (*PW*,i,40). The best known example of Coleridge's careful attention to such detail is the reference to a 'stranger', with its note of explanation, in *Frost at Midnight* (*PW*,i,240-1). Snatches of reading or personal knowledge like this seem to have a particular importance for Coleridge in the corroboration of accuracy; there is the odd satisfaction with which he records, in a note to line 74 of *This Lime-Tree Bower my Prison*, about a rook that 'flew creeking' overhead, that 'Some months after I had written this line, it gave me pleasure to find that Bartram had observed the same circumstance of the Savanna Crane.' And he goes on to quote a relevant passage from Bartram. But a more significant example from the same poem is Coleridge's concern to render exactly the quality of impression made by

> The dark green file of long lank weeds,
> That all at once (a most fantastic sight!)
> Still nod and drip beneath the dripping edge
> Of the blue clay-stone.

> (ll.17-20)

The first line here was footnoted in the earliest published version of *This Lime-Tree Bower my Prison* (the poem first appeared in 1800, in the second volume of Southey's *Annual Anthology*):

The *Asplenium Scolopendrium*, called in some countries the Adder's Tongue, in others the Hart's Tongue, but Withering gives the Adder's Tongue as the trivial name of the *Ophioglossum* only.

(*PW*,i,179)

William Withering's standard *Arrangement of British Plants* (1796) had corrected a mistake made in a poem that was not actually published until some months after the composition of *This Lime-Tree Bower my Prison*. The poem was *Melancholy* (dated ? 1794 by E.H. Coleridge, presumably on internal evidence; it first appeared in the *Morning Post*, 12 December 1797), which included a reference to 'The dark green Adder's Tongue', glossed by Coleridge in the *Morning Post* as

A Plant found on old walls and in wells and moist hedges.—It is often called the Hart's Tongue.

(*PW*,i,74)

The point seems trivial, but Coleridge was genuinely anxious to get the detail right. Quoting the poem in a letter to Sotheby of August 1802, he referred the 'dark green' of *Melancholy* to the '*Asplenium Scolopendrium,* more commonly called the Hart's Tongue' (*CL*,ii,856). And in *Sibylline Leaves* he was still making the point:

A botanical mistake. The plant I meant is called the Hart's Tongue, but this would unluckily spoil the poetical effect.

(*PW*,i,74)

The unease that Coleridge felt over his inability to fit his 'poetical effect' ('adder' helped to intensify the atmosphere of Gothic menace in *Melancholy*) into the external framework of botany, is most suggestive. Like *The Eolian Harp, This Lime-Tree Bower my Prison* was very carefully worked up by Coleridge between its first significant draft, soon after Charles Lamb's visit to Nether Stowey in June 1797, and publication in 1800. The 'dark green file of long lank weeds' that strikes Coleridge as 'a most fantastic sight' in the published version, does not appear at all in the manuscript sent to Southey in July 1797, or in the slightly different version sent to Lloyd around the same time.[26] It may be suggested that Coleridge took this detail, which provides a climax for the crucial passage (ll.5-20) that enables *This Lime-Tree Bower my Prison* to lift in tone, from his drama *Osorio* (written at the request of Sheridan, and then rejected by him). Coleridge was working on the second half of *Osorio* throughout the summer of 1797; the opening of Act IV includes this description spoken by Osorio:

> A jutting clay-stone
> Drips on the long lank weed that grows beneath;
> And the weed nods and drips.
>
> (*Osorio*,IV,i,18-20)

This was doubtless something that Coleridge had actually seen; but the Thomsonian diction has gone, and this descriptive language is made by Coleridge to serve a relationship with nature that is quite different. The visualisation is intense, but so too is Thomson's; the real shift in emphasis is from object to subject, from the plant to its altered and altering reflex in Coleridge's perception of it. And this points to a more fundamental development in poetic language between Thomson and Coleridge, a shift in the poet's sense of audience, his sense of the authority which his values carry. The eighteenth-century perspectives on nature were shared, and were articulated through the confident, and often, in its given limitations, quite successful use of a common language, in prescribed literary forms. 'Stock diction' was informed by a principle of definition that assigned its objects their appropriate places in a received philosophical scheme.

A continual alertness to the demands of decorum, appropriate tone, was the natural corollary of a confidence in shared values. It is precisely in the use of tonal development, in the presentation of an *evolving* state of mind that implies the relative and provisional status of external reality, that Coleridge's poetry effects a radical modification of its tradition. In this sense, Coleridge diverges not only from Thomson and his followers, but from Wordsworth too. Wordsworth, like Thomson and Cowper and other poets who used the blank-verse meditative manner stemming from Milton, most often worked in a tonal unit of the verse paragraph; in Coleridge's most successful blank verse it is the whole poem that works as a finished, self-consistent unit of tone. The eighteenth-century satirists were expert at an ironic manipulation of decorum which tended to form the most serious jokes in their poetry, and Wordsworth, scrupulous to preserve the 'relative dignity and worth' of all his different moments, is not so very far from this, especially in that rhetorical device of sharply contrasted tones that is common in the *Prelude:*

> Visionary Power
> Attends upon the motions of the winds
> Embodied in the mystery of words.
> There darkness makes abode, and all the host
> Of shadowy things do work their changes there,
> As in a mansion like their proper home;
> Even forms and substances are circumfus'd
> By that transparent veil with light divine;
> And through the turnings intricate of Verse,
> Present themselves as objects recognis'd
> In flashes, and with a glory scarce their own.

> Thus far a scanty record is deduced
> Of what I owed to Books in early life;
> Their later influence yet remains untold;
> But as this work was taking in my thoughts
> Proportions that seem'd larger than had first
> Been meditated, I was indisposed
> To any further progress at a time
> When these acknowledgements were left unpaid.
>
> (*Prelude,* V, 619-37)

This stumbling to a halt has an extraordinary effect. The tonal contrast, Wordsworth's control of our response, insists on an opposition, a pervasive ambivalence, that wavers between unknown modes of being and the crashingly commonplace, between a nature majestically appropriated to articulate the personal past and a nature stubbornly external, more acting than acted on. One of these poles is not radically different from Thomson's passionate field-naturalist's love of nature, but couched in the terms of Wordsworth's powerfully self-conscious originality, his

> consciousness of the infinite variety of natural appearances which had been unnoticed by the poets of any age or country, so far as I was acquainted with them.[27]

Wordsworth was able to balance this solidity with an unflinching representation of the self-conscious mind, its mysterious transfiguring, symbolising powers, that took him beyond Coleridge's poetic range. Coleridge was always terrified of doubt, even before an audience he knew he could trust; Wordsworth though, confident, allowed an impressive centrality to the ambiguity of his experience. At really critical moments it is absorbed into his grammar:

> . . . a sense sublime
> Of something far more deeply interfused,
> Whose dwelling is the light of setting suns,
> And the round ocean, and the living air,
> And the blue sky, and in the mind of man,
> A motion and a spirit, that impells
> All thinking things, all objects of all thought,
> And rolls through all things.
>
> (*Tintern Abbey*, ll.96-103)

The construction of the sentence fuses Wordsworth's 'sense sublime' with the 'something' that it is conscious of. That 'sense' is 'in the mind of man', but we cannot determine whether or not this equates it with the 'something' that is also there. It is as if Wordsworth's experience of the world outside himself is displayed in the parallel situation—or is it the same situation?—of a mind conscious of itself as something separate. The famous passage in the *Prelude* that describes Wordsworth's crossing of the Alps centres on a similarly ambiguous grammatical construction, again in the context of a tonal contrast that enacts the elements in tension:

> Hard of belief, we question'd him again,
> And all the answers which the Man return'd
> To our inquiries, in their sense and substance,
> Translated by the feelings which we had
> Ended in this; that we had cross'd the Alps.
>
> Imagination! lifting up itself . . .
>
> (*Prelude*, VI,520-25)

Wordsworth comes to a recognition of the imagination's 'Power', with its 'strength of usurpation',

> when the light of sense
> Goes out in flashes that have shewn to us
> The invisible world
>
> (*Prelude*,VI, 534-6)

Coleridge does not render this dual relationship with nature, at once extinguishing and illuminating the objects of sense. Nature in the conversation poems has no single meaning, but its variety of significance is quite unlike the static classification of Thomson, or the solid awareness through which Wordsworth moves. A rigid, sharply differentiating decorum of tone is foreign to the conversational idiom, which allows nature to shade through a spectrum of significance, in a process determined by the poet's developing consciousness. Our sense of this process, a dialectic of self and nature, is controlled by Coleridge's mastery of tone, which registers his unfolding states of mind with their concomitant activities of intellect. The authority for nature's value inheres entirely in tonal context, as all values in the conversation poems are constituted from the material of a specific, temporal, localised, personal experience. The meaning of Coleridge's 'dark green file of long lank weeds' is controlled by their place, their moment, in a developing experience.

In this perspective Coleridge's nature appears acutely personalised, and subordinate to his determining consciousness. This is a view that needs careful qualification; for we must notice too that the upward movement of the conversation poems, while originating in an ascending interaction of intellect and emotion that implies the relativity of judgement, yet arrives at values that Coleridge certainly offers as objective. The dominant and most consistently defining characteristic of the conversation poems is their presentation of a basically mechanistic view of the world—man learns benevolence, his own potential for good, from the influence of external nature—which is authenticated by a rhetoric that points towards idealism, the creative power of the mind. We must return to this point, which indicates a very considerable importance for the conversation poems. English writing, from Sterne's Uncle Toby to Joyce's Earwicker, embodies a fundamental shift in its presentation of the basis of knowledge, and action. In *Finnegans Wake* the whole of history, in every conceivable dimension, has become the dream of a single consciousness. And Coleridge's work, the conversation poems in particular, has its important place in the movement of literary culture towards that modernism.

The retirement convention can yield us further perspectives on this achievement. The natural philosophical interests of eighteenth-century nature poetry, typified in James Thomson's work, have changed significantly in Coleridge; but he was of course still fascinated by science, and read widely not only in Erasmus Darwin but also the *Philosophical Transactions* (as Lowes demonstrated), as well as taking a lively and intelligent interest in the work of his scientist friends in Bristol, Thomas Beddoes and Humphrey Davy amongst them. This is the Coleridge, amusingly brilliant, a compulsive punster, excellent company, that Wordsworth remembered in his *Stanzas written in my pocket-copy of Thomson's 'Castle of Indolence'*. The poem is a beautiful evocation of Coleridge's positive, attractive qualities that emerge ·stronger against the dark background of his political and psychological life:

> Noisy he was, and gamesome as a boy;
> His limbs would toss about him with delight,
> Like branches when strong winds the trees annoy.
> Nor lacked his calmer hours device or toy
> To banish listlessness and irksome care;
> He would have taught you how you might employ
> Yourself; and many did to him repair,—
> And certes not in vain; he had inventions rare.
>
> Expedients too, of simple sort he tried:
> Long blades of grass, plucked round him as he lay,
> Made, to his ear attentively applied,
> A pipe on which the wind would deftly play;
> Glasses he had, that little things display,
> The beetle panoplied in gems and gold,
> A mailèd angel on a battle-day;
> The mysteries that cups of flowers enfold,
> And all the gorgeous sights which fairies do behold.
>
> He would entice that other man to hear
> His music, and to view his imagery

(ll.47-65)

It is intriguing that Wordsworth should have cast this memory in Thomson's Spenserian stanzas. The style introduces a pastoral quality of antique distance which is pleasantly dissipated by the detailed, half-rapt evocation of a real personal past; but the poem as a whole reminds us of the *Castle of Indolence* itself, in particular a passage towards the end of the first Canto (stanza LVII following) where Thomson makes lightly veiled reference to friends, Collins, Armstrong, Lyttelton, whose company and work he enjoys.[28] Wordsworth remembered the Somerset days with Coleridge as a version of the sweet retirement epitomised in Thomson's first Canto; and this was in spite of the fact that another aspect of Wordsworth's great originality was his presentation of a rural life genuinely outside the conventional perspectives of the retirement tradition. The break with this tradition emerges in part through a more austere awareness of economic reality, in a poem like *The Last of the Flock* for example (a fairly explicit attack on the administration of the poor law), or, more subtly, in *Michael* ('A Pastoral Poem'). Wordsworth had in a sense been anticipated in this awareness, notably by Crabbe, who was yet inhibited by an enlightenment morality that managed to find the poor badly off, but not more so than the rich in a long-term Christian view of man's generally sinful condition; there is a very considerable development between the self-sufficient integrity of Wordsworth's narratives, and the literary consciousness that defined Crabbe's arguments:

> I grant indeed that fields and flocks have charms
> For him that grazes or for him that farms;
> But when amid such pleasing scenes I trace
> The poor laborious natives of the place,
> And see the mid-day sun, with fervid ray,
> On their bare heads and dewy temples play;
> While some, with feebler heads and fainter hearts,
> Deplore their fortune, yet sustain their parts—
> Then shall I dare these real ills to hide
> In tinsel trappings of Poetic pride?
> (*The Village* (1783), Bk I.ll.39-48)

Coleridge, just as firmly conscious of the tradition, could fall into just this idiom; in *Reflections on having left a Place of Retirement:*

> The sluggard Pity's vision-weaving tribe!
> Who sigh for Wretchedness, yet shun the Wretched,
> Nursing in some delicious solitude
> Their slothful loves and dainty sympathies!

(ll.56-9)

And in *The Nightingale:*

> . . . youths and maidens most poetical,
> Who lose the deepening twilights of the spring
> In ball-rooms and hot theatres, they still
> Full of meek sympathy must heave their sighs
> O'er Philomela's pity-pleading strains.

(ll.35-9)

The social concern that benevolent nature fosters became an increasingly dominant emphasis in retirement poetry, but it remains obvious, certainly in Coleridge's poetry, that the delicious appeal of nature was not diminished by its power of moral education, even where this meant a turning of the thoughts away from retirement and back to society. This experience of nature, very characteristic in eighteenth-century retirement poetry, was clearly pleasurable, epicurean rather than stoic; the turning away from nature involved was not a chastening of the senses. Let us return to the terms that have been proposed to describe nature poetry in the eighteenth century, the hypothesis of a basically dual response to nature, either pleasurable and celebratory, or soberly regretful (two forms of guilt), the attitudes of *L'Allegro* and *Il Penseroso*. The conversation poems are remarkable in drawing on both modes of response, in encompassing an experience of nature that is both warmly immediate, of the senses, *and* serenely beyond nature, expressive of a delicate and accessible spirituality. Coleridge's poetry is most extraordinary in the deliberate use of *darkening* nature, typically the setting for a stoic renunciation of sense, as the mediator of man and God; in the conversation poems we approach Coleridge's God through sensory experience, but we do not leave the experience itself behind. In the tradition of retirement poetry, at least in the English poets, these elements, nature as an experience valuable in itself, and nature as merely the path to a higher value, are opposed.

Thomson's *Castle of Indolence* reflects in its two parts the opposition of sweet retirement to the harsh world of Adam's curse, and reflects in this opposition the formal presentation of a dichotomy between image and value, between the sensory and the moral. The issue is raised directly in the opening of the second canto:

> Escaped the castle of the sire of sin,
> Ah! where shall I so sweet a dwelling find?

The pleasure of nature carried a taint of sin. Marvell's ineffably sinister, malevolently purposive nature in *The Garden* marvellously exemplifies the Christian difficulty in feeling secure about simple pleasures of the sense:

> What wond'rous life in this I lead!
> Ripe Apples drop about my head;
> The luscious Clusters of the Vine
> Upon my Mouth do crush their Wine;
> The Nectaren, and curious Peach,
> Into my hands themselves do reach;
> Stumbling on Melons, as I pass,
> Insnar'd with Flow'rs, I fall on Grass.
>
> (ll.33-40)

We court again the original disaster by such an abandonment to sweet nature. Marvell's brilliantly lascivious diction identifies which fall it is that the grass receives. Why Christian morality should be so wary of pleasure is a very interesting question, and certainly a very difficult one; the social structures that generated its spiritual disposition had much to gain from an imperative of dutiful abnegation, the moral urgency of toil without distraction. But it is easier to stay with specific cases; Thomson, in *The Castle of Indolence*, makes explicitly the case for a wariness of nature because it is dangerously pleasant, inviting indolence. His epigraph to the second Canto corrects the appeal of 'false luxury' embodied in the (much more attractive) first Canto:

> The Knight of *Art* and *Industry*,
> And his atchievements fair;
> That, by this Castle's overthrow,
> Secured, and crownèd were.

Thomson was a master of the literary picturesque, which was one way of containing the reality of the pleasure in nature; by imposing on it an illusory order, putting a frame round it:

> Sometimes the pencil, in cool airy halls,
> Bade the gay bloom of vernal landskips rise,
> Or Autumn's varied shades imbrown the walls:
> Now the black tempest strikes the astonished eyes;
> Now down the steep the flashing torrent flies;
> The trembling sun now plays o'er ocean blue,
> And now rude mountains frown amid the skies;
> Whate'er Lorrain light-touched with softening hue,
> Or savage Rosa dashed, or learnèd Poussin drew.
>
> (Canto I, Stanza XXXVIII)

The immediate sensory experience of nature, the sense of a simple wonder, a real and sudden excitement of discovery, was constrained by rules of interpretation. In Dyer, the problems that this raised are striking:

> Now I gain the mountain's brow,
> What a landscape lies below!
> No clouds, no vapours intervene,
> But the gay, the open scene
> Does the face of nature show,
> In all the hues of heaven's bow!
> And, swelling to embrace the light,
> Spreads around beneath the sight.
>
> (*Grongar Hill*, ll.41-8)

Dyer had a painter's training in Italy which enters all of his poetry (perhaps most extensively in *The Ruins of Rome*); but, like Gilpin, Dyer was also a parson. The octosyllabics that suit very well Dyer's painterly lyrical enthusiasm in response to the visual beauty of nature, seem absurdly light when they are made to carry a commonplace morality. Parts of *Grongar Hill* are almost like a parody of Denham or Pope in their trite banality; what strikes us now is an incongruously comic inadequacy of response, like the sermons that parsons in Jane Austen might have given, anxious for cards:

> And see the rivers how they run,
> Through woods and meads, in shade and sun,
> Sometimes swift, sometimes slow,

> Wave succeeding wave, they go
> A various journey to the deep,
> Like human life to endless sleep!
> Thus in Nature's vesture wrought,
> To instruct our wandering thought;
> Thus she dresses green and gay,
> To disperse our cares away.
>
> (ll.93-102)

The pleasure of nature is sobered by this characteristic movement from aesthetic to moral design. In Denham, the interposition between nature and observer of a blurring Christian perspective is more acceptable, because Denham is altogether more confidently substantial in his presentation of this 'perpetual trick of *moralizing* everything',[29] and its social basis. The Thames in *Coopers Hill* (1642) provides a model for countless insights like Dyer's, quoted above:

> Thames, the most lov'd of all the Oceans sons,
> By his old Sire to his embraces runs,
> Hasting to pay his tribute to the Sea,
> Like mortal life to meet Eternity.[30]
>
> (*Coopers Hill*, ll.161-4)

In Gilpin, writing in the second half of the eighteenth century, the trick can seem very feeble:

> Rivers often present us with very moral analogies; their characters greatly resembling those of men. The violent, the restless, the fretful, the active, the sluggish, the gentle, the bounteous, and many other epithets, belong equally to both. The little stream, which divides the valley of Cambeck, suggested the analogy.[31]

The air of modest discovery is barely sensible, but at least it heightens the contrast with Denham; the moralising habit of mind appears increasingly inadequate towards the end of the eighteenth century because the society to which it had accommodated nature had changed. The moral analogy surprises Gilpin, as if it were a rare fern, or a curious shell. Denham's impressive solidity draws strength from an established and received scheme of things that did not hold any surprises:

> Though deep, yet clear, though gentle, yet not dull,
> Strong without rage, without ore-flowing full.
>
> (ll. 191-2)

The style mirrors a considered balance of contrasts, a funda-
mental stability of orientation, the security of a firm moral and
political framework. *Coopers Hill* is a celebration of the
Monarchy which uses nature to sanction the conception of a
hierarchic order in the Creation. The poem had a considerable
influence, on the particular poetry that Dr Johnson labelled
'topographical',[32] and most notably on Pope's *Windsor Forest,*
which was itself a celebration of the Augustan Anne who
sealed an empire-building peace with the Treaty of Utrecht in
1713.[33] Pope's poem represents a significant heightening in
the tension between nature as moral and political hieroglyphic
(borrowing I.A. Richards' terms, we could say that nature had
the function of vehicle in a Divine metaphor), and nature as a
direct source of sensory pleasure, affective outside any meta-
physical framework. The tension is registered in Pope's acknow-
ledgement of visual nature, an experience which is controlled
by emphasis on the design in Creation; but the design is closer
to Bridgeman, and Kent, and Capability Brown, than to God:

> There, interspers'd in Lawns and opening Glades,
> Thin Trees arise that shun each others Shades.
> Here in full Light the russet Plains extend;
> There wrapt in Clouds the blueish Hills ascend:
> Ev'n the wild Heath displays her Purple Dies,
> And 'midst the Desart fruitful Fields arise,
> That crown'd with tufted Trees and springing Corn,
> Like verdant Isles the sable Waste adorn.
>
> (ll. 21-8)

As one critic has noted, 'Pope's conscious references to colour
in *Windsor Forest* are carried to a pitch never before attained by
any poet';[34] but this quality is countered by an idealising
perspective (the style, too, is classically balanced) that will lead
into the literary picturesque. And Pope's nature is also
modified by an aspect of the Christian tradition that had been
most powerfully realised in Milton. *Windsor Forest* begins with a
nod to Milton:

> The Groves of *Eden*, vanish'd now so long,
> Live in Description, and look green in Song
>
>                                   (ll.7-8)

Art could restore a fallen perception of nature, could reconstitute a prelapsarian purity which made the original loss more poignant, the future restoration more intensely desirable. Nature could be expressive of the golden inaccessibility central to Christianity, and its classical appropriations. The literary image of nature, in its Christian context, imposed a further illusory distance between nature and the observer; as a convention, employed with perfunctory ease, in Waller for example:

> Of the first Paradise there's nothing found;
> Plants set by Heaven are vanished, and the ground;
> Yet the description lasts; who knows the fate
> Of lines that shall this paradise relate?
>                         (*On St. James's Park, as lately*
>                         *improved by His Majesty*, ll.1-4)

and in Milton, in *Paradise Lost,* as a pervasive quality of vision that marvellously preserves, everywhere in the description of the garden, a nostalgic unreality, a majestic sorrow of loss. The passage that develops *Genesis* 2:10, for example, works by sombre implication in tracing the courses of the four paradisal rivers:

> . . . the nether flood,
> Which from his darksome passage now appears,
> And now divided into four main streams,
> Runs diverse, wandering many a famous realm
> And country whereof here needs no account,
> But rather to tell how, if art could tell,
> How from that sapphire front . . . .
>                         (*Paradise Lost,* IV, ll.231-7)

We are reminded, as always, that art is, after all, only a means that we have to render the illusion of what might have been; the decision not to go into those realms and countries is more subtle. 'His decision', comments Professor Fowler, 'extricates him from a thorny choice between at least eight conflicting theories . . . .;[35] but the precise location of the rivers is surely not the important point. The reference to a history that 'here needs no account' is rueful, grimly carrying the full weight of intervening disasters which have parted Milton, and the rest of us, from his perfect garden. The Christian chastening of pleasure in nature employed a perspective as deceptively idealising as the picturesque. And, like the picturesque, this way of seeing came increasingly in the eighteenth century to feel the pressure of the real sensory presence of nature. A representation of nature that stressed the observer's fallen perception gave way to a more direct response that could take either of the forms we have indicated; a melancholic gloom that tended to distract the eye, or an optimistic confidence in the healing, educative power of nature, operating through the senses to create a spirit of benevolence that would prepare society for its ultimate Divine destination. Charles Cotton's pleasant, rambling poem *The Wonders of the Peak* (1681) is representative of the transition from paradise as a standard against which nature palls, to paradise as in nature to a degree beyond the power of art. A strongly renunciatory attitude can still be present, reminiscent of the harsh and barren nature, palpably beyond the walls of the first garden, that we find in Renaissance paintings of the Expulsion, or the wilderness:

> The Groves, whose curled Brows shade ev'ry Lake
> Do everywhere such waving Landskips make,
> As Painters baffled Art is far above,
> Who waves and Leaves could never yet make move ...
> To view from hence the glitt'ring Pile above ...
> Environ'd round with Nature's Shames and Ills,
> Black Heath, wild Rock, bleak Crags and naked Hills,
> Who is it but must presently conclude
> That this is Paradise, which seated stands,
> In midst of Deserts, and of barren Sands?[36]

These shames and ills had become much harder to see for Thomson and Dyer; by the middle of the eighteenth century they could in fact be thought of as essential to the finest, most magnificent parts of nature's appeal. And the focus on physical nature is manifestly clearer even in those poets who took to a bizarre extreme the appropriate moods of nature at twilight. Young and Blair wrote poetry that seems now really unbalanced in its obsession with death (especially Young); but still the nature that ushered in meditation of a wilfully pessimistic cast set its scenes with a clarity that strained the idealising Christian perspective. Thomas Parnell's *Night-Piece on Death* (first published in Pope's selection of 1722, *Poems on Several Occasions*), which is in its chosen idiom an interesting and distinctive poem, demonstrates the keen vision that could be blended with thoughts of death:

> How deep yon Azure dies the Sky!
> Where Orbs of Gold unnumber'd lye,
> While thro' their Ranks in silver pride
> The nether Crescent seems to glide.
> The slumb'ring Breeze forgets to breathe,
> The Lake is smooth and clear beneath,
> Where once again the spangled Show
> Descends to meet our Eyes below.
> The Grounds which on the right aspire,
> In dimness from the View retire:
> The Left presents a Place of Graves,
> Whose wall the silent Water laves.
> That Steeple guides thy doubtful sight
> Among the livid gleams of Night.
> There pass with melancholy State,
> By all the solemn Heaps of Fate,
> And think, as softly-sad you tread
> Above the venerable Dead,
> *Time was, like thee they Life possest,*
> *And Time shall be, that thou shalt Rest.*

(ll. 9-28)

The moral here is literally embedded in the landscape, like Gray's in the *Elegy*; indeed, the similarity to Gray is quite marked in other ways too, for both poets effect a composition of place (with the picturesque exhortation to observe)[37] which is also a composition of mood potent enough ultimately to supplant the context in nature. Gray's statement of composed resignation, the defeated moralist's quiet impersonal bitterness, begins to emerge as nature actually disappears:

> Now fades the glimmering landscape on the sight,
> And all the air a solemn stillness holds . . ..

(*Elegy*, ll. 5-6)

It is just such a moment that Coleridge starts from in *Frost at Midnight*, and in *This Lime-Tree Bower my Prison* too the approach to sunset, beckoning the poet beyond his sensory awareness, begins in sadness and frustration. But Coleridge's values are in fact to be constituted from the particular moment, with its particular physical conditions; the moralist has been driven right back on to his own creative resources by the closing down of a public audience, with its invitation to the statement of familiar public values. And in *The Nightingale* Coleridge shows himself to be fully conscious of this situation.

A further convention of retirement that Coleridge uses in the conversation poems is their directly personal manner of address. This quality was noted in G.M. Harper's essay that first identified the conversation poems as a distinctive kind:

> These are his Poems of Friendship. They cannot be even vaguely understood unless the reader knows what persons Coleridge has in mind. They are, for the most part, poems in which reference is made with fine particularity to certain places. They were composed as the expression of feelings which were occasioned by quite definite events. Between the lines, when we know their meaning, we catch glimpses of those delightful people who formed the golden inner circle of his friends in the days of his young manhood: Charles Lamb, his oldest and dearest, Mary Lamb, practical Tom Poole, William and Dorothy Wordsworth in their days of clearest vision and warmest enthusiasm, and in the later pieces Mrs Wordsworth and Sarah Hutchinson her young sister. They may all be termed, as Coleridge himself names one or two of them, Conversation Poems, for even when they are soliloquies the sociable man who wrote them could not even think without supposing a listener. They require and reward considerable knowledge of his life and especially the life of his heart.

Harper went on to characterise the conversation poems as 'among the supreme examples of a peculiar kind of poetry', a kind that also includes 'Ovid's 'Cum subit illius tristissima noctis imago', and several of the Canti of Leopardi'.[38] As an early critical account of the conversation poems Harper's essay is certainly important, even with its atmosphere of belles-lettres; but we can specify antecedents for Coleridge's 'Poems of Friendship' less exotic than Ovid and Leopardi. The conversation poems presume a convention of personalised address very common in retirement poetry. Amongst the earliest English poets to take nature as a major theme was Anne Finch,

Countess of Winchilsea, whose work was admired by Wordsworth as providing (together with the Pope of *Windsor Forest*) an exception to 'the poetry intervening between the publication of the 'Paradise Lost' and the 'Seasons' ', which in Wordsworth's view, 'does not contain a single new image of external nature'.[39] Wordsworth was thinking of Anne Finch's *A Nocturnal Reverie,* easily her best-known poem; but she wrote a number of very accomplished poems, including a *Petition for an Absolute Retreat* which demonstrates the Christian context of private friendship in retirement:

> Give me there (since heaven has shown
> It was not good to be alone)
> A partner suited to my mind,
> Solitary, pleas'd, and kind;
> Who, partially may something see
> Preferr'd to all the world in me,
> Slighting, by my humble side,
> Fame and splendour, wealth and pride.
> When but two the earth possessed,
> 'Twas their happiest days and best:
> They by bus'ness, nor by wars,
> They by no domestic cares,
> From each other e'er were drawn,
> But in some grove, or flow'ring lawn
> Spent the swiftly flying time,
> Spent their own and nature's prime
> In love—that only passion given
> To perfect man, whilst friends with heaven.
>
> (ll. 104-21)

The basic impulse here is clearly sexual, if heavily muted. But the formal representation of this impulse becomes a motif that runs right through eighteenth-century nature poetry. James Thomson invokes his 'Amanda' at intervals throughout *The Seasons,* and a poem as absolutely typical of the retirement themes as John Pomfret's *The Choice* (1700) necessarily includes 'the fair' as an ingredient of country delight.[40] It is particularly interesting that so many eighteenth-century poets should not only refer to women under pastoral names, 'Amanda', 'Dorinda' and so on, that reduce them to a wholly idyllic status, but that the women are in fact largely significant in nature poetry as an absence, an unrealised desire that tempers the pleasure in nature and introduces a distracting sadness. Dyer's *Country Walk* ends on a representative note of complaint:

> But, oh! how bless'd would be the day,
> Did I with Clio pace my way,
> And not alone and solitary stray!
>
> (ll. 154-6)

Coleridge's *Eolian Harp*, which partly succeeds and partly fails to marry the pleasure and the meaning of nature, begins with the presence of the woman: 'My pensive Sara!' This very simple expedient immediately prevents any possibility of the merely habitual sobriety of feeling in nature, a feeling pervasive, for example, in Bowles. Bowles's preface to his *Sonnets and other Poems* (1796), a book that Coleridge appears more or less to have committed to memory, explains that many of the poems

> can be considered in no other light, than as exhibiting occasional reflections which naturally arose in his mind, chiefly during various excursions, undertaken to relieve, at the time, depression of spirits.

And Bowles is ready to broaden this dark hint:

> They who know [the author], know the occasion of them to have been real; to the publick he might only mention the sudden death of a deserving young woman . . . .[41]

The absent loved-one was one characteristic means of importing into the poet's response to nature a stoic gravity. It was a strategy particularly popular in the sonnets written by English poets in the second half of the eighteenth century; Bowles was the most popular exponent of the form (his *Fourteen Sonnets* (1789) was of course a powerful early influence on Coleridge, and on Wordsworth and Southey),[42] but little work has been done on the tradition in which Bowles was writing, a tradition that appears to stem from the revival of the Miltonic sonnet initiated by Thomas Edwards, the friend of Richardson.[43] The eighteenth-century sonnet has a special interest in relation to the conversation poems, which we can return to in a moment.

Obviously, the conversation poems are not all addressed to ladies; but the direct address to friend, rather than lover, absent or present, is a convention of retirement poetry that starts in Horace; the address to Charles Lamb in *This Lime-Tree Bower my Prison*, for example, in its context of an opposition of town to country, is a descendant of the Horatian idiom of the *Epistle*, I,10:

> To Fuscus, lover of the city, I, a lover of the country, send greetings. In this one point, to be sure, we differ much, but being in all else much like twins with the hearts of brothers—if one says 'no', the other says 'no' too—we nod a common assent like a couple of old familiar doves.
>
> You keep the nest; I praise the lovely country's brooks, its grove and moss-grown rocks. In short: I live and reign, as soon as I have left behind what you townsmen with shouts of applause extol to the skies.[44]

The attitudes of Lamb and Coleridge to city life plainly do not fit this passage; but there is a fundamental similarity of style that goes with the freedom and informality of conversation between friends. For Horace this informal rhetoric, a classically poised withdrawal from the great public style, can take on a critical weight in carrying the values of the small, cultivated group; but still, these values are public, and that small group could maintain a clear sense of their public function, their social duty. Just as in the poetry of Pope, the great English Horatian, Horace's informal style serves a moral sense that sought to restore social values that the society itself would not question. Coleridge's private poetry is much more radically dislocated from its social context, and this throws on to the language that holds the isolated group together a very great importance. Coleridge's most impressive successes in the conversational idiom find their structure in a perfect control of tonal development that depends on the security of audience that the isolated group provides, and that does not depend at all on any sense of the received public morality, of those sentiments that, as Dr Johnson said of Gray's *Elegy*, 'find an echo in every bosom'.[45]

We have established that several characteristic features of the conversation poems, their private mode of address, the opposition of town to country, their heightening response to nature that culminates in philosophical generalisation, are common to the tradition of retirement naturalised in English poetry after

the civil war. Coleridge's philosophical speculation is Christian
in basis and celebrates the presence of a benevolent God
operating in nature. Eighteenth-century nature poetry often
reached precisely similar conclusions. We may return again to
Thomson for an example of the typical development of
response to nature; the passage from *Spring* that builds to a
climax as

> We feel the present Deity, and taste
> The joy of God to see a happy world!
>
> (ll.902-3)

is prepared for by an account of the consciousness of God that
contemplation of his works brings:

> Inspiring God! who, boundless spirit all
> And unremitting energy, pervades,
> Adjusts, sustains, and agitates the whole.
> He ceaseless works alone, and yet alone
> Seems not to work; with such perfection framed
> Is this complex, stupendous scheme of things.
> But, though concealed, to every purer eye
> The informing Author in his works appears:
> Chief, lovely Spring, in thee and thy soft scenes
> The smiling God is seen—while water, earth,
> And air attest his bounty, which exalts
> The brute-creation to this finer thought,
> And annual melts their undesigning hearts
> Profusely thus in tenderness and joy.
>
> (ll.853-66)

The 'finer thought' embraced specifically social forms; in
*Autumn,* for example, Thomson describes the feelings inspired
by 'Philosophic Melancholy', when 'The desolated prospect
thrills the soul':

> Ten thousand thousand fleet ideas, such
> As never mingled with the vulgar dream,
> Crowd fast into the mind's creative eye.
> As fast the correspondent passions rise,
> As varied, and as high—devotion raised
> To rapture, and divine astonishment;
> The love of nature unconfined, and, chief,
> Of human race; the large ambitious wish

> To make them blest; the sigh for suffering worth
> Lost in obscurity; the noble scorn
> Of tyrant pride; the fearless great resolve;
> The wonder which the dying patriot draws,
> Inspiring glory through remotest time;
> The awakened throb for virtue and for fame;
> The sympathies of love and friendship dear,
> With all the social offspring of the heart.
>
> (ll.1014-1029)

Thomson derives these various 'awakened throbs' for 'all the social offspring of the heart', a broad humanitarian social concern, from his recognition of the divine scheme in nature. It is a response that is typical in the eighteenth-century poetry that Coleridge knew best in the 1790s, certainly in the work of Mark Akenside, whom Coleridge quotes perhaps more frequently than any other poet.The first version of Akenside's *Pleasures of the Imagination* (1772) ends with a weighty reiteration of the poem's central point; the 'attentive mind' knows harmony, within itself and with its environment, by the influence of nature's harmony. And this leads to an emulation of the 'Eternal Maker', 'Beneficent and active':

> Would the forms
> Of servile custom cramp her generous powers?
> Would sordid policies, the barbarous growth
> Of ignorance and rapine, bow her down
> To tame pursuits, to indolence and fear?
> Lo! she appeals to Nature, to the winds,
> And rolling waves, the sun's unwearied course,
> The elements and seasons; all declare
> For what the Eternal Maker has ordain'd
> The powers of man; we feel within ourselves
> His energy divine; he tells the heart,
> He meant, he made us to behold and love
> What he beholds and loves, the general orb
> Of life and being; to be great like him,
> Beneficent and active. 'Thus the men
> Whom Nature's works can charm, with God himself
> Hold converse; grow familiar, day by day,
> With his conceptions, act upon his plan;
> And form to his, the relish of their souls.
>
> (Book III, ll.615-33)

Coleridge's attempts, in the conversation poems, to formulate

the significance of his experience of nature, are not far from
Akenside, at least in the sense that his formulations can have if
we abstract them from the poetic context. They have a similar
background in Locke and Hartley, and they are essentially
mechanistic in implication. Nature urges benevolence, pity for
men and kindness to animals (we remember Coleridge's brave
attempt to talk to the animals, in *To a Young Ass*), the same
lessons that Thomson had learnt. The important point here is
that retirement quite conventionally pointed back to society;
nature could insist on the value and necessity of social action.
Coleridge's version of retirement in the conversation poems
concentrates on the kind of consciousness that nature could
inspire, but this was not to deny any social dimension, but
rather to stay at the heart of things; individual consciousness is
the only necessary condition of social change. Nature did not
have to be a retreat, in the sense of withdrawal from conflict,
although, increasingly as the eighteenth century wore on, the
poet in nature seems to embrace an exhausted tranquillity that
comforts the defeated moralist. Gray's *Elegy* catches this state of
mind with perfect clarity, and in Cowper particularly the effort
of the moralist drives him back to nature, or more exactly,
away from society, in a condition near to collapse:

> Oh for a lodge in some vast wilderness,
> Some boundless contiguity of shade,
> Where rumour of oppression and deceit,
> Of unsuccessful or successful war,
> Might never reach me more.
> (*The Task*, Book II, 'The Time-Piece',
> ll. 1-5)

This is close to the melancholy that led the eighteenth-century
poets so often beyond nature, and society, altogether, simply to
thoughts of death. But Cowper at his most serious (and it is fair
to add that seriousness in Cowper is often not the intent; subtly
understated parody of Milton is a strength of *The Task*) persists,
precariously, in a conscientiously reasoned optimism, anticipat-
ing Wordsworth's later poetry, that sobers the business-like
confidence of the enlightenment to a humane gravity. It is a
gravity opposed to slavery, to commerce and the various
pollutions of city life, and to exclusive solitudes, enforced or
adopted, where

> the nat'ral bond
> Of brotherhood is sever'd as the flax
> That falls asunder at the touch of fire.
> ('The Time-Piece', ll.9-11)

It seems not to have been recognised that it was this characteristic humanitarian concern that helped to make the sonnets of Bowles so attractive to the young radical Coleridge. In 1796 Coleridge compiled a small anthology, *Sonnets from Various Authors*,[46] for private circulation. He included three sonnets by Bowles; 'At Dover, 1786' is representative:

> Thou, whose stern spirit loves the awful storm,
> That, borne on Terror's desolating wings,
> Shakes the high forest, or remorseless flings
> The shivered surge; when rising griefs deform
> Thy peaceful breast, hie to yon steep, and think,—
> When thou dost mark the melancholy tide
> Beneath thee, and the storm careering wide,—
> Tossed on the surge of life how many sink!
> And if thy cheek with one kind tear be wet,
> And if thy heart be smitten, when the cry
> Of danger and of death is heard more nigh,
> Oh, learn thy private sorrows to forget;
> Intent, when hardest beats the storm, to save
> One who, like thee, has suffered from the wave.[47]

The appeal of Bowles for Coleridge in the mid-90s would have been quite as much a matter of sentiment as of style; indeed, there seems little in the inverted syntax, the latinate diction, the crowded adjectives and adverbs, to qualify Bowles as the pioneer of that 'sweet and indissoluble union between the intellectual and the material world' that Coleridge talks of in his 'Introduction' to the anthology. At least, such a large claim for Bowles is unlikely if we take it as a reference to style, but understandable as praise of Bowles's 'heart', the sympathetic humanity that his sonnets almost always display and recommend. And Coleridge would have found this quality firmly based in a consciousness nurtured and trained by nature. His 'Introduction' to *Sonnets from Various Authors* in fact provides the best approach to the conversation poems, in its emphasis on the private and inward sources of value, and on the development of this personal base for judgement in relationship with nature. It is even reasonable to suggest that the conversational idiom itself, as it first becomes recognisable in *The Eolian Harp*, a pre-Wordsworthian poem, grows out of Coleridge's interest in the sonnet. 'The Sonnet', Coleridge states in his 'Introduction', 'is a small poem, in which some lonely feeling is developed' (*PW*,ii,1139):

> In a Sonnet ... we require a development of some lonely feeling, by whatever cause it may have been excited; but those Sonnets appear to me the most exquisite, in which moral Sentiments, Affections, or Feelings, are deduced from, and associated with, the scenery of nature.

Coleridge's discussion is particularly interesting in its attempt to establish the sonnet as a means to confer unity on subjective, and therefore potentially closed experience:

> It is limited to a *particular* number of lines, in order that the reader's mind having expected the close at the place in which he finds it, may rest satisfied; and that so the poem may acquire, as it were, a *Totality*,—in plainer phrase, may become a *Whole*.

Coleridge's 'Introduction' manages to give the impression, short as it is, that its author has brought considerable learning to bear on the sonnet form; and this too is interesting, because it takes us back to the problem of audience, to the difficulty that Coleridge found in the effort to mediate his experience. Coleridge's learning is a pose. The 'Introduction' opens in a key of authoritative command of the subject:

> The composition of the Sonnet has been regulated by Boileau in his Art of Poetry, and since Boileau, by William Preston, in the elegant preface to his Amatory Poems: the rules, which they would establish, are founded on the practice of Petrarch. I have never yet been able to discover either sense, nature, or poetic fancy in Petrarch's poems; they appear to me all one cold glitter of heavy conceits and metaphysical abstractions.

Coleridge could not read Italian at all at this time, and his French too was weak, by his own admission.[48] William Preston would anyway make a strange companion, as an Irish grub-street hack, for Boileau and Petrarch; Coleridge brings him in because much of the learning in the 'Introduction' to the anthology is taken from the 'Essay, Introductory to Sonnets and other Love Poems', in Preston's *Poetical Works* (1793). Even the criticism of Petrarch's conceited manner is borrowed from Preston.[49] Coleridge was led to this kind of trick by a desperate and tragic insecurity; the same insecurity that informs his discussion of poetry, in the 'Introduction' to *Sonnets from Various Authors* and also in the 'Preface', written earlier in 1796, to *Poems on Various Subjects*. Coleridge was deeply concerned to make the connection between 'some lonely feeling', and 'the reader's mind'. He would have been impressed by one passage in particular at the end of Preston's 'Essay':

> The sonnet will ever be cultivated by those who write on tender and pathetic subjects. It is peculiarly adapted to the situation, of a man violently agitated, by a real passion, and wanting composure and vigour of mind, to methodize his thoughts, and undertake a work of length. The sonnet, from its shortness, and its dwelling simply on a single thought, is fitted to express a momentary burst of passion, and its tender and plaintive melody is calculated to accompany affecting and mournful sentiments, by congenial sounds.[50]

Coleridge may have had this passage in mind when he wrote the 'Preface' to *Poems on Various Subjects*, which engages directly with the problem of an audience for his poetry of private experience:

> Compositions resembling those of the present volume are not unfrequently condemned for their querulous egotism. But egotism is to be condemned then only when it offends against time and place, as in an History or an Epic Poem. To censure it in a Monody or Sonnet is almost as absurd as to dislike a circle for being round. Why then write Sonnets or Monodies? Because they give me pleasure when perhaps nothing else could. After the more violent emotions of Sorrow, the mind demands solace and can find it in employment alone; but full of its late sufferings it can endure no employment not connected with those sufferings. Forcibly to turn away our attention to other subjects is a painful and in general an unavailing effort.
>> 'But O how grateful to a wounded heart
>> The tale of misery to impart;
>> From others' eyes bid artless sorrows flow
>> And raise esteem upon the base of woe!'

> The communicativeness of our nature leads us to describe our
> own sorrows; in the endeavour to describe them intellectual
> activity is exerted; and by a benevolent law of our nature from
> intellectual activity a pleasure results which is gradually
> associated and mingles as a corrective with the painful subject of
> the description. True! it may be answered, but how are the
> PUBLIC interested in your sorrows or your description? We are
> for ever attributing a personal unity to imaginary aggregates.
> What is the PUBLIC but a term for a number of scattered
> individuals of whom as many will be interested in these sorrows
> as have experienced the same or similar.

(*PW*,ii,1136)

We may notice in passing how, once again, many of Coleridge's
most influential critical tenets develop out of the experience of
social dislocation in the 1790s. The insistence in the passage
quoted on the necessity for criticism to bear always in mind the
intention in a work of art, the given limitations and scope of
the particular form, reappears in Coleridge's mature critical
writings as a central emphasis; in *Biographia Literaria*, for
example:

> The first lesson of philosophic discipline is to wean the student's
> attention from the DEGREES of things, which alone form the
> vocabulary of common life, and to direct it to the KIND
> abstracted from *degree*.[51]

It is an emphasis that forms one more dimension in Coleridge's
general effort to make common ground between opposed
parties, writer and critic, poet and audience. Coleridge resolved
his personal difficulty in the 1790s simply by refusing to
acknowledge the reality of a cultivated audience for poetry;
and this is in a positive sense what the conversation poems
actually do, by constituting a private audience of 'scattered
individuals', and by celebrating in the poetry itself the values of
the small group so constituted as a standard against which
society, the 'PUBLIC', may be judged. The 'totality' of the best
conversation poems is achieved in a control of tone that, again,
depends on a private audience (Coleridge's sentence in the
passage quoted, beginning with 'The communicativeness of our
nature . . ..', is as close as he comes to an explicit account of the
tonal structure of the conversation poems); the sonnet, as a
means to the mediation of loneliness, proves too limiting, much
too arbitrarily formal. But it does help Coleridge to build and
shape his own, distinctive style, as an examination of the
genesis of *The Eolian Harp* will show.

# VI
# The Conversation Poems

## THE EOLIAN HARP

A disproportionate amount of critical attention has been devoted to *The Eolian Harp,* the earliest of Coleridge's conversation poems. The reasons are not hard to find; it is a problematic and not wholly successful poem, that raises quite unavoidably the difficulty of Coleridge's 'philosophy' in its relation to his poetry. *The Eolian Harp,* more than any of the other conversation poems, is overtly concerned with abstract ideas, and this concern is enormously complicated by Coleridge's various additions to the poem, in particular the passage first published in the *Errata* of *Sibylline Leaves:*

> O! the one Life within us and abroad,
> Which meets all motion and becomes its soul,
> A light in sound, a sound-like power in light,
> Rhythm in all thought, and joyance every where—
> *(PW,*i,101)

It seems very likely that Coleridge wrote this passage in 1817 (its inclusion in the *Errata* of *Sibylline Leaves* (1817) obviously suggests that Coleridge wrote it after his reading of the final proofs); his philosophical interests had developed in great complexity, over twenty-one years, since the poem's first publication in 1796, in *Poems on Various Subjects,* and it is not credible that he should have achieved, in the addition of four lines, a seamless reconciliation of opposed philosophical positions. It has nevertheless proved to be the case that almost all commentators on the poem have used the text as it appears in E.H. Coleridge's edition of the *Poetical Works,* often without any mention of the problems that this, Coleridge's own final text, raises in the attempt to make sense of the poem's ideas. The poem has consequently become a gold-mine of arcane and recherché 'sources' and 'analogues', and an important case in the argument for the essential continuity of Coleridge's

philosophical development towards the idealism of his mature
prose writings. The poem has been overloaded with a weight of
scholarly reference, of precisely the kind that the poem itself
loses patience with:

> Meek Daughter in the Family of Christ,
> Well hast thou said and holily disprais'd
> These shapings of the unregenerate mind,
> Bubbles that glitter as they rise and break
> On vain Philosophy's aye-babbling spring.

If a detailed and perfectly self-consistent reading of the poem
in its final form is possible, then M.H. Abrams has produced an
account (which takes properly into consideration all the
versions of the poem) that could hardly be bettered, in its
range of learning or the splendidly sustained lucidity of its
argument.[1] But if Professor Abrams has indeed found the
right approach, then Coleridge's poem is unfortunately closed
to most readers, and must be regarded as a dazzling exercise in
philosophical subtlety. The account that follows will read the
poem as a product of Coleridge's mind in the 1790s, and will
consequently exclude reference to all modifications of the text
made by Coleridge after 1803 (the date of the third edition of
Coleridge's *Poems*, which included the last version of *The Eolian
Harp* before the appearance of *Sibylline Leaves*, fourteen years
later).

It may be useful to give the text of *The Eolian Harp* as
Coleridge first published it in 1796:

### EFFUSION XXXV
#### Composed August 20th, 1795, at Clevedon, Somersetshire.

> My pensive SARA! thy soft cheek reclin'd
> Thus on mine arm, most soothing sweet it is
> To sit beside our cot, our cot o'er grown
> With white-flower'd Jasmin, and the broad-leav'd Myrtle,
> (Meet emblems they of Innocence and Love!)
> And watch the clouds, that late were rich with light,
> Slow-sad'ning round, and mark the star of eve
> Serenely brilliant (such should Wisdom be)
> Shine opposite! How exquisite the scents
> Snatch'd from yon bean-field! and the world *so* hush'd!
> The stilly murmur of the distant Sea
> Tell us of Silence. And that simplest Lute

Plac'd length-ways in the clasping casement, hark!
How by the desultory breeze caress'd,
Like some coy Maid half-yielding to her Lover,
It pours such sweet upbraidings, as must needs
Tempt to repeat the wrong! and now its strings
Boldlier swept, the long sequacious notes
Over delicious surges sink and rise,
Such a soft floating witchery of sound
As twilight Elfins make, when they at eve
Voyage on gentle gales from Faery Land,
Where *Melodies* round honey-dropping flowers
Footless and wild, like birds of Paradise,
Nor pause nor perch, hov'ring on untam'd wing.


And thus, my Love! as on the midway slope
Of yonder hill I stretch my limbs at noon
Whilst thro' my half-clos'd eyelids I behold
The sunbeams dance, like diamonds, on the main,
And tranquil muse upon tranquillity;
Full many a thought uncall'd and undetain'd,
And many idle flitting phantasies,
Traverse my indolent and passive brain
As wild and various, as the random gales
That swell or flutter on this subject Lute!
And what if all of animated nature
Be but organic Harps diversly fram'd,
That tremble into thought, as o'er them sweeps,
Plastic and vast, one intellectual Breeze,
At once the Soul of each, and God of all?
But thy more serious eye a mild reproof
Darts, O beloved Woman! nor such thoughts
Dim and unhallow'd dost thou not reject,
And biddest me walk humbly with my God.


Meek Daughter in the Family of Christ,
Well hast thou said and holily disprais'd
These shapings of the unregenerate mind,
Bubbles that glitter as they rise and break
On vain Philosophy's aye-babbling spring.
For never guiltless may I speak of Him,
Th'INCOMPREHENSIBLE! save when with awe
I praise him, and with Faith that inly *feels*;
Who with his saving mercies heal'ed me,
A sinful and most miserable man
Wilder'd and dark, and gave me to possess
PEACE, and this COT, and THEE, heart-honor'd Maid![2]

An asterisk after the word 'inly' (1.52) directed the reader to a note at the end of the volume, a quotation in French from *'la Citoyenne Roland'*; in *Poems* (second edition, 1797) Coleridge placed this note at the end of the poem itself, and he also abandoned the division into three verse paragraphs, but otherwise the 1797 text is identical.³ Two other early forms of the poem exist; an early draft of sixteen-and-a-half lines which is probably Coleridge's first version, and a draft of sixty-two lines which is a revision of the text in *Poems on Various Subjects* intended for the second edition of 1797 (*PW*,ii,1021-1023). Coleridge never published either of these drafts (they first appeared in E.H. Coleridge's edition of 1912). A number of changes were made in the poem in the third edition of 1803, and these are discussed below. References to the poem in the discussion that follows are to the text of 1796, unless otherwise stated.

I

The discourse of philosophy requires a rigorous control of the semantic field that its vocabulary activates. Poetic discourse usually works under a different kind of control; significance in poetry is not absolutely determined within a given logical structure, but allows for relationships between words that may constitute statements not consistent with the 'argument'. It is an endless and fruitless endeavour to read Coleridge's poetry as if it were philosophy; the poetry contains statements of philosophical conviction, certainly, but they cannot be evaluated as such within the poetic context.

The poem displays a metaphoric structure that is not consistent in the terms of philosophical discourse. This is not necessarily a problem, as we are dealing with poetry and not philosophy. But it is in fact problematic in *The Eolian Harp* because the poem contains statements that appear to invite an examination of its philosophical consistency.

The poem develops through six distinct passages that, with the exception of the last, are unified by their common reference to the action of the wind on a wind-harp. Lines 1-12 describe Coleridge and Sara seated beside their honeymoon cottage in Clevedon, as evening quietens the landscape. The next five lines uncover a delicate sexuality in the relationship that is imaged in the effect of a 'desultory breeze' on

> that simplest Lute
> Plac'd length-ways in the clasping casement
>
> (ll. 12-13)

Sara is conventionally posed in the manner of an Epithalamium, both nervous and brightly curious of the imminent sexual experience. G.M. Matthews has suggested a psychological basis for the traditional pose:

> In a conventional Epithalamium, the desire and misgiving which both partners feel are polarized on to a reluctant bride, with her mock-modest virgin attendants, and an avid groom, incited by his troop of wanton boys.[4]

Coleridge's use of the convention does not employ much of the classical form (and we have seen that this is quite characteristic); certainly a troop of wanton boys and attendant virgins would have disturbed the tranquillity of Clevedon. But the 'desire and misgiving' present in the relationship bear interestingly on the succeeding passage in Coleridge's poem. The atmosphere of sexuality, present explicitly and heightened by certain words, 'caress'd', 'half-yielding', 'sweet', 'tempt' (and perhaps even 'length-ways' and 'clasping' in line 13, although these are rather neutralised by the matter-of-fact 'casement'), is briefly intensified before the poem floats off into a dreamy vision of fairies and paradise:

> And now its strings
> Boldlier swept, the long sequacious notes
> Over delicious surges sink and rise,
> Such a soft floating witchery of sound
> As twilight Elfins make, when they at eve
> Voyage on gentle gales from Faery Land,
> Where *Melodies* round honey-dropping flowers
> Footless and wild, like birds of Paradise,
> Nor pause nor perch, hov'ring on untam'd wing.
>
> (ll. 17-25)

One critic has remarked of this passage that it

seems to carry out with greater subtlety a purpose similar to that of the allegorizing in the first section of the poem: it dematerializes, as it were, the beauty of the harp's melody.[5]

But the melody is not all that is 'dematerialized'; Coleridge has possibly gone a little too far, now that the object of the wind's, and the lover's, caresses feels itself, herself, 'Boldlier swept', producing effects that 'Over delicious surges sink and rise'. The elfins and birds of paradise serve to dematerialize the sexual situation. This first movement of the poem (marked in 1796 both paragraph division) is thus headed off by Coleridge's uncertainty in his audience, his anxiety not to embarrass Sara. He had already used the language of 'Faery Land' to deal with a potentially worrying domestic tension, in *Lines in the Manner of Spenser*, where Coleridge's lateness for a meeting with Sara is blamed on a 'laughing Elfin'. The second movement of the poem, from line 26 to the end, will be headed off by Sara in a similar way, as she chastens Coleridge's increasingly adventurous philosophical speculations. *The Eolian Harp* is limited by its audience; Sara will not let Coleridge be quite himself. And the poem demonstrates the very close relationship in Coleridge's mind between intellectual freedom and emotional, here explicitly sexual, security.

In the fourth passage of the poem, Coleridge describes to Sara his characteristic habit of mind in similar moods of 'tranquillity'. And yet it is perhaps not entirely accidental that he now pictures himself alone:

> And thus, my Love! as on the midway slope
> Of yonder hill I stretch my limbs at noon
> Whilst thro' my half-clos'd eyelids I behold
> The sunbeams dance, like diamonds, on the main,
> And tranquil muse upon tranquillity;
> Full many a thought uncall'd and undetain'd,
> And many idle flitting phantasies,
> Traverse my indolent and passive brain
> As wild and various, as the random gales
> That swell or flutter on this subject Lute!
>
> (ll.26-35)

Coleridge has prepared a difficulty for himself here, and for his interpreters too, because we are no longer sure how far the central, recurring image of the harp is actually a unifying presence in the poem. We need first to bear in mind the next passage of the poem, its most explicit philosophical statement:

> And what if all of animated nature
> Be but organic Harps diversly fram'd,
> That tremble into thought, as o'er them sweeps,
> Plastic and vast, one intellectual Breeze,
> At once the Soul of each, and God of all?
>
> (ll.36-40)

Coleridge's unused draft revision of 1797 appears to provide an acceptable gloss on this passage:

> And what if All of animated Life
> Be but as Instruments diversly fram'd
> That tremble into thought, while thro' them breathes
> One infinite and intellectual Breeze,
> And all in diff'rent Heights so aptly hung,
> That Murmurs indistinct and Bursts sublime,
> Shrill discords and most soothing Melodies,
> Harmonious from Creation's vast concent—
> Thus *God* would be the universal Soul,
> Mechaniz'd matter as th'organic harps
> And each one's Tunes be that, which each calls I.
>
> (*PW*,ii,1022-3)

Both passages regard the mind, as part of 'animated nature' or of 'animated Life', as passive in perception and acted upon by a manifestation of God. The Creation is subject to a power that is external to it. H.W. Piper has shown that Coleridge would have been familiar with this model of God's relation to the Creation, in the literature of Unitarian controversy and particularly in the work of Joseph Priestley, which Coleridge undoubtedly knew and admired. Priestley had put the mechanists' case for the externally controlling influence of God very clearly, in *Matter and Spirit* (1782):

> The Divine Being and his energy are absolutely necessary to that of every other being. His power is the very *life and soul* of everything that exists; and strictly speaking *without him we* ARE, as well as *can* DO *nothing*. . . . On his will I am entirely dependent for my *being* and all my *faculties*. My sphere, and degrees of influence on other beings and things, is *his* influence. I am but an instrument in his hands for effecting a certain part of the greatest and most glorious of purposes.[6]

Coleridge was on his own constantly repeated declaration a Unitarian, and a Necessitarian, throughout the period in which *The Eolian Harp* was written, and his use of the wind-harp as an image of the passive mind under God's influence seems reasonably straightforward. But there is some slight room for doubt in the passage, lines 36-40, that Coleridge retained in the poem as published in 1796 and 1797. Does he mean that the 'intellectual Breeze' that acts upon the 'organic Harps' of 'animated nature' is actually a property contained within the 'Harps'? Line 40 at least, 'At once the Soul of each, and God of all', might seem to suggest this possibility. The possibility has been expanded by C.G. Martin, who consequently suggests Ralph Cudworth, the seventeenth-century Cambridge neo-platonist, as an influence on the ideas of the poem. Martin stresses Coleridge's use of the word 'plastic', which he relates to Cudworth's use of the term 'plastic nature' in his *True Intellectual System of the Universe* (1743), a book that Coleridge had borrowed from the Bristol Public Library more than once.[7] Mr Martin quotes in support of his argument from a letter Coleridge wrote to Thelwall, 1 December 1796:

> Dr Beddoes, & Dr Darwin think that *Life* is utterly inexplicable, writing as Materialists—You, I understand, have adopted the idea that it is the result of organized matter acted on by external Stimuli.—As likely as any other system; but you *assume* the thing to be proved—the '*capability* of being stimulated into sensation' *as* a *property* of organized matter—now 'the Capab.' &c is *my* definition of *animal Life*—Monro believes in a plastic immaterial Nature—all-pervading—
> And what if all of animated Nature
> Be but organic harps diversely fram'd
> That tremble into *thought* as o'er them sweeps
> Plastic & vast &c—                              (*CL*,i,294)

The letter continues in increasingly light-hearted vein, which Mr Martin acknowledges but does not quote (except very briefly); it may be helpful though to bear in mind the rest of Coleridge's discussion, when we come to consider the view that *The Eolian Harp* (written about one year earlier than the Thelwall letter) is an expression of neo-platonic ideas, and that as such it points forward to later developments in Coleridge's thought:

(by the bye—that is my favourite of *my* poems—do *you* like it?)
Hunter that the *Blood* is the Life—which is saying nothing at
all—for if the blood were *Life*, it could never be otherwise than
Life—and to say, it is *alive*, is saying nothing—& Ferrar believes
in a *Soul*, like an orthodox Churchman—so much for Physicians
and Surgeons—Now as to the Metaphysicians, Plato says, it is
*Harmony*—he might as well have said, a fiddle-stick's end—but I
love Plato—his dear *gorgeous* Nonsense! And *I, tho' last not least,
I*, do not know what to think about it—on the whole, I have
rather made up my mind that I am a mere *apparition*—a naked
Spirit!—And that Life is I myself I! which is a mighty clear
account of it.

(*CL*,i,295)

Could it be that Coleridge has only introduced the passage
from his own poem in order to indulge in a little showing off
('by the bye . . . .')? That would be harmless enough; if we are to
take the quotation as a serious indication of what Coleridge
meant in his lines, then the obvious conclusion must be that the
source of the ideas should be sought, not in Cudworth, or
Priestley, but in the work of Alexander Monro, which has
apparently not been received by Coleridge's commentators as
an appealing possibility.[8] The letter is certainly engaging in its
freely conceded bewilderment, and indeed Coleridge's attitude,
in the passage quoted, to the various explanations of 'Life', is
not unrelated to the conclusion of *The Eolian Harp* itself, which
does after all decide that philosophy is not necessarily a helpful
or an appropriate activity. It is quite possible that Coleridge did
know something about Cudworth when he wrote the poem,
and though Mr Martin's evidence is not wholly convincing (the
specific 'source' in Cudworth that he suggests for the harp
image seems pretty remote),[9] the context that he provides in
Cudworth's thought does help to sort out a meaning for lines
36-40 of Coleridge's poem. Cudworth's *True Intellectual System*
signifies by the term 'plastic nature' the shaping agency by
which nature evolves, through which it realises the benevolent
purposiveness of God. God uses nature in this way in order not
to have to occupy himself with such 'drudgery'. Coleridge
would not have quarrelled with such a conception, in 1795 or
in 1796; indeed, there is nothing inherent in Cudworth's ideas
on 'plastic nature' inconsistent with Coleridge's Unitarian,
materialist position learnt from Hartley and Priestley. Cud-

worth held that 'plastic nature' is 'lodged in all particular souls of animals, brutes, and men . . . .' and also that there is 'a general plastic or spermatic principle of the whole universe distinct from this higher mundane soul'.[10] As one commentator has put it, Cudworth 'was trying so to conceive the operation of nature as to get around the difficulties inherent in a mechanical system'.[11] It is possible that the 'animated nature' of *The Eolian Harp*, line 36, is conceived by Coleridge as 'organic Harps' that are acted upon by an 'intellectual Breeze', 'Plastic and vast,' that is an *external* influence in the terms of the harp metaphor, but in fact an *internal* agency (the 'Soul' of 1.40) of God's purposiveness. Coleridge's language, unphilosophical as it is, allows for this reading.

But there is a further difficulty in Coleridge's use of the harp metaphor, which takes us back to the earlier passage of lines 26-35 which describe the poet's musings on a hillside at noon. Geoffrey Grigson begins his entertaining essay on 'The Harp of Aeolus' in the belief that

> by [the harp's] aid and more accurately than with the investigations of any English or American scholar of romanticism, one can think oneself back into the romantic mood.

His essay traces the various literary uses of the wind-harp in eighteenth-century writing, finally arriving at Coleridge's poem, in which the instrument 'has ceased to be a drunkard's toy, and becomes dignified into an image by which the deepest relations in the dualism of man and nature can be explored'.[12] We have already seen that Coleridge's use of the harp to image his sense of the relation between nature and God is not altogether straightforward; the poem raises more acutely the question of precisely what Coleridge's sense of this relation was in lines 26-35. We can agree with Mr Grigson that the harp, in Coleridge's poem, is made to raise important questions of the mind's function in perception, but whether or not Coleridge is deliberately raising these questions, or whether he is simply not thinking with absolute clarity, is a serious problem in any reading of the poem. We must assume that, in the relevant passage, Coleridge thinks of himself as the harp; therefore something else must be the wind, and something else again the music produced by the action of the wind on the harp:

> Full many a thought uncall'd and undetain'd,
> And many idle flitting phantasies,
> Traverse my indolent and passive brain
> As wild and various, as the random gales
> That swell or flutter on this subject Lute!

(ll.31-35)

Mr Martin's comments on these lines deserve quoting at length:

> Here the harp is the 'passive brain', and the 'random gales' playing upon it are represented in 'many a thought uncall'd and undetain'd, / And many idle flitting phantasies,'. But this invites questions to which the lines give no answer. Where do the mental activities begin? Unlike the divine 'intellectual breeze', they cannot simply be shown as source-less, yet the source is not given. If thoughts and fantasies exist independently of the lute-brain, what does the wind-harp analogy contribute? Why, in fact, introduce it? Or, since Coleridge did introduce it, when the gale of thought and fantasy traverses the strings of the lute, what kind of music results? If nothing happens to the thoughts and fantasies, then the metaphor is empty; but if the lute contributes a new element, if the music genuinely differs from the gale which creates it, what new meaning does it have? The lines, in fact, contrive to suggest that the mind's contents are both (1) the wind which *causes* the music and (2) the music which is the *effect* of the wind. This ambiguity distracts attention from the real vagueness as to where the thoughts come from, and what part in thinking them is played by the passive brain. The lines evade the very problem they seem to be exploring, the nature of consciousness, the real connexion between thought and brain.

And Mr Martin goes on to conclude that 'the harp image is thus being used in two different ways, to represent two different positions'.[13] This very cogent statement of the problem is unanswerable in its own terms; lines 36-40 of *The Eolian Harp* offer a model of perception in which the brain is passive, its knowledge structured from without, and the harp image is perfectly appropriate. But lines 31-35 appear to suggest that knowledge is structured, effectively created, within the mind. Perhaps Coleridge would not have seen the problem, because it might be argued that the 'thoughts and phantasies' are, properly speaking, simply the music produced by the lute-brain in response to sensations, such as experience of the external world (in terms of the metaphor, the wind):

> And thus, my Love! as on the midway slope
> Of yonder hill I stretch my limbs at noon
> Whilst thro' my half-clos'd eyelids I behold
> The sunbeams dance, like diamonds, on the main,
> And tranquil muse upon tranquillity.

(ll.26-30)

But certainly it is not clear whether Coleridge intends this passage to function as the wind required by the metaphor of the harp. Coleridge's vagueness does, though, allow one interesting effect to emerge in the poem, an effect that points forward to the great conversation poems; the materialist position of the poem's explicit philosophical formulation is authenticated by a mental activity that supposes the creative power of the mind. The development of the poem is relatively successful in the terms of its rhetorical structure, even though this makes for serious confusion in the matter of Coleridge's philosophical position.

If we take Mr Marin's approach one stage further, and consider the consistency of Coleridge's use of the harp metaphor throughout the entire poem, then we are confronted with some very odd identifications. The rigour of philosophical discourse demands that if A = B, and C = B, then A and C are also equivalent. Thus the 'intellectual breeze' of line 39 is equivalent to the beautiful landscape that Coleridge experiences in lines 26-30 (assuming that this landscape is intended by Coleridge as the 'wind' of his metaphor). This would make good sense from the point of view of Coleridge's Hartleian position. But if we look back to the earlier part of the poem, with its two separate uses of the metaphor, then we realise, firstly, that the passage following line 17, with its elfins and birds of paradise, is in fact a description of the harp's music alone. Perhaps the gentle gales on which the elfins 'voyage' are thought of as causing them to produce the melodies that are like fabulous birds; but that would imply that the gales not only propel the elfins but travel quite a lot faster than them, which is having cake and eating it. But the important question is whether Coleridge identified these 'gentle gales' with the 'intellectual breeze' of God (if indeed the 'gentle gales' actually do perform as wind in one version of the harp metaphor). Our second realisation is more startling, for the first appearance of the metaphor in the poem is undoubtedly related to Coleridge's amorous play with Sara, and it is very hard to believe that Coleridge would have identified his sexual advances with the 'Plastic and vast' influence of God on the creation.

The poem is unsatisfactory because its central metaphor is made to do rather too much work, but this fault is magnified disproportionately by the endeavour to find a perfect unity in Coleridge's intellectual position. Efforts to make him a neoplatonist in the poem, encouraged by the four lines introduced in 1817, make for even wilder confusion. Arguments for Coleridge's informed interest in the neoplatonists, as early as the mid-1790s, are essentially implausible in the light of all evidence that survives, in letters, notebooks, and published work; Coleridge read a great deal, and thought about his reading, which certainly involved an acquaintance with Plato ('his dear *gorgeous* nonsense') and his commentators, but his dominant interests and commitments before the trip to Germany were defined against a background of English radical thought that was inseparable from the Unitarian standpoint. Coleridge enjoyed the discussion of ideas, and his current reading is always on or just beneath the surface of his writing in all its forms. And where there is a wealth of material in the 1790s relating to Unitarianism and its materialist philosophy, references to Platonic and neoplatonic thought are fugitive and fragmentary. The germs of a future interest are easy enough to find, and Coleridge was never disposed to rest contented with any given commitment of his early years. But this does not imply the existence of any substantial interest in, or knowledge of ideas that he came later to espouse. There are passages in Coleridge's poetry of the 1790s that suggest elements of later platonism, assimilated with other things and transmitted through secondary sources of various kinds. *Religious Musings* and *The Destiny of Nations* in particular point to a common jumbled inheritance that Coleridge would have shared with Priestley, or could have found, for example, in the work of Thomas Taylor. An approach to Coleridge's poetry like that of A.E. Powell, in her *Romantic Theory of Poetry*, which begins with the assertion that 'between 1795 and 1798 probably, Coleridge studied Plato, Plotinus, Proclus, Ficino, Boehme and Spinoza', is irresponsible and profoundly unhelpful. The proposition that from these philosophers (and the Cambridge Platonists are added in a note) Coleridge drew his first 'philosophical inspiration' is demonstrably not the case, and to assert that, in the poetry of the 1790s Nature is represented by Coleridge as 'the chief means of intercourse with the One'[14] is to ignore the experience offered by the poetry in favour of a highly debatable claim for Coleridge's commitment to an abstraction that is anyway unverifiable in the terms provided by the poetry. This is the crucial point; the philosophical passages in the poetry are at once statements of belief, and attempts to register emotions at a high pitch, that is to say, they are expressive of *feeling*. And Coleridge cannot be expected to have established a language that can adequately express, at one and the same time, both a philosophical speculation and the whole state of mind, with its antecedent intellectual and emotional development, that enabled him to feel confident in the presence of a benevolent divinity.

The philosophical 'sources' of the conversation poems do not help us to read them, and the exigencies of poetic language anyway render a necessary precision, in establishing the provenance and logical context of any given idea, quite impossible. Powell, followed by later critics,[15] suggested a specific source for the central image of *The Eolian Harp* in Plotinus, *Ennead* IV,iv,41. The passage in Plotinus does mention 'a musical string', and 'a lyre'; but it is clear that the lyre in Plotinus is a plucked instrument, and that it is used to exemplify one point in a long argument that has no bearing on Coleridge's poem.[16] It is questionable, in fact, whether Coleridge would have found Plotinus, in the mid-1790s, a particularly congenial figure, with his stern rejection of the private and domestic affections that were absolutely central to Coleridge's happiness, not to speak of his philosophy.[17]

Mr Martin has suggested a specific source for the harp in Cudworth; H.W. Piper, most plausibly, cites a passage from Priestley.[18] Coleridge may have the last word, as he used lines 36-40 of *The Eolian Harp* in the twelfth of his *Philosophical Lectures*, delivered in 1819, to illustrate the point that 'the mind may be defined as a subject which is its own object'; or rather, to illustrate the position of Berkeley in its bearing on that point:

> ... the idealist, concedes a real existence to one of the two terms [i.e. 'subject' and 'object' as elements of perception] only—to the *natura naturans,* in Berkeley's language, to God, and to the finite minds on which it acts, THE NATURA NATURATA, or the bodily world, being the result, even as the tune between the wind and the Aeolian harp. I remember when I was yet young this fancy struck me wonderfully, and here are some verses I wrote on the subject . . . .[19]

Are we to assume that the passage in the poem of 1796 (possibly 1795) has been, all along, about Berkeley? The language, it seems, may be made to bear any variety of philosophical disposition; Coleridge's cavalier appropriation of his own lines (is there again, as in the letter to Thelwall, something of self-display in the way the poem is brought in?) really makes nonsense of the effort to be precise in the identification of the philosophy of his poetry.


## II

It is most likely that Coleridge took over the wind-harp as an increasingly common property of eighteenth-century poetry. Thomson described the device in two stanzas of *The Castle of Indolence* (Canto I, XL-XLI) which emphasised its apparent testimony to a designing and creative presence in the creation superior to anything human; the music was 'Wild warbling Nature all, above the reach of Art!' Thomson also wrote an 'Ode on Aeolus's Harp',[20] and Collins remembered Thomson's association with the instrument in his *Ode Occasioned by the Death of Mr Thomson* (1749), lines 5-12. The term 'Aeolian harp' already carried associations of poetic creativity, from the classical identification of poet with singer—lyre and lyric poet went naturally together—and from the 'Aeolian' mode in Greek music. The opening lines of Gray's *Progress of Poesy* (1757) were thus misunderstood by one contemporary reviewer as a reference to the wind-harp:

> Awake, Aeolian Lyre, awake,
> And give to rapture all thy trembling strings.[21]

But *The Eolian Harp* has a good deal more than this in common with Coleridge's reading in eighteenth-century poetry. Its connections with the sonnet are particularly interesting.

It has recently been pointed out by Professor Fruman that Coleridge's earliest efforts as a poet are characterised by their remarkable variety of form:

> What is particularly noteworthy in the early canon is its technical diversity. Not only is practically every one of the poems Coleridge wrote before he was twenty-five structurally different from the others, but no clear affinity is revealed for any particular line length or rime pattern. Tumbling over each other are anthems and monodies, sonnets and odes, epigrams and other *jeux,* imitations of Milton, Gray, Collins, Casimir, Anacreon, *Ossian*, Rogers, and Bowles, besides a sprinkling of translations and paraphrases from other sources.

Professor Fruman is neither quite fair here, nor quite accurate. It is not so very peculiar to find this mixture of contemporary fashion and taste in a young poet (Professor Fruman does briefly concede this),[22] but Coleridge's early canon does actually display a marked predilection for one form, the sonnet. On a simple count, using E.H. Coleridge's edition of the *Poetical Works*, Coleridge wrote forty-eight sonnets, and at least ten other poems that are near to being sonnets. All but a handful were written before 1802, and the great majority were produced between 1789 and 1796. Coleridge's privately circulated anthology of 1796, *Sonnets from Various Authors,* included four of his own poems, and demonstrates how many of Coleridge's friends, Southey, Lloyd, and Lamb, were also interested in the form. Many, more eminent contemporaries had turned their hand to that 'development of some lonely feeling' (as Coleridge described it in the Preface to his Anthology) that could become 'a *Whole*' in the sonnet. The example of Bowles was of course dominant, but Coleridge had also read Thomas Warton, and Charlotte Smith, and Anna Seward; he could drop into exactly the manner, a regretful sense of the beauty in nature that provides an ironic setting for nostalgia or thwarted desire, that was typified in these poets (the convention of the absent lover has already been noticed):

> Ah! what a luxury of landscape meets
> My gaze! Proud towers, and Cots more dear to me,
> Elm-shadow'd Fields, and prospect-bounding Sea!
> Deep sighs my lonely heart: I drop the tear:
> Enchanting spot! O were my Sara here!
>                 (*Lines . . .climbing . . .Brockley*
>                       *Coomb, PW*,i,94)

These lines, very reminiscent of Thomas Warton, are Coleridge's own version (written some months before the first draft of *The Eolian Harp*) of a common conventional means to the withdrawal from sensory pleasure. It is precisely this convention of the absent lover that *The Eolian Harp*, most clearly in its first, near-sonnet form, manages to avoid, even with all the temptations (of melancholy, Christian stoicism) offered by twilight. Some contemporaries of Coleridge had taken to morbid extremes the melancholy of their sonneteering; Thomas Russel, whose *Sonnets and Miscellaneous Poems* had appeared posthumously in 1789 (one of his poems appeared in *Sonnets from Various Authors*), apparently died of a heart broken by one 'Delia', a lady of aristocratic station whose affection for Russel had been 'jostled' out of her, in the words of a biographer, by 'horse-jockies, valets and gamblers'.[23] And John Codrington Bampfylde, also represented in Coleridge's anthology, had lost his reason in the course of an impossible passion for the niece of Sir Joshua Reynolds.[24] Bampfylde's sonnets are not all as grim as his history; 'Written at a Farm' (1778), for example, demonstrates how *The Eolian Harp* opens in a very recognisable vein of epicurean pleasure in nature. Coleridge's poem is much more interesting in its blending of stoic elements with the pleasure, but it nevertheless clearly owes something to the taste for a neat and brief expression of some received response to a conventional situation:

> Around my porch and lonely casement spread
> The myrtle never sear and gadding vine
> With fragrant sweetbriar love to intertwine;
> And in my garden's box-encircled bed
> The pansy pied and musk-rose white and red,
> The pink, the lily chaste, and sweet woodbine
> Fling odours round: thick woven eglantine
> Decks my trim fence; in which, by silence led,

> The wren hath wisely built her mossy cell,
> Sheltered from storms in courtly land so rife,
> And nestles over her young and warbles well.
> 'Tis here, with innocence in peaceful glen,
> I pass my blameless moments, far from men;
> Nor wishing death too soon, nor asking life.[25]

We can still discern here the traditional motifs of retirement, but the poem rests for its effect on the evocative qualities of the descriptive langauge itself. Coleridge's opening of *The Eolian Harp* will take this a stage further, but the context of that opening is unmistakably a blend of the various idioms he discovered in the contemporary sonnet. Charles Lamb had written a sonnet in 1795 that comes closer still to the mood of *The Eolian Harp*; Lamb's poem describes the imaginary projection of an experience (this is something very characteristic in the conversation poems) that is otherwise very close to Coleridge:

> Methinks how dainty sweet it were, reclin'd
> Beneath the vast out-stretching branches high
> Of some old wood, in careless sort to lie,
> Nor of the busier scenes we left behind
> Aught envying. And, O Anna! mild-eyed maid!
> Beloved! I were well content to play
> With thy free tresses all a Summer's day,
> Losing the time beneath the greenwood shade.
> Or we might sit and tell some tender tale
> Of faithful vows repaid by cruel scorn,
> A tale of true love, or of friend forgot;
> And I would teach thee, lady, how to rail
> In gentle sort, on those who practice not
> Or love or pity, though of woman born.[26]

Lamb's poem ends on a typical note of mild and generalised social concern which was one implication of God's benevolent presence in nature. This emphasis is not strong in the first published version of *The Eolian Harp*, though certainly it lies behind Coleridge's thankfulness in God's 'saving mercies' at the end of the poem. Coleridge did, however, bring out the full implications of God's harmony realised through individual consciousness, a process which issued in love, in his version of *The Eolian Harp* that appeared in *Poems* (third edition 1803):

> Methinks, it should have been impossible
> Not to love all things in a World like this,
> Where e'en the breezes of the simple Air
> Possess the power and Spirit of Melody![27]

The subjunctive tense reinforces the latency of this potential for good in nature; human consciousness continues in fact to obstruct the divine scheme, by removing itself into urban civilisation and away from the natural sources of benevolence. Coleridge used this passage in 1803 to replace the lines on elfins and birds of paradise, and there is little doubt that they are a much more impressive attempt to deal with the necessity of sublimating the sexual relationship with Sara. The movement from private affection to universal benevolence is effected without strain or embarrassment.

One of Coleridge's own sonnets seems to have provided the specific point of departure for *The Eolian Harp*. *To the Evening Star* may be, as one critic has argued, an essay in neo-platonic thought,[28] but if a date around 1790 is correct it makes perfectly good sense as a youthful and entirely abstracted attempt to deal with the embarrassments of adolescent sexuality:

> O meek attendant of Sol's setting blaze,
> I hail, sweet star, thy chaste effulgent glow;
> On thee full oft with fixed eye I gaze
> Till I, methinks, all spirit seem to grow.
> O first and fairest of the starry choir,
> O loveliest 'mid the daughters of the night,
> Must not the maid I love like thee inspire
> *Pure* joy and *calm* delight?
> Must she not be, as is thy placid sphere
> Serenely brilliant? Whilst to gaze a while
> Be all my wish 'mid Fancy's high career
> E'en till she quit this scene of earthly toil;
> Then Hope perchance might fondly sigh to join
> Her spirit in thy kindred orb, O Star benign!
> (*PW*,i,16-17)

The reality of Sara, promising more substantial delight, released in Coleridge all the energies generated by his intense idealisations of domestic life, but his honeymoon poem obviously began, in part at least, as a reworking of this sonnet. *The*

*Eolian Harp* first appeared as 'Effusion XXXV'; Coleridge explained the term 'effusion' in his Preface to the volume of 1796:

> I could recollect no title more descriptive of the manner and matter of the Poems—I might indeed have called the majority of them Sonnets—but they do not possess that *oneness* of thought which I deem indispensible (sic) in a sonnet . . ..
>
> (*PW*,ii,1137)

Of the thirty-six 'Effusions' in *Poems on Various Subjects*, more than half actually are sonnets (including three, numbers 11, 12, and 13, by Lamb), and a fair proportion of the remaining poems hover around the form. The best conversation poems develop out of 'some lonely feeling', but the feeling is only a starting point, in *This Lime-Tree Bower my Prison*, and *Frost at Midnight*, for an ascending rhetorical structure that is fulfilled in a vision of community. This rhetoric, that Coleridge is feeling his way towards in the early conversation poems, has its most specific beginnings in the sonnet. But Coleridge had gone well beyond the contemporary fashion with the composition of *The Eolian Harp*, which attempts a *'oneness'* of greater scope, developing out of a subtlety quite new in the descriptive language of poetry.


### III


Coleridge's physical presence in the landscape, the sensory agencies of his experience of nature, are established simultaneously with a composition in the picturesque manner; a detail in the foreground which gradually recedes pleasantly to the sea. It is twilight, but the fading light and encroaching silence are realised with a quiet serenity that does not go beyond the experience itself. The gradual formation of place is achieved in terms that also unfold the quality of Coleridge's mood; the connection between mood and place is inherent in their common language:

> My pensive Sara! thy soft cheek reclin'd
> Thus on mine arm, most soothing sweet it is

> To sit beside our cot, our cot o'er grown
> With white-flower'd Jasmin, and the broad-leav'd Myrtle,
> (Meet emblems they of Innocence and Love!)
> And watch the clouds, that late were rich with light,
> Slow-sad'ning round, and mark the star of eve
> Serenely brilliant (such should Wisdom be)
> Shine opposite! How exquisite the scents
> Snatch'd from yon bean-field! and the world *so* hush'd!
> The stilly murmur of the distant Sea
> Tells us of Silence.
>
> (ll.1-12)

First touch, then sight, smell, sound; and Sara is at the beginning and end of Coleridge's receptivity to sensation, his ability to organise sense impressions to an expressive unity ('My pensive Sara . . . Tells *us* of Silence'). The explicit identifications that Coleridge makes, the emblematic plants, the star of eve's serene brilliance like Wisdom, are not quite in key (they are in fact omitted in 1803); Innocence and Love are appropriate on a honeymoon (a 'treaclemoon', as Byron called it), but they are quite sufficiently present in the poem without a formal acknowledgement that trivialises the descriptive language, and threatens it with imposed limitations of significance that are foreign to the subtle, unstated connectedness for which it allows. The opening passage of *The Eolian Harp* allows Coleridge's sympathy with the landscape—the way in which his mood, like the range of his sensory experience, is defined by it—to emerge, without the necessity for any formal acknowledgement of what is happening. But we do not think of nature as determining of consciousness, because Coleridge has also established the relationship with Sara as a condition of his receptivity. The private context, not pointed out but simply present, releases the potential for positive relationship with the whole range of Coleridge's experience. The simple and unclotted diction resists any impulse to channel and control this experience by reference to an order outside or abstracted from the particular objects of description. Those objects take on a significance that is exclusively defined by the poetic context, the connections established in the verse. There is Coleridge and Sara, and there is Coleridge and Sara in the landscape, and the quality of both relationships is informed by love; the more embracing love is God's, present in the breeze that animates (foreshadowed in the breeze that carries the scent of the bean-field), the influence that teaches benevolence; but Coleridge can only approach a sense of the whole human community (the implication of benevolence) through the particular and private love for Sara. And it is the particular and private audience constituted in Sara that allows Coleridge's style a manner that can *arrive* at values that are embracing from a rhetorical point of departure that is characteristically limited and particular.

The movement of the verse, Coleridge's fine control of the personal tone, underpins the development from private to public, from a happiness resting on the security of private relationship, to a more encompassing happiness in the security of values that are generally accessible. An initially regular caesural pause, strengthened by grammar that dissipates the force of the line-endings, relaxes the constraints of the blank verse and establishes an easy, unexcited rhythm; the movement is easily quickened to register Coleridge's intensifying responses, by a sharpening of the caesurae and slight but definite variations in the placing of the pause. Exclamation marks, perhaps just a little strident, and the italicised '*so* hush'd', force the tone onto a higher level of emotional and intellectual engagement that finally rests on the steady rhythm of lines 11-12:

> The stilly murmur of the distant Sea
> Tells us of Silence.

Coleridge has prepared for the introduction of the wind-harp by a brief concentration on sound; the silence of the immediate surroundings is brought out by the sea's audibility, a distant sound that we assume would not normally be heard. The harp comes in as a counterpoint to the distant 'stilly murmur', thus establishing one more connection, with its implications of an underlying connectedness in the variety of Coleridge's experience.

The wind-harp to which Coleridge now turns his attention becomes a dominant metaphor, used, as we have seen, in various ways, for all but the final sixteen lines of the poem. The basic structure of *The Eolian Harp* shares certain broad characteristics with all the conversation poems; there is an ascending movement of emotion and intellect, carefully registered by Coleridge's distinctive handling of the blank verse as a constant modification of tone. This movement is arrested at certain moments, usually corresponding to a more or less excited tonal pitch that has carried Coleridge beyond the particular objects of his experience, and the specific private audience of his language. There is then a return to those particular conditions, or to a different but related set of particulars, but the private context is now charged with our heightened sense of the potential that Coleridge can generate out of such moments. *The Eolian Harp* reaches a first climax at line 25, with the sublimation of the sexual relationship between Coleridge and Sara. Lines 17-25 introduce an entirely imaginary dimension that completes the expansion of all horizons which began in a movement from 'cot', to 'clouds', to 'the star of eve', and then to the 'bean-field' and the distant sea beyond. It is unfortunately clear that the elfins passage, with its indulgent blend of the marvellous with the whimsical, cannot really lead anywhere; the lines display an intricate musicality of diction which is rather wasted on their essentially irrelevant status in the developing poem:

> And now its strings
> Boldlier swept, the long sequacious notes
> Over delicious surges sink and rise,
> Such a soft floating witchery of sound . . ..
>
> (ll. 17-20)

Coleridge uses this highly concentrated play on sound to extraordinary effect in his best poetry, where it compounds the pervasive atmosphere of an informal relatedness between phenomena apparently quite distinct, and discrete. This quality of sound is present in *The Eolian Harp*, but like the descriptive manner established in the opening lines of the poem, it is an effect not absolutely subordinated to the overarching structure that develops out of an elaborate interplay between mood and idea.

The poem turns back at line 26 to the private context, with Coleridge imagining himself alone at noon on a sunlit hillside (this point is marked by a new paragraph in 1796). Coleridge again employs a movement of verse that is mimetic of his heightening response, but the passage, lines 26-35, does not take such care to be comprehensive in evocation both of the landscape and its mode of affectiveness through the senses. There is, again, a gradual expansion out from the particular context to embrace, finally, 'all of animated nature'. Again this movement of expansion is arrested, at line 41, and the poem moves back at last to Sara, returning to the particular conditions of the opening lines, 'PEACE, and this COT, and THEE, heart-honor'd Maid!' A.S. Gerard has described this movement of arrested expansion as 'the heartbeat rhythm',[29] and has employed the terms 'systole' and 'diastole' to designate the alternate expansion and contraction that is characteristic in the structure of the conversation poems.[30] These terms do have a certain usefulness, but they leave awkwardly out of account the cumulative effect of a repeatedly arrested expansion; we become increasingly conscious of the potential that the private context has for Coleridge, so that he can in the end rest on a return to the conditions of the poem's beginning, which are charged with a *latent* value that needs no explicit formulation at all. The conversation poems share as a group the same final atmosphere of quiet intensity, a very powerful and beautifully understated sense of the private, and local, and domestic values that Coleridge had come to regard, for all the various reasons that we have already discussed, as especially attractive. G.M. Harper first noted the 'return' of the conversation poems,[31] and most commentators have discussed Coleridge's use of the device. It is perhaps curious that M.H. Abrams does *not* discuss this aspect of the conversation poems in his *Natural Supernaturalism*, which is in effect a study of cyclical form in Romantic art; he concentrates his discussions of Coleridge on *The Ancient Mariner*, the *Dejection Ode,* and *Biographia Literaria,*[32] but his argument is conducted within a framework of reference to the social context of Romanticism that makes assumptions fundamentally different from those of the present argument. Coleridge's emphasis on the transcendant value of the private and the domestic does not necessarily imply that his creative thought has been forced back into this narrow sphere of operation. The conversation poems return to their particular conditions, but the potential generated in those conditions reaches beyond them; the public is finally implicit in the private, which represents for Coleridge both the source of constructive social values, and the model of a society that might realise those values in its own organisation. Coleridge's poetry is not the triumph of a crushed revolutionary spirit, but the form in which that spirit could maintain a stern resistance.

*The Eolian Harp* is not a completely successful poem; too much of the poem is given to a ratiocinative habit of mind that does not leave enough room to the verse itself. It is probably Coleridge's use of the harp image itself that is at the heart of the problem; Coleridge's variations on the metaphor are simply too inventive, starting too many hares, so that he cannot really hold the poem together. And the poem's conclusion does recognise this, but too late to solve the problem in terms of the poetic structure. Coleridge rejects the speculations of the poem on obviously fabricated grounds of Christian piety that are foreign to the whole cast of his mind. The limited, myopic piety that consequently emerges is projected onto Sara (unfairly, perhaps, but certainly prophetic), and couched in a disappointing declamatory manner that invites, a little smugly, the solemn approval of the Christian public. Sub-Miltonic inversions, capitalisations, a florid diction and cramped rhythmic movement, and a clumsy double negative, spoil what is nevertheless a most significant achievement in the development of the conversational idiom. Coleridge takes the opportunity to domesticate for his public, flooded as they are by sentiments to approve, a passage from the jacobin martyr Madame Roland, which he appended as a note to line 52; Dykes Campbell wrote this off as 'of no interest',[33] and critics of the poem have apparently taken him at his word.[34] But it surely *is* remarkable that Coleridge should so oddly have persisted in whispering the nature of his convictions, just as he is using exactly the poetic manner that he could not avoid in talking straight to the public, or at least, in claiming to agree with what he conceived the 'reading public' to believe. Coleridge's inability to deal with the direct address to this public issued in two serious failures, *Religious Musings* and *The Destiny of Nations*; and this same inability also spoilt his next serious attempt at a conversation poem, *Reflections on having left a Place of Retirement*.

## REFLECTIONS ON HAVING LEFT A PLACE OF RETIREMENT

### I

*Reflections on having left a Place of Retirement* has not attracted a great deal of critical attention. In contrast to estimates of *The Eolian Harp*, its shortcomings have not seemed sufficiently interesting; William Empson's laconic dismissal of most of the poem is representative:

> The two concluding paragraphs of this poem have been omitted since they add nothing to its chief interest which is in lines 24-40. Written in 1795 before anything comparable in Wordsworth's poetry, they describe the peculiar experience which was to become the basis of much of his best verse: a moment of mystical intensity, based on the beauty of the landscape, and supported by virtually pantheist ideas.[1]

It is at least arguable that *Reflections* is perhaps the least understood of all Coleridge's poems. It is not a success, by any criteria, but it can be rescued from the limbo it currently inhabits in critical esteem; its failure is a radical failure of the relationship between Coleridge and his audience, and as such the poem is very interesting indeed, because it confirms the absolute dependance of the conversational idiom on a secure sense of audience.

The text itself presents no problems like those of *The Eolian Harp,* and references are to the text of E.H. Coleridge, unless otherwise stated. The poem has a context, in Coleridge's life and thought, that has been totally ignored, and the poem is most easily approached through an effort to establish this context. This effort incidentally argues for a new dating of the poem that pushes the period of its completion forward some five or six months from the currently accepted date of around November 1795. The evidence for a new dating of the poem, in or after April 1796, is certainly not absolutely conclusive, but there is more material to support a later, rather than an earlier date, and the argument that follows will assume that *Reflections* was indeed composed in or after April 1796.

The poem is dated 1795 by E.H. Coleridge (and all other editors) on the basis of its biographical reference. This basis has been explained by C.G. Martin, in an essay that proposes a possible source for *Reflections* in William Crowe's topographical poem *Lewesdon Hill* (1786): 'Coleridge wrote 'Reflections on having left a Place of Retirement' in the winter of 1795 after he and Sara had returned from the Clevedon cottage, probably by mid-November.' The 'place of retirement' obviously does refer to Clevedon, sharing the same low cot and quiet dell, jasmine and myrtle, as the setting of *The Eolian Harp*. The opening descriptive passages of the two poems are in fact remarkably similar; similar enough even to suggest that Coleridge simply reworked the opening of *The Eolian Harp*, and incorporated it into *Reflections*. Mr Martin identifies the 'Mount sublime' in *Reflections*, from which Coleridge enjoys the 'goodly scene', as Dial Hill, 'rising about three hundred feet above Clevedon and mentioned in Baedeker as a 'point of view''.[2] His essay is primarily concerned to point out some very general similarities of structure, and one or two more particular similarities of diction and phrasing, between *Reflections* and Crowe's *Lewesdon Hill*. A connection between the two works is plausibly established, though, while granting that lines 26-42 of *Reflections* in particular may owe something to Coleridge's reading of Crowe, there are still very considerable differences between the two poems, of length (Crowe's poem is a great deal longer than Coleridge's), and of quality in the versification, that Mr Martin's essay does not make sufficiently clear. Nevertheless, it may be worthwhile to pursue Coleridge's connection with Crowe and *Lewesdon Hill*, because it takes us into areas that are helpful in the consideration of *Reflections*.

Mr Martin regards the parallels that he has discovered between the two poems as evidence for a date of the poem in 1795. We know from George Whalley's list of Coleridge's borrowings from the Bristol Library that he almost certainly read *Lewesdon Hill* between 2 and 10 March 1795.[3] Mr Martin notes that Crowe, 'of ultra-whig, pro-republican sympathies', and well-known at Oxford for his political opinions and eccentricity, may well have been known to the undergraduate Southey. His Crewian Oration to the University was delivered in 1788 as a celebration of the centenary of the Glorious

Revolution, and like Dr Price he was ready to prolong his applause in the following year, in welcome of the Revolution in France.[4] But even if Coleridge had not heard of Crowe before borrowing his poem from the Bristol Library, *Lewesdon Hill* would have won his approval on the strength of the attitudes expressed in it; at least it is Mr Martin's argument that the Coleridge of March 1795 would have found much to approve in the poem. Crowe praises Washington and the Corsican patriot Pasquale Paoli, both examples of the kind of hero that Coleridge himself admired. There is an attack on mechanist psychology, which Mr Martin suggests would have caught the eye of Coleridge who, although at that time a declared necessarian, may have found this interesting as pointing in the direction he was later to take: 'Crowe's emphatic declarations in favour of free will and moral responsibility might therefore have had the additional interest of articles of faith towards which Coleridge was already dimly working.' Mr Martin also makes the further suggestion that *Lewesdon Hill* may have been useful to Coleridge as a stylistic model, 'a descriptive-meditative blank verse poem written in a relatively simple and unliterary style'.[5] Coleridge recalled a debt to Crowe's poetic style in *Biographia Literaria,* where he is mentioned briefly as a name ('though known to me at a somewhat later date') to be added to that of Bowles.[6] This acknowledgement is very odd; it might almost sound like the strongest evidence of some Coleridgean 'debt' to Crowe, if we add to the inherent implausibility of Crowe's status as a 'stylistic model' (his poetry, including *Lewesdon Hill,* barely rises above an utterly pedestrian turgidity), Coleridge's habit of making provision, in the vaguest terms, for any eventual uncovering of some petty plagiarism. Mr Martin almost seems disposed to class Crowe with Cowper, which is not a fair comment on the level of Coleridge's critical discrimination. Mr Martin finally concurs with Coleridge's editors in dating *Reflections* towards the end of 1795, with the acknowledgement of one difficulty in this interpretation of the parallels with Crowe's poem: 'Coleridge's loan of [*Lewesdon Hill*] was short, and one can only conjecture that he *did* read *Lewesdon Hill,* and that he read it with sufficient attention to remember it several months later when he wrote 'Reflections'.'[7]

Such a strained assumption woul be unnecessary if there was

any reason to suppose that *Reflections* may have been written in the early months of 1796, because Coleridge in fact borrowed Crowe's poem from the Bristol Library for a second time, on 30 December 1795, and kept it until the end of January.[8] And there are reasons to suppose a later date for Coleridge's poem, because *Reflections,* in the form in which it first appeared in the *Monthly Magazine* of October 1796, shares a number of interests and ideas, rather too many for simple coincidence, with the fifth number of Coleridge's magazine *The Watchman*, issued on 2 April 1796. This does not rule out the possibility of Coleridge's interest in *Lewesdon Hill.* On the contrary, it rather strengthens the common ground shared by the Coleridge of *Reflections*, and William Crowe. Mr Martin, in establishing the kind of interest that Crowe's poem would have had for Coleridge, notes, as we have already seen, its passages in praise of Washington and Pasquale Paoli, and its censure of mechanist psychology. He includes also in his argument the poem's general denunciation of militarism. Coleridge's anti-militarism was made explicit and public in his lecture 'On the Present War', delivered in Bristol in February 1795, and published in November in *Conciones ad Populum*.[9] But he is as firmly opposed to war throughout the pages of the *Watchman*, turning against the French for their military aggression.[10] General Washington is mentioned once by Coleridge in a letter to Southey of July 1794 (*CL*,i,89), but not at all in the lectures of 1795; he was an obvious choice for a patriot hero, but does not emerge as one until the *Watchman*, indeed the very issue, the fifth, in which Coleridge first mentions William Crowe.[11] Coleridge does not mention Paoli at all in the records that survive from the 1790s, though he certainly knew about the contemporary situation in Corsica.[12] The censures of mechanist psychology would undoubtedly have caught Coleridge's eye in March 1795; in December 1794 he had called himself 'a compleat Necessitarian', and had claimed to

> understand the subject almost as well as Hartley himself—but I go further than Hartley and believe the corporeality of thought—namely, that it is motion—
>
> (*CL*,i,137)

The letter is light-hearted, and Coleridge goes on to poke fun at Priestley's extension of Hartley's ideas (though it is beyond question that Coleridge had a serious and committed interest in Priestley, in 1794 and 1795), but he retained the greatest respect for Hartley at least until September 1796, when his first son was born and named after the philosopher. But by the end of March 1796 Coleridge was openly critical, almost scornful of Priestley.[13] The early months of 1796 suit better than November 1795 a Coleridge 'dimly working' towards 'new articles of faith' (though it is still the case that this way of thinking about Coleridge's intellectual development implies a peculiar gift of foresight—as if he could stand back to observe his own intellectual development—that is not evident in the contemporary records); in fact the Coleridge of March and April 1796 would altogether have found 'the moral-political cast of *Lewesdon Hill* . . .both familiar and pleasing'.[14]

Perhaps the most significant feature of the textual history of *Reflections* is the fact that it was not included in *Poems on Various Subjects*, which appeared in April 1796. It is hard to believe that Coleridge could not find a place for this comparatively impressive poem in his first published volume of poetry, if, that is to say, the poem existed in anything like finished form. *Religious Musings* was the last poem printed in *Poems on Various Subjects*, and Coleridge was still working on it in 'early March 1796': 'The Religious Musings are finished, and you shall have them on Thursday' (*CL*,i,187).[15] Coleridge placed, *The Eolian Harp* and *Reflections* consecutively in the 1797 *Poems* (a grouping preserved in all the subsequent editions that appeared in Coleridge's lifetime); the two poems appear side by side in *Sibylline Leaves* under the general heading 'Meditative Poems in Blank Verse', under which heading Coleridge in fact included all the conversation poems. But the arrangement of poems in *Sibylline Leaves* is not chronological (in spite of Coleridge's later claims to prefer a chronological arrange-ment).[16] *Reflections* follows naturally on *The Eolian Harp*, as a kind of sequel to it, and it is obvious that *Reflections* is about Coleridge's departure from Clevedon. This does not necessar-ily argue that the poem was written at the time of his departure; all the conversation poems imply or state a specific time and location that goes with their direct personal address, but this is a dimension of their rhetoric, and not biographical evidence. Coleridge liked to encourage the sense that many of his poems were the products of a single burst of creative energy, but we know that he actually took great pains, certainly with the conversation poems (there are a number of significant textual variants in most of the poems). And the settings of the conversation poems, naturally as they seem to flow out of a moment's real experience, are carefully composed as a function of the rhetoric. Geoffrey Grigson has drawn attention to Coleridge's astonishing luck, for example, in *The Eolian Harp*, when he can enjoy the scent of a bean-field in blossom, in late August.[17]

Professor Whalley's list of Bristol Library borrowings shows that, on 2 March 1795, and again on 30 December 1795, Coleridge took out 'Poetical Tracts Vol. 3'. This was *Miscellaneous Poems*, a set of three volumes, bound up by the library, of various separately published poems by different authors. Volume 3 contained nine separate works, amongst them *Lewesdon Hill*.[18] Perhaps Coleridge chose the volume because it contained two works on the slave trade, Hannah More's *Slavery* (1788) and Ann Yearsley's *Poems on the Inhumanity of the Slave Trade* (Ann Yearsley, 'the milk-maid poetess', was a protegée of Hannah More's). But it is reasonable to assume that Coleridge read through the whole volume, which opens with Thomas Russel's *Sonnets and Miscellaneous Poems*. A 'Lecture on the Slave Trade' was delivered by Coleridge on 16 June 1795, and he published the lecture in slightly different form in the fourth *Watchman*, on 25 March 1796.[19] Coleridge wanted to jog his memory about something in December 1795; possibly he wanted another look at Crowe's poem, or a look at Russel for his projected anthology of *Sonnets from Various Authors*. Most probably, he wanted to look at material for a revision of his lecture on the slave trade, with a view to including it in the magazine he was about to launch. Certainly, it is fascinating to turn to the *Watchman* as a link between Coleridge's interests and state of mind, and the poetry that he was writing early in 1796.

The *Watchman* that appeared on Saturday 2 April 1796, is a characteristic mixture of borrowed and original material. Coleridge was beginning to feel the strain of producing an issue each eighth day, and contributions from the newspapers were becoming increasingly evident by the end of March.[20]The fifth issue contained, as usual, reports of foreign and domestic affairs extracted from politically sympathetic papers, the *Star* and the *Morning Chronicle*; there were a few poems contributions from friends and acquaintances, a book review, a reply to a correspondent. William Gilbert, a poet and barrister known and admired by Coleridge in Bristol, contributed an essay entitled 'The Commercial Academic', which aimed at establishing in the public mind a proper sense of the value of commerce as an essentially benevolent activity, a source of happiness for both trader and customer:

> Happiness is the cause and object of commerce, as every individual is the best judge of his own wants, or in other words of what will contribute to his own happiness, and as national commerce can only be carried on to supply the wants and promote the happiness of individuals, it follows, that every restraint laid upon commerce is a restraint laid upon our own happiness.[21]

If we can judge from Coleridge's editorial preface to Gilbert's essay, he sensed something less than satisfactory in this argument:

> The Editor returns his grateful acknowledgements to Mr G——rt for the following ESSAY, and will anxiously expect the remaining Numbers. The Editor is not perhaps equally convinced of the uses of Trade; but this small difference of opinion by no means lessens his admiration or gratitude. Mr G discovers much general knowledge, and when his reasonings are not perhaps unimpregnably solid, even then they are ingenious, and uniformly conveyed in a style luminous and elegant.[22]

*Reflections* opens with a description of the scene of retirement, a 'little landscape', very similar to the opening lines of *The Eolian Harp*; the first published version of the poem then focussed briefly on the effect of the retired scene on a passer-by from Bristol, out on a Sunday walk:

> Once I saw
> (Hallowing his Sabbath-day by quietness)
> A wealthy son of Commerce saunter by,
> Bristowa's citizen—he paus'd and look'd

> With a pleased sadness and gaz'd all around,
> Then eye'd our cottage and gaz'd round again,
> And said it was *a blessed little place*.
>
> (*PW*,i,106)

Coleridge put it a little stronger in the revised text of the 1797 *Poems*:

> Once I saw
> (Hallowing his Sabbath-day by quietness)
> A wealthy son of Commerce saunter by,
> Bristowa's citizen: methought, it calm'd
> His thirst of idle gold, and made him muse
> With wiser feelings: for he paus'd . . . .
>
> (ll.9-14)

Gilbert's essay discusses the importance of gold bullion.[23] 'The Commercial Academic' would naturally have no authoritative claim as a 'source' of this passage; Coleridge is exemplifying the kind of social effectiveness that a retired life in nature can have, and the particular example may perfectly well appear to be a quite arbitrary choice. Following Gilbert's essay, in the same fifth issue of the *Watchman*, is an extract (on the need for a review of the game laws) probably contributed by William Frend, the Unitarian don who had been sacked for his principles, and whose trial Coleridge had attended at Cambridge. *Reflections* has a moment of resolute determination to enter the sphere of action as a Unitarian:

> I therefore go, and join head, heart, and hand,
> Active and firm, to fight the bloodless fight
> Of Science, Freedom, and the Truth in Christ.
>
> (ll.60-62)

Coleridge did not need Frend to remind him that he was a Unitarian, of course, and this resolution would doubtless have been as firm without the inspiration of his early hero. Next after the extract communicated by Frend is a review, by Coleridge, of Count Rumford's *Essays, Political, Economical, and Philosophical*, the first volume of which appeared in 1796. The review is a good one; soon after writing it Coleridge was hoping to make money by selling plans to 'Rumfordize' Bristol,

Birmingham, and Manchester (Rumford had invented a fire-place that did not smoke).[24] Coleridge prefaced his review of the *Essays* with a passage of verse (unidentified in the *Watchman*) from William Bowles's *On Mr Howard's Account of Lazarettos:*

> These, Virtue, are they triumphs, that adorn
> Fitliest our nature, and bespeak us born
> For loftiest action; not to gaze and run
> From clime to clime; or batten in the sun,
> Dragging a drony flight from flow'r to flow'r,
> Like summer insects in a gaudy hour;
> Nor yet o'er love-sick tales with fancy range,
> And cry "'Tis pitiful, 'tis passing strange!"
> But on life's varied views to look around,
> And raise expiring sorrow from the ground:—
> And he—who thus hath borne his part assign'd,
> In the sad fellowship of human kind,
> Or for a moment sooth'd the bitter pain
> Of a poor brother—has not liv'd in vain.[25]

These lines make an interesting comparison with the first seventeen lines of the third verse paragraph of *Reflections:*

> Ah! quiet Dell! dear Cot, and Mount sublime!
> I was constrain'd to quit you. Was it right,
> While my unnumber'd brethren toil'd and bled,
> That I should dream away the entrusted hours
> On rose-leaf beds, pampering the coward heart
> With feelings all too delicate for use?
> Sweet is the tear that from some Howard's eye
> Drops on the cheek of one he lifts from earth:
> And he that works me good with unmov'd face,
> Does it but half: he chills me while he aids,
> My benefactor, not my brother man!
> Yet even this, this cold beneficence
> Praise, praise it, O my Soul! oft as thou scan'st
> The sluggard Pity's vision-weaving tribe!
> Who sigh for Wretchedness, yet shun the Wretched,
> Nursing in some delicious solitude
> · Their slothful loves and dainty sympathies!

(ll.43-58)

The two passages are very similar in their basic contrast between active, socially-mediated benevolence, and passive, self-indulgent sensibility. There are local similarities of phrasing and idea, most strikingly between Bowles's 'And raise expiring sorrow from the ground' (which is implicitly a reference to the subject of his poem, the work of the prison reformer John Howard), and Coleridge's

> Sweet is the tear that from some Howard's eye
> Drops on the cheek of one he lifts from earth.

The tear of compassion was possibly suggested by the two lines in Bowles's poem that immediately follow the passage quoted by Coleridge in the *Watchman*:

> But 'tis not that Compassion should bestow
> An unavailing tear on want or woe.

Bowles's 'sad fellowship of human kind' are akin to Coleridge's 'unnumber'd brethren' who toil and bleed, and the 'brother man' of *Reflections* echoes Bowles's 'poor brother'; 'The sluggard Pity's vision-weaving tribe... nursing... Their slothful loves and dainty sympathies' are as lazy as those in Bowles's poem who spend their time, 'Like summer insects in a gaudy hour', 'Dragging a drony flight from flow'r to flow'r', and cry "tis pitiful'. Coleridge makes an interesting mistake in his quotation of Bowles's poem in the *Watchman*, in the substitution of 'batten in the sun' where Bowles's original has 'flutter in the sun'. In *Reflections* Coleridge uses 'pampering' ('to over-indulge or 'feed' (any mental appetite, feeling, or the like)': *OED* 'pamper' Ic *fig*), in describing the 'coward Heart's' selfish indulgence in 'feelings', and it is possible that Coleridge projected this idea back onto his Bowlesian model by mis-remembering 'batten' for 'flutter' in a related context ('to thrive, grow fat, prosper (*esp* in a bad sense, at the expense or to the detriment of another); to gratify a morbid mental craving': *OED* 'batten' $v^1$, Ic *fig*).

Coleridge's reference to John Howard in *Reflections* takes us back to the notion of 'benevolence' (the word is weaker in current usage that it was in the late eighteenth century—it expressed an attitude that has really disappeared, with the particular relations of class that made such an attitude possible). In the *Watchman* review of Count Rumford Coleridge celebrates Howard, with Rumford, as Britons exemplary in their benevolence. And it is not surprising that Coleridge should have associated these models of social concern with William Lisle Bowles, whose appeal for Coleridge lay, at least in part, in the gentle colouring of social concern that informs the sensibility of his poetry. Bowles wrote two relatively long poems about the prison reformer, *On Mr Howard's Account of Lazarettos*, and *On the Grave of Howard*, and many other poems, for example his *Verses to the Philanthropick Society*, and *The African*, which amplify a quality that Coleridge discovered in his sonnets, a sensibility turned outwards as an active response to suffering (a quality distinct from the ludicrous disabling grief of Henry Mackenzie's hero in *The Man of Feeling* (1771)). We have already seen that eighteenth-century nature poetry developed the response to nature as a sense of God's benevolent presence and design, and that this development was mediated most importantly for Coleridge through Bowles's work (though he would have found it a central emphasis in Thomson and Akenside). In December 1796 Coleridge could confidently present John Thelwall's wife with a gift of Bowles's *Sonnets, and other Poems* (4th edition, 1796), writing on the fly-leaf

> I entreat your acceptance of this Volume, which has given me more pleasure, and done my heart more good, than all the other books, I ever read, excepting my Bible.
>
> *(CL,*i,287)

Coleridge felt that he could fit Bowles into the scheme of his radicalism; writing to Southey in July 1794, and apparently casting round for a suitable motto that Southey had asked him to suggest for some poems (the *Botany-Bay Eclogues*), Coleridge thought of Bowles's *Verses on the Philanthropick Society*. The train of thought that this initiates in Coleridge's mind establishes some important connections:

> For a motto! Surely my memory has suffered an epileptic fit. A Greek Motto would be pedantic—These Lines will perhaps do.
>
> > All mournful to the pensive Sage's eye
> > The Monuments of human Glory lie:
> > Fall'n Palaces crushed by the ruthless haste
> > Of time, and many an Empire's silent waste
> > But where a Sight shall shuddering Sorrow find
> > Sad as the ruins of the human mind?
> >
> > Bowles

A Better will soon occur to me— Poor Poland! They go on sadly there. Warmth of particular friendship does not imply absorption. The nearer you approach the Sun, the more intense are his Rays—yet what distant corner of the System do they not cheer and vivify? The ardour of private Attachments makes Philanthropy a necessary *habit* of the Soul. I love my *Friend*— such as *he* is, all mankind *are* or *might be*! The deduction is evident—. Philanthropy (and indeed every other Virtue) is a thing of *Concretion*—Some home-born Feeling is the *center* of the Ball, that rolling on thro' Life collects and assimilates every congenial Affection.

(*CL*,i,86)

'The ruins of the human mind' are far sadder than the ruined 'Monuments of human Glory', because all the forms that shape and express consciousness, including forms of social organisation ('Poor Poland!'), must find their basis in human creativity. 'Private Attachment', inseparable for Coleridge from the 'home-born Feeling' of stable familial community, is the precondition of 'Philanthropy', socially effective action. The contrast in *Reflections* between benevolence and the sensibility of the 'sluggard Pity's vision-weaving tribe' concerned Coleridge very deeply in the middle years of the 1790s. Rumford, like Howard, was a fine example of the active, unselfish sensibility of the kind embodied in Bowles's poetry; Coleridge's review of Rumford quotes an example from the *Essays* of his 'expansive benevolence':

However selfish pity may be, *benevolence* certainly springs from a more noble origin. It is a good-natured, generous sentiment, which does not require being put to the torture in order to be stimulated to action. And it is this sentiment, not pity, or compassion, which I would wish to excite. Pity is always attended with pain; and if our sufferings at being witnesses of the distresses of others, sometimes force us to relieve them, we can neither have much merit, nor any lasting satisfaction, from such involuntary acts of charity; but the enjoyments which result from acts of genuine benevolence are as lasting as they are exquisitely delightful.[26]

These are precisely the issues that concern Coleridge in *Reflections*. And they concern him elsewhere, too, in 1796. He wrote a poem addressed to Charles Lloyd, probably in December 1796; after meeting Lloyd, Coleridge had written about him to Thomas Poole:

> Charles Lloyd wins upon me hourly—his heart is uncommonly pure, his affections delicate, & his benevolence enlivened, but not sicklied, by sensibility.
>
> (*CL*,i,236)

Lloyd moved in with the Coleridges as a sort of paying disciple, but his charm rapidly wore off. He became 'ill' in November: 'his distemper (which may with equal propriety be named Somnambulism, or frightful Reverie, or *Epilepsy from accumulated feelings*) is alarming', Coleridge complained to Poole (*CL*,i,257). *Addressed to a Young Man of Fortune* was written as an admonition from mentor to devotee (it is not surprising that the relationship turned so sour), and Coleridge was plainly irritated by the wealthy Lloyd, who had abandoned himself to 'an indolent and causeless melancholy' (*PW*,i,157; one of Lloyd's contributions to Coleridge's *Poems* of 1797 was entitled 'The Melancholy Man'):[27]

> Hence that fantastic wantonness of woe,
> O youth to partial Fortune vainly dear!
> To plunder'd Want's half-shelter'd hovel go,
> Go, and some hunger-bitten infant hear
> Moan haply in a dying mother's ear:
> Or when the cold and dismal fog-damps brood
> O'er the rank church-yard with sear elm-leaves strew'd,
> Pace round some widow's grave, whose dearer part
> Was slaughter'd, where o'er his uncoffin'd limbs
> The flocking flesh-birds scream'd! Then, while thy heart
> Groans, and thine eye a fiercer sorrow dims,
> Know (and the truth shall kindle thy young mind)
> What nature makes thee mourn, she bids thee heal!
> O abject! if, to sickly dreams resign'd,
> All effortless thou leave Life's commonweal
> A prey to Tyrants, Murderers of Mankind.
>
> (*PW*,i,157-8)

The tone is slightly confused by Gothic elements, but Coleridge's meaning is clear; nature teaches philanthropy by conditioning a natural reaction to suffering. This education can be encouraged (the function of the familial community in retirement) and leads to a specifically political awareness, or it can be wilfully resisted, by indulgence in the self-centred sensibility of melancholy, the luxuriant emotionalism censured in Rumford's *Essays*, and in Coleridge's *Reflections* too. A related distinction between kinds of sensibility is also important in *The Nightingale*; it is implicit in the poem addressed to Lloyd, and in *Lines to W.L.*,[28] Coleridge relates it to the domestic ideal:

> While my young cheek retains its healthful hues,
> And I have many friends who hold me dear,
> L——! methinks, I would not often hear
> Such melodies as thine, lest I should lose
> All memory of the wrongs and sore distress
> For which my miserable brethren weep!
> But should uncomforted misfortunes steep
> My daily bread in tears and bitterness;
> And if at Death's dread moment I should lie
> With no beloved face at my bedside,
> To fix the last glance of my closing eye,
> Methinks such strains, breathed by my angel-guide,
> Would make me pass the cup of anguish by,
> Mix with the blest, nor know that I had died!
>
>                                        (*PW*,i,236)

Even art can be damaging for the wrong kind of consciousness. In this poem the art is music, but a notebook entry of 1796 conceives of a similar negative function for poetry; 'Poetry—excites us to artificial feelings—makes us callous to real ones'.[29] Poetry has a positive aspect that is stressed in the *Lines to W.L.*, for art is a part of nature and can heal like her when 'uncomforted misfortunes' destroy the basis of philanthropy, a Hartleian basis in private affection. Coleridge's anxiety about the security of that basis in his own life is only just beneath the surface of *Lines to W.L.*; we are reminded of the enduring potency of the domestic ideal in Coleridge's life and poetry, and of the way in which that potency was strengthened by Coleridge's conviction that the domestic community in nature lead directly to benevolence. In the 'Introductory Address' to *Conciones ad Populum* he had stated succinctly his conception of the process:

> The searcher after Truth must love and be beloved; for general Benevolence is a necessary motive to constancy of pursuit; and this general Benevolence is begotten and rendered permanent by social and domestic affections. Let us beware of that proud Philosophy, which affects to inculcate Philanthropy while it denounces every home-born feeling, by which it is produced and nurtured. The paternal and filial duties discipline the Heart and

prepare it for the love of all Mankind. The intensity of private attachments encourages, not prevents, universal Benevolence.[30]

These issues were the subject of public debate. In May 1796, for example, an 'Enquirer' essay in the *Monthly Magazine* (the magazine—'journal of the Dissenters, the Unitarians—radicals in religion and politics alike'[31]—to which Coleridge sent *Reflections*) discussed the question 'Is Private Affection inconsistent with Universal Benevolence?'[32] We have already considered Coleridge's position on this issue in the 1790s, in the context of his attitudes to Hartley and Godwin. And it is clearly the case that these issues provide a very helpful context for *Reflections on having left a Place of Retirement.* Coleridge became particularly concerned about the social implications of his own way of life, the relationship of public and private, in 1796, when his marriage, with its increased economic pressures, and the gradual emergence of local hostility to radicals, forced the issue in a very material way. His writings testify to a newly immediate concern; and the fifth *Watchman* brings different aspects of the problem together in a way that may have lead, directly or indirectly, to *Reflections*. Coleridge mentions William Crowe for the first time in that number of the *Watchman*, just as he quotes from the Bowles poem that also appears to enter into *Reflections*;[33] and there are other details that may have contributed material to Coleridge's poem. *Reflections* may well have existed in some form (the opening at least already existed, in the form of the opening lines of *The Eolian Harp*), and perhaps Coleridge discovered a way of fusing an 'imitation' of Bowles with an 'imitation' of Crowe. He did not publish *Reflections* in *Poems on Various Subjects*; the date of the poem's composition was more probably around April 1796, than November 1795.

II

The basic structure of *Reflections on having left a Place of Retirement* is in one aspect a fairly straightforward representation of the relationship between a domestic community in nature, and benevolence, an active engagement with society.

The opening verse paragraph, lines 1-26, establishes the pleasant setting in nature of Coleridge's home, and the private happiness with his 'sweet Girl'. The verse again works by making unstated connections; the response to a bird's song quietly asserts Coleridge's love for Sara as paradigmatic of an embracing reciprocity in experience. The effect of the song, and the effect of Sara, are equally 'inobtrusive', and equally imply a unity (sometimes the bird may be seen as well as heard, but its visual presence is not a condition of the song's effect) in apparently circumstantial details:

> Oft with patient ear
> Long-listening to the viewless sky-lark's note
> (viewless, or haply for a moment seen
> Gleaming on sunny wings) in whisper'd tones
> I've said to my Beloved, 'Such, sweet Girl!
> The inobtrusive song of Happiness,
> Unearthly minstrelsy! then only heard
> When the Soul seeks to hear; when all is hush'd,
> And the Heart listens!'
>
> (ll. 18-26)

Coleridge here repeats more explicitly an effect that we recognise from *The Eolian Harp*, and that he uses again in the later conversation poems; the creative effect of a properly attuned consciousness of nature is displayed in the capacity for increasingly fine auditory discrimination. Local sounds fade away to allow the emergence of distant, or fainter, or more delicate sounds. There is most characteristically a gradual fall into silence that is broken by some auditory detail that initiates the growth of consciousness into a state of mind capable of registering connection, the 'dim sympathies' of *Frost at Midnight*.

The second verse paragraph of *Reflections* enacts the more strenuous effort necessary to achieve a sense of the full potential in nature, the true extent of its capacity to manifest the presence of God. The verse realises this strenuous effort by charting Coleridge's increasingly difficult, but increasingly excited ascent to a point of view; the climb itself is implied by the widening and lengthening perspective that Coleridge can command as he gets highter and higher. The difficulty of the effort is at first very great in relation to the pleasure ('steep',

'stony', 'perilous toil'), but is at last swamped by the 'luxury' of
the sheer scope of vision:

> But the time, when first
> From that low Dell, steep up the stony Mount
> I climb'd with perilous toil and reach'd the top,
> Oh! what a goodly scene! *Here* the bleak mount,
> The bare bleak mountain speckled thin with sheep;
> Grey clouds, that shadowing spot the sunny fields;
> And river, now with bushy rocks o'er-brow'd,
> Now winding bright and full, with naked banks;
> And seats, and lawns, the Abbey and the wood,
> And cots, and hamlets, and faint city-spire;
> The Channel *there*, the Islands and white sails,
> Dim coasts, and cloud-like hills, and shoreless Ocean—
> It seem'd like Omnipresence! God, methought,
> Had built him there a Temple: the whole World
> Seem'd *imag'd* in its vast circumference:
> No *wish* profan'd my overwhelmed heart.
> Blest hour! It was a luxury,— to be!

(ll. 26-42)

The passage marks a very considerable advance in the range of
Coleridge's blank verse descriptive poetry. The transition from
the comparatively limited consciousness of the 'low Dell', less
limited towards the end of the first verse paragraph, to the
vision that may encompass 'the whole World', is effected by a
gradual raising of tonal pitch; each subtle elevation of tone
creates the possibility of a correspondingly greater intensity of
mental life, which in its turn contributes to the tonal ascent.
There is a remarkable control in the gradual acceleration of
pace in the verse, where the increasing rapidity with which
details in the scene accumulate, reined in at just the critical
point on 'The Channel *there*', culminates in an elevated calm, a
breathless, arrested confrontation with the view in its entirety.
The composition of the scene is evidently in the picturesque
manner, the eye led back by a river (the passage suggests quite
strongly the work of Claude Lorraine), taking in an Abbey, to
the background of mountains and shoreline. This picturesque
quality, reinforced by the urgent injunctions to observe, *'Here'*,
*'There'*, enables Coleridge to insist on the physical reality, the
sensational presence of nature, even as it leads him to a
luxurious confidence in the designing creator beyond his

sensory experience. The description ends by suggesting the boundless, illimitable quality of his vision, and of the landscape, but without denying its physicality:

> Dim coasts, and cloud-like hills, and shoreless Ocean—.

It is puzzling that Coleridge should proceed to reject this vision in the next verse paragraph. Certainly he seems to reject both kinds of experience of nature that the poem has displayed:

> Ah! quiet Dell! dear Cot, and Mount sublime!
> I was constrain'd to quit you.
>
> (ll.43-4)

We must return to this puzzle a little later.

Coleridge now turns to consider different kinds of response to social suffering. This is a logical development; nature can, in his experience of it, imply 'the whole world', and it was Coleridge's stated conviction that benevolence, the concern to alleviate the suffering of others, was best learnt from nature, in the educative security of 'private attachment'. The Unitarian resolve of lines 60-62 is perfectly consistent with the direction of the poem as a whole:

> I therefore go, and join head, heart, and hand,
> Active and firm, to fight the bloodless fight
> Of Science, Freedom, and the Truth in Christ.

And the poem maintains this consistency to the end. The final verse paragraph, lines 63-71, refers us back to the conditions of the opening lines; the sentiment is explicitly levelling, in fact suggesting the millennial atmosphere of early revolutionary fervour. The retired familial community in nature does not only foster a social conscience, but it also provides a model of social organisation:

> Yet oft when after honourable toil
> Rests the tir'd mind, and waking loves to dream,
> My spirit shall revisit thee, dear Cot!
> Thy Jasmin and thy window-peeping Rose,
> And Myrtles fearless of the mild sea-air,
> And I shall sigh fond wishes—sweet Abode!
> Ah!—had none greater! And that all had such!
> It might be so—but the time is not yet.
> Speed it, O Father! Let thy Kingdom come!

Our return to the initial context of retirement is now charged with a sense of its revealed potential, the latent power that Coleridge has uncovered in his ideal.

But something has gone wrong with the poem. There are very serious lapses of style, and equally serious contradictions in the attitude of the poem. And it is interesting that these two kinds of failure are very closely related in the poem. It may be helpful to look closely at the third verse paragraph, which represents the most sustained of the poem's stylistic lapses:

> Ah! quiet Dell! dear Cot, and Mount sublime!
> I was constrained to quit you. Was it right,
> While my unnumber'd brethren toil'd and bled,
> That I should dream away the entrusted hours
> On rose-leaf beds, pampering the coward heart
> With feelings all too delicate for us?
> Sweet is the tear that from some Howard's eye
> Drops on the cheek of one he lifts from earth:
> And he that works me good with unmov'd face,
> Does it but half: he chills me while he aids,
> My benefactor, not my brother man!
> Yet even this, this cold beneficence
> Praise, praise it, O my Soul! oft as thou scann'st
> The sluggard Pity's vision-weaving tribe!
> Who sigh for Wretchedness, yet shun the Wretched,
> Nursing in some delicious solitude
> Their slothful loves and dainty sympathies!

The lines deteriorate into Coleridge's worst declamatory manner. There are ugly compressions of grammar, personified abstractions, and a strident, almost hysterical quality in the tone. This failure of tone undercuts any conviction in the sentiment; we feel that Coleridge is posing, and there is almost a possibility that some actual sense of guilt is being covered up, not the attempt at a business-like deflation of impassioned climax in the preceeding lines ('Was it right . . .?'), but in the attack on retirement in the last lines of the quoted passage. Certainly, the distinction between the 'slothful loves and dainty sympathies' of 'The sluggard Pity's vision-weaving tribe' (with poets apparently amongst them), and Coleridge's own 'feelings all too delicate for use', is rather fine. Coleridge's personal security, in the esteem of his audience, is threatened, by a spill-over effect in the vehemence of his attack on the wrong kind of retirement. His kind was all right (it has taken him back into society, after all) in its own terms: 'I was constrain'd to quit you' does not necessarily imply anything wrong in the scenes that are left; if anything, the implication is regretful. Coleridge loses control of the style simultaneously with the movement of the poem's address out from the private audience of retirement, to a public audience; the social dimension of retirement introduces the necessity for a public rhetoric that Coleridge is too nervous, personally and politically, to sustain. He meets exactly the same difficulty in *Fears in Solitude* (where he copes with it a little more successfully); it had already emerged as a difficulty in the conversational idiom, in *The Eolian Harp*. He will avoid the public dimension altogether in *This Lime-Tree Bower my Prison, Frost at Midnight,* and *The Nightingale.*

The audience that Coleridge intends for *Reflections* is never quite clear. In the poem, Coleridge seems to be talking primarily to the scene of retirement itself. But the poem expresses a resolution for public commitment to the problems of society; it was a resolution that Coleridge found it impossible to maintain in fact, and in the poem too he cannot carry off the frank statement of his social ideals. They evaporate into third-rate oratory. Colridge first published *Reflections* in the *Monthly Magazine*, but even before an audience of fellow dissenters and radicals he played nervously with an apologetic title: 'Reflections on entering into active life. A Poem which affects not to be Poetry.' Coleridge was worried that the conversational idiom would not impress favourably as 'poetry' in the received public sense of contemporary fashion. We have already seen how the bright Tories of the *Anti-Jacobin* seized on the opportunity to ridicule the levelling implications in a diction and rhythm nearer to ordinary speech than 'the language of the classical and neo-classical models. In *Reflections*, it is exactly at the moment of commitment to society that his poetic language lapses into turgid conventions of approved practice.

*Reflections* is not a total failure. In the first half of the poem Coleridge achieves the characteristic qualities of the conversational style, but he also suffers a sobering lesson in the limits of that style, which were indeed co-extensive with the social limits of retirement itself. In the 1797 *Poems*, he changed the title to focus attention back onto the retirement, and away from 'active life'. He also introduced a motto from Horace, *'Sermoni Propriora' (Satire* I, iv, 1.42; the error of *'propriora'* for *'propiora'* stayed in all subsequent editions).[34] The Latin tag was conventionally applied to verse that took as its subject some aspect of public or political life that was not properly, in the received sense, a subject for poetry at all.[35] And Coleridge took care after 1796 to assume a private and specified audience as a function of the rhetoric of his best conversation poems.

## THIS LIME-TREE BOWER MY PRISON

On 7 July 1797, Charles Lamb arrived in Nether Stowey for a week's holiday with Coleridge and his family. The Wordsworths were already there, and efforts were made to bring Poole and Cottle into the party.[1] But the party was a little spoilt for Coleridge, as he explained to Southey in introduction to *This Lime-Tree Bower my Prison*:

> Charles Lamb has been with me for a week—he left me Friday morning.— / The second day after Wordworth came to me, dear Sara accidently emptied a skillet of boiling milk on my foot, which confined me during the whole time of C. Lamb's stay & still prevents me from all *walks* longer than a furlong.—While Wordsworth, his Sister, & C. Lamb were out one evening; / sitting in the arbour of T. Poole's garden, which communicates with mine, I wrote these lines, with which I am pleased—
>
> (*CL*,i,334)

The emerging strain in Coleridge's marriage is implicit in that 'dear Sara'; Sara no doubt showed up badly beside the newly arrived Dorothy Wordsworth, who had impressed Coleridge: 'Her information various—her eye watchful in minutest observation of nature—and her taste a perfect electrometer' (*CL*,i,330-31). Coleridge's own eye for the minute details of nature clearly grew more watchful under the influence of Dorothy and her brother, and the poem that he wrote during their stay with Lamb displays a new keenness of visual awareness. *This Lime-Tree Bower* also manifests a fresh intensity in the potential of Coleridge's ideal retirement, which may perhaps have developed in part out of a growing sense of the

actual shortcomings in his domestic life, the irritations that
were to loom large in his life with Sara. We have noticed
already that Coleridge's most cherished ideals intensified in
their appeal as they became more difficult actually to sustain in
reality.

The text of *This Lime-Tree Bower* that Coleridge included in
his letter to Southey of 7 July 1797 underwent considerable
revision before its eventual publication in Southey's *Annual
Anthology* of 1800. Coleridge sent an intermediate version to
Charles Lloyd, in a letter which is now lost, but which is quoted
in the notes to James Dykes Campbell's edition of the poems.[2]
It is obvious that *This Lime-Tree Bower*, in its finished form, was
not dashed down by Coleridge as he waited for his friends to
return from their walk. At least part of the poem was worked
up from a verse fragment written by Coleridge more than a
year earlier; the Gutch notebook contains these lines, dated by
Kathleen Coburn around March 1796:

> The Sun (for now his Orb Gan slowly sink)
> Shot half his rays aslant the heath, whose flowers
> Purpled the mountain's broad & level top,
> Rich was his bed of Clouds: & wide beneath
> Expecting Ocean smiled with dimpled face.[3]

This fragment provided Coleridge with a basis for six lines of
*This Lime-Tree Bower:*

> Ah! slowly sink
> Behind the western ridge, thou glorious Sun!
> Shine in the slant beams of the sinking orb,
> Ye purple heath-flowers! richlier burn, ye clouds!
> Live in the yellow light, yet distant groves!
> And kindle, thou blue Ocean!
>
> (ll.32-37)

But this is not the only clue to Coleridge's careful realisation
of a pre-meditated design in the poem; H.W. Piper has pointed
out the relationship between *This Lime-Tree Bower*, and Words-
worth's *Lines left upon a Seat in a Yew-Tree*,[4] a poem which was
first published in the 1798 *Lyrical Ballads* (placed after *The
Ancient Mariner* and *The Foster Mother's Tale*, and immediately
before *The Nightingale*), but which Wordsworth had started

possibly while still at school. It is probable that Wordsworth composed most of the poem in its first published form early in 1797.[5] There is an obvious similarity of phrasing in the two poems; Wordsworth's *Lines* describe how a lonely figure in retirement finds certain experiences of nature overwhelming:

> And lifting up his head, he then would gaze
> On the more distant scene; how lovely 'tis
> Thou seest, and he would gaze till it became
> Far lovelier, and his heart could not sustain
> The beauty still more beauteous.

(ll.30-34)

Coleridge's poem appears deliberately to recall these lines, in the climax to the second verse paragraph. There is an identical development of response to the distant landscape, from the beautiful to the intensely beautiful; and the repetition of 'gaze' in both passages is particularly suggestive:

> So my friend
> Struck with deep joy may stand, as I have stood,
> Silent with swimming sense; yea, gazing round
> On the wide landscape, gaze till all doth seem
> Less gross than bodily; and of such hues
> As veil the Almighty Spirit, when yet he makes
> Spirits perceive his presence.

(ll.37-43)

It may be that Coleridge is slipping in a graceful compliment to his visitor in this reminiscence; he certainly made no secret of his admiration for Wordsworth's *Lines*,[6] and there is another passage in *This Lime-Tree Bower* that seems an acknowledgement of Wordsworths's influence:

> I have lost
> Beauties and feelings, such as would have been
> Most sweet to my remembrance even when age
> Had dimm'd mine eyes to blindness!

(ll.2-5)

These lines were not in the earliest surviving version that Coleridge sent to Southey, though, and it is reasonable to assume that the references to Worsworth are carefully placed in *This Lime-Tree Bower*, and have a more important function in the poem than merely verbal reminiscence.

Coleridge's period of close friendship with the Wordsworths began in Nether Stowey. He had entered on the period of happiness in a closed, familial community, living in retirement, that constituted, as we have seen, his most successful attempt to establish the kind of community that Pantisocracy would have involved. Wordsworth's *Lines left upon a Seat in a Yew-tree* would have had a special interest for Coleridge, as they are about a man, gifted with 'no common soul', who has turned from the 'neglect' of the world to a self-absorbed retirement:

> In youth, by genius nurs'd,
> And big with lofty views, he to the world
> Went forth, pure in his heart, against the taint
> Of dissolute tongues, 'gainst jealousy, and hate,
> And scorn, against all enemies prepared,
> All but neglect: and so, his spirit damped
> At once, with rash disdain he turned away,
> And with the food of pride sustained his soul
> In solitude.—Stranger! these gloomy boughs
> Had charms for him; and here he loved to sit,
> His only visitants a straggling sheep,
> The stone-chat, or the glancing sand-piper;
> And on these barren rocks, with juniper,
> And heath, and thistle, thinly sprinkled o'er,
> Fixing his downward eye, he many an hour
> A morbid pleasure nourished, tracing here
> An emblem of his own unfruitful life.
>
> (ll. 12-29)

These lines are followed by the vision of a 'distant scene', more beautiful than the lonely man's heart can 'sustain', that seems to be invoked in *This Lime-Tree Bower*. And then Wordsworth's poem considers the response to nature in terms that Coleridge must have found particularly striking (he had been working on *Reflections* in the early months of 1797, for inclusion in the second edition of his *Poems*):

> Nor, that time,
> Would he forget those beings, to whose minds,
> Warm from the labours of benevolence,
> The world, and man himself, appeared a scene

> Of kindred loveliness: then he would sigh
> With mournful joy, to think that others felt
> What he must never feel: and so, lost man!
> On visionary views would fancy feed,
> Till his eyes streamed with tears. In this deep vale
> He died, this seat his only monument.

(ll.34-43)

The final verse paragraph of Wordsworth's poem moves powerfully into condemnation of a consciousness that is wilfully closed to the influence of nature; the most serious failure that follows from this is a failure to realise the love that 'true knowledge' leads to:

> The man, whose eye
> Is ever on himself, doth look on one,
> The least of nature's works, one who might move
> The wise man to that scorn which wisdom holds
> Unlawful, ever. O, be wiser thou!
> Instructed that true knowledge leads to love,
> True dignity abides with him alone
> Who, in the silent hour of inward thought,
> Can still suspect, and still revere himself,
> In lowliness of heart.

(ll.51-60)

Wordsworth has made explicit the quality of this 'love' as a state of mind to which 'The world, and man himself' may appear 'a scene/Of kindred loveliness', which may inspire 'the labours of benevolence'. *This Lime-Tree Bower* enacts the development from retirement, in its apparent loneliness, its introspective, limiting oppression, to the 'joy' that asserts connectedness, and enables an enlivening and creative response to 'the wide landscape'. Coleridge's poem uncovers the potential in his domestic retirement, and it is possible that it does so partly in response to the condemnation of his commitment to the 'deep vale' that he may have considered implicit in *Lines left upon a Seat in a Yew-tree*.[7]

Coleridge achieves a more dramatic representation of the potential in retirement, in *This Lime-Tree Bower,* by accentuating the movement of expansion, from the particular and the private to an assertion of values that could transcend the narrow limits of their basis, a movement that had also defined the rhetorical structure of *The Eolian Harp*. The ascending development of tone becomes more striking because it now begins at a level of emotional and intellectual activity that is noticeably lower in pitch. *The Eolian Harp* begins with a descriptive passage that hints at the melancholy so often associated with nature at twilight; Coleridge observes the clouds 'that late were rich with light', but avoids the inference of fading glory that could lead to thoughts of death. The clouds are 'slow-sadd'ning round', but again the potential ambiguity in the epithet (the clouds sadden in appearance, and simultaneously sadden the observer) is ignored, for Coleridge insists on the positivity his circumstances can yield, and insists also that the experience of nature need not take him beyond sense; the sources of his happiness are in sensory experience, and the values that he is moving towards encompass the physical world. The appearance of the evening star does not function as an invitation beyond sense, as it had done in the early sonnet *To the Evening Star* that Coleridge incorporated details from into the opening of *The Eolian Harp*:

> On thee full oft with fixed eye I gaze
> Till I, methinks, all spirit seem to grow.
>
> (*PW*,i,16)

The opening of *This Lime-Tree Bower does* allow an initial dominance to the familiar mood of melancholy as evening falls on the natural scene, because this initial lowness of spirit provides a context for the upward movement of emotion and intellect that emerges more clearly, and more impressively, against a background at first much darker:

> Well, they are gone, and here must I remain,
> This lime-tree bower my prison! I have lost
> Beauties and feelings, such as would have been
> Most sweet to my remembrance even when age
> Had dimm'd mine eyes to blindness! They, meanwhile,
> Friends, whom I never more may meet again,
> On springy heath, along the hill-top edge,
> Wander in gladness . . .
>
> (ll. 1-8)

Coleridge's depression is given quite a strong emphasis, strong enough almost to seem indulgently self-pitying, wilfully miserable. We remember Wordsworth's character in *Lines left upon a Seat*, seated amongst the 'gloomy boughs', where 'Fixing his downward eye',

> He many an hour
> A morbid pleasure nourished, tracing here
> An emblem of his own unfruitful life.
>
> (ll. 27-29)

Coleridge thinks of the bower as a prison; there is a maudlin disposition to dwell on the attractions of the experiences he will miss, abandoned by friends whom he quite unreasonably fears that he 'may never meet again'. The verse itself at first suggests a futile energy, an effort to pull himself together that Coleridge has no real heart in, and which ends abruptly with a helpless gesture towards the unanswerable constraint of his circumstances: 'This lime-tree bower my prison!' The movement then slackens to a relaxed measure that we recognise from *The Eolian Harp*, but gradually quickens as Coleridge exercises an increasingly tight control over the caesural pauses, stronger and more frequent, which ascends to a new steadiness, by the end of the first verse paragraph, that confirms Coleridge's new level of mood, now receptive and potentially creative, with its concomitant capacity for intellectual strength.

By line 20, Coleridge has lifted himself out of the poem's dark beginning, and is ready to move into the affirmations of the second and third verse paragraphs. The reciprocal action of mood and intellect that characterises the ascending tonal pitch of the poem reflects a special quality of Coleridge's experience, that we meet from time to time in the notebooks. He could sometimes seize on a given set of particulars, and so construe them as to initiate an extraordinary burst of mental energy that transforms those particulars, and also his own mood. An entry in the Gutch notebook demonstrates the action of this energy:

> Misfortunes prepare the heart for the enjoyment of Happiness in a better state. Life & sorrows of a religious & benevolent man is as its April Day— (his pains & sorrows fertilizing rain)—the Sunshine blends with every shower—and look! how full and lovely it lies on yonder hills![8]

The note anticipates Coleridge's affirmation, later in *This Lime-Tree Bower*, of his capacity to 'lift the soul', and to experience a 'lively joy' in the contemplation of an ideal joy, an envisaged, imaginable joy that, in the terms of actual experience, 'we cannot share'. Coleridge's joy is a joy of the possible, the potential; and it is always bound up, in his poetry, with his ideal community of friends and family in retirement. Coleridge's joy in *This Lime-Tree Bower* is realised vicariously through his imaginative creation of what his friends experience on their walk.

There is no doubt that Coleridge's depression in the opening lines of the poem is a controlled rhetorical effect. It is in fact rather overdone in the version sent to Southey—the self-pity is almost laughably exaggerated—and the passage in which Coleridge first follows his friends out on their walk is too brief; there is not enough scope for the tone properly to develop:

> Well—they are gone: and here must I remain,
> Lam'd by the scathe of fire, lonely & faint,
> This lime-tree bower my prison. They, meantime,
> My friends, whom I may never meet again,
> On springy heath, along the hill-top edge,
> Wander delighted, and look down, perchance,
> On that same rifted Dell, where many an Ash
> Twists its wild limbs beside the ferny rock,
> Whose plumy ferns for ever nod and drip
> Spray'd by the waterfall.
>
> (*CL*,i,334-35)

The Lloyd version is very close to this text, except that Coleridge has dropped the over-statement of 'Lam'd by the scathe of fire, lonely & faint';[9] but in the first published text Coleridge achieves perfectly the transition from maudlin introspection to an excited awareness of the positive experience offered by nature for his friends:

> They, meanwhile,
> My Friends, whom I may never meet again
> On springy heath, along the hill-top edge,
> Wander in gladness, and wind down, perchance,
> To that still roaring dell, of which I told;
> The roaring dell, o'erwooded, narrow, deep,
> And only speckled by the mid-day sun;

> Where its slim trunk the ash from rock to rock
> Flings arching like a bridge;—that branchless ash,
> Unsunn'd and damp, whose few poor yellow leaves
> Ne'er tremble in the gale, yet tremble still,
> Fann'd by the water-fall! and there my friends
> Behold the dark green file of long lank weeds,
> That all at once (a most fantastic sight!)
> Still nod and drip beneath the dripping edge
> Of the dim clay-stone.[10]

The language of natural description is at once minute in observation, and exactly expressive of Coleridge's developing mood, with its emerging potential to register a pervasive unity between phenomena, and between natural phenomena and the perceiving self. One significant feature of this text is Coleridge's obviously deliberate introduction of the word 'still', here used three times in twelve lines. The opposite connotations of the word, 'fixed, unmoving', but also 'ever, continually', underpin the development in Coleridge's mood from static, barren introspection, to the dynamic growth in consciousness that is effected in the description of an imagined experience. This development is implicit in almost every detail. There is, firstly, just the suggestion of a qualification of the morbid anticipation that Coleridge may never again meet his friends, because as the sentence unfolds there is at least the possibility that it is only *there*, on the heath, and the hill-top edge, that they may not visit again together. The descent into the roaring dell picks up Coleridge's mood, that is to say, he projects his inner darkness onto the scene in which he imagines his friends to be. But the intensity and increasing excitement of the visualisation lifts the tone up from darkness, and issues in the fascinated contemplation ('a most fantastic sight!') of a scene from which Lamb and the Wordsworths can then be conceived by Coleridge to emerge, into the wide view, beneath an open sky. This emergence is also a sudden entry into silence, that signal, in the conversation poems, of heightened receptivity, from the 'roaring' of the dell. There is a revealed connectedness in the structure of the dell itself, pointed deftly in the bridging tree that Coleridge's syntax actually throws across the line-ending:

> . . . its slim trunk the ash from rock to rock
> Flings arching like a bridge . . ..
>
> (ll. 12-13)

And the initial absence of light, 'only speckled by the mid-day sun',[11] 'unsunn'd', is counteracted by a striking emphasis on colour that Coleridge returns to later in the poem. The 'branchless ash' is perhaps suggestive of Coleridge himself, in his melancholy and abandoned aspect of the poem's opening. That aspect of Coleridge is supplanted by the new mood into which he has developed through the descriptive passage in the first verse paragraph, just as the ash-tree takes on a different kind of significance from its connective function in the context of the whole natural scene.

The poem now moves out, with Coleridge's imagination of his friends' journey, to a wider view, that is yet bound to the image of the dell by its unity, revealed in the descriptive language as essentially a unity of visual design:

> Now, my friends emerge
> Beneath the wide wide Heaven—and view again
> The many-steepled tract magnificent
> Of hilly fields and meadows, and the sea,
> With some fair bark, perhaps, whose sails light up[12]
> The slip of smooth clear blue betwixt two Isles
> Of purple shadow!
>
> (ll. 20-26)

The newly realised potential in Coleridge's state of mind is co-extensive with the progressive widening of horizons on his imagined journey; here, the horizon is all but boundless, and Coleridge can proceed to claim an encompassing vision of unity in nature that is also a tacit assertion of his common experience that is shared with Charles Lamb. Lamb and Coleridge are merged into a single consciousness; their past, with its deprivations, is held in common, and now Coleridge envisages Lamb's rich pleasure in the sunset with a degree of intensity (the intensity of response is suggested in the intensity of light reflected and radiated from the sun) that physical presence could not surpass:

> Yes! they wander on
> In gladness all; but thou, methinks, most glad,

> My gentle-hearted Charles! for thou hast pined
> And hunger'd after Nature, many a year,
> In the great City pent, winning thy way
> With sad yet patient soul, through evil and pain
> And strange calamity! Ah! slowly sink
> Behind the western ridge, thou glorious Sun!
> Shine in the slant beams of the sinking orb,
> Ye purple heath-flowers! richlier burn, ye clouds!
> Live in the yellow light, ye distant groves!
> And kindle, thou blue Ocean!

(ll.26-37)

The city, with its inescapable obstructions to the proper influence of nature, is now the truer prison; Lamb, like Coleridge as a schoolboy, has lived 'In the great City pent'. The sunset description is particularly interesting, in that it appears to prepare for a conviction that the landscape is independantly *alive*; 'Live in the yellow light', 'kindle, thou blue Ocean'. Again, it is clear that Coleridge's response is still developing; his mood, with its given level of intellectual activity, is constantly arriving at new possibilities in the meaning of his experience. The sunset, it may be, confers on the landscape an appearance of independent life, under the rapidly changing effects of light. But this immediately changes, in the earliest version of the poem, to an assertion that the landscape is indeed alive. And yet the context of this assertion, with its assumption of objective and universal validity, points to a conception of the landscape that insists on the relative and provisional status of Coleridge's judgements. The poem's opening carries an equal authority in expressing an almost antithetical conviction. Still, the climax of vision, in the version sent to Southey, claims an autonomous life for the landscape:

> So my friend
> Struck with joy's deepest calm, and gazing round
> On the wide view, may gaze till all doth seem
> Less gross than bodily, a living Thing
> That acts upon the mind, and with such hues
> As cloathe the Almighty Spirit, when he makes
> Spirits perceive His presence!

(*PW*,i,335)

The precise character of Coleridge's philosophical position in these lines is very difficult to establish. A note in the Southey letter to the phrase 'the wide view', 'You remember, I am a *Berkleian*', is too vague to be of much use, and though Coleridge may certainly have had in mind something he had read in Berkeley, in the quoted passage, the poem as a whole simply does not provide an adequate context for precision of a technical kind in the question of philosophy. One critic has remarked of Coleridge's note that it

> asks us to look outside the poem to a philosophical system for understanding. Instead of appearing to be the form in which an experience is realized, the lines seem rather an attempt to translate prior philosophical concepts into the terms of an experience.[13]

This is a fair comment on Coleridge's note, which indeed implies a lack of confidence in the language of the poem as an adequate expression of a 'Berkleian' position. We could read this position into the poem; Berkeley's *Theory of Vision* (1709) had described how the individual spirit perceives the spirit of God, just as it perceives other spirits, by an assumption of the *animus mundi* that is necessary to render intelligible the existence of things not perceived by any finite mind, and changes in things which are not produced by any finite agency. Coleridge's careful attention to colour in *This Lime-Tree Bower* might support such a reading. But there are confusions in the poem that do not encourage the search for a coherent philosophy. The repetition of 'spirits' does not help, where the word must clearly mean two separate things in each usage; Coleridge may mean by 'Almighty Spirit' the divine as it appears in nature, and then the second spirit would refer to such spirits as Lamb and Coleridge himself. But the usage in fact appears to be metaphorical; the response of Lamb and Coleridge to the landscape is *like* the response of 'spirits' to a manifestation of 'the Almighty Spirit'. William Empson, introducing his choice of the text in the Southey letter for his selection of Coleridge's verse, chooses the second alternative, with its implication of 'spirit' in the sense of the neoplatonists, as a being somewhere between man and God in the scale of things:

> When he wrote it, he meant that the spirits of Nature see God
> fairly often, but only in the passive way that we men see
> spirits—that is, when they choose to become visible.[14]

This reading could be supported by Coleridge's phrase 'Less
gross than bodily', where 'gross', signifying that which is thicker
than spiritual substance, would imply a scale of being between
divine substance and material substance. But what then
becomes of Coleridge's allusion to Berkeley? Without that hint,
the passage might seem to arrive at a commonplace of
Christian contemplation; God manifests his glory in nature,
and Coleridge would have been familiar with the imagery of
clothing in this context from the *Psalms*.[15] It remains clear that
Coleridge is celebrating the recognition, which he shares with
Lamb, of an external influence on the mind that brings 'joy's
deepest calm'. There is nothing in the passage essentially
inconsistent with Coleridge's persisting interest in Hartley,
though his conception of the difficulties involved in
Associationism was undoubtedly sharpening, and his attempts
to account for the educative process implicit in perception grew
increasingly unmanageable in their complexity, their sense of
the problems. The text of the *Annual Anthology* introduced one
further confusion into the climactic passage of lines 37-43, and
this was a confusion of grammar:

> So my friend
> Struck with deep joy may stand, as I have stood,
> Silent with swimming sense; yea gazing round
> On the wide landscape, gaze till all doth seem
> Less gross than bodily, a living thing
> Which acts upon the mind and with such hues
> As cloathe the Almighty Spirit, when he makes
> Spirits perceive his presence.

> (*PW*,i,180)

The grammatical status of 'gaze' is uncertain; the mood may be
subjunctive, or imperative, and its subject may be Lamb, or
Coleridge. And this is Coleridge's *revision*, so that we would
expect a clarification, rather than further chaos in a passage
that was already quite sufficiently complex. But the revision
works, in terms of the poetic context; the whole poem has built
towards this climax of vision, and it is the sense of community,
between Coleridge and Lamb, between them both and the

landscape, that is important, and not the exact intellectual affiliation of the insight. The grammar now develops the implications of 'swimming sense', and the whole passage enacts a final intensity in the quality of vision by an actual blurring of contours, emotional, intellectual, even grammatical, that carries the ascent of tone to its highest pitch.

The poem now arrests this tonal ascent, with its widening of horizons, and returns to the particular context of Coleridge's garden bower in Nether Stowey. The potential of the limited, local, personal circumstances, that had seemed at first so disastrously limiting, can now emerge. The sunset that he had envisaged for his friends is now realised in the private context, and the silence that ushers in a higher insight ('silent with swimming sense') is present for Coleridge too, and broken by the tiny detail of auditory experience that testifies to new awareness:

> A delight
> Comes sudden on my heart, and I am glad
> As I myself were there! Nor in this bower,
> This little lime-tree bower, have I not mark'd
> Much that has sooth'd me. Pale beneath the blaze
> Hung the transparent foliage; and I watch'd
> Some broad and sunny leaf, and lov'd to see
> The shadow of the leaf and stem above
> Dappling its sunshine! And that walnut-tree
> Was richly ting'd, and a deep radiance lay
> Full on the ancient ivy, which usurps
> Those fronting elms, and now, with blackest mass
> Makes their dark branches gleam a lighter hue
> Through the late twilight: and though now the bat
> Wheels silent by, and not a swallow twitters,
> Yet still the solitary humble-bee
> Sings in the bean-flower!

>                                    (ll.43-59)

Coleridge has earned this state of mind, and his first acknowledgement of the change wrought in himself, 'and I am glad', recalls the state of mind he has projected onto his friends; 'They, meanwhile ... Wander in gladness', 'Yes! they wander on/In gladness all', 'thou, methinks, most glad,/My gentle-hearted Charles!'. Gladness and joy are clearly related in the poem, and it is very important to realise the basis of this

happiness that is generally recognised as a distinctive quality of
Coleridge's experience. It is a state of mind that is receptive to
the beauty in nature, and it is often associated with the process
by which this receptivity is displayed,. in the poetry that
registers a growth into that receptivity. The dazzling visual
complexity of Coleridge's description of the light in the bower,
its simple testimony to an informing presence in nature, is an
implicit celebration of the creative power that has emerged in
the poet's experience; the bower was always there, but to see
the unifying presence in its visual design implies something
conferred by the poet. The climax of the poem claims an
external divinity in nature that constitutes the highest form of
experience, but that knowledge is arrived at through a process
that throws the emphasis onto the creative power of the mind
itself.

The dual character of joy is fundamental in Coleridge's
poetry; it is a state of mind in which the poet feels himself at
one with the physical world, and the human community, but
this ultimate connectedness in things is the culmination of a
process that begins, for Coleridge, in a strictly local and
personal context, and a private and strictly limited community.
It is a condition that bears the whole pressure of Coleridge's
social experience, growing out of a retirement, an isolation,
that was at once enforced and adopted, at once a concession to
the superior power of reaction, and an assertion of the
potential in nature and private attachment. The possibilities
that Coleridge felt able to generate in the enforced limitations
of his early life emerge in a quiet confidence, and a courageous
acceptance of the only path to joy left open by his social
context:

> Henceforth I shall know
> That Nature ne'er deserts the wise and pure;
> No plot so narrow, be but Nature there,
> No waste so vacant, but may well employ
> Each faculty of sense, and keep the heart
> Awake to Love and Beauty! and sometimes
> 'Tis well to be bereft of promis'd good,
> That we may lift the soul, and contemplate
> With lively joy the joys we cannot share.
>
> (ll.59-67)

Coleridge wins through to this joy by a sustained act of sympathetic imagination, a determined effort to share in the experience of his friends, and the success of his effort holds out a promise of wider sympathies, a connectedness of the whole human community in its environment of nature. *This Lime-Tree Bower* closes on a beautiful dying fall, prepared for throughout the poem in the fading light of the sun, that returns to Lamb, to whom the whole poem has been addressed.[16] The rook provides one last connection in the experience of the two friends, a connection 'deemed' by Coleridge; the connections are there if we create them, and the optimism of this final assertion is counter-pointed by an eerie suggestion of possibilities closed down (it is 'the last rook') as the sun prepares to disappear:

> My gentle-hearted Charles! when the last rook
> Beat its straight path along the dusky air
> Homewards, I blest it! deeming its black wing
> (Now a dim speck, now vanishing in light)
> Had cross'd the mighty Orb's dilated glory,
> While thou stood'st gazing; or, when all was still,
> Flew creeking o'er thy head, and had a charm
> For thee, my gentle-hearted Charles, to whom
> No sound is dissonant which tells of Life

Again, the orchestration of sound and silence serves to discriminate between levels of awareness; Lamb, certainly the ideal figure of Coleridge's imagined journey in the poem, represents a consciousness 'Awake to Love and Beauty', open to the connectedness in things.

*This Lime-Tree my Prison* is an important poem. It shows us, with *Frost at Midnight*, the experience that was central to an emerging distance, in English culture, between the poet and his audience. Coleridge's joy finds its basis in a private community; the *Letter to Sara*, with its identification of joy as the condition on which experience depends for its positive significance, will associate joy, almost exclusively, with the small domestic community, of family and friends, that Coleridge had lost after Nether Stowey. The *Letter to Sara* uses the word 'joy' fourteen times; five occurrences are in the closing passage that begins

> O Sara! we receive but what we give,
> And in *our* Life alone does Nature live.

The remaining nine usages of the word all preceed these lines, and all relate to Coleridge's special happiness in the company of friends and loved ones, and his children. We have seen that 'joy' is associated throughout Coleridge's poetry with domesticity and retirement, and there is no doubt that the word had for him a positive and unmistakable resonance of security in personal relationship and a stable home. Coleridge learnt in the 1790s that he could turn only to this limited sphere in the effort to realise the values by which he sought to live. Society as a whole could no longer offer him a home.

## FROST AT MIDNIGHT

The conversation poems have most often been read in a context supplied by Coleridge's own later writings, critical and philosophical, that bear on his Christian account of the pervasive unity that he conceived to inform experience. The best commentaries on *This Lime-Tree Bower* and *Frost at Midnight* have employed a critical framework derived from Coleridge's later thought; usually, in fact, the endeavour has been to illustrate that thought by reference to the way in which the earlier poetry works.[1] This kind of approach, often valuable in its own terms, is not the present concern; the terms of the present discussion have been established in the context of Coleridge's contemporary social experience in the 1790s, although this does carry the implication that Coleridge's later thought, with its manifest relation to the earlier poetry, was determined to an unrecognised extent by the formative social experience of the nineties.

*Frost at Midnight* is dated 'February 1798' in E.H. Coleridge's edition of the poems, and the poem was undoubtedly written before Coleridge's trip to Germany. But Coleridge himself omitted this date from the last editions of his poetry that were published in his lifetime, and we can assume that he did so because the poem did not exist, in its received form, until 1829. His revisions of *Frost at Midnight* between its first appearance, in a quarto pamphlet together with *France: An Ode* and *Fears in Solitude* in 1798, and the text of the 1829 *Poetical Works* are more substantial than the changes he made in *This Lime-Tree*

*Bower* and *The Eolian Harp*. A reading of the poem in its contemporary context of 1798 might therefore seem inappropriate, because a number of the poem's distinctive effects do not emerge until some thirty years later. But while Coleridge's revisions consistently improve the design of the poem, they do not significantly affect the explicit theme, or the dominant atmosphere. The relation of *Frost at Midnight* to its context in Coleridge's experience of the 1790s is not obscured by later improvements in the text, and the discussion that follows will make reference to the final form of the poem, as it appears in E.H. Coleridge's edition.

*Frost at Midnight* begins in calm. A windless stillness, registered at once by the quiet movement of the verse, held back in two strong pauses, on 'ministry' and 'wind', is disturbed only by low sounds that alternate with silence, in a pattern familiar from *The Eolian Harp* and *This Lime-Tree Bower*:

> The Frost performs its secret ministry,
> Unhelped by any wind. The owlet's cry
> Came loud—and hark, again! loud as before.
> The inmates of my cottage, all at rest,
> Have left me to that solitude, which suits
> Abstruser musings: save that at my side
> My cradled infant slumbers peacefully.
>
> (ll. 1-7)

The diction carries an elusive resonance. The frost has something beautiful to make; 'ministry' implies the agency of the frost, its operation under a higher command, and its minute, unnoticeable action has an urgency, almost a fugitive quality, in the epithet 'secret'. 'Performs' subtly reinforces the sense of a task to be done, a task that is at once lonely and isolated, introspective and wary, and yet very important, full of potential and implication; like the task of a secret agent. 'Unhelped' sustains the implication of an absorbed, patient, solitary agency, hinting at something indomitable, a quiet insistence in the process that will create the patterns of the frost, out of the cold night. Coleridge does not mention the frost again until the very end of the poem, but the unstated identification of its action with his own activity in the poem needs no further emphasis. This connection is of a typical order, a function of the connective habit of mind displayed throughout the poem. The creative potential of the frost is finally uncovered in the end of the poem, like Coleridge's own creativity, emerged in its final form. But the necessary condition of this potential is darkness, a midnight solitude in which the development of tone, that forms the poem, may begin. *This Lime-Tree Bower* begins with a melancholy that is carefully placed in the rhetorical structure, and the effect is repeated in *Frost at Midnight*. Coleridge's relation to the objects of his experience is threatened. The 'owlet's cry' is a remote token of the outside world from which he is withdrawn, and Coleridge settles into the distracted, directionless self-absorption of one still thoughtfully awake, when his companions have fallen asleep. The 'abstruser musings' that preoccupy Coleridge distance him even from the sleeping child at his side, wrapped in an inaccessible serenity. And the calm that follows this loss of personal contact carries the threat of loneliness, of a stark separateness in human relations:

> 'Tis calm indeed! so calm, that it disturbs
> And vexes meditation with its strange
> And extreme silentness.
>
> (ll.8-10)

This is like the calm in *The Ancient Mariner*; there is the sense that Coleridge is foreign in his environment, that he has no place in it, and this faintly carries over the suggestions of 'secret ministry', as though Coleridge were a spy in an alien country, working alone, under cover, to change it for the better. The reality of Coleridge's introspective reverie is dominant over his context in the community, and in nature; and his displacement from that context, the self-isolating character of his consciousness of it, reduces the community and the place to a passive and unmeaning spectacle (like the effect of a silent film):

> Sea, hill, and wood,
> This populous village! Sea, and hill, and wood,
> With all the numberless goings-on of life,
> Inaudible as dreams!
>
> (ll.10-13)

But there is already a quickening excitement in the movement

of the verse, a direction that is offered by the very intensity of
Coleridge's self-awareness, the consciousness of his own isola-
tion. The 'populous village', the 'numberless goings-on', are
like an invitation to participate, to create the connectedness
that is wanting. M.H. Abrams has noticed 'the rhythm of the
seemingly unnoticed breathing of a sleeping infant' that
informs the movement of the poem,[2] but this rhythm is not
constant, because in *Frost at Midnight*, as in the other conversa-
tion poems, slight variations in the pace of the verse, effected
by the weight and placing of pauses in the caesurae and at
line-endings, control the gradual ascent of tone which registers
Coleridge's characteristic interaction of thought and emotion.
The new excitement in Coleridge's consciousness, a restlessness
that is positive rather than constrained, is registered overtly in
the exclamation marks after 'village' and 'dreams', more subtly
in the intensified deliberateness in the repetition of 'Sea, and
hill, and wood'. The growth into connective consciousness
begins in Coleridge's awareness of constraint, the limited
circumstances of his small cottage in Nether Stowey. By
building a relationship with these circumstances he will gener-
ate the capacity to find a greater unity, encompassing a general
connectedness between men, between man and nature, bet-
ween present, past, and future. The matrix of this unity is
Coleridge's retirement.

The dark, uneasy mood persists, but it fades as the creative
impulse gains in strength. Coleridge's very unquietness sup-
plies the way to positive awareness, because he finds for it 'a
companionable form':

> the thin blue flame
> Lies on my low-burnt fire, and quivers not;
> Only that film which fluttered on the grate,
> Still flutters there, the sole unquiet thing.
> Methinks, its motion in this hush of nature
> Gives it dim sympathies with me who live,
> Making it a companionable form,
> Whose puny flaps and freaks the idling Spirit
> By its own moods interprets, every where
> Echo or mirror seeking of itself,
> And makes a toy of Thought.

(ll. 13-24)

Coleridge's low spirits, like the 'low-burnt fire', are enlivened by the image of his consciousness offered in the motion of the film on the grate; and just as the rook in the closing lines of *This Lime-Tree Bower* had been 'deemed' a confirmation of Coleridge's unity with his friends, so this too is a conferred unity. The positive impulse of Coleridge's awareness, 'me-thinks', is what 'gives' the object of experience its 'dim sympathies'. This unifying awareness is still frail, as it is the 'puny' and intermittent quality of the film with which Coleridge identifies. And the unity is clearly not discovered but made, because the image is of the kind produced by an 'echo or mirror', a passive reflex. The poem will later affirm the external reality of the image, something to discover rather than make, in its celebration of the 'eternal language' that God 'utters' in nature. But the creative and defining power of the mind is implicit in the development of thought and emotion that leads to this affirmation. The 'toy' that Coleridge makes of thought, by the close of the verse paragraph, enables a relieving lightness of tone, a sense that the threatening element in his solitude is mastered, and that his musings have now the innocent creativity of a child's play. The movement back to his own schooldays, then back to the present and his baby Hartley, then forward to the future childhood of his son, is thus prepared for, delicately foreshadowed, in the preceeding movement of thought.

Humphrey House, whose comments on *Frost at Midnight* still remain amongst the best accounts of the poem, has pointed out that lines 13-24 in particular, and the whole of the first verse paragraph in general, display a 'most striking likeness' to a passage in the fourth book of William Cowper's *The Task*.[3] There is no need to rehearse the similarities and differences between the two poems, which are fully discussed by House; lines 286-310 of 'The Winter Evening' describe Cowper's habit of firegazing, and he mentions the 'stranger', and an 'indolent vacuity of thought', and the frost outside. In Cowper's poem 'the fancy weaves / Her brittle toys'. The tone is playful, relaxed, and unserious, and the description does not lead to anything that bears a further similarity to *Frost at Midnight*. Professor Fruman has argued for Coleridge's plagiarism in the matter of these similarities, but this is not really the kind of

activity that is at issue.⁴ Coleridge would have found a great
deal to admire in the fourth book of Cowper's poem, during
the winter of 1797-1798, in the cottage at Nether Stowey;
before Cowper's poem turns to its description of the firegazing,
that was undoubtedly in Coleridge's mind when he began *Frost
at Midnight*, there is an account of the particular pleasures that
winter brings:

> Thou hold'st the sun
> A pris'ner in the yet undawning east,
> Short'ning his journey between morn and noon,
> And hurrying him, impatient of his stay,
> Down to the rosy west; but kindly still
> Compensating his loss with added hours
> Of social converse and instructive ease,
> And gath'ring, at short notice, in one group
> The family dispers'd, and fixing thought,
> Not less dispers'd by day-light and its cares.
> I crown thee king of intimate delights,
> Fire-side enjoyments, home-born happiness,
> And all the comforts that the lowly roof
> Of undisturb'd retirement, and the hours
> Of long uninterrupted evening, know.
>                    ('The Winter Evening', ll. 129-143)

This kind of domestic security in retirement underpins
Cowper's happiness by his fireside, and would have appealed
most strongly to Coleridge's own conviction of the value in
secure retirement. *Frost at Midnight* takes off from a basis
provided in Cowper's poem, just as *Reflections on having left a
Place of Retirement* and *This Lime-Tree Bower*, appear to start in
Coleridge's response to the work and ideas of another. The
*Letter to Sara* has a similar basis, in Wordsworth's *Immortality
Ode;* and Coleridge's creative derivativeness must be regarded
as a literary equivalent of his dependency on others for
happiness and stability, the potential that he was able to
develop out of what he felt to be a sympathetic audience.

Professor Fruman has shown that the earliest version of
lines 13-24 in *Frost at Midnight* is even closer, in details of
phrasing, to Cowper's poem. The original version is less
satisfactory because the self-consciousness is too overt, too
much an attempt to account for the process of thought that is
involved. Max Schulz has argued that Coleridge's succeeding

versions of the passage are increasingly less explicit;[5] the poem's final subtlety depends on a pervasive understatement in the way that connections are established, so that Coleridge's developing consciousness is manifest in the unity that it makes of experience. At first, the poem was too concerned to assert rather than demonstrate

> Methinks, its motion in this hush of nature
> Gives it dim sympathies with me who live,
> Making it a companionable form,
> With which I can hold commune. Idle thought!
> But still the living spirit in our frame,
> That loves not to behold a lifeless thing,
> Transfuses into all its own delights,
> Its own volition, sometimes with deep faith
> And sometimes with fantastic playfulness.
> Ah me! amus'd by no such curious toys
> Of the self-watching subtilizing mind,
> How often in my early school-boy days
> With most believing superstitious wish,
> Presageful, have I gazed upon the bars . . . .[6]

The revisions that were incorporated into this passage when the poem appeared in the *Poetical Register* of 1808-9 merely compound the impression of random speculation, and Coleridge did not begin to move towards the more suggestive restraint of the final version until *Sibylline Leaves:*

> Methinks, its motion in this hush of nature
> Gives it dim sympathies with me who live,
> Making it a companionable form,
> To which the living spirit in our frame,
> That loves not to behold a lifeless thing,
> Transfuses its own pleasures, its own will,
> And makes a toy of Thought.[7]

But this too says more than is necessary, and reduces the effect of spontaneous development which contributes an unobtrusive delicacy of form to the poem, the apparent effortlessness of its unfolding. The received text that first appeared in 1829 achieves the proper balance of meditation and reflection, a balance which supports the ascending interaction of experience and response through which the poem takes on its shape.

In the second verse paragraph, Coleridge turns from the

particular time and place of the poem's opening, to a memory
of his childhood:

> But O! how oft,
> How oft, at school, with most believing mind,
> Presageful, have I gazed upon the bars,
> To watch that fluttering *stranger!* and as oft
> With unclosed lids, already had I dreamt
> Of my sweet birth-place, and the old church-tower,
> Whose bells, the poor man's only music, rang
> So sweetly, that they stirred and haunted me
> With a wild pleasure, falling on mine ear
> Most like articulate sounds of things to come!
> So gazed I, till the soothing things, I dreamt,
> Lulled me to sleep, and sleep prolonged my dreams!
>
> (ll.23-35)

The lines establish an unexpected continuity in Coleridge's
experience; it is as if the enlivening realisation of 'dim
sympathies' between poet and flame was indeed simply the
confirmation of an existing relationship, something discovered,
and not made, after all. The 'stranger' points to a continuity in
time, relating Coleridge's memory, in his cottage, of a moment
in childhood, to the child Coleridge's memory, in school, of a
still earlier moment. And as this unity in experience emerges,
so the poem simultaneously telescopes out in range; a long
receding temporal perspective is quite suddenly introduced in
the memory within a memory, which will also become a
forward temporal perspective as Coleridge contrasts his past
childhood with the future childhood that awaits Hartley. A
connectedness is thus suggested, not only in the continuity
between Coleridge and his earlier self, but between his present
self and the sleeping baby at his side. As the unifying impulse
in consciousness strengthens, so the apparently discrete ele-
ments in experience multiply and lead to a constantly more
comprehensive unity. The threatening solitude of Coleridge's
cottage at midnight is now revealed as a condition of his whole
life, which is implied in the superstition of the 'stranger' itself;
earlier versions of the poem had carried a note to the phrase
'only that film', which explained the superstition:

> In all parts of the kingdom these films are called *strangers* and
> are supposed to portend the arrival of some absent friend.
>
> (*PW*,i,240)

The absence of relatedness has provided a context for
Coleridge's gradual heightening of awareness, that begins in
the first verse paragraph with that very 'stranger' traditionally
held to portend the imminent breaking of loneliness. Col-
eridge's memory, in the second verse paragraph, is now
working to account for that initial, threatening solitude; its
sources are in the past, in the original failure to draw
nourishment from a secure childhood in nature. The schoolboy
memory of an earlier childhood, a dream of 'soothing things',
creates a fleeting image of the lost potential in the fatally
damaging estrangement from the rural community of his
birth-place and family home:

> . . . my sweet birth-place, and the old church-tower
> Whose bells, the poor man's only music, rang
> From morn to evening, all the hot Fair-day,
> So sweetly, they they stirred and haunted me
> With a wild pleasure, falling on mine ear
> Most like articulate sounds of things to come!

Here, in Coleridge's Hartleian terms, were the sources of
positive relation to the community; in private attachment, and
the direct experience of nature. But the London schoolboy was
cut off from these bases of happiness:

> So gazed I, till the soothing things, I dreamt,
> Lulled me to sleep, and sleep prolonged my dreams!
> And so I brooded all the following morn,
> Awed by the stern preceptor's face, mine eye
> Fixed with mock study on my swimming book:
> Save if the door half opened, and I snatched
> A hasty glance, and still my heart leaped up,
> For still I hoped to see the *stranger's* face,
> Townsman, or aunt, or sister more beloved,
> My play-mate when we both were clothed alike!
>
> (ll. 34-43)

The classical austerity of 'preceptor' will be contrasted with the
teacher that Coleridge intends for Hartley, the 'Great universal
Teacher' of God, working through 'The lovely shapes and
sounds intelligible' of nature. And Coleridge's determination
properly to nurture his son's developing consciousness con-
trasts, more tragically, with the sad deprivation implicit in his

own boyhood hope if a visit from some relative, perhaps from the sister to whom he had once been so close.

But the self-knowledge that Coleridge's heightened awareness has brought does not issue in bitterness; the third verse paragraph turns to anticipate Hartley's future with a serene confidence. Coleridge will realise his own lost potential in the development of his son's consciousness:

> Dear Babe, that sleepest cradled by my side,
> Whose gentle breathings, heard in this deep calm,
> Fill up the interspersèd vacancies
> And momentary pauses of the thought!
> My babe so beautiful! it thrills my heart
> With tender gladness, thus to look at thee,
> And think that thou shalt learn far other lore,
> And in far other scenes! For I was reared
> In the great city, pent 'mid cloisters dim,
> And saw nought lovely but the sky and stars.
> But *thou*, my babe! shalt wander like a breeze
> By lakes and sandy shores, beneath the crags
> Of ancient mountain, and beneath the clouds,
> Which image in their bulk both lakes and shores
> And mountain crags: so shalt thou see and hear
> The lovely shapes and sounds intelligible
> Of that eternal language, which thy God
> Utters, who from eternity doth teach
> Himself in all, and all things in himself.
> Great universal Teacher! he shall mould
> Thy spirit, and by giving make it ask.
>
> (ll.44-64)

Again, as in *This Lime-Tree Bower*, Coleridge has won 'gladness' through a realisation of the potential in his small circle of family and friends. The sympathetic identification that he achieves with them transforms the constraint of retirement into a basis for positive and unifying awareness, that can accommodate the whole range of experience. *Frost at Midnight* steadily increases the range of its temporal and spatial perspectives, until the poem arrives at a level of tone that may sustain the serene confidence in God's controlling influence that is celebrated in the closing lines of the third verse paragraph. The 'deep calm' no longer 'disturbs / And vexes meditation', but rather allows Hartley's 'gentle breathings' to emerge as a rhythmic complement to Coleridge's movements of thought.

The conviction in the healing agency of nature, contrasted with
the 'great city' in which Coleridge had been imprisoned ('pent'),
will be substantiated in the context that domestic retirement
offers for Hartley. And his future experience will be a type of
the unobtrusive reciprocity, the 'dim sympathies', that Col-
eridge has uncovered in the poem. The 'mirror' that has been
discovered in the 'stranger', the intensifying, inter-reflective
quality in Coleridge's distinctive complementary development
of thought and emotion, has foreshadowed the revelation of a
universal reciprocity, in nature, and between nature and man:

> . . . *thou*, my babe! shalt wander like a breeze
> By lakes and sandy shores, beneath the crags
> Of ancient mountain, and beneath the clouds,
> Which image in their bulk both lakes and shores
> And mountain crags . . ..
>
> (ll.54-58)

This climactic vision does not take Coleridge beyond sense; the
emphasis on colour in *This Lime-Tree Bower* insists on the basis
of Coleridge's optimism in the real, physical context, and in
*Frost at Midnight* too the process of growth, towards an
affirmation of the potential for good in experience, is a process
of gradual attunement to the value of what is really there,
always affective in potential. And yet the central paradox of the
great conversation poems is that this benevolent purposiveness
in nature is manifestly dependent on consciousness; the
materialist universe is a product of the mind, and the
intelligible shapes and sounds that Hartley will learn to 'see and
hear' remain meaningless until their significance is 'deemed'.
Coleridge anticipates that God will 'mould' Hartley's spirit, and
'by giving make it ask'. But the poem has shown that this
external benevolence depends on the creative projection of the
mind, Seeking out 'companionable form'. This ambiguity is the
expression of a fundamental opposition in Coleridge's experi-
ence in the 1790s, the opposition of social ideals, with their
theoretical basis of an external and benevolent design in the
frame of things, to social reality, with its testimony to the
imperious sway of institutions sanctioned by dominant
economic and social groups. The reality of Coleridge's social
ideal, physical as he held it to be in basis, was constrained to the

status of an emotional and intellectual conviction, something that Coleridge *believed*.

*Frost at Midnight* returns finally to simple description, and to the frost of the opening line:

> Therefore all seasons shall be sweet to thee,
> Whether the summer clothe the general earth
> With greenness, or the redbreast sit and sing
> Betwixt the tufts of snow on the bare branch
> Of mossy apple-tree, while the nigh thatch
> Smokes in the sun-thaw; whether the eave-drops fall
> Heard only in the trances of the blast,
> Or if the secret ministry of frost
> Shall hang them up in silent icicles,
> Quietly shining to the quiet Moon.
>
> (ll.65-74)

The lines are an exceptionally fine realisation of the unity, the subtle reciprocity, that has emerged in Coleridge's experience. The implication of universality generates an atmosphere of apocalyptic promise; 'all seasons', 'general earth', the triumphant comprehensiveness of 'Whether . . .whether . . .or if'. But it is in the quality of the diction itself that Coleridge most powerfully suggests the wholeness of nature, running right through the great sweep of seasonal cycles. The sources of this effect in the diction are inseparable from the movement of the verse, which displays a perfectly balanced composure, developing out of the quiet, confident precision of 'Therefore . . ..'; the high concentration of assonance, and consonantal rhymes on 's', on 'm' and 'n', and most particularly on 'th', combine to a completely natural musicality, an apparently unconsidered aural complexity. The unity is a product of linguistic patterning, that can relate the most distant phenomena; as in the effortless return—completing the transforming growth of consciousness into real awareness of the circumstantial, and completing too the increasing particularity of the final descriptive lines—to the frost itself, with its ministry, secret like Coleridge's. The finally pervasive reciprocity, that Coleridge is now a part of too, may be established in the simple reflective pattern of epithets:

> Quietly shining to the quiet Moon.

The whiteness of the frost is a reflection of the moon's light—an 'echo' or 'mirror'—but also itself a source in the ostensible visual experience. And the silence of their interchange is a part of Coleridge's creative receptivity, his quiet confidence in a unity to which he belongs. The silence is both a condition and a product of that awareness of belonging, a silence that falls, as in the other conversation poems, only to usher in sound 'that tells of life'.

## FEARS IN SOLITUDE

In *Fears in Solitude* Coleridge tries again, as he had done in *Reflections on having left a Place of Retirement*, to restore the values of the conversation poems to society. The two poems have much in common; both begin and end in retirement, and both attempt a directly public address in central sections that are stylistic failures. Coleridge used the same apology for the style of each poem, by assigning them to the genre of *'sermoni propriora'*; an undated autograph MS of *Fears in Solitude* identified the kind to which Coleridge felt the poem belonged:

> N.B. The above is perhaps not Poetry—but rather a sort of middle thing between Poetry and Oratory—sermoni propriora.—Some parts are, I am conscious, too tame even for animated prose.
>
> (*PW*,i,257)

The broad structural similarity between *Fears in Solitude* and *Reflections* is confirmed in various details, like the lark that sings unseen, and the 'burst of prospect', from a hill-top, that 'seems like society.' And both poems betray the same anxiety about audience that Coleridge signals by a degeneration into a stridently declamatory manner, the poor imitation of Miltonic style that ruins *Religious Musings*. But *Fears in Solitude* does not lapse as badly as *Reflections*; it is in many ways a remarkable, and a courageous poem, that comes close to success in the attempt to mediate between private and public idioms. Swinburne found in the poem 'a tepid dilution of sentiment, a rancid unction of piety,'[1] and certain passages do undeniably suggest the embarrassments of *Reflections*, and the closing lines of *The Eolian Harp*. But *Fears in Solitude* is easily Coleridge's best public poem, not simply in the sustained effort to move beyond the narrow audience of retirement, but in the poem's real concern to make the values of that audience recognisable and generally available.

Most critics pass over the poem in silence, or notice briefly the fine conversational qualities of its opening and closing paragraphs. An exception is Carl Woodring, whose thoughtful account finds *Fears in Solitude* Coleridge's best 'political' poem:

> ... the argument gains unobtrusive force through an antithetical, epigrammatic balance and thrust in the sentences; by use of monosyllabic and colloquial words; by a marked pattern of vowel and consonantal sounds, bold in initial and internal alliteration; by a rocking and sliding variety in the pauses; and, in its general progress, by rapid changes of pace. A simplicity and ease of movement, eroding the antithetic precision, dissolves the individual line-units into flowing paragraphs, with the freedom newly discovered by Coleridge and Wordsworth. Betrayed by the Revolution, they have found a liberty in which a poet can have faith.[2]

But this very sensitive analysis contrasts oddly with some other of Professor Woodring's remarks; he notes that *Fears in Solitude* falls midway between the 'torrential effusion' of *Religious Musings*, and the style of the conversation poems, and concludes that 'its metrical texture is finer than that of either conversational or hysterical extremes'. And yet his account of the metrical texture of *Fears in Solitude* suggests very strongly that the style of the poem is a development of the conversational idiom itself; it differs only in the absence of tonal control as a structural principle, because *Fears in Solitude* proceeds, at least throughout the central section of lines 29-202, at a consistently maintained level of tone that prohibits the distinctive ascending development of *This Lime-Tree Bower* and *Frost at Midnight*.The form of those poems is determined by the ascending interaction of thought and emotion, registered in a steady ascent of tone, that enables a final return to the transformed particularities that had constituted the condition of growth. 'The conversation poems', comments Professor Woodring, 'lack that suggestion of a poet talking to himself

which is winningly present in *Fears in Solitude,* the suggestion of
intimate disclosure within the self, which actually widens the
imagined audience beyond a conversational circle.'[3] But it is
not the case that Coleridge is 'talking to himself' in the poem,
though certainly its audience is not that circle of the conversa-
tion poems; the address of *Fears in Solitude* is quite explicit at
several points: 'my countrymen!', 'O Britons! O my brethren!',
'Oh dear Britain! O my Mother Isle!' We can agree with
Professor Woodring that '*Fears in Solitude* is a representative
Romantic poem', in its 'novel simplicity of style and structure,
the subdued articulation of its movement, and its approach
through subjective mood to public theme.'[4] But we need a
clearer sense of the achievement that it represented for
Coleridge; the characteristically Romantic poetic style that
Professor Woodring calls 'a liberty in which a poet can have
faith' was no escape from the social context of England in the
1790s, because that style constituted in itself an identification
with party, as the writers of the *Anti-Jacobin* knew perfectly
well. Coleridge picks his way with great care, in *Fears in Solitude,*
through all the pitfalls of party rage. But poetic style was not a
means to avoid the tensions of a nation polarised in opposition,
any more than retirement could make Coleridge's social
anxiety disappear. Retirement, and style, were two forms of
response to tension, and their special character in Coleridge's
life and work was always a function of his social experience.

The first twenty-eight lines of *Fears in Solitude* adumbrate the
distinctive features of Coleridge's conversational manner. The
blank verse moves from easy, unexcited description to a serene
confidence generated in Coleridge's emerging receptivity;
silence and sound alternate to bring out the auditory dimen-
sion of heightening awareness, and there is a beautifully clear
visual sense, of colour and the effects of light. It is again late
afternoon (the poem will end with a sunset), but the emphasis
on physical sensation holds us within the limits of sense, with
the implication of God's benevolent influence through the
forms of nature. We recognise familiar elements of the diction
that Coleridge has already established in the conversational
idiom; 'sweet', combing the sensory response with a fine
pleasure that is physical, and emotional, and intellectual at
once; the 'dell' or 'nook'; the 'joy' that Coleridge experienced in

consciousness of a secure basis for his outward, embracing growth of head and heart:

> A green and silent spot, amid the hills,
> A small and silent dell! O'er stiller place
> No singing sky-lark ever poised himself.
> The hills are heathy, save that swelling slope,
> Which hath a gay and gorgeous covering on,
> All golden with the never-bloomless furze,
> Which now blooms most profusely: but the dell,
> Bathed by the mist, is fresh and delicate
> As vernal corn-field, or the unripe flax,
> When, through its half-transparent stalks, at eve,
> The level sunshine glimmers with green light.
> Oh! 'tis a quiet spirit-healing nook!
> Which all, methinks, would love; but chiefly he,
> The humble man, who, in his youthful years,
> Knew just so much of folly, as had made
> His early manhood more securely wise!
> Here he might lie on fern or withered heath,
> While from the singing lark (that sings unseen
> The minstrelsy that solitude loves best),
> And from the sun, and from the breezy air,
> Sweet influences trembled o'er his frame;
> And he, with many feelings, many thoughts,
> Made up a meditative joy, and found
> Religious meanings in the forms of Nature!
> And so, his senses gradually wrapt
> In a half sleep, he dreams of better worlds,
> And dreaming hears thee still, O singing lark,
> That singest like an angel in the clouds!
>
> (ll.1-28)

But Coleridge's sense of a wider audience is discernible, rather as it affects the opening passage of *Reflections;* retirement assumes an ambiguous function, forming at once the basis of social concern, and the means to a delightful, relieving escape from social pressure. In *Reflections* the positive social dimension is blurred by Coleridge's attempt to share the perspective of society itself on his retirement:

> It was a spot that you might aptly call
> The Valley of Seclusion!
>
> (ll.8-9)

In *Fears in Slitude* too the idea that retirement is an indulgent, socially remote 'half sleep', a kind of dream, is certainly present. But the dream is of 'better worlds', and it is nourished by the 'sweet influences' of 'the forms of Nature', and these were real enough; Coleridge is trying to adjust his commitments in relation to the assumptions he anticipated in a public audience, but he cannot obscure the palpable relation between his retirement, 'spirit-healing' and conscious of 'better worlds', and the long, directly public statement of his attitudes to English society as a whole.

*Fears in Solitude* is dated by Coleridge 'Nether Stowey, April 20, 1798', and is subtitled 'written in April 1798, during the alarm of an invasion'. The alarm had developed out of French military operations in Switzerland, in the early months of 1798, and this period marked a turning point in popular attitudes to the war with France; England was no longer the aggressor, and this made the position of those opposed to the war much more uncomfortable. We have seen that Coleridge tried in a number of poems, notably *France: an Ode*, and *Recantation: Illustrated in the story of the Mad Ox*, to justify his opposition to the war, an opposition now transformed by the sweep of events into a viciously alienating conviction in the context of English society, a literally treasonable attitude. Coleridge manages in *Fears in Solitude* to avoid almost completely the turgid, overblown diction and imagery, the hysterical note, that was his usual defence. The poem is based in a security that produces its patiently reasonable rhetoric, its brave refusal to panic. Coleridge appears not to make concessions; the attack on his countrymen begins in firm conviction, and yet there is an insistence on Coleridge's own place in the community and the guilt:

> We have offended, Oh! my countrymen!
> We have offended very grievously,
> And been most tyrannous.

> (ll. 41-43)

This is an orator's trick: 'We've all been wrong; let me be the first to admit it.' Coleridge uses the plural pronoun constantly in the poem. The objects of his attack are 'vice', 'wretchedness', 'pollutions'; abstract evils, that allow Coleridge to keep in obscurity the specific evils of social practice. The second verse paragraph, lines 29-86, is in fact directed against Imperialism, slavery, political corruption, the abuse of Christianity by its agents, and the indiscriminate administering of oaths. Coleridge can assume with his audience that these things are inherently bad, because he does not specify persons or practices. The criticism of oath-taking is particularly interesting, because Coleridge would at this time have felt very powerfully the threat of the loyalty-oath, which was a tacit consent to conscription. It is the one oath that is *not* mentioned:

> Oh! blasphemous! the Book of Life is made
> A superstitious instrument, on which
> We gabble o'er the oaths we mean to break;
> For all must swear—all and in every place,
> College and wharf, council and justice-court;
> All, all must swear, the briber and the bribed,
> Merchant and lawyer, senator and priest,
> The rich, the poor, the old man and the young;
> All, all make up one scheme of perjury,
> That faith doth reel.
>
> (ll.70-79)

The success of Coleridge's strategy in the poem, his implication that evil is really something external to society, that has infected it like a disease, from which Coleridge himself suffers with his countrymen, enables the balance and poise that is sustained in the tone. There are lapses, but they stand out against the general level of control:

> Forth from his dark and lonely hiding-place,
> (Portentous sight!) the owlet Atheism,
> Sailing on obscene wings athwart the noon,
> Drops his blue-fringed lids, and holds them close,
> And hooting at the glorious sun in Heaven,
> Cries out, 'Where is it?'
>
> (ll.81-86)

But the endeavour to make common ground becomes more difficult in the third and fourth verse paragraphs, when Coleridge turns to the war itself. This is the issue that is potentially most damaging to his position in the community of the nation; it is in the implications of his attitude to France, and all that the Revolution had stood for, that the crisis comes.

But Coleridge does not attack, or defend, the war with France; the poem is simply anti-war, and his criticism is of the failure of the English properly to realise the horrors of war. If a reckoning, an invasion, is coming, it will come as a consequence of this failure to understand the reality of war in terms of human suffering:

> Therefore, evil days
> Are coming on us, O my countrymen!
> And what if all-avenging Providence,
> Strong and retributive, should make us know
> The meaning of our words, force us to feel
> The desolation and the agony
> Of our fierce doings?
>
> (ll. 123-29)

The retribution of Providence will be directed not against the bad cause of the English, but against their failure to realise the gravity of their actions. Nevertheless, Coleridge can proceed to exhort the men of England, in the strongest patriotic terms, to defend their country against a now enraged enemy. He is striking a very fine balance, between a forthright assertion of the interests he shares with his own nation, and a precarious persistence in mitigating the aggression of the French by the suggestion that they have been goaded into retaliation:

> Sons, brothers, husbands, all
> Who ever gazed with fondness on the forms
> Which grew up with you round the same fire-side,
> And all who ever heard the sabbath-bells
> Without the infidel's scorn, make yourselves pure!
> Stand forth! be men! repel an impious foe,
> Impious and false, a light yet cruel race,
> Who laugh away all virtue, mingling mirth
> With deeds of murder; and still promising
> Freedom, themselves too sensual to be free,
> Poison life's amities, and cheat the heart
> Of faith and quiet hope, and all that soothes,
> And all that lifts the spirit! Stand we forth;
> Render them back upon the insulted ocean,
> And let them toss as idly on its waves
> As the vile sea-weed, which some mountain-blast

> Swept from our shores! And Oh! may we return
> Not with a drunken triumph, but with fear,
> Repenting of the wrongs with which we stung
> So fierce a foe to frenzy!
>
> (ll. 134-53)

These lines suggest a fundamental ambiguity in *Fears in Solitude*; the poem is about a nation under threat, partly through its own faults, from a foreign power, but it is also about Coleridge's retirement, under threat from the nation. Coleridge's retirement, with all the force of a social and personal ideal that it contained, is used as an image of the good heart of the nation, but it is at the same time actually under threat from the misconceptions and corruptions of that nation. Coleridge's fears are both for and of his society. His presentation of the French actually identifies them with the English society that has been displayed in the poem; and he does indeed hint that the French have been driven to their excesses by England, 'the wrongs with which we stung / So fierce a foe to frenzy!' When Coleridge goes on to condemn the 'restless enmity' of the Jacobins, and the 'mad idolatry' of the Tories, he seems to steer a sensible middle course of the kind that he could expect his audience to approve; but he identifes the real problem of society in its 'own folly and rank wickedness', and even while he includes himself in this deep-rooted sickness, the 'radical causation', it remains a fundamental and essentially self-isolating criticism:

> I have told,
> O Britons! O my brethren! I have told
> Most bitter truth, but without bitterness.
> Nor deem my zeal or factious or mistimed;
> For never can the courage dwell with them,
> Who, playing tricks with conscience, dare not look
> At their own vices. We have been too long
> Dupes of a deep delusion! Some, belike,
> Groaning with restless enmity, expect
> All change from change of constituted power;
> As if a Government had been a robe,
> On which our vice and wretchedness were tagged
> Like fancy-points and fringes, with the robe
> Pulled off at pleasure. Fondly these attach
> A radical causation to a few

Poor drudges of chastising Providence,
Who borrow all their hues and qualities
From our own folly and rank wickedness,
Which gave them birth and nursed them. Others, meanwhile,
Dote with a mad idolatry; and all
Who will not fall before their images,
And yield them worship, they are enemies
Even of their country.

(ll. 153-75)

Coleridge needed his country. He had not the resources to sustain the alienation from it that was forced on him. He needed to belong to the community, to be approved by it, and find a recognisable identity within it. He conceived of the nation ideally, in the image of his retirement, and its failure to substantiate this ideal is manifest in *Fears in Solitude*. The poem builds to a climax that represents the ideal country, a great family, receptive to the guiding, educative 'sweet sensations' of nature. It is an ideal threatened by the real nation in which Coleridge lived, and the 'filial fears' that he has tried to dispel in the poem, are fears of that terrible dislocation of the real from the ideal, as much as they are fears of a French invasion. The 'vengeful enemy' is France, but it is also the nation beyond Nether Stowey, those 'brethren' who found Coleridge, just as his real brothers had, an unacceptable man. The passage quoted above continues with Coleridge's quiet sadness at the label of 'enemy' conferred on him by his countryman:

Such have I been deemed.—
But, O dear Britain! O my Mother Isle!
Needs must thou prove a name most dear and holy
To me, a son, a brother, and a friend,
A husband, and a father! who revere
All bonds of natural love, and find them all
Within the limits of thy rocky shores.
O native Britain! O my Mother Isle!
How shouldst thou prove aught else but dear and holy
To me, who from thy lakes and mountain-hills,
Thy clouds, thy quiet dales, thy rocks and seas,
Have drunk in all my intellectual life,
All sweet sensations, all ennobling thoughts,
All adoration of the God in nature,
All lovely and all honourable things,
Whatever makes this mortal spirit feel

> The joy and greatness of its future being?
> There lives nor form nor feeling in my soul
> Unborrowed from my country! O divine
> And beauteous island! thou hast been my sole
> And most magnificent temple, in the which
> I walk with awe, and sing my stately songs,
> Loving the God that made me!—
>                                    May my fears,
> My filial fears, be vain! and may the vaunts
> And menace of the vengeful enemy
> Pass like the gust, that roared and died away
> In the distant tree: which heard, and only heard
> In this low dell, bowed not the delicate grass.
>                                    (ll.175-202)

The poem thus recedes back into the security of Coleridge's retirement, which has provided the terms of his ideal vision of England, and the poetic voice that achieves a direct mode of public address. Coleridge sustains his public style because the poem in a sense supposes simply the conversational audience, family and friends, on a national scale. *Fears in Solitude* at least confirms for Coleridge the potential of his retirement, the confidence and the social example that it can yield. His return to it, in the final verse paragraph, is a return to the sources of value; to the large social perspective that it can offer:

> Now farewell,
> Farewell, awhile, O soft and silent spot!
> On the green sheep-track, up the heathy hill,
> Homeward I wind my way; and lo! recalled
> From bodings that have well-nigh wearied me,
> I find myself upon the brow, and pause
> Startled! And after lonely sojourning
> In such a quiet and surrounded nook,
> This burst of prospect, here the shadowy main,
> Dim-tinted, there the mighty majesty
> Of that huge amphitheatre of rich
> And elmy fields, seem like society—
> Conversing with the mind, and giving it
> A livelier impulse and a dance of thought!
>                                    (ll.207-20)

and to the real home, shared with a small circle of friends, in nature, that was to Coleridge a constrained form of his social ideal, a limited kind of freedom:

And now, beloved Stowey! I behold
Thy church-tower, and, methinks, the four huge elms
Clustering, which mark the mansion of my friend;
And close behind them, hidden from my view,
Is my own lowly cottage, where my babe
And my babe's mother dwell in peace! With light
And quickened footsteps thitherward I tend,
Remembering thee, O green and silent dell!
And grateful, that by nature's quietness
And solitary musings, all my heart
Is softened, and made worthy to indulge
Love, and the thoughts that yearn for human kind.

(ll.221-32)

## THE NIGHTINGALE

Coleridge published *The Nightingale* in *Lyrical Ballads*. The poem forms part of an interesting sequence with which the volume opened; first came *The Rime of the Ancyent Marinere,* then *The Foster-Mother's Tale,* extracted from Coleridge's drama *Osorio.* These were followed by Wordsworth's *Lines left upon a Seat . . .,* and then came *The Nightingale;* 'A Conversational Poem, Written in April 1798'. This all but completes the sum of Coleridge's contribution to the joint production with Wordsworth. *The Nightingale* is followed by *The Female Vagrant* and *Goody Blake and Harry Gill,* and the character of the volume changes with Wordsworth's emerging dominance. But there is a basic unity of interest in *Lyrical Ballads*, a thematic concern that is always present in the work of both poets, and in the two distinctive kinds of poetry that they included in their volume, the blank verse meditative and descriptive poetry, and those poems that are actually cast in ballad form, in their metre and stanzaic arrangement. They all attempt to display the constitutive power of the mind, the creative element in perception. And they portray, additionally, the destructive effect that a self-absorbed mode of perception can have, in particular the destructive effect that it can have on the social relations of the self, the relation of the individual to other men, and the relation of the self to nature. We know that Wordworth and Coleridge carried their discussions together into poetry; the sequence formed by Coleridge's *The Mad Monk*, Wordsworth's *Immortality Ode*, and Coleridge's *Letter to Sara* and the *Dejection Ode*, is a case in point.[1] Something similar appears to be happening in the opening sequence of poems in *Lyrical Ballads*, especially when we recall the close connections between Wordsworth's *Lines left upon a Seat*, and a poem of Coleridge's that was not included in *Lyrical Ballads*, *This Lime-Tree Bower my Prison*. The poems that lead up to *The Female Vagrant* are each concerned with the necessity to discriminate between positive and negative kinds of consciousness, and they are concerned in particular to show the positive kind of consciousness that can connect man's relation to nature with his relation to the human community. This connective consciousness, a distinctive property of all the conversation poems, is a central theme of *The Nightingale*.

The invitation to melancholy that was conventionally associated with twilight is explicitly rejected in *The Nightingale*. We have seen that Coleridge had used the potentially saddening effects of late afternoon and evening already, to insist on his final confidence in the positive potential that he could create in his limited personal context. *The Nightingale* begins just after sunset:

> No cloud, no relique of the sunken day
> Distinguishes the West, no long thin slip
> Of sullen light, no obscure trembling hues.
>
> (ll. 1-3)

This is deliberately suggestive of the conventional reaction to night, in 'relique', 'sunken', 'sullen', and 'obscure'. But the impulse to melancholy is simultaneously countered by the clarity of Coleridge's visual imagination, which effectively re-creates the sunset that is in fact over. With this kind of serene confidence in the pleasure of nature, Coleridge can master quite effortlessly the threat of melancholy; the divine plan is manifest everywhere, in the connection between stream and shower, between shower and clouds:

> Come, we will rest on this old mossy bridge!
> You see the glimmer of the stream beneath,
> But hear no murmuring: it flows silently,

O'er its soft bed of verdure. All is still,
A balmy night! and though the stars be dim,
Yet let us think upon the vernal showers
That gladden the green earth, and we shall find
A pleasure in the dimness of the stars.

(ll. 4-11)

The reciprocity is mirrored in an unobtrusive echoing on sounds, 'glimmer', 'balmy', 'dimness' (the sequence is supported by slighter echoes, 'mossy', 'stream', 'dim'), and 'verdure', 'vernal'. Coleridge's experience, the composed, receptive happiness of his mood, is very directly a shared experience, that gains strength from his sense of the sympathy of his small audience of close friends: 'Come, we will rest . . ..' The descriptive language is also a composition of this mood; the showers 'gladden' the earth, just as the dimness of the stars offers a 'pleasure' for Coleridge and his friends. Again, the silence is broken by a sound that confirms Coleridge's positive awareness:

And hark! the Nightingale begins its song,
'Most musical, most melancholy' bird!
A melancholy bird? Oh! idle thought!
In Nature there is nothing melancholy.
But some night-wandering man, whose heart was pierced
With the remembrance of a grievous wrong,
Or slow distemper, or neglected love,
(And so, poor wretch! filled all things with himself,
And made all gentle sounds tell back the tale
Of his own sorrow) he, and such as he,
First named these notes a melancholy strain.

(ll. 12-22)

The good in nature can be perverted by a failure of consciousness, like the wrong-headedness that Wordsworth condemns in *Lines left upon a Seat;* and like the low spirits that Coleridge develops away from in *This Lime-Tree Bower* and *Frost at Midnight. The Nightingale* too develops away from melancholy, but as something that is always outside Coleridge's personal mood in the poem, it cannot function within the context of tonal ascent: *The Nightingale* is consequently rather too discursive, because Coleridge does not structure the poem around a development of consciousness into real awareness. There is a lack of direction in the development of the poem, a rambling quality that is certainly expressive of Coleridge's serenity, but which he himself sensed to make its experience finally inaccessible, not fully realised in the poetic context. There is no dominant organising principle at work in the poem, and when Coleridge sent his manuscript to Wordsworth for comment, he acknowledged this flaw in a jokey rhyme:

> In stale blank verse a subject stale
> I send *per post* my *Nightingale*;
> And like an honest bard, dear Wordsworth,
> You'll tell me what you think, my Bird's worth.
> My own opinion's briefly this—
> His *bill* he opens not amis;
> And when he has sung a stave or so,
> His breast, & some small space below,
> So throbs & swells, that you might swear
> No vulgar music's working there.
> So far, so good; but then, 'od rot him!
> There's something falls off at his bottom.
> Yet, sure, no wonder it should breed,
> That my Bird's Tail's a tail indeed
> And makes its own inglorious harmony
> Æolio crepitû, non carmine.

(CLi,406)

But while the poem is a little shapeless in comparison with the best of the conversation poems, there is still a design in the apparently random movement of ideas. There is not the steady ascent of emotion and thought into a level of awareness that reveals connectedness, and the poem cannot take advantage of the structural unity, the shape, that is conferred in that ascent. But the poem is about connectedness; it seeks to display the subtle inter-relations between natural phenomena, and between man and nature.

The endeavour is confused, though, by what one critic has called the 'ironic complexity' of the poem, a complexity that depends on 'the reader recognising what pitfalls are skirted', as Coleridge constantly suggests conventionally melancholic atmospheres and settings, in order to subvert the expectations thus established.[2] This object of the poem is perfectly obvious in Coleridge's reference to *Il Penseroso*, and is more subtly present in the opening descriptive passage and its mood.

Coleridge specifies the failure properly to respond to nature as a product of metropolitan sophistication; melancholy was a convention sustained by city-dwellers who could scarcely expect themselves to know better, cut off from 'the influxes / Of shapes and sounds and shifting elements':

> And many a poet echoes the conceit;
> Poet who hath been building up the rhyme
> When he had better far have stretched his limbs
> Beside a brook in mossy forest-dell,
> By sun or moon-light, to the influxes
> Of shapes and sounds and shifting elements
> Surrendering his whole spirit, of his song
> And of his fame forgetful! so his fame
> Should share in Nature's immortality,
> A venerable thing! and so his song
> Should make all Nature lovelier, and itself
> Be loved like Nature! But 'twill not be so;
> And youths and maidens most poetical,
> Who lose the deepening twilights of the spring
> In ball-rooms and hot theatres, they still
> Full of meek sympathy must heave their sighs
> O'er Philomela's pity-pleading strains.
>
> (ll.23-39)

Coleridge opposes to this failure of consciousness in the metropolitan community (a failure which issues in that useless, self-indulgent social consciousness, 'pity', that he had criticised in *Reflections*), the receptivity fostered in his small community of friends (the Wordsworths) and family (Hartley, later in the poem) in nature:

> My Friend, and thou, our Sister! we have learnt
> A different lore: we may not thus profane
> Nature's sweet voices, always full of love
> And joyance!
>
> (ll.40-43)

But the poem continues to 'skirt' conventional responses; in particular, Coleridge seems unable to resist the Gothic atmosphere, with its pervasive implication of undisclosed horrors, that he had encountered in 'Monk' Lewis and Mrs Radcliffe:

> And I know a grove
> Of large extent, hard by a castle huge,

> Which the great lord inhabits not; and so
> This grove is wild with tangling underwood,
> And the trim walks are broken up, and grass,
> Thin grass and king-cups grow within the paths.
>
> (ll.49-54)

This is surely not parody; the atmosphere that Coleridge evokes here, with skilful economy, does not appear to be qualified by any ironic context. We have stumbled across a narrative in the classic Gothic manner, full of threads that lead off into murky secrets; why is the castle uninhabited? what can have happened to the 'great lord'? why is the place so run down? But these invitations to speculate are of course quite empty, even though Coleridge returns to the ghostly narrative again:

> A most gentle Maid,
> Who dwelleth in her hospitable home
> Hard by the castle, and at latest eve
> (Even like a Lady vowed and dedicate
> To something more than Nature in the grove)
> Glides through the pathways.
>
> (ll.69-74)

But Coleridge's purpose *is* ironic. These clever cameos of Gothic titillation set up a conventional expectation of the bizarre and fantastic events that involve this 'gentle Maid' (the sexuality of Gothic romance was evidently its main appeal); but no absurd fictions await her in the grove, even if her breathless anticipation is not disappointed. She finds no more than 'Nature in the grove', but that is a real experience worth more than anything that the fiction could have offered.

She finds the nightingales. Coleridge's poem uncovers the multiple relationships, of harmony, constituted in the songs of the nightingales, and between the nightingales and the moon, and finally between Hartley and the moon, with its unstated implication of something common in the responses of Hartley and the nightingales. Nevertheless, it is difficult to resist the sense that Coleridge has been caught up himself in the appeal of the Gothic conventions; their atmosphere is present in the poem a little too substantially, and Coleridge allows it an authenticity that obscures what must be an ironic intention.

Two entries in the Gutch notebook suggest that Coleridge had planned a poem about Hartley and the nightingales; at least, the connection that is established in *The Nightingale* is implicit in Coleridge's notes, written at around the same time in late 1797. One note is the record of a real incident:

> —Hartley fell down & hurt himself—I caught him up crying & screaming—& ran out of doors with him.—The Moon caught his eye—he ceased crying immediately—& his eyes & the tears in them, how they glittered in the Moonlight![3]

A few entries later Coleridge is working on the passage of verse that became lines 43-49 of *The Nightingale:*

> —The merry nightingale
> That crowds & hurries & precipitates
> With fast thick warble his delicious notes;
> As he were fearful, that an Apirl Night
> Would be too short for him to utter forth
> His love-chant, and disburthen his full soul
> Of all its music!—[4]

But the entries that surround these two in the Gutch notebook show that Coleridge was working on *Frost at Midnight* at the same time; and in particular on the final verse paragraph:

> The subtle snow in every breeze rose curling from the Grove, like pillars of cottage smoke.[5]

Coleridge was clearly working towards the effects of weather in lines 65-74 of *Frost at Midnight,* and just before the passage that went into *The Nightingale* he wrote this:

> The Sun-shine lies on the cottage-wall
> Ashining thro' the snow—[6]

It seems not to have been noticed that the episode of Hartley's fall, and his glittering eyes in the moonlight, may have suggested to Coleridge the ending of the original published version of *Frost at Midnight*:

> . . . whether the eave-drops fall
> Heard only in the trances of the blast,

> Or whether the secret ministry of cold
> Shall hang them up in silent icicles,
> Quietly shining to the quiet moon,
> Like those, my babe! which ere tomorrow's warmth
> Have capp'd their sharp keen points with pendulous drops,
> Will catch thine eye, and with their novelty
> Suspend they little soul; then make thee shout,
> And stretch and flutter from thy mother' arms
> As thou wouldst fly for very eagerness.
>
> (*PW*,i,242-3)

Here Coleridge implies an analogy between the reciprocity of frost and moon, and the reciprocity between Hartley and the frost, and, as in the notebook passage, it is the evidence of a benevolent, educative design in the response of the child to the influences of nature that fascinates Coleridge. Humphrey House criticized the original ending of *Frost at Midnight*, in terms that remind us of *The Nightingale*, with its very similar ending:

> This was a stopping rather than an end; for once the vista of new domestic detail was opened there was no reason why it should not be indefinitely followed, with increasing shapelessness. This was informal and conversational as family talk. The decision to stop at line 74 was one of the best artistic decisions Coleridge ever made.[7]

We can agree that Coleridge was right to finish the poem in a return to the frost with which it began. But we can on the other hand appreciate that the original ending was more than merely arbitrary; the further connectedness that it implied, between Hartley's experience and Coleridge's own, between Hartley's relation to nature and an internal relation between natural phenomena, does strengthen the pervasive network of relationships that *Frost at Midnight* works to uncover. In *The Nightingale*, a similar domestic detail quite successfully integrates various elements in the poem that appear to be distinct, and it may in fact be the case that Coleridge abandoned the original ending of *Frost at Midnight* at least partly because he found a better use for the Hartley incident in *The Nightingale*.

Coleridge's first description of the nightingales confirms the joyful positive awareness of nature that he shares with the

Wordsworths. The mutuality between friends finds a kind of celebration in the song of the birds:

> My Friend, and thou, our Sister! we have learnt
> A different lore: we may not thus profane
> Nature's sweet voices, always full of love
> And joyance! 'Tis the merry Nightingale
> That crowds, and hurries, and precipitates
> With fast thick warble his delicious notes,
> As he were fearful that an April night
> Would be too short for him to utter forth
> His love-chant, and disburthen his full soul
> Of all its music!
>
> (ll.40-49)

Coleridge turns next to the effect of the birds' songs, as he has heard them in the 'grove / Of large extent, hard by a castle huge':

> But never elsewhere in one place I knew
> So many nightingales; and far and near,
> In wood and thicket, over the wide grove,
> They answer and provoke each other's song,
> With skirmish and capricious passagings,
> And murmurs musical and swift jug jug,
> And one low piping sound more sweet than all—
> Stirring the air with such a harmony,
> That should you close your eyes, you might almost
> Forget it was not day! On moonlight bushes,
> Whose dewy leaflets are but half-disclosed,
> You may perchance behold them on the twigs,
> Their bright, bright eyes, their eyes both bright and full,
> Glistening, while many a glow-worm in the shade
> Lights up her love-torch.
>
> (ll.55-69)

The independent songs merge into a single 'harmony'; Coleridge distinguishes the separate sounds as elements within a unity of effect that transforms the night. It is important to notice that the eyes of the birds, visible in the moonlight and counterpointed by the light from the glow-worms, in a kind of visual equivalent to the audible harmony, are given a special emphasis. 'Their bright, bright eyes' are 'glistening' in the pale light, and Coleridge will return to this detail in a different context, in the final verse paragraph of the poem.

The adventure that awaits the 'gentle Maid' in the grove introduces a third description of the nightingales, which points forward again, in very direct terms, to the 'father's tale' that ends the poem:

> ... she knows all their notes,
> That gentle Maid! and oft, a moment's space,
> What time the moon was lost behind a cloud,
> Hath heard a pause of silence; till the moon
> Emerging, hath awakened earth and sky
> With one sensation, and those wakeful birds
> Have all burst forth in choral minstrelsy,
> As if some sudden gale had swept at once
> A hundred airy harps! And she hath watched
> Many a nightingale perch giddily
> On blossomy twig still swinging from the breeze,
> And to that motion tune his wanton song
> Like tipsy Joy that reels with tossing head.
>
> (ll.74-86)

The moon's influence, a visual dimension, awakens the audible response of the nightingales in a synaesthetic unity that issues in 'Joy'. The image of the wind-harps confirms the Associationist basis from which Coleridge would have rationalised the effect. It is characteristic of the conversation poems that when Coleridge turns to Hartley's response to the moon, in the final verse paragraph, the 'dim sympathy' that he shares with the nightingales, in their response, is a connection that remains unstated, simply implicit in the whole statement of the poem:

> Farewell, O Warbler! till to-morrow eve,
> And you, my friends! farewell, a short farewell!
> We have been loitering long and pleasantly,
> And now for our dear homes.—That strain again!
> Full fain it would delay me! My dear babe,
> Who, capable of no articulate sound,
> Mars all things with his imitative lisp,
> How he would place his hand beside his ear,
> His little hand, the small forefinger up,
> And bid us listen! And I deem it wise
> To make him Nature's play-mate. He knows well
> The evening-star; and once, when he awoke
> In most distressful mood (some inward pain
> Had made up that strange thing, an infant's dream—)

> I hurried with him to our orchard-plot,
> And he beheld the moon, and, hushed at once,
> Suspends his sobs, and laughs most silently,
> While his fair eyes, that swam with undropped tears,
> Did glitter in the yellow moon-beam! Well!—
> It is a father's tale: But if that Heaven
> Should give me life, his childhood shall grow up
> Familiar with these songs, that with the night
> He may associate joy. —Once more, farewell,
> Sweet Nightingale! once more, my friends! farewell.
>
> (ll.87-110)

Coleridge has brought together here all the central values of the conversation poems. The voice is serene, self-possessed, optimistic; it is confident in the values that are shared with a small and intimate group in nature, 'my friends', 'my dear babe', a group that belongs to its environment, finding their 'dear homes' in retirement. The highest value that is sustained by this group is their awareness of nature, in its benevolence, the 'joy' that it can teach. But this joy in the conversation poems is an experience that is always based, not solely in a positive consciousness of nature, but in the special kind of·community that formed the basis of Coleridge's positive consciousness. On 14 September 1798, worried about the possibility of conscription, and the reception of *Lyrical Ballads,* upset by a quarrel with Charles Lloyd and Lamb, and excited by the new intellectual horizons of German thought, Coleridge sailed for Hamburg from Yarmouth. He left behind his family in the cottage at Nether Stowey, and all the friends and places associated with the eighteen months of his life in that small community. It was a life that he was never to regain.

# ABBREVIATIONS

| | |
|---|---|
| *BL* | S. T. Coleridge, *Biographia Literaria*, ed. J. Shawcross, 2 Vols. (Oxford, 1907). |
| *Bristol Borrowings* | George Whalley, 'The Bristol Library Borrowings of Southey and Coleridge, 1793-8', *The Library*, iv (1949), pp.114-31. |
| Campbell | *The Poetical Works of Samuel Taylor Coleridge*, ed. J. Dykes Campbell (London 1893). |
| *CL* | *The Collected Letters of Samuel Taylor Coleridge*, ed. E.L. Griggs, 6 Vols., (Oxford, 1956-71). |
| *CN* | *The Notebooks of Samuel Taylor Coleridge*, ed. Kathleen Coburn, 5 Vols. (each in 2 parts, 3 volumes published) (London, 1957-). |
| *Friend* | S.T. Coleridge, *The Friend*, ed. B. Rooke, 2 Vols., 1969 (*The Collected Coleridge*, Vol. IV). |
| *Hazlitt Works* | *The Complete Works of William Hazlitt*, ed. P.P. Howe, 21 Vols. (London, 1930-34). |
| *Lectures 1795* | S.T. Coleridge, *Lectures 1795: On Politics and Religion*, ed. Peter Mann and Lewis Patton, 1971 (*The Collected Coleridge*, Vol. I.). |
| *Prelude* | William Wordsworth, *The Prelude, Text of 1805*, ed. E. de Selincourt, rev. Stephen Gill (London, 1970). |
| *Prose Works* | *The Prose Works of William Wordsworth*, ed. W.J.B. Owen and Jane Smyser, 3 Vols. (Oxford, 1974). |
| *PW* | *The Complete Poetical Works of Samuel Taylor Coleridge*, ed. E.H. Coleridge, 2 Vols. (Oxford, 1912). |
| *Watchman* | S.T. Coleridge, *The Watchman*, ed. Lewis Patton, 1970 (*The Collected Coleridge*, Vol. II). |
| *WPW* | *The Poetical Works of William Wordsworth*, ed. E. de Selincourt and Helen Darbishire, 5 Vols. (Oxford, 1940-49). |

**NOTES**

# Introduction

1. W.H. Auden, *Collected Longer Poems* (London 1968), pp.98-99.
2. M.H. Abrams, *Natural Supernaturalism: Tradition and Revolution in Romantic Literature* (London, 1971), pp. 333-4. The quotation is from *New Year Letter (Collected Longer Poems*, p.102).
3. P.B. Shelley, *Poetical Works*, ed. T. Hutchinson (1905) (London 1968), pp. 33-4.
4. *Hazlitt Works*, xi, p.34.
5. Ibid. xi, pp. 37-38.
6. Ibid. xi,p.87.
7. Ibid. v,p.161.
8. Ibid. v,pp.162-3.
9. For Professor McFarland's virulent attack on Professor Fruman's *Coleridge the Damaged Archangel* (London, 1971), see 'Coleridge's Plagiarisms Once More: A Review Essay', *Yale Review*, lxiii (1974), pp.254-86. 'Coleridge's Anxiety' appeared as a contribution to *Coleridge's Variety*, ed. J. Beer (London, 1974), pp. 134-65. This collection of essays was conceived as a 'reply' to Professor Fruman's arguments; cf. 'Preface and Acknowledgements', p.viii.
10. Thomas McFarland, *Coleridge and the Pantheist Tradition* (Oxford and New York, 1969).
11. E.S. Shaffer, *'Kubla Khan' and The Fall of Jerusalem* (Cambridge, 1975), p.2.
12. Lucien Goldmann, *The Hidden God* (Paris, 1955), trans., 1964, p.12.
13. Raymond Williams, *The Long Revolution* (London, 1961), p.62.
14. *Prose Works*,i,p.116.

# Coleridge and the French Revolution

1. *Watchman*,pp.127-30, 199-201.
2. *Morning Post*, April 16 1798; cf. *PW*,i,243. See D.V. Erdman, 'Coleridge as Editorial Writer', in *Power and Consciousness*, ed. C.C. O'Brien and L. Vanech (London, 1969), pp.183-201.
3. James Gillman, *Life of Coleridge* (London, 1838), p.55.
4. *Hazlitt Works*, xvii,p.113; Fruman, *Coleridge the Damaged Archangel*, p.467,n.106.
5. Gillman, *Life of Coleridge*, p.54.
6. William Rough to Henry Crabb Robinson, August 31 1835, quoted by Edith J. Morley, 'Some Contemporary Allusions to Coleridge's Death', in *Coleridge: Studies by several hands on the hundredth anniversary of his death,*

ed. E. Blunden and E.L. Griggs (London, 1934),pp.91-95,p.93.

7. *Gentleman's Magazine*, December 1834, May 1838; quoted in L. Hanson, *The Life of S.T. Coleridge; the Early Years* (London, 1938),p.33.

8. E.P. Thompson, 'Disenchantment or Default? A Lay Sermon', in *Power and Consciousness*, ed. C.C. O'Brien and L. Vanech, pp. 149-81,p.150.

9. Richard Price, *A Discourse on the Love of our Country, &c.* (London 1789).

10. Richard Price, *Observations on the Nature of Civil Liberty, &c.* (London, 1776),p.95.

11. Richard Price, *A Discourse on the Love of our Country*, pp. 50-51.

12. C. Kegan Paul, *William Godwin, his friends and acquaintances*, 2 Vols. (London, 1876),i,p,69.

13. See Cecil Roth, *Nephew of the Almighty* (London, 1933); E.P. Thompson, *The Making of the English Working Class* (London 1963), Penguin edition, pp. 123-30; P.M. Zall, 'The Cool World of Samuel Taylor Coleridge: Richard Brothers—The Law and the Prophet', *Wordsworth Circle*, iv (1973), pp.25-30.

14. Anthony Lincoln, *Some Political and Social Ideas of English Dissent, 1763-1800* (London, 1938), p.127, see also the chapter on Priestley in Basil Willey, *The Eighteenth Century Background* (London, 1940).

15. Joseph Priestley, *Essay on the First Principles of Government* (London, 1771),p.122.

16. Joseph Priestley, *Letters to Burke* (London, 1791),p.237.

17. *CN*, 133 and note.

18. *CL*,i,187.

19. Fruman, *Coleridge the Damaged Archangel*, pp.243-45.

20. M.H. Abrams, *Natural Supernaturalism*, pp.327-28.

21. For the distinction between 'patriot hero' and 'patriot sage', see Carl Woodring, *Politics in the Poetry of Coleridge* (Madison, Wisc., 1961).

22. *Watchman*, pp.22-23.

23. Ibid. pp.235-38.

24. Ibid. pp.269-73.

25. Mario Praz, *The Hero in Eclipse in Victorian Fiction* (London, 1965),p.39.

26. Ibid. pp.3-5.

27. Ibid. p.40.

28. Ibid. p.41.

# Domesticity and Retirement in Coleridge's Poetry

1. Sister Eugenia Logan, 'Coleridge's Scheme of Pantisocracy and American Travel Accounts', *PMLA*, xlv (1930),pp.1069-84.

2. George Whalley, *Coleridge and Sara Hutchinson and the Asra Poems* (London, 1955),p.113.

3. Fruman, *Coleridge the Damaged Archangel,* pp.13-25.

4. Cf. J. Smyser, 'Coleridge's Use of Wordsworth's Juvenilia', *PMLA*, lxv (1950),pp.419-26.

5. See Woodring, *Politics in the Poetry of Coleridge,* pp. 119-22.

6. Byron, *English Bards and Scotch Reviewers* (London, 1809), ll.261-64; *Coleridge's Verse: A Selection,* ed. W. Empson and D. Pirie (London 1972), p. 16.

7. M.H. Abrams, *Natural Supernaturalism,* pp. 265-66.

8. See H.W. Piper, *The Active Universe* (London, 1962), pp.29-59.

9. *Lectures 1795,* p.xliii.

10. Geoffrey Carnall, *Robert Southey and his Age* (Oxford, 1960), p.31.

11. Woodring, *Politics in the Poetry of Coleridge,* p.197.

12. The text that appeared in the *Morning Chronicle,* December 30 1794, was amongst other things an explicit attack on George III; *PW*,i,76.

13. Jack Simmons, *Southey* (London, 1945),pp.57-58.

# Pantisocracy and the Theory of Retirement

1. On Pantisocracy, see J.R. MacGillivray, 'The Pantisocracy Scheme and its Immediate Background', *Studies in English by members of University College, Toronto* (collected by Principal Malcolm Wallace) (Toronto, 1931),pp.131-69; Sister Eugenia Logan, 'Coleridge's Scheme of Pantisocracy and American Travel Accounts'; and especially L.W. Deen, 'Coleridge and the Sources of Pantisocracy: Godwin, the Bible, and Hartley', *Boston University Studies in English* (New York, 1961), pp.232-45. There are interesting accounts in two books by H.N. Fairchild, *The Noble Savage* (New York, 1928), and *The Romantic Quest*(New York, 1931); in L. Hanson, *Life of S.T. Coleridge: The Early Years* (London, 1938); and in Carnall, *Robert Southey and his Age.*

2. For Coleridge's influence on Godwin, see Kegan Paul, *William Godwin*,i,p.357.

3. William Godwin, *Enquiry Concerning Political Justice,* ed. F.E.L. Priestley, 3 Vols. (Toronto, 1964), iii,p.146 (Bk II, ch.ii). The text of 1798 substituted 'father' and 'brother'; cf. i,pp. 127-8.

4. Mrs Henry Sandford, *Thomas Poole and his Friends,* 2 Vols. (London, 1888),i, pp. 100-101.

5. Jack Simmons, *Southey*,p.30.

6. Max Beerbohm, *The Poet's Corner,* (London, 1904), plate 13.

7. Sandford, *Thomas Poole and his Friends,* i,p.97.

8. Ibid.i,p.103.

9. John Poole's comment was recorded by Cornelia Crosse, *Red Letter Days,* 1892; quoted in Berta Lawrence, *Coleridge and Wordsworth in Somerset* (Newton Abbot, 1970),p.65.

10. Simmons, *Southey*,p.29.

11. Carnall, *Robert Southey and his Age*, p.16.

12. Sandford, *Thomas Poole and his Friends*, i,p.105.

13. For details of these debts, see Fruman, *Coleridge the Damaged Archangel*,pp.16,444 (note 22).

14. Simmons, *Southey*,p.28.

15. Carnall, *Robert Southey and his Age*, p.17.

16. Sandford, *Thomas Poole and his Friends*, i,p.98.

17. Robert Southey to Tom Southey, September 20 1794, *Life and Correspondence of Robert Southey*, ed. C.C. Southey, 2nd edition, 6 Vols. (London, 1849-50), i, pp. 220-21; also, *CL*,i 98-99.

18. Sandford, *Thomas Poole and his Friends*,i. p.98.

19. Godwin, *Political Justice*, ed. F.E.L. Priestley, i, pp.206-7 (Bk.III, ch. iii).

20. Ibid.i,pp.14-15 (Bk I,ch.iii).

21. Ibid.ii,pp.507-8 (BkVIII, ch.viii).

22. See F.E.L. Priestley's comments on the 'modifications of doctrine' that followed Godwin's experience of life with Mary; ibid.iii,p.87.

23. *Life and Correspondence of Robert Southey*, ed. C.C. Southey, i,pp.220-21.

24. Joseph Priestley, *Hartley's Theory of the Human Mind* (London, 1775), pp.xvi-xvii.

25. Hartley, *Observations on Man, his Frame, his Duty, and his Expectations*, 2 Vols. (London, 1749),i,pp.369-70 (Ch.III, section iii).

26. Ibid.i,pp.419-20 (Ch. IV, section i).

27. Ibid.i,pp.472-3 (Ch.IV,section iv).

28. On Coleridge's apparently limited first-hand knowledge of Godwin's work, see *Lectures 1795*,p.lxviii.

29. Cf. Coleridge's note to *Religious Musings*,1.315,*PW*,i,121.

30. See the essay on 'Modern Patriotism', *Watchman*,pp.98-100.

31. Hartley, *Observations on Man*,i,p.ii (Introduction).

32. Ibid.i,p.114 (Ch.I,section iii); cf. note to *Religious Musings*, 1.43,*PW*,i,110.

33. Ibid.i,p.496 (Ch.IV,section vi).

34. My account of the Unitarian element in Coleridge's radicalism is indebted to L.W. Deen, op. cit., and to Peter Mann's introduction to the 'Lectures on Revealed Religion', in *Lectures 1795*, pp.liii-lxxx.

35. *Lectures 1795*,pp.125-6. The editorial notes to the second lecture indicate the considerable extent of Coleridge's debt to Lowman.

36. Ibid.pp.226-7.

37. Ibid.p.128.

38. Ibid.pp.8-11.

39. Ibid.pp.12-13. With Coleridge's assertion that the true patriot 'is hopeless concerning no one', cf. William Empson: 'Pantisocracy differed from Democracy, I judge from the derivation, in believing that even an aristocrat might be trusted, after conversion and repentance'. *Coleridge's Verse: a Selection*,pp.16-17.

40. Cf. *Religious Musings*, ll.45-49, PW,i,III.

41. 'To Jane: the Recollection', ll.41-52.

42. *Lectures 1795*, pp.217-18.

43. Coleridge, *On the Constitution of the Church and State* (1830), Everyman edition, ed. John Barrell (London, 1972), p.36.

44. *BL*,i,I.

45. Cf. *CL*,i,342: 'has [Poole] not already almost alienated, certainly very much cooled, the affections of some of his relations, by his exertions on *my* account?'

46. Sandford, *Thomas Poole and his Friends*, i,pp.97-98.

47. Godwin, *Political Justice*, ed. F.E.L. Priestley, ii,pp.191-200 (Bk.V,ch.xxii).

48. Edmund Burke, *Relections on the Revolution in France* (1790), Penguin edition, ed. C.C.O'Brien (London, 1970),p.135.'

49. See John Barrell's lucid account of Coleridge's arguments in *On the Constitution of the Church and State*, pp.viii-xxxi.

# Politics and the Problem of Audience

1. *Lectures* 1795,p.I; cf., e.g., John Colmer, *Coleridge, Critic of Society* (Oxford, 1959),p.23, and J.R. de J. Jackson, *Method and Imagination in Coleridge's Criticism* (London, 1969),pp.21-47.

2. *Specimens of the Table Talk of the Late Samuel Taylor Coleridge*, ed. H.N. Coleridge (London, 1835) September 12 1831.

3. Coleridge, *On the Constitution of the Church and State*,p.9.

4. *Friend*,i,pp.I, 163,407.

5. Marginal note in Sarah Hutchinson's copy of *Poems*, 1803, in Cornell University Library. *The Cornell Wordsworth Collection*, ed. G.H. Healey (Ithaca, New York, 1957), p.264, quoted in *Friend*,ii,p.25 Note 5.

6. *Lectures 1795*,p.5.

7. Ibid.p.4.

8. Quoted on A. Cobban, *The Debate on the French Revolution 1789-1800* (London, 1950), p.50.

9. Burke, *Reflections on the Revolution in France*, p.99.

10. Mary Wollstonecraft, *Vindication of the Rights of Women*, Penguin edition, ed. Miriam Kramnick (London, 1975), p.91.

11. *Critical Review*, N.S. xiii (April 1795), p.445.

12. Lucyle Werkmeister, 'Coleridge's *The Plot Discovered;* Some Facts and a Speculation', *MP*,lvi (1958-9), pp.254-63.

13. *Lectures 1795*,p.27.

14. *Friend*,ii,pp.21-26.

15. See *CL*,i,435-7.

16. *Friend*,ii,pp.25-26 (Coleridge's note).

17. Robert Southey to Charles Danvers, June 15 1809, *New Letters of Robert Southey*, ed. K. Curry, 2 Vols. (London and New York, 1965),i,p.511.

18. Thelwall's marginal note in his copy of *Biographia Literaria*, quoted

by George Watson, 'The revolutionary youth of Wordsworth and Coleridge', *Critical Quarterly*, xviii (1976), pp.49-66.

19. See e.g., *Friend*,i,p.ii; *BL*,i,p.34. Peacock puts the phrase into Flosky's mouth in *Nightmare Abbey* (London, 1818), Ch VI.

20. *BL*,i,p.121; cf. the letter signed 'Q' in *Monthly Magazine*, xxiv (1819), pp.203-205.

21. G.S. Veitch, *The Genesis of Parliamentary Reform* (London, 1913),p.340.

22. See especially Ch.5, 'Planting the Liberty Tree'; throughout the present chapter I have leant heavily on the work of historians, more particularly P.A. Brown, *The French Revolution in English History* (London, 1918); W.P. Hall, *British Radicalism, 1791-97* (New York, 1912); E.J. Hobsbawm, *Industry and Empire* (London, 1968); S. MacCoby, *The English Radical Tradition 1763-1914* (London, 1952). The volumes by E.P. Thompson and E. Halévy (cited below) are indispensable to a study of the period. There is a wealth of detailed material on radical activity in the 1790's in James Walvin, 'English Democratic Societies and Popular Radicalism, 1791-1800', an unpublished Ph.D thesis submitted in the University of York, 1969.

23. Brown, op. cit., pp.78-81, gives a convenient summary of the events; Coleridge's sonnet is, of course, a reference to Priestley's departure for America in 1794.

24. E. Halévy, *England in 1815* (1913), trans. E.I. Watkins and D.A. Barker (London, 1924), p.245.

25. R.B. Rose, 'The Priestley Riots of 1791', *Past and Present*, No. 18, November 1960, p.84.

26. *Lectures 1795*, p.47.

27. J.R. MacGillivray, 'The Pantisocracy Scheme and its Immediate Background', p.138.

28. Maurice W. Kelly, 'Thomas Cooper and Pantisocracy', *MLN*,xlv (1930), p.182; see also Mary C. Park, 'Joseph Priestley and the Problem of Pantisocracy', *Proceedings of the Delaware County Institute of Science*, xi (1947), pp. 1-60.

29. *Lectures 1795*,pp.34-35.

30. Sandford, *Thomas Poole and his Friends*,i,pp.112-13.

31. MacGillivray, 'The Pantisocracy Scheme and its Immediate Background', pp.148-49.

32. *Watchman*,p.5.

33. G.S. Veitch, *The Genesis of Parliamentary Reform* p.208.

34. P.A. Brown, *The French Revolution in English History*, 2nd ed. (London, 1923),p.54; on the Whig Friends of the People, see Frank O'Gorman, *The Whig Party and the French Revolution* (London, 1967).

35. Cf. *CL*,i,347.

36. Lord Coleridge, *The Story of a Devonshire House* (London, 1905),pp.59-65.

37. *CL*,i,182-84; cf. Thompson, *Making of the English Working Class* (London, 1963),p.150 note I.

38. See R.E. Scholfield, *The Lunar Society of Birmingham* (London, 1963).

39. *Letters 1795*, pp.235-51; *Watchman*,pp.130-40.

40. The petition is reprinted in *Lectures 1795*,p.367.

41. M.G. Jones, *Hannah More* (Cambridge, 1952), p.142.

42. *Life and Correspondence of Robert Southey*, ed. C.C. Southey, i,p.127.

43. Jones, *Hannah More*,pp.125, 138-39.

44. Quoted in Veitch, *The Genesis of Parliamentary Reform*,p.166.

45. Figures for the sales of books are from R.D. Altick, *The English Common Reader* (Chicago, 1957), pp.69-72.

46. *Lectures 1795*, p.149.

47. Sandford, *Thomas Poole and his Friends*,i,pp.34-35.

48. R.K. Webb, *The British Working Class Reader* (London ,1955), p.42.

49. Ibid. p.43. Coleridge had read Paley's book: cf. *CL*,i,48; *CN*,75 note.

50. Thompson, *Making of the English Working Class*, pp.151-52.

51. Lawrence, *Coleridge and Wordsworth in Somerset* (Newton Abbot, 1970),pp.40-41.

52. John Thelwall, *Poems chiefly written in Retirement*, 2nd ed. (London, 1801),pp.xxx-xxxvii.

53. *Specimens of the Table Talk of the late Samuel Taylor Coleridge*, ed. H.N. Coleridge, July 27 1830.

54. *WPW*,i,p.363.

55. John Thelwall to Mrs Thelwall, July 18 1797, Sandford, *Thomas Poole and his Friends*,i, pp.232-33.

56. Thelwall, *Poems chiefly written in Retirement*, p.xlvi.

57. *Hazlitt Works*, iv, p.214 ('Coriolanus', in *Characters of Shakespeare's Plays*).

58. Sandford, *Thomas Poole and his Friends*,i,p.280.

59. Ibid.i,p.33.

60. Ibid.i,p.54.

61. Thomas Poole to S. Purkis, May 10 1797, ibid,i,p.220.

62. Ibid.i,p.222.

63. Ibid.i,p.235.

64. Ibid.i,p251.

65. Thompson, *Making of the English Working Class*,pp.162,183-85.

66. Quoted in Brown, *The French Revolution in English History*,p.157.

67. Burke, *Reflections on the Revolution in France*, e.g., pp.180-81.

68. Quoted in Cobban, *The Debate on the French Revolution 1789-1800* pp.99-100.

69. See J. Steven Watson, *The Reign of George III* (Oxford, 1960), pp.325,361; Brown, *The French Revolution in English History*,p.131.

70. J.A. Colmer, *Coleridge: Critic of Society* (Oxford, 1959),p.4.

71. Hanson, *Life of S.T. Coleridge: The Early Years*, p.208.

72. *BL*, i, 127.

73. *Lectures 1795*, p.60.

74. The facts are presented by A.J. Eagleston, 'Wordsworth, Coleridge, and the Spy', in *Coleridge: Studies by several hands . . .*, pp.73-87.

The essay quotes extensively from correspondence preserved in the Home Office records: other sources are *BL*,i, 126-28: *Life and Correspondence of Robert Southey*, ed. C.C. Southey, ii, p.243; Sandford, *Thomas Poole and his friends*, i,pp.235-43. See also George W. Meyer, 'Wordsworth and the Spy Hunt', *American Scholar*, Winter 1950-51, pp.50-56; and E.P. Thompson, 'Disenchantment or Default? A Lay Sermon'.

75. *BL*, i, 128-29.

76. Eagleston, 'Wordsworth, Coleridge, and the Spy', pp.80-82.

77. *CL*, i, 403-405.

78. Brown, *The French Revolution in English History*, p.86.

79. M.D. George, *Catalogue of Political and Personal Satires . . . in the British Museum*, Vol. vii (1793-1800) (London, 1942), p.280.

80. George, *Catalogue of Political and Personal Satires . . .in the British Museum*, p.468, attributes the *New Morality* to Canning, but L. Rice-Oxley, *Poetry of the Anti-Jacobin* (Oxford, 1924), p.190, attributes the lines on Coleridge to Canning and Frere, and the whole poem to Canning, Frere, Ellis, Gifford, and possibly even Pitt himself.

81. *The Anti-Jacobin; or, Weekly Examiner*, 2 Vols., 4th edition (London, 1799), ii, p.636. Cf. E.V. Lucas, *Charles Lamb and the Lloyds* (London, 1898), pp.68-76.

82. George, *Catalogue of Political and Personal Satires . . .in the British Museum*,pp.468-72.

83. *The Beauties of the Anti-Jacobin* (London, 1799), p.iv.

84. Ibid.p.306.

85. *Anti-Jacobin*,ii, p.653.

86. Ibid.ii, pp.263-69.

87. *Critical Review*, N.S. xii (November 1794), pp.260-62.

88. Ibid. N.S. xiii (April 1795), p.455; N.S. xvi (February 1796), pp.216-17.

89. *British Critic*, vii (May 1796), pp.549-50.

90. *Critical Review*, N.S. xvii (June 1796), pp. 209-12.

91. *British Critic*, xiii (June 1799), pp.662-63; *Critical Review*, N.S. xxvi (August 1799), pp.473-75. The *Analytical Review*, xxviii (December 1798), remained sympathetic in its review of *Fears in Solitude*.

92. *Anti-Jacobin*,i,pp.31-34.

93. Ibid.i,pp.69-72.

94. See e.g., *Lectures 1795*, p.lxv; Colmer, *Coleridge: Critic of Society*,Ch.I.

95. See the 'Essay on Fasts', *Watchman*, pp.51-55. Coleridge estimated that this essay lost him 'near five hundred of my subscribers at one blow'; *BL*,i,120. Cf. *CL*,i,181,189.

96. *Watchman*, p.99.

97. But on the possibility of some real justification for the attack on Gerrald, see Peter Mann, 'Coleridge, Joseph Gerrald, and the Slave Trade', *Wordsworth Circle*, viii (1977), pp.38-46.

# The Literary Context of Retirement

1. Humphrey House, *Coleridge* (The Clark Lectures 1951-52) (London, 1953) p.73.

2. George Watson, *Coleridge the Poet* (London, 1966), pp. 61-84.

3. Walter Jackson Bate, *Coleridge* (London, 1969), pp.43-46; R.H. Fogle, 'Coleridge's Conversation Poems', *Tulane Studies in English*, ix (1959), pp.103-10, p.106; Max F. Schulz, *The Poetic Voices of Coleridge* (Detroit, 1963),pp.73-99.

4. M.H. Abrams, 'Structure and Style in the Greater Romantic Lyric', in *From Sensibility to Romanticism: Essays Presented to Frederick A. Pottle*, ed. F.W. Hilles and H. Bloom (New York, 1965), pp. 527-60; W.K. Wimsatt, 'The Structure of Romantic Nature Imagery', in *The Verbal Icon* (Kentucky 1954), pp. 103-16 (reprinted in *English Romantic Poets: Modern Essays in Criticism*, ed. M.H. Abrams (New York, 1960), pp. 25-36); Richard Haven, *Patterns of Consciousness* (Boston, 1969),pp.43-77; Robert Langbaum, *The Poetry of Experience* (New York, 1957), pp.1-68.

5. *Letters of Charles and Mary Lamb*, ed. E.V. Lucas, 3 Vols. (London, 1935), i,p.55-56.

6. Ibid.i,p.59.

7. Ibid. i, pp.10,16.

8. Wimsatt, op. cit., (in *English Romantic Poets*, ed. Abrams), p.28.

9. Important passages in Horace and Virgil are discussed in the present chapter; see also Martial's tenth Epigram, and the chorus in Seneca, *Thyestes*, II.i for other influential statements of the retirement themes.

10. Langbaum, op. cit., is an excellent discussion of this development. See also Marilyn Butler, *Jane Austen and the War of Ideas* (Oxford, 1975), for interesting material in relation particularly to the novel in the late eighteenth century.

11. *Prose Works*, i,p.128.

12. On *The Thorn*, see S.M. Parrish, *The Art of the Lyrical Ballads* (Cambridge, Mass., 1973), pp.95-114; various critics have approached *The Ancient Mariner* as a dramatisation of the mariner's guilty consciousness: the best-known studies are David Beres, 'A Dream, A Vision, and a Poem: A Psycho-analytic Study of the Origins of the Rime of the Ancient Mariner', *International Journal of Psychoanalysis*, xxxii (1951), pp. 97-116; D.W. Harding, 'The Theme of The Ancient Mariner', *Scrutiny*, ix (1941), pp.334-42 (reprinted in *Experience into Words* New York, 1963); William Empson, 'The Ancient Mariner', *Critical Quarterly*, vi (1964), pp.298-319 (and see Empson's Introduction to *Coleridge's Verse: A Selection*).

13. E.R. Wasserman, 'Nature Moralized: The Divine Analogy in the Eighteenth Century', *ELH*, xx (1953), pp. 39-76, p.39.

14. W.G. Hoskins, *The Making of the English Landscape* (London 1955), Penguin edition, 1970, p. 178.

15. William Gilpin, *Observations, relative chiefly to Picturesque Beauty,*

*Made in the year 1772, on several parts of England; particularly the mountains and lakes of Cumberland and Westmoreland,* 2 Vols. (London, 1786), ii, p.44.

16. Ruskin's major attacks on the picturesque were made in *Modern Painters;* see Martin Price, 'The Picturesque Moment', in *From Sensibility to Romanticism,* ed. Hilles and Bloom, pp.259-92.

17. Payne Knight, *The Landscape,* 2nd ed. (London, 1795) note to Bk. I,ll.257-70.

18. Edmund Burke, *A Philosophical Enquiry into the Origin of our Ideas of the Sublime and Beautiful* (London, 1756), Part 4, Section IX.

19. For a discussion of landscape gardening in this context, see Raymond Williams, *The Country and the City* (London, 1973), Ch.12.

20. Cowper, *The Task,* 1785, Bk. I, 'The Sofa', ll.413-27; Wordsworth, *Prelude,* Bk. XI, ll.121-223; Jane Austen, *Northanger Abbey* (London, 1818), Ch. 14.

21. Ll.580-89 in Warton's translation, *The Works of Virgil,* 4 Vols. (London, 1753-88).

22. On stock diction, see Thomas Quayle, *Poetic Diction, a study of Eighteenth Century Verse* (London, 1924), and the valuable study by John Arthos, *The Language of Natural Description in Eighteenth Century Poetry* (London, 1949). Also, C.V. Deane, *Aspects of Eighteenth Century Nature Poetry* (Oxford, 1935), and G. Tillotson's discussions of eighteenth century poetry in his *Augustan Studies* (London, 1961).

23. Cf. Arthos, *The Language of Natural Description in Eighteenth Century Poetry,* p.75.

24. See Dix Harwood, *Love for Animals and how it Developed in Great Britain* (London, 1928).

25. *Tintern Abbey,* note to line 4. Wordsworth's notes to *Descriptive Sketches* are in very much the same idiom.

26. The Lloyd version is unfortunately lost. It is quoted in Campbell, pp.591-2.

27. Fenwick note to *An Evening Walk, WPW,* i,p.319.

28. Cf. Thomson's *Poetical Works,* ed. J. Logie Robertson (London, 1908), p.307.

29. Coleridge, talking in disenchantment of Bowles, *CL,*ii,864.

30. References are to the text of 1655, the 'B' text, draft IV, in Brendan O'Hehir, *Expans'd Hieroglyphicks, a critical edition of Sir John Denham's Coopers Hill* (Berkeley and Los Angeles, 1969).

31. Gilpin, op. cit., ii, pp.120-21.

32. 'Life of Denham', in Samuel Johnson *Lives of the Poets,* 10 Vols. (London, 1779-81); on topographical poetry, see R.A. Aubin, *Topographical Poetry in XVIIIth Century England* (New York, 1936).

33. *Poems of Alexander Pope* (Twickenham Edition), Vol. I, *Pastoral Poetry and An Essay on Criticism,* ed. E. Audra and A. Williams (London, 1961), pp.131-44.

34. Norman Ault, *New Light on Pope* (London, 1949), pp.87-88.

35. *Poems of John Milton,* ed. A. Fowler and J. Carey (London, 1968), p.624 (note to *Paradise Lost,* IV, ll.233-35).

36.  Charles Cotton, *Poetical Works*, (London, 1770 edition), p.342.

37.  On the picturesque element in the *Elegy*, see Jean Hagstrum, *The Sister Arts* (Chicago, 1958), p.293.

38.  G.M. Harper, 'Coleridge's Conversation Poems', *Quarterly Review*, ccxliv (1925), pp.284-98; reprinted in *Spirit of Delight* (New York, 1928), and in *English Romantic Poets*, ed. Abrams, pp.144-57.

39.  Wordsworth, 'Essay, Supplementary to the Preface' of 1815; *Prose Works*, iii, p.73.

40.  Cf. Thomson, *Spring*, 1.483, *Summer* 1.1401.

41.  Bowles, *Sonnets and other Poems* (London, 1800 edition), pp.v,vii.

42.  On Wordsworth's early enthusiasm for Bowles, See *Recollections of the Table-Talk of Samuel Rogers*, ed. Alexander Dyce (London, 1856); on Southey's see William Haller, *The Early Life of Robert Southey* (New York, 1917).

43.  The only extended discussion of the English sonnet in the eighteenth century is in R.D. Havens, *The Influence of Milton on English Verse* (Boston, Mass., 1961) (revised edition).

44.  Horace, *Satires, Epistles and Ars Poetica* trans. H.R. Fairclough (Loeb Classical Library), (London, 1947), p.315.

45.  'Life of Gray', in Samuel Johnson, *Lives of the Poets*.

46.  For details of *Sonnets from Various Authors*, see *CL*,i,252; *PW*,ii,1138-41.

47.  *Poetical Works of William Lisle Bowles*, ed. Rev. G. Gilfillan, 2 Vols. (London, 1855), i, pp.23-24.

48.  On Coleridge's early knowledge of Italian and French, see the comments in Fruman, *Coleridge the Damaged Archangel*, pp.63-64.

49.  Preston, *Poetical Works*, 2 Vols. (Dublin, 1793),i,pp.257-68; for the criticism of Petrarch, i, pp.262-63.

50.  Ibid. i,p.268.

51.  *BL*,i,108; an excellent account of the importance of genre in Coleridge's criticism is in R.H. Fogle, *The Idea of Coleridge's Criticism* (Berkeley and Los Angeles, 1962), pp.1-17.

# The Conversation Poems

## THE EOLIAN HARP

1.  M.H. Abrams, 'Coleridge's "A Light in Sound": Science, Meta-science, and Poetic Imagination', *Proceedings of the American Philosophical Society*, cxvi (1972), pp. 458-76.

2.  Coleridge, *Poems on Various Subjects* (Bristol, 1796), pp.96-100.

3.  Coleridge, *Poems*, 2nd edition (Bristol and London, 1797), pp.96-99..

4.  G.M. Matthews, 'Shelly's Lyrics', in *The Morality of Art*, ed. D.W. Jefferson, 1969, pp. 195-209, p.201.

5. A.S. Gerard, *English Romantic Poetry: Ethos, Structure and Symbol in Coleridge, Wordsworth, Shelley, and Keats* (Berkeley and Los Angeles, 1968), p.26.

6. H.W. Piper, '"The Eolian Harp" again', *N&Q*, ccxiii (1968), pp.23-25.

7. C.G. Martin, 'Coleridge and Cudworth: A Source for "The Eolian Harp" ', *N&Q*, ccxi (1966), pp.173-76; cf. *Bristol Borrowings*, pp.120,124.

8. Piper, op. cit., identifies 'Monro' as Alexander Monro, eminent surgeon and Professor of Anatomy at Edinburgh, 1720-64. Cf. *DNB*, 'Alexander Monro, *primus*'.

9. Piper's article cited above is a reply to Martin's argument for the influence of Cudworth; Piper had already suggested Coleridge's possible debt to Cudworth in *The Eolian Harp*, in his *The Active Universe*, pp.43-46.

10. For Cudworth's discussion of 'plastic nature', see *The True Intellectual System of the Universe*, ed. Harrison, 3 Vols. (London, 1845), i, pp.246-62.

11. Joseph Warren Beach, *The Concept of Nature in Nineteenth Century English Poetry* (New York, 1936), p.61. On Cudworth see also J.A. Passmore, *Ralph Cudworth, An Interpretation* (London, 1951); and Basil Willey, *The Seventeenth Century Background* (London, 1934).

12. Geoffrey Grigson, *The Harp of Aeolus and other Essays on Art, Literature and Nature* (London, 1947), p.24.

13. Martin, "Coleridge and Cudworth: A Source for "The Eolian Harp"', p.176.

14. A.E. Powell, *The Romantic Theory of Poetry* (London, 1926), pp. 81,85; Powell quotes from *Reflections* and *Frost at Midnight* in support of her argument (p.87).

15. See, e.g., M.F. Schulz, *The Poetic Voices of Coleridge*, pp.86-91; J.D. Boulger, 'Imagination and Speculation in Coleridge's Conversation Poems', *JEGP*, lxiv (1965), pp.691-711.

16. *Enneads*, trans. S. MacKenna, 3rd edition (London, 1956), p.323.

17. For Plotinus on private attachment see *Enneads*, IV, iii, 32.

18. Martin, 'Coleridge and Cudworth: A Source for "The Eolian Harp"', p.175; Piper, '"The Eolian Harp" again', p.24.

19. *The Philosophical Lectures of Samuel Taylor Coleridge*, ed. K. Coburn (London, 1949), p.371.

20. Thomson, *Poetical Works*, p.432.

21. *Poems of Gray, Collins and Goldsmith*, ed. Roger Lonsdale (London, 1969), p.161, note to l.i.

22. Fruman, *Coleridge, the Damaged Archangel*, p.256.

23. *The Poems of Cuthbert Shaw and Thomas Russel*, ed. Eric Partridge (London, 1925), pp.28-30.

24. *DNB*, entry on Bampfylde.

25. Bampfylde's sonnet is reprinted in *Wayside Sonnets 1750-1850*, ed. Edmund Blunden and Bernard Mellor (Hong Kong, 1971), p.5.

26. *Works of Charles and Mary Lamb*, ed. E.V. Lucas, 7 Vols. (London, 1903), v, p.4.

27. Coleridge, *Poems*, 3rd edition (London 1803), p.130.

28. Lucyle Werkmeister, 'Coleridge, Bowles and feelings of the heart', *Anglia*, lxxviii (1960), pp.56-73.

29. A.S. Gerard, *English Romantic Poetry*, p.37.

30. A.S. Gerard, 'The Systolic Rhythm: the structure of Coleridge's conversation poems', *Essays in Criticism*, x (1960), pp.307-19.

31. G.M. Harper, 'Coleridge's Conversation Poems', in *English Romantic Poets*, ed. Abrams, p.148.

32. Abrams, *Natural Supernaturalism*, pp.268-77.

33. Campbell, p.578.

34. R.C. Wendling, 'Coleridge and the consistency of The Eolian Harp', *Studies in Romanticism*, viii (1968-69), pp.26-42, refers in a note to 'the French author Roland', and assumes that 'la citoyenne Roland' was a man (p.28). Coleridge still retained the note in 1803.

# REFLECTIONS ON HAVING LEFT A PLACE OF RETIREMENT

1. *Coleridge's Verse: A Selection*, ed. William Empson and David Pirie, pp.218-19.

2. C.G. Martin, 'Coleridge and Crowe's Lewesdon Hill', *MLR*, lxii (1967), pp.400-406.

3. *Bristol Borrowings*, p.119.

4. C.M. Maclean, 'Lewesdon Hill and its Poet', *Essays and Studies*, xxvii (1941), pp.30-40.

5. Martin, 'Coleridge and Crowe's Lewesdon Hill', p.402.

6. *BL*,i, 10-11.

7. Martin, 'Coleridge and Crowe's Lewesdon Hill', p.400.

8. *Bristol Borrowings*, p.122.

9. *Lectures 1795*, p.22.

10. *Watchman*, pp.269-73.

11. Ibid.p.164.

12. Ibid. p.279; *CL*, i, 250.

13. For Coleridge on Hartley, see *CL*,i, 126,200,245,288; on Priestley, see *CL* i, 192-93.

14. Martin, 'Coleridge and Crowe's Lewesdon Hill', p.401.

15. Cf. Joseph Cottle, *Early Recollections chiefly relating to the late Samuel Taylor Coleridge*, 2 Vols. (London, 1837),ii,p.52.

16. See *Specimens of the Table Talk of the late Samuel Taylor Coleridge*, January 1 1834.

17. Geoffrey Grigson, *The Harp of Aeolus*, p.32.

18. *Bristol Borrowings*, p.119.

19. *Lectures 1795* p.232.

20. See S.F. Johnson, 'Coleridge's *The Watchman*: Decline and Fall', *RES*, N.S. iv (1953), pp. 147-48.

21. *Watchman*, pp.169-70.

22. Ibid. p.168.
23. Ibid. pp.170-72.
24. *CL*, i, 206.
25. *Watchman*, p.175; cf. *Poetical Works of William Lisle Bowles*, i, p.40.
26. *Watchman*, p.178.
27. Coleridge, *Poems*, 2nd edition 1797, p.153.
28. A different version of this sonnet is given in *CL*,i, 352.
29. *CN*, 87.
30. *Lectures 1795*, p.46.
31. Geoffrey Carnall, 'The *Monthly Magazine*', *RES*, N.S. v (1954), pp.158-64,p.158.
32. *Monthly Magazine*, i (May 1796), pp.273-77.
33. Coleridge plagiarised from Bowles more than once: see, e.g., Lucyle Werkmeister, 'Coleridge's 'Anthem' : Another Debt to Bowles', *JEGP*, lviii (1959), pp.270-75; Fruman, *Coleridge the Damaged Archangel*, pp.223ff.
34. Lamb translated Coleridge's epigraph as 'properer for a sermon': *Specimens of the Table Talk of the late Samuel Taylor Coleridge*, July 25 1832.
35. Cf. John Foster, *An Essay on the different nature of Accent and Quantity, &c.* (Eton, 1763): '... unpoetical subjects, in very unpoetic expression, with loose metre, and according to their name, *sermoni propiora*' (pp.201-202). Coleridge borrowed Foster's work from the Bristol Library in October 1796 (*Bristol Borrowings*, p.124). See R.T. Martin, 'Coleridge's use of "*sermoni propriora*"', *Wordsworth Circle*, iii (1972), pp.71-75. It is very characteristic that Coleridge should seek defence in genre.

## THIS LIME-TREE BOWER MY PRISON

1. Hanson, *Life of Coleridge*, pp.157ff; cf. *CL*, i, 330-37.
2. Campbell, p.591.
3. *CN*, 157; cf. *PW*, ii, 990. There are cancelled variants in the text sent to Southey, *CL*,i, 334-36.
4. Piper, *The Active Universe*, pp.80-81.
5. Mark L. Reed, *Wordsworth: The Chronology of the Early Years* (Cambridge, Mass., 1967), p.20. References to *Lines left upon a Seat in a Yew-Tree* are to the text of *Lyrical Ballads*, 1798; see *Lyrical Ballads*,ed. R.L. Brett and A.R. Jones (London ,1963), pp.38-40.
6. A letter from Lamb to Coleridge, written on his return from Nether Stowey, indicates that Coleridge actually recited Wordsworth's poem to Lamb during his stay; *Letters of Charles and Mary Lamb*, i,p.112.
7. Wordsworth's poem was not in fact written with Coleridge in mind, of course; see the Fenwick note, *WPW*,i, p.329.
8. *CN*, 41; cf. *CN* 1512, a very interesting analogous passage.
9. Campbell, p.591.
10. This is the text of the *Annual Anthology*; cf. *PW*,i,´ 179, ll.5-20. Coleridge substituted 'blue' for 'dim' in 1.20, in *Sibylline Leaves*.

11. Coleridge must mean here that the dell is only speckled by the sun, *even* at mid-day; the poem is set between late afternoon and early twilight.

12. In the *Annual Anthology* this line reads 'With some fair bark, perhaps, which lightly touches'; an even more painterly touch.

13. Richard Haven, *Patterns of Consciousness*, p.65.

14. *Coleridge's Verse: A Selection*, ed. William Empson and David Pirie, p.23.

15. Cf. *Psalms* 93, 104.

16. *This Lime-Tree Bower* was 'A Poem Addressed to Charles Lamb, of the India House, London', in the *Annual Anthology; PW*,i,178.

# FROST AT MIDNIGHT

1. See, e.g. R.A. Durr, 'This Lime-Tree Bower my Prison and a Recurrent Action in Coleridge', *ELH*, xxvi (1959), pp.514-30; Richard Haven, *Patterns of Consciousness*, pp.43-77; R.H. Fogle, *The Idea of Coleridge's Criticism*, pp.28-33 (the best discussion of *This Lime-Tree Bower*); R.C. Wendling, 'Dramatic Reconcilation in Coleridge's Conversation Poems', *Papers on English Language and Literature*, ix (1973), pp.145-60; George Gilpin, 'Coleridge and the Spiral of Poetic Thought', *Studies in English Literature*, xii (1972), pp. 639-52; M.G. Sundell, 'The Theme of Self-Realization in "Frost at Midnight"', *Studies in Romanticism*, vii (1967-68), pp.34-39.

2. M.H. Abrams, 'Structure and Style in the Greater Romantic Lyric', p.532.

3. House, *Coleridge*, pp. 72, 78-79.

4. Fruman, *Coleridge, the Damaged Archangel*, pp.305-10.

5. Schulz, *The Poetic Voices of Coleridge*, p.94.

6. Text of quarto pamphlet, 1978, *PW*,i, 240-41.

7. *PW*, i, 241.

# FEARS IN SOLITUDE

1. Swinburne, 'Coleridge', in *Essays and Studies* (London, 1875), pp.259-75, p.271.

2. Woodring, *Politics in the Poetry of Coleridge*, p.190.

3. Ibid. p.189.

4. Ibid.p.193.

# THE NIGHTINGALE

1. See, e.g., Stephen Prickett, *Wordsworth and Coleridge: The Poetry of Growth* (Cambridge, 1970), pp.147-74.

2. R.H. Hopkins, 'Coleridge's Parody of Melancholy Poetry in "The Nightingale"', *English Studies,* xlix (1968), pp.436-41.

3. *CN,* 219.

4. *CN,* 231.

5. *CN,* 217.

6. *CN,* 229.

7. House, *Coleridge,* p.82.

# BIBLIOGRAPHY

The place of publication is London, unless otherwise stated.


## Coleridge

*An Answer to "A Letter to Edward Long Fox, M.D."*, Bristol, 1795.
*Biographia Literaria* (1817), ed. J. Shawcross, 2 vols., Oxford, 1907.
*Coleridge's Miscellaneous Criticism*, ed. T.M.Raysor, 1936.
*Coleridge's Poems*, ed. J.Beer, 1963.
*Coleridge's Shakespearian Criticism*, ed. T.M. Raysor, 2 Vols., 1930.
*Coleridge's Verse: A Selection*, ed. William Empson and David Pirie, 1972.
*The Collected Letters of Samuel Taylor Coleridge*, ed. E.L.Griggs, 6 Vols., Oxford, 1956-71.
*The Complete Poetical Works of S.T.Coleridge*, ed. E.H.Coleridge, 2 Vols., Oxford, 1912
*Conciones ad Populum, or Addresses to the People*, Bristol, 1795.
*The Fall of Robespierre*, [with Robert Southey] Cambridge, 1794.
*Fears in Solitude . . . To which are added, France, an Ode; and Frost at Midnight*, 1798.
*The Friend* (Penrith, 1809-10; 1812; 3 Vols., 1818), Ed. B.Rooke, 1969 (*The Collected Coleridge*, Vol. IV).
*Lectures 1795: On Politics and Religion*, ed. Peter Mann and Lewis Patton, 1971 (*The Collected Coleridge*, Vol. I).
*Lyrical Ballads, with a few other Poems*, [with W.Wordsworth] Bristol and London, 1798.
*Lyrical Ballads* [with W.Wordsworth] (2 Vols., 1800), ed. R.L.Brett and A.R.Jones, 1963.
*A Moral and Political Lecture*, Bristol, 1795.
*The Notebooks of Samuel Taylor Coleridge*, ed. Kathleen Coburn, 5 Vols. (each in 2 parts; 3 volumes published), 1957- .
*On the Constitution of the Church and State, according to the Idea of Each with aids towards a right judgement on the late bill* (1830), ed. J.Barrell, 1972.
*The Philosophical Lectures of Samuel Taylor Coleridge*, ed. Kathleen Coburn, 1949.
*The Plot Discovered; or an Address to the People, against Ministerial Treason*, Bristol, 1795.
*Poems on Various Subjects*, Bristol, 1796.
*Poems by S.T. Coleridge, second edition, to which are now added Poems by Charles Lamb and Charles Lloyd*, Bristol and London, 1797.
*Poems, third edition*, 1803.
*The Poetical Works of Samuel Taylor Coleridge*, 3 Vols., 1828.
*The Poetical Works of Samuel Taylor Coleridge*, 3 Vols., 1829.
*The Poetical Works of Samuel Taylor Coleridge*, 3 Vols., 1834.

*The Poetical Works of Samuel Taylor Coleridge*, ed. J.Dykes Campbell, 1893.

*Specimens of the Table Talk of the late Samuel Taylor Coleridge*, ed. H.N.Coleridge, 1835.

*Sibylline Leaves*, 1817.

*The Watchman* (Bristol, March 1 - May 13 1796), ed. Lewis Patton, 1970 (*The Collected Coleridge*, Vol. II).

## General

Abrams, M.H. 'Coleridge's "A Light in Sound": Science, Metascience, and Poetic Imagination', *Proceedings of the American Philosophical Society*, cxvi (1972).

'The Correspondent Breeze: A Romantic Metaphor', in *English Romantic Poets*, ed. Abrams.

ed. *English Romantic Poets: Modern Essays in Criticism*, New York, 1960.

'English Romanticism: the Spirit of the Age', in *Romanticism Reconsidered*, ed. Frye.

*The Mirror and the Lamp: Romantic Theory and the Critical Tradition*, Oxford, 1953.

*Natural Supernaturalism: Tradition and Revolution in Romantic Literature*, 1971.

'Structure and Style in the Greater Romantic Lyric', in *From Sensibility to Romanticism*, ed. Hilles and Bloom.

Adair, Patricia. *The Waking Dream*, 1967.

Akenside, Mark. *Poetical Works*, ed. Rev. G.Gilfillan, 1854.

Altick, R.D. *The English Common Reader*, Chicago, 1957.

*The Anti-Jacobin; or, Weekly Examiner*, 2 Vols., 4th edition 1799.

Appleyard, J.A. *Coleridge's Philosophy of Literature*, Cambridge, Mass., 1965.

Arthos, John. *The Language of Natural Description in Eighteenth Century Poetry*, 1949.

Aubin, R.A. *Topographical Poetry in XVIIIth Century England*, New York, 1936.

Ault, Norman. *New Light on Pope*, 1949.

Bampfylde, J.C. *Sixteen Sonnets*, 1778.

Bate, W.J. *Coleridge*, 1969.

Beach, Joseph Warren. *The Concept of Nature in Nineteenth Century English Poetry*, New York, 1936.

*The Beauties of the Anti-Jacobin*, 1799.

Beer, J.B., ed. *Coleridge's Variety; Bicentenary Studies*, 1974.

*Coleridge the Visionary*, 1959.

Beres, D. 'A Dream, a Vision and a Poem: A Psychoanalytic Study of the Origins of the "Rime of the Ancient Mariner" ', *International Journal of Psycho-analysis*, xxxii (1951).

Bloom, H. *The Visionary Company*, 1962.

Blunden, E., and Griggs, E.L., eds. *Coleridge: studies by several hands on the hundredth anniversary of his death*, 1934.

Blunden, E., and Mellor, B., eds. *Wayside Sonnets, 1750-1850*, Hong Kong, 1971.

Boulger, J.D. 'Imagination and Speculation in Coleridge's Conversation Poems', *JEGP*, lxiv (1965).

Bowles, William Lisle. *Poetical Works*, ed. Rev G.Gilfillan, 2 Vols., 1855. *Sonnets and Other Poems*, 1800 edition.

Bradley, A.C. *A Miscellany*, 1929.

Brandl, A.L. 'Cowper's Winter Evening und Coleridge's Frost at Midnight', *Archiv*, xcvi (1896).

Brett, R.L., ed. *S.T.Coleridge*, 1971.

Briggs, Asa, *The Age of Improvement*, 1959.

Brinton, Crane. *The Political Ideas of the English Romanticists*, 1926.

Brown, P.A. *The French Revolution in English History*, 2nd ed., 1923.

Burke, Edmund. *A Philosophical Enquiry into the Origin of our Ideas of the Sublime and Beautiful* (1756), ed. J.T.Boulton, 1958.
*Reflections on the Revolution in France* (1790), ed. Conor Cruise O'Brien, 1970.

Burke, Kenneth. *The Philosophy of Literary Form*, Baton Rouge, L.A., 2nd edition 1967.

Butler, Marilyn. *Jane Austen and the War of Ideas*, Oxford, 1975.

Byatt, A.S. *Wordsworth and Coleridge in their Time*, 1970.

Calleo, D.P. *Coleridge and the Idea of the Modern State*, New Haven, Conn., 1966.

Campbell, J.Dykes. *Coleridge: A Narrative of the Events of his Life*, 1894.

Carnall, Geoffrey. 'The *Monthly Magazine*', *RES*, N.S. v (1954).
*Robert Southey and his Age*, Oxford, 1960.

Chambers, E.K. *Coleridge*, Oxford, 1938.

Christie, I.R. *Wilkes, Wyvill and Reform*, 1962.

Cobban, A., ed. *The Debate on the French Revolution 1789-1800*, 1950.
*Edmund Burke and the Revolt against the Eighteenth Century*, 1960.

Coburn, Kathleen, *Coleridge: A Collection of Critical Essays*, Englewood Cliffs, N.J., 1967.
*The Interpenetration of Man and Nature* (Warton Lecture on English Poetry, British Academy), 1963.
'Reflexions in a Coleridge Mirror', in *From Sensibility to Romanticism*, ed. Hilles and Bloom.

Coldicutt, D. 'Was Coleridge the Author of the "Enquirer" Series in the *Monthly Magazine*, 1796-9?', *RES*, xv (1939).

Coleridge, Lord. *The Story of a Devonshire House*, 1905.

Colmer, J.A. *Coleridge: Critic of Society*, Oxford, 1959.

Cone, Carl B. *The English Jacobins*, New York, 1968.

Cottle, Joseph. *Early Recollections chiefly relating to the late Samuel Taylor Coleridge*, 2 Vols., 1837.

Cotton, Charles. *Poems*, ed. J. Beresford, 1923.
*The Wonders of the Peak*, 1681.

Cowper, William. *Poetical Works*, ed. H.Milford, Oxford, 1905.

Crowe, William. *Lewesdon Hill*, 1786.

Cudworth, Ralph. *The True Intellectual System of the Universe* (1743), ed. F.Harrison, 3 Vols., 1845.

Darwin, Erasmus. *The Botanic Garden*, 2 Vols., 1794-5.

Davie, Donald. *Purity of Diction in English Verse*, 1952.

Deane, C.V. *Aspects of Eighteenth Century Nature Poetry*, Oxford, 1935.

Deen, L.W. 'Coleridge and the Sources of Pantisocracy: Godwin, the Bible, and Hartley', in *Boston University Studies in English*, New York, 1961.

Deschamps, Paul. *La Formation de la Pensée de Coleridge, 1772-1804*, Paris, 1964.

Doughty, Oswald. 'Coleridge and a Poet's Poet: William Lisle Bowles', *English Miscellany*, xiv (1963).

Durr, R.A. 'This Lime-Tree Bower my Prison and a recurrent action in Coleridge', *ELH*, xxvi (1959).

Dyson, A.E., ed. *English Poetry: Select Bibliographical Guides*, 1971.

Eagleston, A.J. 'Wordsworth, Coleridge, and the Spy', in *Coleridge: studies by several hands . . .*, ed. Blunden and Griggs.

Empson, William. 'The Ancient Mariner', *Critical Quarterly*, vi (1964).

'The Enquirer', *Monthly Magazine*, i (1796).

Erdman, D.V. 'Coleridge as Editorial Writer', in *Power and Consciousness*, ed. O'Brien and Vanech.

Fairchild, H.N. *The Noble Savage*, New York, 1928.

*The Romantic Quest*, New York, 1931.

Fausset, H.L'Anson, ed. *Minor Poets of the Eighteenth Century* (Dyer, Finch, Green), 1930.

Fitzgerald, Margaret M. *First Follow Nature: Primitivism in English Poetry 1725-1750*, New York, 1947.

Fogle, R.H. 'Coleridge's Conversation Poems', *Tulane Studies in English*, ix (1959).

*The Idea of Coleridge's Criticism*, Berkeley, Calif., 1962.

Fruman, Norman. *Coleridge the Damaged Archangel*, 1971.

Frye, Northrop. 'The Drunken Boat: the Revolutionary Element in Romanticism', in *Romanticism Reconsidered*, ed. Frye.

ed. *Romanticism Reconsidered: Selected Papers from the English Institute*, Columbia, 1963.

Fuller, John. *The Sonnet*, 1972.

Garber, Frederick. 'The Hedging Consciousness in Coleridge's Conversation Poems', *Wordsworth Circle*, iv (1973).

George, M.D. *Catalogue of Political and Personal Satires . . . in the British Museum*, Vol. vii (1793-1800), 1942.

Gérard, A.S. 'Clevedon Revisited: Further Reflections on Coleridge's "Reflections . . .'", *N&Q*, ccv (1960).

'Counterfeiting Infinity: The Eolian Harp and the Growth of Coleridge's Mind', *JEGP*, lx (1961).

*English Romantic Poetry: Ethos, Structure and Symbol in Coleridge, Wordsworth, Shelley, and Keats*, Berkeley and Los Angeles, 1968.

'The Systolic Rhythym: the structure of Coleridge's conversation poems', *EC*, x (1960).

Gilfillan, Rev. G., ed. *Poetical Works of Beattie, Blair, and Falconer*, 1854. ed. *Poetical Works of Goldsmith, Collins, and T. Warton*, 1854.

Gillman, James. *Life of Coleridge*, 1838.

Gilpin, George. 'Coleridge and the Spiral of Poetic Thought', *Studies in English Literature*, xii (1972).

Gilpin, William. *Observations, relative chiefly to Picturesque Beauty, Made in the Year 1772. On several Parts of England; particularly the Mountains, and Lakes of Cumberland and Westmoreland*, 1786.

Godwin, William. *Political Justice* (1793), ed. F.E.L.Priestley, 3 Vols., Toronto, 1946.

Grant, A. *A Preface to Coleridge*, 1972.

Griggs, E.L., ed. *Wordsworth and Coleridge: studies in honour of George Maclean Harper*, Princeton, 1939.

Grigson, Geoffrey. *The Harp of Aeolus and other Essays on Art, Literature and Nature*, 1947.

Hagstrum, Jean. *The Sister Arts*, Chicago, 1958.

Halévy, E. *England in 1815* (1913), trans. E.I.Watkins and D.A.Barker, 1924.

Hall, W.P. *British Radicalism, 1791-97*, New York, 1912.

Haller, William. *The Early Life of Robert Southey*, New York, 1917.

Haney, J.L. *A Bibliography of Samuel Taylor Coleridge*, Philadelphia, 1903.

Hanson, L. *The Life of S.T.Coleridge: The Early Years*, 1938.

Harding, A.J. *Coleridge and the Idea of Love*, 1974.

Harding, D.W. 'The Theme of the Ancient Mariner', *Scrutiny*, ix (1941).

Harper, G.M. 'Coleridge's Conversation Poems', *Quarterly Review*, ccxliv (1925); rptd. in *Spirit of Delight*, New York, 1928, and in *English Romantic Poets*, ed. Abrams.

Hartley, David. *Observations on Man, his Frame, his Duties, and his Expectations*, 1749.

Hartmann, Geoffrey, ed. *New Perspectives on Wordsworth and Coleridge: Selected Papers from the English Institute*, Columbia, 1972.

Harwood, Dix. *Love for Animals and how it Developed in Great Britain*, 1928.

Haven, Richard. 'Coleridge, Hartley, and the Mystics', *Journal of the History of Ideas*, xx (1959). *Patterns of Consciousness*, Boston, 1969.

Havens, R.D. *The Influence of Milton on English Verse*, Boston, Mass., rev. edition 1961. 'Solitude and the Neoclassicists', *ELH*, xxi (1954).

Hazlitt, William. *The Complete Works*, ed. P.P.Howe, 21 Vols., 1930-34.

Hilles, F.W., and Bloom, H., eds. *From Sensibility to Romanticism: Essays Presented to Frederick A. Pottle*, New York, 1965.

Hobsbawm, E.J. *The Age of Revolution 1789-1848*, 1962. *Industry and Empire*, 1968.

Hopkins, R.H. 'Coleridge's Parody of Melancholy Poetry in The Nightingale', *English Studies*, xlix (1968).

Hoskins, W.G. *The Making of the English Landscape*, 1955.
Hough, G.G. *The Romantic Poets*, 3rd edition 1967.
House, Humphrey. *Coleridge* (the Clark Lectures, 1951-2), 1953.
Hussey, Christopher. *The Picturesque*, 1927.
Jackson, J.deJ., ed. *Coleridge: The Critical Heritage*, 1970.
  *Method and Imagination in Coleridge's Criticism*, 1969.
Johnson, S.F. 'Coleridge's *The Watchman*: Decline and Fall', *RES*, N.S.
  iv (1954).
Jones, A.R. 'Coleridge and Poetry: II. The Conversational and other
  Poems', in *S.T.Coleridge*, ed. Brett.
Jones, M.G. *Hannah More*, Cambridge, 1952.
Jordan, Frank, ed. *The English Romantic Poets: A Review of Research and
  Criticism*, New York, 3rd rev. edition 1972.
Kelley, M.W. 'Thomas Cooper and Pantisocracy', *MLN*, xlv (1930).
Knight, Richard Payne. *The Landscape*, 2md edition 1795.
Knights, L.C. *Further Explorations*, 1965.
Lamb, Charles and Mary. *The Letters*, ed. E.V.Lucas, 3 Vols., 1935.
  *The Works*, ed. E.V.Lucas, 5 Vols., 1903-05.
Langbaum, Robert. *The Poetry of Experience*, New York, 1957.
Lawrence, Berta M. *Coleridge and Wordsworth in Somerset*, Newton
  Abbot, 1970.
Leavis, F.R. 'Coleridge in Criticism', *Scrutiny*, ix (1940).
  ed. *Mill on Bentham and Coleridge*, 1950.
  *Revaluation*, 1936.
Lincoln, Anthony. *Some Political and Social Ideas of English Dissent,
  1763-1800*, 1938.
Logan, Sister Eugenia. 'Coleridge's Scheme of Pantisocracy and
  American Travel Accounts', *PMLA*, xlv (1930).
  ed. *Concordance to the Poetry of Samuel Taylor Coleridge*, St. Mary of the
  Woods, Ind., 1940.
Lonsdale, R., ed. *The Poems of Gray, Collins and Goldsmith*, 1969.
Lovejoy, A.O. *Essays in the History of Ideas*, Baltimore, 1948.
Lowes, J.L. *The Road to Xanadu*, 2nd edition 1930.
Lucas, E.V. *Charles Lamb and the Lloyds*, 1898.
MacCoby, S., *The English Radical Tradition 1763-1914*, 1952.
MacGillivray, J.R. 'The Pantisocracy Scheme and its Immediate
  Background', in *Studies in English by Members of University College,
  Toronto* (collected by Principal Malcolm Wallace), Toronto, 1931.
Maclean, C.M. 'Lewesdon Hill and its Poet', *Essays and Studies*, xxvii
  (1941).
Magnuson, Paul. 'The Dead Calm in the Conversation Poems',
  *Wordsworth Circle*, iii (1972).
Margoliouth, H.M. *Wordsworth and Coleridge 1795-1834*, 1953.
Marshall, W.H. 'The Structure of Coleridge's Eolian Harp'. *MLN*,
  lxxvi (1961).
  'The Structure of Coleridge's "Reflections on having left a Place of
  Retirement" ', *N&Q*, cciv (1959).
Martin, C.G. 'Coleridge and Crowe's Lewesdon Hill', *MLR*, lxii

(1967).

'Coleridge and Cudworth: A Source for "The Eolian Harp" ', *N&Q*, ccxi (1966).

Martin, R.T. 'Coleridge's use of "sermoni propriora" ', *Wordsworth Circle*, iii (1972).

Mayo, R. 'The Contemporaneity of the *Lyrical Ballads*', *PMLA*, lxix (1954).

McFarland, T. *Coleridge and the Pantheist Tradition*, Oxford, 1969.

'Coleridge's Anxiety', in *Coleridge's Variety*, ed. Beer.

Meyer, G.W. 'Wordsworth and the Spy Hunt', *American Scholar*, Winter 1950-51.

Milley, H.J.W. 'Some Notes on Coleridge's Eolian Harp', *MP*, xxxvi (1939).

Milton, John. *Poems*, ed. A.Fowler and J.Carey, 1968.

Moorman, Mary. *William Wordsworth: The Early Years 1770-1803*, Oxford, 1957.

More, Hannah. *Village Politics*, 1792.

O'Brien, Conor Cruise and Vanech, L., eds. *Power and Consciousness*, 1969.

O'Gorman, Frank. *The Whig Party and the French Revolution*, 1967.

O'Hehir, Brendan, ed. *Expans'd Hieroglyphicks: a critical edition of Sir John Denham's 'Cooper's Hill'*, Berkeley and L.A., 1969.

Paine, Thomas. *Rights of Man* (1791-2), ed. H.Collins, 1969.

Paley, William. *Reasons for Contentment: addressed to the Labouring Part of the British Public*, 1793.

Park, Mary C. 'Joseph Priestley and the Problem of Pantisocracy', *Proceedings of the Delaware County Institute of Science*, xi (1947).

Parrish, S.M. *The Art of the Lyrical Ballads*, Boston, Mass., 1973.

Partridge, Eric, ed. *The Poems of Cuthbert Shaw and Thomas Russel*, 1925.

Passmore, J.A. *Ralph Cudworth, An Interpretation*, 1951.

Pater, Walter. *Appreciations*, 1889.

Patton, Lewis. 'Coleridge and the "Enquirer" Series', *RES*, xvi (1940).

Paul, C.K. *William Godwin, his friends and acquaintances*, 2 Vols., 1876.

Peacock, T.L. *Nightmare Abbey*, 1818.

Piper, H.W. *The Active Universe*, 1962.

' "The Eolian Harp" again', *N&Q*, ccxiii (1968).

Plotinus. *The Enneads*, trans. S.MacKenna, 3rd edition 1956.

Pope, Alexander. *Poems*, ed. J.Butt (Twickenham Edition), 1963.

Potter, S. *Coleridge and STC*, 1935.

Powell, A.E. *The Romantic Theory of Poetry*, 1926.

Praz, Mario. *The Hero in Eclipse in Victorian Fiction*, 1965.

Preston, William. *Poetical Works*, 2 Vols., Dublin, 1793.

Price, Martin. 'The Picturesque Moment', in *From Sensibility to Romanticism*, ed. Hilles and Bloom.

Price, Richard. *A Discourse on the Love of our Country, &c.*, 1789.

*Observations on the Nature of Civil Liberty, &c.*, 1776.

Prickett, S. *Coleridge and Wordsworth: the Poetry of Growth*, Cambridge, 1970.

Priestley, Joseph. *Hartley's Theory of the Human Mind, on the Principle of the Association of Ideas; with Essays relating to the subject of it*, 1775. *Theological and Miscellaneous Works*, ed. J.T.Rutt, 25 Vols., 1817-31.

Quayle, Thomas. *Poetic Diction, a Study of Eighteenth Century Verse*, 1924.

Raine, Kathleen. *Coleridge* (British Council Pamphlet), 1953.

Read, H. *The True Voice of Feeling*, 1953.

Reed, Amy. *The Background of Gray's Elegy*, New York, 1962.

Reed, Mark L. *Wordsworth: The Chronology of the Early Years*, Cambridge, Mass., 1967.

Reiman, D.H., ed. *The Romantics Reviewed* (Part A, *The Lake Poets*, 2 Vols.), 1972.

Renwick, W.L. *English Literature, 1789-1815*, Oxford, 1963.

Rice-Oxley, L., ed. *Poetry of the Anti-Jacobin*, Oxford, 1924.

Richards, I.A. *Coleridge on Imagination* (1934), rptd. with essay by Kathleen Coburn, Bloomington, Ind., 1950.

Rinaker, C. 'Thomas Edwards and the Sonnet Revival', *MLN*, xxxiv (1919).

Rogers, Samuel. *Recollections of the Table-Talk*, ed. A. Dyce, 1856.

Rose, R.B. 'The Priestley Riots of 1791', *Past and Present*, No. 18, November 1960.

Rostvig, Maren-Sofie. *The Happy Man: Studies in the Metamorphoses of a Classical Ideal*, 2 Vols., Oslo, 1954, 1958.

Roth, Cecil. *Nephew of the Almighty*, 1933.

Rubinstein, J. 'Sound and Silence in Coleridge's Conversation Poems', *English*, xxi (1972).

Rudé, G. *Revolutionary Europe 1783-1815*, 1964.

Rudrum, A.W. 'Coleridge's This Lime-Tree Bower my Prison', *Southern Review*, i (1964).

Russel, Thomas. *Sonnets and Miscellaneous Poems*, Oxford, 1789.

Salingar, L.G. 'Coleridge: Poet and Philosopher', in *The Pelican Guide to English Literature*, Vol. v (*From Blake to Byron*), 1957.

Sandford, Mrs Henry. *Thomas Poole and his Friends*, 2 Vols., 1888.

Schmidt, Michael. 'Coleridge: This Lime-Tree Bower my Prison', *Critical Survey*, vi (1973).

Schneider, Elisabeth. *Coleridge, Opium and 'Kubla Khan'*, Chicago, 1953.

Scholfield, R.E. *The Lunar Society of Birmingham*, 1963.

Schulz, M.F. 'Coleridge, Milton and Lost Paradise', *N&Q*, cciv (1959). 'Oneness and Multeity in Coleridge's Poems', *Tulane Studies in English*, ix (1959). *The Poetic Voices of Coleridge*, Detroit, 1963.

Shaffer, E.S. *'Kubla Khan' and The Fall of Jerusalem*, Cambridge, 1975.

Shelley, P.B. *Poetical Works*, ed. T.Hutchinson (1905) 1968.

Simmons, Jack. *Southey*, 1945.

Smyser, J. 'Coleridge's Use of Wordsworth's Juvenilia', *PMLA*, lxv (1950).

Southey, Robert. *Life and Correspondence*, ed. C.C.Southey, 6 Vols., 2nd edition 1849-50. *New Letters*, ed. K.Curry, 2 Vols., 1965.

*Poems*, ed. M.H.Fitzgerald, Oxford, 1909.
Stallknecht, N.P. *Strange Seas of Thought*, 1945.
Stoll, E.E. 'Symbolism in Coleridge', *PMLA*, lxiii (1948).
Sundell, M.G. 'The Theme of Self-Realization in Frost at Midnight',
    *Studies in Romanticism*, vii (1967-68).
Suther, M. *Visions of Xanadu*, 1965.
Swinburne, A. *Essays and Studies*, 1875.
Thelwall, John. *Poems chiefly written in Retirement*, 2nd edition 1801.
Thompson, E.P. 'Disenchantment or Default? A Lay Sermon', in *Power
    and Consciousness*, ed. O'Brien and Vanech.
    *The Making of the English Working Class*, 1963.
Thomson, James. *Poetical Works*, ed. J.Logie Robertson, 1908.
Thorpe, C.D., Baker, C., and Weaver, B., eds. *The Major English
    Romantic Poets: A Symposium in Reappraisal*, Carbondale, Ill., 1957.
Tillotson, Geoffrey. *Augustan Studies*, 1961.
Traill, H.D. *Coleridge*, 1884.
Veitch, G.S. *The Genesis of Parliamentary Reform*, 1913.
Walsh, W. *Coleridge: The Work and the Relevance*, 1967.
Walvin, James. 'English Democratic Societies and Popular Radicalism,
    1791-1800', unpublished Ph.D thesis, University of York, 1969.
Wasserman, E.R. 'Nature Moralized: the Divine Analogy in the
    Eighteenth Century', *ELH*, xx (1953).
Watson, G. *Coleridge the Poet*, 1966.
    'The revolutionary youth of Wordsworth and Coleridge', *Critical
    Quarterly*, xviii (1976).
Watson, J.R. *Picturesque Landscape and English Romantic Poetry*, 1970.
Watson, J. Steven. *The Reign of George III*, Oxford, 1960.
Webb, R.K. *The British Working Class Reader*, 1955.
Wellek, R. *Concepts of Criticism*, New Haven, Conn., 1963.
Wendling, R.C. 'Coleridge and the consistency of the Eolian Harp',
    *Studies in Romanticism*, viii (1968-69).
    'Dramatic Reconciliation in Coleridge's Conversation Poems',
    *Papers in Language and Literature*, ix (1973).
Werkmeister, Lucyle. 'Coleridge, Bowles and feelings of the heart',
    *Anglia*, lxxviii (1960).
    'Coleridge's 'Anthem': Another Debt to Bowles', *JEGP*, lviii (1959).
    'Coleridge's *The Plot Discovered*: Some Facts and a Speculation', *MP*,
    lvi (1958-59).
Whalley, George. 'The Bristol Library Borrowings of Southey and
    Coleridge, 1793-8', *The Library*, iv (1949).
    *Coleridge and Sara Hutchinson and the Asra Poems*, 1955.
    'Coleridge and Southey in Bristol, 1795', *RES*, N.S. i (1950).
Willey, Basil. *The Eighteenth Century Background*, 1940.
    *Nineteenth-Century Studies: Coleridge to Matthew Arnold*, 1949.
    *Samuel Taylor Coleridge*, 1971.
    *The Seventeenth Century Background*, 1934.
Williams, Raymond. *The Country and the City*, 1973.
    *Culture and Society, 1780-1950*, 1958.

*The Long Revolution*, 1961.

Williams, R.M. 'Coleridge's Parody of Dyer's "Grongar Hill" ', *MLR*, xli (1946).

Wimsatt, W.K. 'The Structure of Romantic Nature Imagery', in *The Verbal Icon*, 1954; rptd. in *English Romantic Poets*, ed. Abrams.

Woodring, C. *Politics in the Poetry of Coleridge*, Madison, Wis., 1961.

Wordsworth, Dorothy. *Journals*, ed. M. Moorman, 1971.

Wordsworth, Dorothy, and William. *The Letters*, ed. E. de Selincourt, 3 Vols., Oxford, 1935-39; rev. edition, Vol. i, ed. C.L.Shaver, 1957; Vol. ii, ed. M.Moorman, 1969; Vol. iii, ed. M.Moorman and A.G.Hill, 1970.

Wordsworth, William. *Poetical Works*, ed. E. de Selincourt and H.Darbishire, 5 Vols., Oxford, 1940-49.

*Prelude, Text of 1805*, ed. E. de Selincourt, rev. Stephen Gill, 1970.

*Prose Works*, ed. W.J.B.Owen and J.Smyser, 3 Vols., Oxford, 1974.

Young, Edward. *The Complaint: or night-thoughts*, 9 Parts, 1742-5.

Zall, P.M. 'The Cool World of Samuel Taylor Coleridge: Richard Brothers - The Law and the Prophet', *Wordsworth Circle*, iv (1973).

# INDEX